The Euro

Governance in Europe
Series Editor: Gary Marks

The Euro

European Integration Theory and Economic and Monetary Union

EDITED BY AMY VERDUN

ROWMAN & LITTLEFIELD PUBLISHERS, INC.
Lanham • Boulder • New York • Oxford

ROWMAN & LITTLEFIELD PUBLISHERS, INC.

cau

Published in the United States of America
by Rowman & Littlefield Publishers, Inc.
An Imprint of the Rowman & Littlefield Publishing Group
4720 Boston Way, Lanham, Maryland 20706
www.rowmanlittlefield.com

12 Hid's Copse Road, Cumnor Hill, Oxford OX2 9JJ, England

Copyright © 2002 by Rowman & Littlefield Publishers, Inc.

An earlier version of chapter 7 was first published by Indiana University Press as R. Amy
Elman, 'Testing the Limits of European Citizenship: Ethnic Hatred and Male Violence',
NWSA 13, 3 (2001): 49–69.

British Library Cataloguing in Publication Information Available

Library of Congress Cataloging-in-Publication Data

The euro : European integration theory and economic and monetary union / edited by
Amy Verdun.
    p. cm.
Includes bibliographical references and index.
ISBN 0-7425-1883-3 (alk. paper) — ISBN 0-7425-1884-1 (pbk. : alk. paper)
    1. Economic and Monetary Union—Congresses. 2. Euro—Congresses. 3.
Monetary unions—European Union countries—Congresses. 4. Monetary policy—
European Union countries—Congresses. I. Verdun, Amy, 1968– II. Series.

HG3942 .E964 2002
332.4'94 21

                    2002017606

Printed in the United States of America

™
⊖ The paper used in this publication meets the minimum requirements of American
National Standard for Information Sciences—Permanence of Paper for Printed Library
Materials, ANSI/NISO Z39.48-1992.

To
Paul, Zoey, and Inez

Contents

Figures and Tables

Abbreviations

AMUE	Association for the Monetary Union of Europe
BDI	Bundesverband der Deutschen Industrie
BoI	Bank of Italy
CAP	Common Agricultural Policy
CBI	Confederation of British Industry
CFDT	Confédération Française Démocratique du Travail
CGT	Confédération Général du Travail
CNFP	Conseil National du Patronat Français
DGB	Deutscher Gewerkschaftsbund
EC	European Community
ECB	European Central Bank
ECJ	European Court of Justice
ECSA	European Community Studies Association
ECSC	European Coal and Steel Community
ECU	European Currency Unit
EEC	European Economic Community
EMS	European Monetary System
EMI	European Monetary Institute
EMU	Economic and Monetary Union
ERM	Exchange Rate Mechanism
ESCB	European System of Central Banks
ETUC	European Trade Union Confederation
EU	European Union
EUN	European Union National
EWL	European Women's Lobby
FN	Front National
FO	Force Ouvrière
IGC	Intergovernmental Conference
IMF	International Monetary Fund
IR	International Relations

MCA   Monetary Compensatory Amounts
OCA   Optimum Currency Area
SEA   Single European Act
SGP   Stability and Growth Pact
SVAR   Structural Vector Auto Regression
TEU   Treaty on European Union
TUC   Trade Unions Congress
UNICE   Union of Industrial and Employers' Confederations of Europe

Acknowledgements

This volume grew out of the conference 'Conceptualising the New Europe: European Monetary Integration and Beyond', which was held at the University of Victoria (UVic) on 15-16 October 1999. The conference inaugurated the new European Studies Program at UVic and brought together scholars from various European countries, the United States, and Canada.

Economic and Monetary Union (EMU) is an exciting research topic. First, it is an interesting case study because of its sheer economic and political importance. Second, the empirical study of EMU puts European integration theories into perspective. Last, but not least, we stand on the eve of the introduction of the euro banknotes and coins—an event that takes the euro out of the realm of theory into day-to-day life. European integration has long been there for the European elites; now the everyday citizen will feel European integration in its most tangible form.

A book project of this magnitude always leaves the editor heavily indebted to a number of persons and institutions. First of all, I thank all conference participants,whose enthusiastic presentations and discussions made for a lively and productive conference. I also thank four UVic graduate students—Konrad Cedro, Robin Kells, Ben Müller, and Lloy Wylie—for helping organise the conference and preparing discussions on the conference papers. I also thank all authors for their dedication to this project in the two subsequent years of revisions. Next, I thank two anonymous reviewers and the series editor, Gary Marks, for insightful suggestions on earlier drafts. Furthermore, I am grateful for the service and support provided by Susan McEachern and April Leo, Rowman & Littlefield. I gratefully acknowledge financial support from the Social Science and Humanities Council Canada (conference grant 646-1999-0020), from the European Community Studies Association Canada (ECSA-C), and from various sources within UVic. A special word of thanks goes to Lloy Wylie for invaluable editorial assistance in preparation of the final manuscript. I am pleased that in more than one way this book is the product of a fruitful interaction between graduate students and academics.

NIR

Chapter 1
INTRODUCTION:
EUROPEAN INTEGRATION, THEORIES, AND GLOBAL CHANGE

Amy Verdun

Fifty years after the Schuman Plan, and at the start of the new millennium, the European Union (EU) stands at the eve of a major transition. It introduced the single currency, the euro, in twelve Member States. It is also considering institutional reform in preparation of the expansion of the EU with countries from Central and Eastern Europe. During these fifty years many attempts have been made to conceptualise the European integration process.

Traditionally the debate in European integration theory has been between the neofunctionalists and the intergovernmentalists (Haas 1958, 1964; Hoffmann 1966; Lindberg and Scheingold 1970, 1971). However, more recently other approaches have gained terrain. The economic and monetary integration process offers an interesting case study on which theories of European integration should be able to shed some light.

This volume brings together scholars who have theorised about European integration as well as scholars with knowledge about the process of economic and monetary integration. The aim is to advance further our understanding of European integration, in particular the economic and monetary integration process using insights derived from European integration theories. The contributors have been encouraged to adopt a variety of different theoretical approaches, such as neofunctionalism, intergovernmentalism, multilevel governance, supranationalism, transactions theory, new institutionalism, constructivist approaches, feminist approaches, knowledge based/ideational approaches, et cetera. The main case study is Economic and Monetary Union (EMU). Our aim is not to test the theories of integration. Rather it is an effort to shed light on the EMU process—one of the most important developments of the past fifty years.

This book focuses on the broader question of what European economic and monetary integration is all about: how European integration theories inform us about the integration process; what dynamics are at stake; who are the core actors; how do they operate; and what factors determine the outcome of the process. EMU offers a case study for the applicability of the theoretical approaches.

This volume addresses three core sets of questions. First, what is the usefulness of the traditional integration theories, i.e., intergovernmentalism and neofunctionalism? How do the more recent approaches (e.g., multilevel governance) differ from these earlier approaches, and how do they contribute to the debate? What should the future generations of European integration theorists focus on? The second set of questions is: what do the theoretical approaches teach us about the European economic and monetary integration process? Do different theoretical approaches shine light on different parts of the picture? The third set of questions asks how the European integration process is embedded in wider global trends. How are specific national factors important for understanding the integration process? Let us turn to each of these questions and briefly reflect on them.

Neofunctionalism and intergovernmentalism have focused attention on the role of actors and structures in the overall integration process. Intergovernmentalists assume that national governments are the core actors and only pursue further integration if it is in the direct interest of 'the state' (Moravcsik 1993a; cf. Milward 1992). In this view, 'the state' (or the 'state executive' or 'national government') is considered to be more or less a unitary actor. More sophisticated analyses seek to explain the preferences of the state by understanding the domestic politics underlying those preferences. More often than not, these preferences are still rather deterministic and focus on the economic interests as they have been voiced by business associations (Moravcsik 1998).

Neofunctionalism, in its various permutations, has focused on why integration happens by including the role of societal actors, functional and political spill-over, and the role of supranational institutions (cf. Burley and Mattli 1993; Corbey 1995; Sandholtz and Stone Sweet 1998; Tranholm-Mikkelsen 1991). Neofunctionalists theorise about the circumstances in which political action moves from the national to the European level. The relevant actors are the governments (at the various levels), the societal actors (that transfer their activities from the national to the European level), and the supranational actors that take over some of the tasks previously performed at the national level and/or act as policy entrepreneurs. The core mechanism in neofunctionalism is spill-over. This concept was later translated and nuanced by neoinstitutionalists into concepts such as 'path dependence' and 'unintended consequences' (cf. Hall and Taylor 1994; Pierson 1996).

More recent approaches, such as multilevel governance (Marks, Hooghe, and Blank 1996; Marks and Hooghe 2000; Kohler-Koch 1996; Eising and Kohler-Koch 1999) focus on how the European integration process happens at the same time at various levels. This approach does not disqualify the role of national governments. In fact it explicitly acknowledges that national governments still play a crucial role. Rather it emphasises that the process happens at different times at different levels, with different actors being important in it. Other theoretical perspectives, such as knowledge-based (Radaelli 1995) and constructivist approaches (Christiansen, Jørgensen, and Wiener 1999), examine how the idea of European integration is embedded in a larger discourse—a larger notion of acceptable ideas, policy choices, and a framing of the issues (cf. Marcussen 1997, 1998, 2000; McNamara 1998; Verdun 1999, 2000b). In a way, these approaches question the basis of 'preferences' that intergovernmentalists take as given and the logic of integration underlying the neofunctionalist views. These approaches try to explain that one needs to place these developments in the European Union within a broader context in order to understand what comes out of the integration process and why it has its specific outcome. Years of European integration studies have taught us that there are different parts of the process that may be best understood by adopting one approach rather than another. At other times an eclectic approach may be useful (Verdun 2000a; and Verdun, this volume).

Let us now turn to the second question, i.e., what do the theoretical approaches teach us about the European economic and monetary integration process? First, it is important to reiterate here that there is no single economic theory that spells out that EMU was inevitable, necessarily desirable, or that it should have taken the form it did (Gros and Thygesen 1998; Taylor 1995). It is, however, remarkable that Robert Mundell received the Nobel Prize for Economics in 1999 for his work on Optimum Currency Areas (OCAs) in the 1960s. It was claimed to have been an important influence on the policy-makers in the EU and to have motivated EMU itself! This reasoning is remarkable because all EMU documents spell out specifically that the eurozone is *not* an OCA, and that many existing federations would not fulfil the criteria of being an OCA (see also Verdun 2000a). As for the political science 'theories', we find that there are a variety of scholars who have examined parts of the process. Some of the chapters in this volume indicate that the EMU process is in part a result of the changes in the global economy and the pace and nature of the wider European integration process. Other chapters show that neofunctionalism and intergovernmentalism alone are unable to give a satisfactory answer to why EMU happened. One needs to move beyond the traditional debate and include a whole range of theories (this will be discussed further in the next chapter). Also, the static image of anticipated behaviour, preferences, and attitudes towards European integration more generally, or EMU in particular, is also outdated. Actors are less uniform in their views, and may change their minds over time. Theories may not always be applicable to all parts of the process, as important factors have been left out of the original debates. This is why theories of globalisation and the role of ideas in policy-making processes need to be included. It is clearly the case that different theoretical approaches illuminate different parts of the process. It seems obvious that we are moving away from parsimonious theory formation to an eclectic approach in the use of theories, with the choice of theoretical approach being highly dependent on the kinds of questions the researcher is posing.

Now turning to the third question, how is the European integration process embedded in wider global trends? The history of EMU shows that the global context is crucial in explaining European integration more generally and EMU specifically (Dyson 1994; Dyson and Featherstone 1999; Verdun 2000a). A brief overview of the history of EMU requires mentioning the failure of the first plan for economic and monetary union: the Werner Plan (Werner Report 1970). It failed due to unfavourable international circumstances and divergent domestic strategies to deal with the challenges of the 1970s. The success of the European Monetary System (EMS) was in part due to the Mitterrand experience in the early 1980s in which it became clear that it was not possible to have 'socialism in one country'. The 1992 programme (or '1992'—which outlined the goals of eliminating all barriers to trade in Europe) was strongly supported by the business community, which saw it as a strategy to cope with global pressures. Business representatives adopted '1992' as a strategy to deal with the increasing lack of competitiveness and the perceived decline of the economic power of Europe vis-à-vis the United States and the Pacific basin. The relaunch of EMU came in the wake of the introduction of the Single European Act (Delors Report 1989).

The process of creating EMU was due to a number of factors, each of which has a global component. The following summary by no means provides a complete list. First, there was the need to build on the successful momentum of European integration in the wake of the completion of the Single Market. The '1992 programme' nicely fits into the wider trend of increasing privatisation and deregulation, i.e., letting the market do the work. Second, there was a perceived need to institutionalise the success of the Exchange Rate Mechanism (ERM) of the EMS to protect it from possible speculative attacks from the increasingly turbulent financial markets. Third, there was a desire to Europeanise the ERM, which was de facto based on German monetary policy hegemony.[1] Fourth, as a result of the decision to liberalise capital markets by 1990 there would be less room for manoeuvre over monetary policy-making (i.e., if one simultaneously tried to maintain a regime of fixed exchange rates). Fifth, increasing 'globalisation' (however defined) implied that a variety of policies became less feasible, or would be less successful if pursued in isolation (that is, without coordination with the policies of others, in particular with those of neighbouring countries and countries with whom significant amounts of trade occurred). Thus globalisation was limiting the scope for choice. Sixth, and finally, the global context had changed with the end of the Cold War and the reunification of Germany. The latter background factors are definitely important for our understanding of why EMU happened. Yet a mere realist account—which places almost all emphasis on these structural, systemic factors—misses the nuances that led to the creation of EMU.

Notwithstanding these wider global trends, the following questions still remain to be answered: why did the member state governments (save that of the UK) agree to create an EMU in 1991; why was this particular type of EMU regime selected; and why did the EMU process not fail in the course of the 1990s? These questions lead us to reflect on the question of whether there are specific national factors important for understanding the integration process. It also poses the question of why EMU has the specific institutional design it has, i.e., an independent central bank that deals with monetary policy but no flanking institution to deal with wider macroeconomic or fiscal policy, as is the case in federal states (see Verdun 1996, 1998a; see also Verdun and Christiansen 2000). The chapters prepared for this volume in one way or another address these questions.

The volume is divided into four parts. Part I deals with European integration theories more generally and individual authors discuss EMU from a broad range of theoretical perspectives. Each of these chapters examines how the conventional European integration theories are in need of a reshuffle. The chapters by Amy Verdun, Dieter Wolf, and Femke van Esch look at various metatheoretical issues. Both Verdun and Wolf discuss the various integration theories and offer different ways to merge or amalgamate the theories. Van Esch's chapter deals with the question of why International Relations theory, in particular the realist approach, has not been able to explain the emergence of EMU. Part II examines EMU using other theoretical lenses. Lloy Wylie looks at constructivist approaches and the role of neoliberalism as a way to analyse the role of the nation state in EMU. Kenneth Dyson offers an analysis of the process leading up to the signing of the Maastricht Treaty in 1991. He analyses, among other things, the importance of cultural and national differences. Amy Elman offers a feminist perspective on European integration more generally and the economic and monetary integration process in particular.

The chapters in Part III deal more specifically with matters that lie at the intersection of economics and politics, and how those matters impact institutions and accountability. The chapters by Erik Jones and Peter Loedel discuss issues of accountability, democracy, and legitimacy and the role of the European Central Bank (ECB). Peter Loedel discusses a broad range of theories and ultimately adopts a multilevel governance model for explaining the independence of the ECB. Erik Jones discusses the logic of having an independent central bank, argues why it was not surprising that this regime was selected, and draws some conclusions about whether a democratic deficit has resulted from the choice of this regime. Patrick Crowley provides us an economist's view. His chapter looks at the Stability and Growth Pact and how it has impacted and will impact the future developments in the EU.

Part IV is dedicated to three country studies. David Howarth examines how the case of France shows the usefulness of various theoretical approaches to EMU. William Chandler offers an evaluation of the role of Germany in the European integration process. Finally, Osvaldo Croci and Lucio Picci offer an analysis of the case of Italy. The country studies show how different the EMU process is in each of these countries (a conclusion consistent with the findings of a study of EMU in small member states; see Jones et al. 1998).

These chapters show how the variety of European integration theories and approaches have merits but at times fall short in explaining why European integration happens. What has become clear, however, is that the starting assumptions are crucial in understanding the validity of the approaches. In particular, what is European integration all about? Is it economics versus politics, as mentioned in some chapters, or is it the process of policy and polity formation at the European level, or both? What causes the European integration process? Is it the result of the actions of states on the basis of state preferences (as is studied in the van Esch chapter), or is the formation of ideas and the construction of social relations important (as emphasised in the chapters by Dyson and Wylie)? What are the domestic reasons for supporting European economic and monetary integration (which can be seen in the three chapters that provide country studies, i.e., the Chandler, Howarth, and Croci and Picci chapters)?

Can any of this be seen separately from the global forces and the wider scene of International Relations and International Political Economy? How have European integration theories dealt with the legacy of intergovernmentalism versus neofunctionalism? To what extent are these two 'ends of the spectrum' still useful, and what do mid-range theories (multilevel governance, constructivism, et cetera) offer as theoretical frameworks for understanding the process? Who are the 'actors' in the process, and to what extent do institutions, regimes, and the international context (globalisation but also wider Europeanisation) affect the EMU process? We will return to these questions throughout the chapters of this volume and summarise our findings in the final chapter.

Note

1. Again, German monetary policy nicely corresponded to the broader beliefs about appropriate aims of policy-making (i.e., supported by the United States, the International Monetary Fund, et cetera). German monetary policy aimed at (i) maintaining low inflation (so-called 'price stability'), (ii) more or less 'balanced budgets', and (iii) an independent central bank pursuing monetary policy. An independent central bank was perceived necessary in order to have the maximum guarantee that the central bank would fulfill its mandate and that politicians would not have access to the printing press (cf. Kaufmann 1995).

I. THE EXPLANATORY POWER OF INTEGRATION THEORIES: EXAMINING ECONOMIC AND MONETARY UNION

F33
F36

Chapter 2
MERGING NEOFUNCTIONALISM AND INTERGOVERNMENTALISM: LESSONS FROM EMU

Amy Verdun

In recent years there have been major debates in European integration studies about what ultimately explains why European integration happens. This is not a new phenomenon. Contending approaches have been around ever since the creation of the first European Community (EC). In the 1950s Ernst Haas developed a theory in which he described the actors and mechanisms that would lead to further integration (neofunctionalism). When in the 1960s the process halted, Stanley Hoffmann identified caveats in the neofunctionalist approach. In turn he identified actors and mechanisms that could promote or obstruct integration (intergovernmentalism). In the 1970s and 1980s these debates died down, only to re-emerge in the 1990s with renewed strength (see also Wolf, this volume).

Currently the debate in the literature is about the usefulness of these traditional and various other recent approaches. The emphasis is on the fact that different theoretical approaches apply to different parts of the integration process. In addition, the usefulness of the approach depends on the level of analysis of the study. Methodological issues also play an important role in determining why certain scholars see the integration process through one theoretical lens or another. Some aim at distilling a limited number of variables that explain the outcome of the process. They want to be able to predict, or to argue with some certainty that they know, what causes what. These studies are appealing in their simplicity and their possible applicability to other cases. Other scholars are more interested in getting

9

the 'story' right. They allow more variables to have an influence. In their view certain circumstances can change importantly the likelihood of some causal links between the variables. As a result their analyses appear rather messy. Though the 'story' these scholars tell may be more convincing, the sceptics remain unconvinced by these studies. They stress that these studies fail to demonstrate general insights that can be learned from these cases for other future similar situations (i.e., the generalisability of the case study) and what variables ultimately caused integration to happen.

This chapter is purposefully provocative. It aims at re-examining the integration theories in light of their usefulness for studying EMU. Different approaches offer different insights into different parts of the integration process. Theories are complementary. I argue that an eclectic mix of theories should be used to analyse the European integration process.

The argument is developed in four steps. First, I argue that the variety of integration theories can be seen as a spectrum, illustrating that the theories differ minimally from some but more from other theories with the extremes at opposite ends. Next, I show that the theories can also be clustered into two groups, which I here name 'neofunctionalist' and 'intergovernmentalist'. The third step is to show that for a full understanding of the European integration process one needs to adopt an eclectic approach whereby the two families of theories are merged. This merger allows the richness of both families of theories to help explain the outcome of the process. The usefulness of this eclectic approach is illustrated with the example of Economic and Monetary Union (EMU). Drawing on both theories, the chapter identifies the actors and mechanisms that are at work in European integration. The argument is not to prove or disprove one particular theory or family of theories but to persuade the reader to consider the benefits of eclecticism. The general argument draws on a broader exploratory study (Verdun 2000a), which did not aim at testing theories, but rather on understanding the EMU process.

The chapter is structured as follows. The first section discusses European integration theories. The second section reviews the theoretical explanations of why EMU happened, followed by a discussion of a case study of EMU in the third section. The fourth section analyses the usefulness of a merged integration theory for understanding the particular case of EMU. The last section draws some conclusions and reflects on the benefits of using an eclectic approach when studying European integration.

European Integration Theories

Although the development of European integration theory is well documented in the literature, for the purpose of this chapter it is worthwhile to restate it very briefly. Neofunctionalists and intergovernmentalism are often displayed as rival theories. In the 1950s neofunctionalism identified interest groups and supranational actors as the key actors in the process of European integration. The motor of integration in this view was functional. This meant that domestic actors (interest groups, trade unions, business associations, et cetera) would discover that they could create policies much more effectively by conducting them at the supranational level. Once one area of policy-making was transferred to the supranational level, other adjacent areas of policy-making would follow (functional spill-over). Domestic actors would thus assume that policies would be conducted at the supranational level and thereby transfer their loyalties to the supranational level (political spill-over). At that level supranational actors would create policies that would further develop the integration process (Haas 1958, 1964; Lindberg and Scheingold 1970, 1971).

In the 1960s intergovernmentalists criticised this view and argued that the role of national governments had been underestimated. It claimed that European integration would only happen if it were in the best interest of national governments. If strong leaders were against integration, it would halt. Thus, neofunctionalism was being criticised for being deterministic and lacking a clear analysis of the role of nation state governments. At this stage a differentiation was being made between 'high' and 'low' politics with the former containing foreign and security policies and the latter consisting of welfare policies (Hoffmann 1966; Haas 1968). The neofunctionalist assumptions were seen as more likely to happen in the area of low politics but unlikely in the area of high politics, as the latter would be seen by national governments as being at the core of national sovereignty.

By the middle of the 1970s the dialogue between Haas and Hoffmann ended. Haas (1975, 1976) acknowledged that neofunctionalism was unable to theorise why European integration could fail. In the early 1980s there was another small contribution when Hoffmann (1982) argued that European integration needed to remain focused on the importance of national sovereignty and Taylor (1983) spelled out once again why neofunctionalism had failed. Carole Webb's contribution probably sums up quite well where the literature stood at that point in time (Webb 1983). It emphasises that both intergovernmentalism and neofunctionalism had failed to incorporate interdependence and global factors. By the middle of the 1980s integration theory appeared to have died out completely.

With the re-emergence of European integration in the late 1980s scholars picked up the debate and started to re-examine the usefulness of both approaches. Moravcsik (1991) reintroduced intergovernmentalism. The role of the state and the national interests of national governments stood at the core of his theoretical approach. In addition, he placed emphasis on the relative strength of some national governments over that of others. At some point he even stated that European integration strengthened the state, making it a more powerful actor than before European integration (Milward 1992; Moravcsik 1994, 1998). Various authors revamped neofunctionalism in one way or another (Burley and Mattli 1993; Corbey 1993, 1995; Mutimer 1989; Tranholm-Mikkelsen 1991). They did not reintroduce the determinism of neofunctionalism but did emphasise the importance of functional spill-over and the role of supranational actors and interest groups. In addition, European integration scholars introduced a large variety of other approaches, which they claimed were distinct from the earlier two theories. These approaches, however, did have aspects in common with the earlier approaches, but ultimately they did not combine the exact actors and integration mechanisms in the same way as the traditional theories had done. The new approaches were also different in that they identified a level of analysis or domain for which their approach was applicable (for a discussion see Peterson 1995). Let us now turn to those newer approaches and briefly discuss what they consist of.

Multilevel governance examines the role of a variety of actors in the policy-making process. It argues that the national government obviously remains a crucial actor but that considerable progress in the integration process can be found when examining the various levels of governance and the variety of actors that participated in the policy-making process (Marks, Hooghe, and Blank 1996). A historical institutionalist approach focuses on the role of institutions and works with the mechanism of path-dependence (Bulmer 1994; Pierson 1996). It is rather broad in its analysis and focuses on the longer-term. Domestic politics approaches emerged. They focus on how the domestic scene provides information that can help observers understand the behaviour of national state executives in international bargaining. Furthermore this approach also focuses on how the specific domestic context in each country can be significantly different to influence the outcome of the process (Bulmer 1983; Huelshoff 1994).

Wolfgang Wessels (1997) has introduced a complicated scheme that suggests why the integration process has its waxing and waning. He refers to this approach as a 'Fusion thesis'. A number of different approaches have explored the neofunctionalist's interest in the role of experts and technocrats. Network analysis examines how the role of networks (i.e., actors most involved in a particular area of policy-making) influences European integration (Börzel 1997; Kohler-Koch 1996). When a particular policy outcome is being promoted over a long period of time one could study the role of a so-called 'advocacy coalition' (Sabatier and Jenkins-Smith 1993; Sabatier 1998). According to these studies advocacy coalitions can be very influential in the policy-making process. If a community of experts holds similar normative beliefs and aims at certain policy outcomes, one can identify an epistemic community (Haas 1992; Verdun 1999). It can help national governments solve problems regarding international agreement on which they may have general agreement but still have problems regarding the details. A more recent approach is the so-called 'Laguna Beach approach' (named after the beach close to the university where the scholars met to discuss their project). This approach examines the importance of transaction costs for understanding the integration process. It also stresses that the integration process does indeed logically follow the decisions made earlier (Stone Sweet and Sandholtz 1997, 1998). Another set of approaches that recently has received more attention is constructivism. They identify how the very nature of perceived national interests and the scope for European integration is itself embedded in a larger 'construction' of what 'national interests' are or what 'Europe' would be (Christiansen, Jørgensen, and Wiener 1999). Finally, Liberal intergovernmentalism focuses on the importance of the national state executives and how the bargaining between them is at the core of understanding the treaty negotiations (Moravcsik 1998).

Each of these approaches identifies slightly different mechanisms and actors at work. They each also direct their attention to slightly different parts of the process. I now want to make a provocative suggestion. I think it is possible, without doing them too much injustice, to map these approaches on a spectrum based on how they view the European integration process. I shall look at two main dichotomies: (1) the role of other actors versus the role of the state; and (2) the role of automaticity and path-dependence versus no automaticity.

On the right hand side of the spectrum I shall put those approaches that consider integration occurring because national member state governments want it. The approaches on the right-hand side also refute the idea that there is any automatic process. The further right on the spectrum, the more the approach focuses on the importance of the state and on the lack of automaticity in the integration process. On the left-hand side of the spectrum I shall place those theories that downgrade the role of the state and consider other actors (interest groups, elites, networks, supranational actors) also to be important. Also on this side of the spectrum are the approaches that assume that there are certain automatic mechanisms at work (such as spill-over, path-dependence, et cetera). The results are illustrated in figure 2.1.

This spectrum illustrates how each of the various approaches focuses on slightly different aspects of the integration process and on different actors and mechanisms. Now that we have put the approaches on a spectrum, I will be even more daring and make another provocative simplification. If one wanted to

Figure 2.1: The Spectrum of Integration Theories

Note: Approaches that see integration determined by national Member State governments' preferences and bargaining are placed on the extreme right hand of the spectrum. Those theories that downgrade the exclusive role of the state and emphasise the role of other actors (interest groups, elites, networks), as well as the role of some kind of automatic mechanisms (such as spill-over, etc.), are placed on the left hand of the spectrum.

reduce the approaches to their very basics and examine their position on a number of issues we could actually reintroduce two families of theories. For the sake of simplicity I shall name them 'neofunctionalist' and 'intergovernmentalist' families.

The two families differ in which actors they consider to be of primary importance, as well as what the primary integration mechanism is (i.e., what drives integration). The neofunctionalist family comprises nine approaches: (classical) neofunctionalism, historical institutionalism, constructivism, the epistemic community approach, the policy networks approach, the advocacy-coalition approach, the Laguna Beach approach, the fusion thesis, and the multilevel governance approach. It sees the important actors as a colourful melange of non-state actors, supranational actors, and governments. They consider each national member state government to be only one of many influential actors (albeit an important one). The neofunctionalist family considers the integration mechanism to have some automaticity, which is due to functional spill-over, technocratic knowledge, path-dependence, and unintended consequences. Integration happens as a result of policy-making with a large variety of actors involved.

The intergovernmentalist family consists of four approaches: the domestic politics approach, the two-level games approach, liberal intergovernmentalism, and

Figure 2.2: Two Large Families of Theories

Neofunctionalist family	Intergovermentalist family
• Neofunctionalism • Historical institutionalism • Constructivism • Epistemic community approach • Advocacy-coalition approach • Policy networks approach • Laguna Beach approach • Fusion-thesis • Multilevel governance	• Domestic politics • Two-level games • Liberal intergovernmentalism • Intergovernmentalism
Actors: A variety of non-state actors are crucial actors. The national Member State government is just one of many influential actors. The influence of supranational actors is considerable.	*Actors:* The national state government is the crucial actor. The domestic situation informs the national state preferences. Some states are 'stronger' than others. The influence of supranational actors is limited.
Mechanism: There is some automaticity in the integration process due to functional spill-over, technocratic knowledge, etc. Integration happens as a result of policy-making with a large variety of actors involved.	*Mechanism:* There is no automaticity in the process; the safeguarding of national state interests is the crucial mechanism determining the outcome of the integration process. Integration happens due to bargaining among key actors, in particular national governments.

(classical) intergovernmentalism. The intergovernmentalist family considers the member state governments to be the crucial actors. The domestic situation, actors, and institutions are only important insofar as they inform the preferences of the national government as well as their relative strength in the bargaining process. Some national member state governments (in particular the larger ones) are considered to be much 'stronger' than others. The intergovernmentalist family considers the integration mechanism to have no inherent move forward or backward; there is no automaticity. The safeguarding of national state interests is the crucial mechanism determining the outcome of the integration process.

The final provocative step I would like to suggest now is to merge the two families of theories. Let us, for a moment, consider why it might be attractive to merge the neofunctionalist and intergovernmentalist families. Neofunctionalism's strength lies in the fact that in addition to national bureaucracies it sees a role for domestic actors and supranational actors. It emphasises the role of elites and technocratic expertise. It identifies the need for more efficient policies as the route to integration, which in this view would be done by conducting them at the supranational level. Once one policy area has been transferred there are mechanisms that make it attractive to transfer other areas of policy-making as well. It also envisages that European integration has some automatic 'forward' drive inherent in the process.

Intergovernmentalism focuses exactly on the remainder of the process. It examines the role of national governments. It looks at how integration happens by examining how national governments benefit from integration. The earlier work by Hoffmann did not identify exactly how governments determined what were 'the national interests'. Moravcsik's liberal intergovernmentalism, however, has looked at the domestic (economic) interests of business groups and others in order to be able to better understand the preference formation of national governments vis-à-vis European integration.

Given that each approach focuses at such different parts of the process it is not difficult to see how both theories can be merged (or to extend the metaphor, 'marry the families of theories'). From the neofunctionalist family we adopt the idea that interest groups, business associations and trade unions, technocrats, and lobbyists as well as supranational actors are important in order to understand European integration. Furthermore, from the findings of the more recent literature in that tradition we may want to be inspired and add a few more actors to this list, i.e., policy networks, elite groups, and committees, and also to stress the importance of certain ideas and the effects of socialisation. From the intergovernmentalist family we can take the importance of national governments and their specific strength in the bargaining process. The importance of appreciating the domestic context in order to understand the position of a national government or national government representative is very useful as well.

Yet we notice an apparent contradiction as far as what the approaches see as the integration mechanism. Does integration have an automatic forward momentum, as neofunctionalism assumes, or not, as intergovernmentalism predicts? Probably it is safe to say that there is always a 'zeitgeist' or dominant paradigm present that influences the process, as well as the scholars studying the integration process, at a given point in time. For example, during the early 1980s it appeared as if the integration process had lost its momentum. By contrast, in the late 1980s the integration process had just been given a boost. As for the effect of history or earlier bargaining on the subsequent integration process, it is reasonably uncontroversial to state that earlier decisions have an effect on the integration process. This can be traced back in the path-dependence or functional spill-over concepts. Yet there is no guarantee that integration will at all times 'go forward', which is the point made convincingly by the intergovernmentalist family. It will be for future researchers to determine what criteria and conditions influence this mechanism.

Finally, the overall criticisms on both of these theories, namely their failure to incorporate changes in the global economy, will have to be dealt with. The importance of understanding interdependence will have to be introduced to obtain the desired merged theory (on the importance of including external factors in integration theories see Rosamond 1995 and Webb 1983). What we now have is what I have elsewhere called an eclectic approach of European integration (Verdun 2000a). It combines elements of both traditions to appreciate the full richness of the process. What now occurs is the need to identify which actors and mechanisms may be most important at which times to explain why integration happens. In my view it is not necessary to determine this beforehand. A variety of case studies in the past, and no doubt countless in the future, will empirically determine when these actors and mechanisms are most crucial. Integration theories should be used for understanding empirical cases as well as the basic principles of European integration. Theory is not a holy thing in itself (see Strange 1994).

An additional question to be addressed is the level of analysis. There are obviously different roles to be played by the various actors depending on what process one is studying. If one wanted to understand the outcome of the implementation process of EU policy-making one would give more weight to local officials, interest groups, and other actors who are immediately involved. Likewise, domestic groups, European interest groups, and technocratic experts influence the creation of an EU regulation. By contrast, during the grand bargaining of member state governments about treaty changes, obviously a much larger role is being played by national governments.

So, what is the usefulness of an eclectic theory that merges the two rival integration theories? Well, it offers a theoretical approach that can take seriously all elements of the integration process. The following two sections will look at the usefulness of the eclectic approach for the case of Economic and Monetary Union (EMU). The next section reviews the existing explanations of why EMU happened. It is followed by a discussion of an empirical case study of EMU, looking at perceptions of EMU as held by domestic actors in three EU member states.

Review of the Theoretical Explanations of EMU

Economic and Monetary Union (EMU) was incorporated in the Treaty on European Union (TEU) in February 1992, which came into force in November 1993. The creation of an EMU in the EC had been attempted before in the 1970s, but had failed due to various domestic and international reasons (see Kruse 1980; Tsoukalis 1977). Many scholars have analysed why EMU occurred in the 1990s. Interestingly, there are almost as many explanations of the EMU process as there are integration theories. Yet it is not difficult to group the explanations together roughly in either a 'neofunctionalist' or an 'intergovernmentalist' explanation. Let us take a number of these explanations together and group them into two large categories. First, we shall discuss explanations that emphasise spill-over, learning, path-dependence, the role of supranational actors, experts, and interest groups. We shall refer to this group of explanations as being part of the 'neofunctionalist' family. Second, we shall look at explanations that focus on the role of national governments, domestic politics, and two-level games as being part of the 'intergovernmentalist' family.

The first version of why EMU happened (that of the 'neofunctionalist' family) focuses on how EMU should be seen in the broader context of European integration. EMU comes into being after the European Monetary System (EMS) has operated quite successfully for a few years. During this time, the EMS had become a political symbol of successful European integration. Moreover, EMU also followed the Single European Act (SEA), the plan to complete the Internal Market by 1992 and capital liberalisation in the EC (Sandholtz 1993). Various supranational actors, and in particular the then European Commission president Jacques Delors, were influential in putting EMU on the agenda (Ross 1995). The Commission (Directorate General for Economic and Financial Affairs) helped provide studies that supported the view that EMU was the next logical step in the broader integration process (Commission of the EC 1990, 1991). In addition, EMU re-emerged at a time when monetary experts in national governments, central banks, and other institutions realised that national sovereignty in the area of monetary policy had become limited by interdependence (Andrews 1993, 1994). The success of the EMS and the desire for EMU was based on a common understanding about how monetary and exchange rate policy could be best safeguarded (Dyson 1994; Marcussen 1997, 1998a, 1998b, 2000; McNamara 1998). In particular, the French government had drawn some important lessons from its experiment of 'socialism in one country' and realised that co-ordination was the name of the game.

Various scholars have also emphasised the role of identity. It shows how the basic premises of national identity are engraved in self-images held over time about Europeanness (Engelmann et al. 1997). Monetary experts from the member states were influential in this process. They formed part of a community of experts who had been meeting in committees for decades. Eventually a group of central bankers, Commission officials, and a few 'independent experts' was asked to draft a proposal. Their report—the Delors Report—was ultimately the basis of the text on EMU that came into the Treaty on European Union (Verdun 1999).

In a number of countries the restructuring process of the welfare state and the continuous processes of liberalisation and deregulation were making it difficult for national governments to make necessary adjustments. Though the situation differed across the EU Member States, domestic actors warmly welcomed the 'disciplinary effects' of EMU in assisting them to argue for the need to restructure (Featherstone 1996; Jones, Frieden, and Torres 1998; Verdun 2000a).

The second version of the explanation of why EMU happened (that of the 'intergovernmentalist' family) focuses on how EMU was in the interests of the national governments. Although the above factors were in the background, according to this explanation, one cannot understand EMU without looking at the role of national governments. In this view the crucial moment is the final bargaining in the Council meetings in which heads of states and governments agreed to EMU. A deal was only possible because it served the interests of the large Member States. Moravcsik (1998), for example, argues that to understand EMU one needs to understand the interests of large member states, (in particular France, Germany, and the UK).

Other authors have made similar points. To understand why France was in favour of EMU one needs to understand the position of France before EMU. That country had to deal with a dominant position of Germany in the EMS and its de facto hegemony over monetary policy (Howarth 2000). The position of the UK can also only be understood by putting it in historical perspective. It had suffered from late entry into the EU and realised that it could only influence the outcome by being part of the negotiations. Hence even though the UK government was concerned over EMU, it kept on bargaining and participating in fear of losing influence over the process if others went on alone (Verdun 2000a). Grieco (1995) places this all in a realist perspective and examines how countries favoured EMU to regain power lost to the Bundesbank. Garrett (1993) provides a similar analysis. In his view Germany dominated the outcome of the process because of its dominant position before EMU came on the agenda. Another dimension of the interests of the national states in EMU should be found in their response to global change and change in ideas over the role of the government. In some countries the national governments used EMU to provide a straightjacket to restructure the domestic welfare state (Featherstone 1996; Jones et al. 1998; Verdun 2000a). A two-level games perspective (Putnam 1988) has been adopted by various authors to explain the interplay between national governments and the domestic constituency, as well as national governments and the international arena (Dyson 1994; Wolf and Zangl 1996). It has been adopted to explain how the national government in Italy has used EMU to strengthen its position vis-à-vis domestic actors (Featherstone 1996).

For a full understanding of the EMU process, one needs to examine it from both perspectives. Indeed some authors have already adopted an eclectic approach. Eclecticism offers the researcher a way to examine the process at various levels of analysis and through the role of a variety of actors and mechanisms. By examining the process with only one approach, one may be able to come up with a partial explanation of part of the process, but not the whole picture.

It is of course understandable that scholars have been tempted to look at the process and examine theories that seem competing. They are interested in finding clear answers. One way to do this is to argue that one theory is more capable at explaining the process than another is. In doing so one tests hypotheses derived from both theories and judges which one fits best. In a sense social scientists suffer from being 'scientists' in that they are tempted to adopt the scientific method used in other fields of science, such as to use tests to see which theory is better able to explain the results of the testing. As is well known, the problem in social science research is that pure testing as is done in laboratories is impossible. Moreover, there are so many factors involved in any given situation and no situation is ever really similar to another. The hypothesis testing method often means that one has to make many assumptions about the actors one is studying, the level of analysis, and the process and mechanisms at stake. By defining the research project in a certain way, the research design ends up favouring one theoretical approach over another. The two theories discussed here look at different parts of the process and assume that different actors are important and that different mechanisms are at work. Integration is however happening all the time at different levels with different actors. Thus, I argue here that the various theories complement each other. One's perspective is limited if one only looks at one part of the process with the analysis of one of the two families of theories.

Lessons from Perceptions of EMU

As stated above the theoretical framework adopted for the present study is a so-called 'eclectic approach' of European integration, which tries to explain why integration happens. It is eclectic in that it adopts elements from both the intergovernmental and the neofunctional families of theory. From the intergovernmentalist family it adopts the claim that national governments try to promote 'national interests' through the European integration process. The eclectic approach also applies this claim to societal actors, and suggests that their attitudes to European integration also have to do with the fact that they perceive European integration as a useful instrument for influencing policy-making in order to protect their interests. From the neofunctionalist family the eclectic approach takes on the idea that policy-making can indeed *spill-over* into other policy areas, and that there inevitably is an important role for experts and technocrats in the policy-making process, as well as domestic and supranational actors. In response to the critics of both theories (Rosamond 1995; Webb 1983), the eclectic approach incorporates the importance of the effects of globalisation and interdependence. Hence, from the international political economy literature it borrows the assertion that increasing globalisation and its results—e.g., the reduction in national policy autonomy—strongly influence the policy-making process and hence international cooperation, and in our case European integration (see inter alia Pauly 1992; Strange 1994).

Hence, this 'eclectic approach' is an attempt to explain the progress towards further European integration by taking domestic, European, and global factors into consideration. It examines how the European (monetary) integration process became considered as (part of) the solution to existing problems.

Let us now turn to a specific case study of perceptions of EMU.[1] In the early 1990s a research project was conducted to study the perceptions of domestic actors and EU officials on EMU. The aim was to understand whether EMU was considered desirable and, if so, under what conditions. It also hoped to understand how EMU served or frustrated the interests of each of these actors. The domestic actors selected were trade unions, employers' organisations, central banks, and Ministries of Finance in Britain, France, and Germany. The perceptions of various EU actors were investigated as well, but below we shall discuss only the results of the research on the perceptions of domestic actors.[2] Because there were very few policy documents, it was chosen to conduct interviews based on semi-structured questionnaires. They were held in the spring of 1991 and repeated in the autumn of 1992. In total seventy-five interviews were held.

The main results of the 1991 interviews were that monetary authorities in the three countries held very similar views with respect to the earlier EMU plans and the EMS. However, in that year they held substantially different views with respect to conditions under which EMU was desirable, in particular concerning the restrictions on budgetary and fiscal policies. All monetary authorities agreed to the blueprint set out in the Delors Report (1989). They accepted that EMU implied having a single monetary authority that would be solely responsible for monetary policy with the single mandate of guaranteeing price stability. Even though France, and especially Britain, faced difficulties (in that their central banks would have to become politically independent), the monetary authorities of these two countries nevertheless accepted the fact that the new European monetary authority needed to be independent to be effective. In 1991, the British monetary authorities did not want any formal limits on fiscal freedom (see, e.g., Leigh-Pemberton 1990a, 1990b). The French counterparts wanted the limits, but wanted the introduction of these limits to be compensated for by a transfer of power of economic policy-making to the Community level (see also Lagayette 1990, 1991). German monetary authorities proposed rules on budgets and no transfer of economic sovereignty.

These matters were settled in the 1992 Maastricht Treaty. In the second round of interviews in late 1992 interviewees were asked if they were satisfied with the EMU design as set out in the treaty. All monetary authority officials explained that the formal policy of their organisation or institution was that they were very content with the section on EMU in the Maastricht Treaty, even though the officials personally criticised some elements.

The British monetary authorities were happy with the Maastricht Treaty, as they had secured an 'opt-out' from joining the single currency and from the Social Chapter. They would have preferred not to have had the 3 percent and 60 percent limits on the budgetary deficits and debt levels, but argued that these rules were much less restrictive than the objectives that the British had set out for themselves. The difference between the Bank of England and the Treasury became obvious in their general attitude towards EMU. The Bank of England saw EMU as an objective to be included in the long-term strategy of the bank. The Treasury still had grave doubts about whether Britain would ever join EMU.

The French monetary authorities in general were very positive about the EMU articles in the treaty. They had made some concessions, but the EMU part of the treaty contained all the elements the French thought were important. It ensured the issuing of a single currency based on price stability. The fact that economic policy-making in the treaty would have to follow the principle of subsidiarity, which here meant that it would remain at the level of the member state, no longer seemed to be a problem for the French. When asked her personal opinion, an official of the French Finance Ministry argued that a lot still needed to be done on the institutional side, especially concerning the role of economic policy-making, and the role of the Community budget (and of parliamentary decision-making).

The German authorities felt that the treaty very much followed their proposals, as they had obtained all they hoped for: a politically independent European monetary authority, with a single mandate to secure price stability. Limits had been placed on national budgetary deficits and the timetable would push member states to become ready to join.

As regards the effects of EMU on other policy areas, the monetary authorities in both 1991 and 1992 shared the view that once EMU and the Internal Market would be fully operational, national fiscal and social policies would come under market pressure. It would be very difficult to have systems that varied considerably across national boundaries, but moreover, it would be impossible to maintain a system that was not consistent with maintaining competitiveness. The French monetary authorities were perhaps the ones that foresaw the smallest change to occur in social policies.

The employers' organisations in the three countries, if taken together as a single group of actors, held the most positive view about EMU of all actors questioned both in 1991 and 1992. In 1991 they emphasised the need for a single currency in Europe for economic efficiency, and to strengthen the role of Europe and the European single currency in the world economy. They were generally hesitant to accept that any social regulation accompany the move towards the final stages of EMU. In 1992 they welcomed the treaty and were hopeful about it. In all three countries the national employers' confederations perceived EMU as implying a strengthening of the deregulated single market, the introduction of a single currency, very small transfer payments, and low fiscal and social regulation. In other words, 'letting the market do the work'. They were all very much against tax increases, or more generally, against a 'centralist', strongly regulated Europe.

The Confederation of British Industry (CBI) was very much in favour of EMU. However, in 1991 it was opposed to binding rules on budgetary deficits and public debt. In 1992 it changed this view and suggested that these were healthy norms. The Conseil National du Patronat Français (CNPF) was split over EMU. The elites dealing with EMU as well as its president were in favour, but a minority within the French *patronat*, mainly consisting of Gaullists, was opposed. Thus the CNPF did not formally take a political position. However, the majority was very much in favour. The president gave a very positive personal statement in support of EMU. Also, the CNPF did publish joint statements with its German counterparts in support of EMU (BDI-CNPF 1990). The German Bundesverband der Deutschen Industrie (BDI) was also in favour of EMU. It welcomed the further integration of monetary policies and the introduction of a single currency. However, of all employers' organisations, it was the one most concerned about the possible regional implications of EMU. Reflecting on the experience of German reunification it wondered to what extent the treaty should also have focused on economic convergence (see also BDI 1990; BDI and DGB 1990).

Trade unions have come a long way from opposition to, and scepticism about, the European integration project in the 1970s, to gradual support of European integration in the 1980s, to full support towards the end of the 1980s. The trade unions saw EMU as a way of reinforcing their position in European policy-making. They realised that the role of trade unions in the national domain had diminished during the 1980s. They felt that their job could not be done effectively by remaining focused only at the national level. Moreover, due to globalisation and further financial interdependence, policies made purely at the national level were becoming ineffective. In the view of the trade unions, it was becoming more and more important to coordinate, or at least to have full knowledge about similar policies conducted in other member states. Finally, the awareness had arisen that policies initiated at the European level by the European Trade Union Confederation (ETUC) were becoming increasingly important. In general it was thought that the voice of trade unions would not be heard if they opposed the process. They hoped that a constructive contribution would make it possible for them to influence agenda setting. With this in mind their strongest input was to make sure the Social Chapter was included in the Maastricht Treaty, and to secure some redistributing funds to regions that might lose out when EMU becomes fully operational (see for example ETUC 1990, 1991, 1992).

There were some differences among the various national trade unions. The Trade Unions Congress (TUC) in Britain, the three French trade union confederations, Confédération Française Démocratique du Travail (CFDT), Force Ouvrière (FO) and the Confédération Général du Travail (CGT), and the German Deutscher Gewerkschaftsbund (DGB) all held different views on whether EMU was desirable. Nevertheless, all recognised that the room for manoeuvre for trade unions has become very limited in recent years. With the exception of the two communist/left-wing French trade union confederations FO and CGT, who were still sceptical about this capitalist project, the trade unions in the three countries accepted EMU. They realised that no matter how much criticism one may have on the exact details of the EMU plans of the Community, it is better to participate in the drawing up of the plans than stand outside the process arguing against it (see DGB 1990a, 1990b). If trade unions only oppose the process, arguing that it is imperfect, national decision-makers will definitely not take any notice of the unions. Moreover, EMU was seen as offering an important window of opportunity for trade unions to become institutionalised at the European level in European governance and for shaping the future of macroeconomic policy-making in the EU.

Thus, monetary authorities and social partners all perceived the total EMU package to be desirable, albeit under various different conditions and aiming at various objectives. Even among functionally similar organisations divergent views are held.

When do actors 'behave' according to the characteristics of their 'function' and when do they behave according to those of the 'country'? It can be stated that the Finance Ministry of each country generally propounds the position of that 'national government'. In Britain the Treasury stressed the need to take part in the negotiations and restrict its outcome to the very minimum. Simultaneously it was arguing the need to perpetuate the possibility of joining EMU eventually. In France the Finance Ministry voiced a very strong, almost unconditional, desire to create EMU. Even though it claimed there is a need to create some kind of 'economic government', it did not fight strongly for this objective during the Maastricht negotiations. The German Finance Ministry favoured EMU as long as its main objective was price stability, and as long as participating countries' economies could 'prove' to be converging as expressed by the performance of their monetary indicators. The other German motive was to show the other Member States that Germany was committed to Europe.

Within every country some actors were more in favour of joining EMU while others were more reluctant. After a discussion of the attitudes of the actors within the countries, it is clear that the French were the most positive and the British the most reserved. In table 2.1 these attitudes are pictured schematically.

Table 2.1: Attitudes Towards EMU

	Pro-EMU		Cautiously Pro-EMU			Reluctant	Opposed
France	FFM	BdF	CNPF[1]	CFDT	CNPF[1]	FO	CGT
Germany		GFM		BDI	DGB	BB	
Britain			CBI	BoE	TUC	HMT	

1.The CNPF is divided about the desirability of EMU, which is illustrated in the table by categorising it twice.

Abbreviations: BB (Bundesbank), BdF (Banque de France), BDI (German employers' organisation), BoE (Bank of England), CBI (Confederation of British Industry), CFDT (Confédération Française Démocratique du Travail), CGT (Confédération Générale du Travail), CNPF (Conseil National du Patronat Français), DGB (Deutscher Gewerkschaftsbund), FFM (French Finance Ministry), FO (Force Ouvrière), GFM (German Finance Ministry), HMT (Her Majesty's Treasury), TUC (Trades Unions Congress).

The table illustrates that the French actors are on the whole the most positive (if the views of two French trade unions CGT and FO are left aside) followed by the Germans and lastly the British. Within the three countries there is a spread in support for EMU. This scheme needs to be used with great caution, as it reflects an estimation of the actors' perceptions on EMU. Caution is especially needed as actors do not hold an equally positive/negative view on all issues related to EMU. Likewise, the views have undergone minor changes over time. On the whole it seems true to say that the German and French Finance Ministries pushed the process forward, whereas the British Treasury tried to hold it back. The Banque de France was very positive, whereas the Bank of England, and certainly the Bundesbank held more reservations. The employers' organisations seemed generally more in favour of EMU than the trade unions in their respective countries. The French and the British were more in favour than the German employers' organisation, mainly because the German employers' organisation held stronger reservations about the conditions under which they would agree to EMU. The trade unions followed the same pattern as the Finance Ministries: the French are the most in favour, the British the most reluctant. They were concerned about the possibility of EMU being introduced without proper cushioning.

Limits of Neofunctionalism and Intergovernmentalism for Understanding EMU: The Need to Adopt an Eclectic Theory

The question raised here was why and how integration takes place? The two main schools of thought that were discussed above are neofunctionalism and intergovernmentalism. The two hold different assumptions about why integration happens, who the decisive actors in the process are, and what mechanisms lead to further integration. It is now appropriate to recapitulate their assessment of the integration process.

The neofunctionalists hold the view that the integration process starts in some policy areas because some actors, whether societal groups, experts, or government bureaucracies, consider it functionally practical to settle issues in these policy areas at the supranational level. These issues would concern technical matters that are not politically sensitive areas of policy-making. As soon as integration has successfully taken place in one policy area, it will eventually require the integration of other policy areas (spill-over). It seems to have an internal dynamic that is monitored in part by a supranational authority. Yet, it is not fully automatic. The actors will notice that the policy areas that were transferred to the supranational level have been looked after successfully. Some policy areas will now be more difficult to handle at the national level in isolation from cooperation with other states and soon thereafter it will prove to be handy to transfer more decision-making capacity to the supranational level. This is the spill-over mechanism.

The intergovernmentalists take the national governments as the dominant and decisive actors. The integration process develops as a logical consequence of interstate bargaining. The larger member states, in particular Britain, France, and Germany, play a dominant role in this interplay. In contrast to the neofunctionalist assumption, societal groups are thought to play at most an indirect role. They can only influence the outcome by lobbying, and persuading their national governments to take their interests into account when defining 'the' national interests. In contrast to the neofunctionalist theory, it is assumed that the integration process does not have any internal dynamic, neither through integration spill-over from one policy to another, nor path-dependence, nor the workings of a supranational authority. If there appears to be spill-over it would be coincidence. European integration only happens when member state governments decide that they want to embark on further integration because of domestic interests heading in that direction. If the policy objectives of various dominant member states converge, then one can expect coordination of policies and eventually, perhaps, integration. This can happen more easily if national policies and strategies have started to converge, as governments have abandoned earlier policies, and adopted successful policies of other countries. Yet, in the intergovernmentalist view even the globalisation process has not been identified as having caused the integration process. It is still argued that the exact outcome of the coordinated policy, or indeed integration, results primarily from the interstate bargaining process.

When examining how these schools of thought view the European economic and monetary integration process, we find that each of the two conventional theories taken by itself is only partially successful in anticipating the progress of the integration process. The neofunctionalists would predict that economic policies should be an easy subject for integration. To a certain extent this is actually what happened. The 'economic' part of the development of the Community has kept the integration train moving forward. Even though on several occasions in the history of economic and monetary integration the EC plans did not materialise, some projects have been unexpectedly successful. The EMS set up in 1979 survived its childhood and miraculously only ran into difficulties in 1992-93. The impact and speed of the completion of the Internal Market, as was set out in the Single European Act of 1985, was perhaps an even better example of the neofunctionalist concept of policy decisions on technical matters being taken at a higher level. In turn, these decisions would eventually trigger the need for other policy issues to be settled at the supranational level. Finally, EMU was set up to incorporate a monetary policy that would aim at price stability and eventually to supply a single currency. The latter would safeguard the benefits of the Internal Market. These last two integration projects—the Internal Market programme and the EMU project—were considered at the outset to be highly technical matters that could better be arranged at the supranational level, rather than having national politicians conduct individual national policies.

From our case of EMU we have seen that all kinds of actors played an important role in creating EMU. Domestic interest groups such as trade unions saw the national domain as being unable to deal with their problems. The employers' organisations saw EMU as a way to institutionalise neoliberal principles and keep out too much government intervention in the market economy at the European level. Experts were involved in drafting the blueprint of EMU. Moreover, even the intergovernmental negotiations were conducted by experts who were fully aware of the sensitivities of the national governments of other member states. The representatives of the Ministries of Finance had been participating in many EU committee meetings, and thus were fully immersed in the collective knowledge about 'proper' policy-making. These observations all sound very much like neofunctionalist thinking. But there is another story to be told.

How would the intergovernmentalists interpret the same facts? Their focus would be on the bargaining of the national governments to safeguard their interests, and whether the domestic policy objectives of the member states would happen to coincide. The outcome of any bargaining would not contain more than the lowest common denominator, or, if it would contain more, it would have been a result of the greater bargaining power of the larger states. Hence, referring to the same examples, the EMS was successful because the member states participating in it had started to converge policy objectives. Important contributions to its success were the policy experiences of France (1981-83) and Italy in the mid- and late 1980s. These countries discovered that it was necessary to try to keep inflation under control, and during the course of the 1980s they started using the EMS framework to funnel policies to meet the inflation and exchange rate objectives. Moravcsik's analysis of the EMU bargaining process focuses on the final negotiations at the Intergovernmental Conference, and how EMU served the interests of the state leaders. His analysis sees the role of any other actor or mechanism to be negligible (Moravcsik 1998).

Turning back to the discussion of neofunctionalism, the fact is that it can very eloquently explain the dynamics of integration considering only its theoretical concepts of spill-over and the evidence, that is, the renewed move towards European integration. However, neofunctionalist thought does not identify two of the main motives for the renewed interest in integration. My study of EMU shows that the move towards EMU is triggered by three causes. In addition to the spill-over effect there are two other causes (Verdun 2000a).

First, the member states (social partners as well as central banks and national governments) saw EMU as a solution to the problem of the lack of national policy autonomy. This situation had resulted from the change in the global economy, rather than from a response to the integration processes itself. In preference to fighting each other, they felt that they needed to unite the European interests in order to stand up to the rest of the world, in particular to the Pacific Basin and the United States. The intergovernmentalists have better understood this mechanism, and have often referred to 'policy objective convergence'.

Second, another result of the awareness that the global economy had changed was that member states drew the conclusion that their domestic economies were too rigid, making a flexible adjustment to the external changes very difficult. It was politically problematic to address these issues at the national level, as it implied reducing the benefits that industry and labour had received from the state.

Politicians who needed to restructure public finances and the welfare state found themselves having to sell very unpopular measures. It was considered much easier to restructure the economy by focusing on the benefits of European integration, and by using European integration to legitimise the need for change. Neofunctionalist theory had not anticipated these two aspects related to the changes in the international global economy as being decisive in creating the momentum for renewed interest in European integration.

Intergovernmentalists failed to recognise that the support of the European economic and monetary integration project by the societal groups made it very easy for the governments to develop the EMU plans. An exception in this regard is Andrew Moravcsik's Liberal Intergovernmentalist approach that *does* incorporate a role for domestic economic interests. Yet in his analysis they only affect national government interests and preference formation (Moravcsik 1998), but do not affect preference formation at the EU level. Also, he does not see any independent influence on the process from any societal actor other than the national governments. In the case of EMU, however, national and European employers' organisations and trade union confederations have very actively promoted the European objective at both the national and the European level. The umbrella organisation of trade unions, ETUC, and the European organisation of employers' organisations, UNICE, played a significant role in getting the message across that they favoured the deepening of European integration objective, albeit under some specific conditions (see, e.g., UNICE 1990a, 1990b). The support from societal actors served as additional legitimation to national governments for surrendering sovereignty to the supranational level. ETUC and UNICE were aiming at securing their own interests by conducting policies at the European level when they realised that it would no longer suffice to focus exclusively at the national level.

The intergovernmentalists also do not envisage the fact that the spill-over was indeed taking effect, albeit *in parallel* with the globalisation process. All actors considered it impossible to turn back the clock. For example, the success of the EMS and the '1992' project made actors want to secure its full benefits by creating the EMU project. The capital liberalisation of July 1990 polarised the choice. The Delors Committee decided to let the first stage of EMU coincide with the decision already taken to liberalise capital. All in all, the European leaders would either be moving beyond the EMS or risk having to move back. The domestic actors in Britain, France, and Germany realised that it is imperative to accept a whole package deal, which was carefully negotiated, and that there is no easy way back.

In Conclusion:
Merging European Integration Theories and the Future (Use) of Integration Theories in EU Studies

This chapter has argued that the European integration theories need to be merged in order for us to obtain a better picture of the actors involved in the European integration process as well as the mechanisms at work. Recent approaches to European integration offer additional insights into the integration process. This chapter placed all those theories on a spectrum examining their view on the role of state actors, other actors, and whether or not the integration mechanism was to a certain degree automatic. Subsequently the theories were placed in two categories, and two large families of integration theories were introduced. Theories were grouped into a neofunctionalist family and an intergovernmentalist family. In order to get a more complete picture of how integration happens the chapter proposed to merge the theories.

Based on the case of EMU one can see how adopting the view of the neofunctionalist family or the intergovernmentalist family influences the analysis of the integration process, and that the whole story can only be seen if both are taken together. Each offers its own valuable insights into the process of creating EMU and the actors and mechanisms involved. In a case study of perceptions of EMU, as held by domestic actors, the usefulness of both approaches was once again highlighted. However, it became clear that integration theories developed in the 1950s and 1960s fall short in understanding the importance of the changed role of the external world, the global economy, and increasing interdependence. The integration theories will have to keep reflecting on the broader trends in the global economy, be they in the areas of common ideas, paradigms and regimes, or the actual power struggle at the geopolitical level. Thus, the eclectic theory of integration incorporates that dimension as well into its view of European integration.

What does this all mean for the future of EU studies and the usefulness of integration theories? The view held here is that it will be up to the researchers of EU studies to determine when which actors are most important, and when which mechanisms are most salient in any given part of the process at any given level of analysis at any point in time. However, for an overall picture of the multifaceted integration process one needs to adopt eclecticism.

Notes

1. This case study draws on the findings reported in Verdun (2000).

2. The EU actors studied were the European Commission (Directorate General for Economic and Financial Affairs and the Delors Cabinet) and the Economic and Social Committee. In addition interviews were conducted with various European interest organisations, such as the European Trade Union Confederation (ETUC), the European employers' organisation (UNICE), and the Association for the Monetary Union of Europe (AMUE)—an organisation of big business representatives strongly in favour of the creation of EMU.

F33
F36

Chapter 3
NEOFUNCTIONALISM AND INTERGOVERNMENTALISM AMALGAMATED: THE CASE OF EMU

Dieter Wolf

There is probably no other research area in political science that has more often been decried as dead, obsolescent or inadequate than the realm of research on theories of European integration. And yet, no other political scientific research area seems to have witnessed more revivals, reformulations and 'bringing-back-ins' than this scientific research agenda (see also Verdun, chapter 2 this volume). From the glorious heights of the 1950s and 1960s (Haas 1958; Hoffmann 1966) to its self-critical 'obsolescence' (Haas 1975) and the seemingly definitive labelling as insufficient in its explanatory power (Webb 1983), the roller-coaster of the theories of integration started toward new summits in the late 1980s and early 1990s (Sandholtz and Zysman 1989; Moravcsik 1991; Tranholm-Mikkelsen 1991). From its renewed assurance of a lively existence (Moravcsik 1993a, 1994; Garrett 1992; Burley and Mattli 1993; Corbey 1995) integration theory was again harshly criticised for being not powerful enough in explaining the existing empirical evidence of the development of European integration (Cram 1996; Kaltenthaler 1997; Alter 1998; Mattli and Slaughter 1998). Again, it seems to be fashionable in political scientific research on European politics to start with the short yet strong statement that neofunctionalism and intergovernmentalism are too reductionist in their analysis, do not explain certain empirical facts and, thus, are to be cast aside in order to open the road for more comprehensive perspectives.

Against the background of this renewed argument of obsolescence it is especially important to explain why one is still attempting to continue the ride on the roller-coaster and why history has not yet closed the books on this kind of political scientific research. The aim of this chapter is not to question the validity of most of the critical remarks against current theories of European integration. In fact, it agrees with the two main criticisms. It is undeniably true that the European Union has developed into some kind of 'political system' (Hix 1999) and, thus, should be analysed with theories, methods and instruments from comparative politics (Hix 1994, 1996; Caporaso 1998), looking for answers to questions of political power and legitimacy. At the same time, even the most sophisticated recent analyses based on neofunctionalism, supranationalism or intergovernmentalism (Corbey 1995; Sandholtz and Stone Sweet 1998; Moravcsik 1998) do not manage to refute unequivocally the central critique against these approaches since the debates of the 1960s and 1970s.

With respect to neofuctionalism, this major critique focuses on the accusation of a non-political determinism and holism, which can still be detected in Corbey's (1995) 'dialectical functionalism' or Burley and Mattli's (1993) judicial version of the approach. Neofunctionalism, so the argument goes, offers no room for voluntary decision-making of even the central actors in European integration, but rather assumes that structural necessities will inevitably lead to more integration. With respect to intergovernmentalism, even its most elaborate accounts (Moravcsik 1998; Scharpf 1997; Zangl 1999) still face the central critique of reductionism, since they offer refined decision-making and interest aggregation theories against the background of game theoretic concepts, while still lacking a genuine interest theory. Interests and preferences are exogenous to the model and have to be assessed in each case on the basis of the empirical evidence available.

If that is the case, why this chapter? Why provide a renewed attempt to reformulate neofunctionalism and intergovernmentalism? It seems necessary to deal with the question of 'why' European integration exists and develops at least as long as the Community is in the process of deepening and widening integration. Even if one agrees with Wallace (1983) that, in the perspective of comparative politics, the results of intergovernmental conferences can be viewed as 'constitutional policies', it is not enough to ask how these policies came about, which power distribution they reflect and how legitimate they are. Rather, there is still ample room for the traditional question of why European integration is still in the process of deepening and widening, which are the critical 'engines' and 'brakes' of this process, and what could be seen as the ultimate goal of the whole endeavour. This chapter maintains that there is a possibility to amalgamate the two major theories of European integration, neofunctionalism and intergovernmentalism, into one coherent approach on a sound theoretical basis and beyond the often advocated simple addition of their findings (Wessels 1997; Niemann 1998). It argues that with this amalgamation it is possible to counter most of the central criticisms against both approaches and, thus, to extract synergetic benefits in order to improve the explanatory power with respect to European integration.

In order to present its argument the chapter takes four steps. First, it offers a systematic ordering of the different empirical-analytical theoretical approaches to European integration in order to clarify the contents of the multitude of black boxes labelled 'intergovernmentalism' or 'neofunctionalism' and to reformulate the central premises and hypotheses of these two traditional theories of European integration. One of the central problems of this debate on theories of European integration is the sometimes extremely confusing use of the labels 'supranationalism' and 'neofunctionalism'. This resulted in a wild array of presumably 'neofunctional' hypotheses in the literature. Hence, first it is critically necessary to sort and restructure the theoretical arguments. Second, the chapter offers the promised amalgamated approach including a set of hypotheses with respect to European monetary integration. It will be shown that intergovernmentalism and neofunctionalism can be amalgamated on a sound (meta) theoretical basis and that the resulting new approach is also able to address the major theoretical shortcomings of the traditional explanations for European integration. Third, it shows the plausibility of the new approach by applying the hypotheses to two cases of European monetary integration: the decision to accept the Werner Plan in 1971 and the failure to follow up on this decision in the early 1970s. It is impossible in the context of this chapter to offer more than a preliminary assessment of the explanatory power of the amalgamated approach to European integration. Finally, the paper outlines the prospects of this new approach with respect to two important research aims:

(a) The theoretically sound combination of neofunctionalism and intergovernmentalism beyond the simple eclectic addition of their results and beyond holism or reductionism.

(b) The introduction of a genuine interest theory for rational choice approaches, in this case a functional interest theory for European integration.

What Is Neofunctionalism and What Is Intergovernmentalism? An Attempt to Structure the Debates

For years it seemed the necessary prerequisite of any scholar of European integration to present an overview of the theoretical landscape of the research area. This practice occurred either in order to show a recognition of the monumental debates or to lay the foundations for a wholesale rejection of these discussions as inadequate and unsatisfactory. This chapter does not aim at either one of these goals. Rather it attempts to structure the debates according to their theoretical contents in order to present a careful map of this theoretical landscape and to extract the major hypotheses of the two central theoretical approaches to the explanation of European integration.

In her dissertation on the 'Origins of the Single Market' Nicola Fielder (1997) summarises her review of Sandholtz and Zysman (1989) with the following words:

> It is difficult to classify Sandholtz and Zysman either as neorealists or as neofunctionalists . . . at times it is not quite clear where they stand. However, their theory includes elements of both neorealistic and neofunctionalist explanations, but the emphasis is perhaps slightly on the neofunctionalist side (1997: 25).

Is it possible to sort this out?

In order to get to the core one has first to introduce two important distinctions in the realm of political scientific research on European integration. First, as already mentioned, the research field was divided around the question of 'why' integration developed on the one hand and the question of 'how' policies are made and implemented in the context of the multilevel political system on the other (Zürn 1995; Jachtenfuchs and Kohler-Koch 1996; Jachtenfuchs 2001). The first question relates mostly to theories of international politics, whereas the second question is most often answered on the basis of approaches stemming from comparative politics. This chapter restricts itself to the first question.

The second differentiation relates to the question of rational positivist versus reflexive constructivist approaches to the understanding or explanation of European integration (Hollis and Smith 1991; Pollack 2001). Particularly in the second half of the 1990s constructivist and reflectivist approaches became prominent in research on international cooperation and, thus, also found their way into the study of European integration. Although these analyses argue convincingly to broaden the theoretical perspective beyond the positivist realm (Cameron 1995; Risse-Kappen 1996; Verdun 1999; Diez 1999) this chapter confines itself to the rationalist empirical and analytical perspective on European integration.

Table 3.1: Categorisation of Positivist Theoretical Approaches to European Integration

Mode of Explanation	Level of Analysis	
	intergovernmental	supranational
functional	1	2
intentional	3	4

In this positivist perspective on European integration it is possible to identify two dimensions in order to distinguish the theoretical arguments of various approaches to the explanation of European integration. On the one hand, these approaches focus either on the intergovernmental or the supranational as the appropriate level of the analysis. On the other hand, these approaches offer different modes of explanation: intentional or functional.[1] This leads to the matrix in table 3.1.

1. Functional Intergovernmentalism

The analyses in this sector are heavily based on neorealist arguments. State governments are the central actors of European integration and they have to secure (or improve) their relative position vis-à-vis other member governments. Grieco (1995, 1996) in particular and also Hoffmann (1993) to some extent, argue that—even after the end of the Cold War—European integration can only be understood in terms of relative gains. Thus, monetary integration is considered to be the means for France and Italy to improve their 'voice' in monetary matters and to emancipate themselves from German domination, that is, from the hegemony of the German Bundesbank. According to this perspective, member state governments have to consider their relative power position vis-à-vis other member states and, thus, inescapably face structural requirements and functional necessities, which do not provide any major room for political manoeuvre. These structural and functional requirements determine the preference structures of the national governments and, thus, their ability to enter into cooperative agreements. The governments only enter into such co-operation if they are able to extract relative gains in power or welfare.

2. Functional Supranationalism

The approaches in this sector include most of the classic functional or neofunctional arguments of the 1960s and 1970s (Mitrany 1966; Haas 1958; Lindberg 1963; Schmitter 1969) as well as several 'bringing-back-ins', reformulations or extensions of the early 1990s (Tranholm-Mikkelsen 1991; Burley and Mattli 1993; Beukel 1994; Gabriel 1995; Corbey 1995). These arguments are built on two major theoretical foundations. On the one hand, they use Emil Durkheim's (1893) notion of functional differentiation as the central source of modernisation. Durkheim traces the development of modern societies to increasing sectoralisation, segmentation and specialisation, which increases the efficiency of social and economic processes, but also increases the mutual interdependence of each of the sectors, segments or specialised areas. Powered by this functional differentiation (and its efficiency gains) and coerced by the resulting interdependence, industrialised societies are forced into cooperation

and coordination of their sectors and segments. If the exchanges and externalities transgress state borders, this cooperation and coordination have to follow.
On the other hand, functional supranationalists assume pluralist societies with
multiple interest and preference structures, which lead to the formation of
different, competing interest groups and social movements with the aim to lobby
and influence the political sphere (parties, parliaments, governments,
administrations, even courts) in order to realise the preferred goals.

With respect to European integration these basic premises led Mitrany
(1948) and Haas (1955, 1968) to the belief that increasing trans-border exchange
will inevitably force national governments to introduce supranational regulations
and to cooperate in the complex management of transnational social and
economic interdependence. Integration can start in technical sectors, for
example, the postal services or telecommunications sector. However, cooperation even in such apolitical—and hence uncontroversial—sectors tends to
spill-over into further cooperative arrangements. Structural and functional
pressures not only deepen the level of integration of the respective policy area
but also widen the realm of cooperation into other, connected policy areas (and
to other countries in Europe). Supranational institutions act as catalysts of these
processes and—finally—will take over political responsibilities from the
national governments. At this time the citizens of the member states will transfer
their loyalty to these new common institutions.

Thus, the central explanatory factors are increasing transnational interdependence and functional spill-over which force the governments to cooperate, to
create common institutions and, finally, to transfer major competences to this
new political level. In this perspective, the governments of the member states do
not have any substantial room for manoeuvre in their decision to cooperate.
Rather, the structural and functional necessities of increasingly interdependent
societies coerce them into similarly increasing degrees of cooperation,
coordination and integration. Even supranational institutions cannot escape this
basically deterministic path towards common political decision-making. The
reason is that they are only able to catalyse the removal of barriers and these
supranational institutions are considered the final destination for all major
political competences in the Community.

3. Intentional Intergovernmentalism

This sector of the matrix combines the major critics of neofunctionalism
both in the 1960s (Hoffmann 1964, 1966; Aron 1964) as well as their successors
in the 1990s (Morvacsik 1991, 1993, 1994, 1998; Garrett 1992, 1993, 1995).
Hoffmann harshly criticised the neofunctionalists for their basically deterministic perspective on integration and for their holistic view on member governments. Hoffmann became more critical especially after the 'empty-chair' crisis
of 1965-66, in which de Gaulle boycotted the Council and forced the partners
into accepting unanimous decision making as the core principle of European

politics for some twenty years. This move back to unanimity was not explainable by transnational interdependence and functional spill-over.[2] Thus, Hoffmann argued, member state governments and their interests represent the central explanatory element of European integration.

Morvacsik and Garrett, in particular, reformulated this perspective in the 1990s. Integration in their view is the result of converging governmental interests. They argue that European integration will prosper, deepen and widen its realm, as long as these interests are converging. As soon as these interests start to diverge, the integration process will be stalled or even reversed. Member state governments aggregate their interests through a complex process of internal bargaining with major societal interest groups and actors. However, since—from a national perspective—European politics is still considered to be part of foreign policy, member governments are able to increase their room of manoeuvre vis-à-vis their constituencies via intergovernmental cooperation. Bargaining behind closed doors and information advantages offer the governments the possibility to claim the positive effects of cooperation for themselves ('credit-claiming') but to blame the European level for disadvantages, shortcomings or additional burdens ('scape-goating'), even if the government itself did not veto the decision in the bargaining process. Thus, Moravcsik concludes, European integration is dependent on the will of the national executives and strengthens their position vis-à-vis their societies (Moravcsik 1994; Moravcsik and Nicolaidis 1999).

The engine of integration is clear: convergence of voluntaristic interests of the member governments. There is no room for deterministic structural or functional pressures since transnational interdependence and intergovernmental cooperation increases rather than decreases the room of manoeuvre for the governments (Moravcsik 1999, 2000).

4. Intentional Supranationalism

The research convoked in this sector of the matrix represents a comparatively new strand of political scientific research on European integration. Starting with the seminal article of Sandholtz and Zysman (1989) these scholars accept the intergovernmental critique on the deterministic character of functional spill-over but utter their disbelief in the central role of member state governments in European integration and particularly in the wholly nationally oriented process of interest aggregation. Rather, Sandholtz (1992) and Stone Sweet and Brunell (1998) argue that voluntaristic interests are certainly the core of the explanation and that national governments have the final decision about major changes of the European treaties, but that the interests of the member governments are heavily influenced by decisions made at the supranational level. According to the reasoning of 'intentional supranationalism' the European Commission and the European Court of Justice play an important role in initiating new European policies and in developing European cooperation.

Through their entrepreneurial behaviour and the already acquired competences in various policy fields these common institutions are able to change the interest structure of the member governments and to induce major steps to deepen and widen the area of cooperation in the Community (Sandholtz 1996; Sandholtz and Stone Sweet 1999; Tallberg 2000).

In pursuing this goal the Commission was and is able to enlist the support of important national and transnational interest groups which put additional pressure on their governments to strengthen the European level and to transfer political competences to the supranational decision making bodies. Thus, member governments are part of a multilevel governance system and sometimes face coalitions of supra- and sub-national actors in order to pressure them into engaging in or accepting common solutions for different social, economic and political problems (Jabko 1999).

In this perspective the engine of European integration is to be found in the voluntaristic interests of supra- and sub-national actors which are able to influence the interest structure of member state governments and, thus, give new impulses to the deepening and widening of European integration.

Critiquing the Theoretical Debates

Against the background of this differentiation of various positivist approaches to the explanation of European integration it seems appropriate to make several critical remarks on the theoretical debates of the last ten years. First, not everything which is labelled 'neofunctionalist' is really a neofunctionalist argument. The best example of this misunderstanding is the debate between Sandholtz and Zysman (1989) and Moravcsik (1991, 1993a). It is simply wrong to assert that anyone who is advocating a more pronounced role for supranational actors automatically has to be considered a neofunctionalist. Although Haas in his seminal work *The Uniting of Europe* (1958) extensively deals with supranational actors and transnational interest groups, his central theoretical argument rests on the concept of functional spill-over and the (quasi-) inevitability of increasing degrees of cooperation until finally the supranational European institutions win over the loyalty of the population. Sandholtz, Zysman and Stone Sweet (until recently) rejected any notion of this spill-over concept but rather rested their case on the ability of common institutions to change the interest structure of member state governments.[3] The dispute between Sandholtz and Moravcsik was not about 'functional spill-over' versus 'converging interests' but rather about 'wholly national interest formation' versus the ability of the Commission and the Court to alter the interests of their national principals. Hence, the difficulty of Fielder (1997) to subsume Sandholtz and Zysman (1989) under neofunctionalist or intergovernmentalist labels is understandable. They belong to neither one of these two camps.

Second, even after several reformulations and extensions of the original concepts of neofunctionalism and intergovernmentalism there seems to be no answer to the central critique of each of the two approaches. Although Corbey's (1995) 'dialectical functionalism' is able to account for the 'stop-and-go' pattern of European integration over the last forty years, it still contains a deterministic perspective since the actors involved do not possess any room for manoeuvre and, hence, no capability for any voluntaristic decision making. In this analysis the integration process is still quasi inevitable. It might only take more time to reach the final goal and proceed in an uneven fashion. Intergovernmentalism, however, still lacks any comprehensive theory of interest generation and development. In this perspective, interests are exogenous to the model and have to be assessed separately in each empirical case. Even Moravcsik's most elaborate treatment of interests and preferences (Moravcsik 1998; Moravcsik and Nicolaidis 1999) only presents a theory of interest aggregation from national societal actors to national governments and, finally, to the international negotiations. The sources and contents of these interests, however, are still exogenous to the model.

Third, the label 'functional institutionalism', which some scholars (most recently Sandholtz 1996) have attached to intergovernmentalist arguments in the tradition of Keohane (1984) and Moravcsik, is extremely misleading. Keohane's argument is not holistically functionalist but solidly voluntaristically intentional. He simply argues (in the tradition of Wright 1971) that state actors are able to recognise the beneficial functions of common institutions and, thus, are interested in creating them. The explanation rests on the intentions and preferences of the actors and not on the straight-jacket of structural or functional necessities.

Fourth, the renewed harsh critique of Alter (1998) or Mattli and Slaughter (1998) of the inadequacy of theories of integration for the explanation of recent developments in European politics—especially the role of the European Court of Justice—is essentially correct but fundamentally ill-directed since it crosses the boundaries between the 'why' question of integration theory and the 'how' question of comparative politics. What Alter is asking for in particular is an answer to the question of power and legitimacy in European politics and not an explanation of the way European integration came about (Rosamond 2000).

Neofunctionalism and Intergovernmentalism: The Sets of Empirically Testable Hypotheses

Following this structure of different premises and theoretical arguments it is now possible to delineate the major hypotheses of the two central traditional approaches to the explanation of European integration. Based on the premises of neofunctionalism (functional differentiation, pluralism, spill-over, functional necessities) it is possible to formulate two major hypotheses:

(a) The socio-economic structures of the member states are the most important factors to explain European integration. Their form and development determine to a large extent the realisation and contents of European cooperation and the supranational institutional setting. Integration is deepening and widening if the functional pressure to cooperate emanates from an adjoining, already Europeanised policy area, or from an already Europeanised sector of the same policy field, and if the most important socio-economic factors (of the policy field) on national level in the medium term show a tendency to converge on a common level. The stronger the functional pressure for cooperation and the higher the degree of convergence, the higher the level of integration to be reached, and the more competences to be transferred to the European level.

(b) Political-administrative structures both on the national or supranational level only play a catalytic role with respect to the functional pressures for integration. They strengthen the integration process if they have already acquired some political competences in the policy area.

For intergovernmentalism (intentional intergovernmentalism), Moravcsik (1993a, 1998) argues that state governments aggregate national interests (with considerable room for manoeuvre) and that they enter into intergovernmental cooperation if the interests of the participating governments converge on certain questions. The exact contents of the policies are the result of a bargaining process between these governments. Moravcsik argues that in this bargaining process governments do possess advantages which are either able a) to remove negative externalities; or b) to change policies desired by other governments; or c) to distribute resources in which other governments are interested (Moravcsik 1993a: 499). The more the government is in command of such options the better is its bargaining position and vice versa. The bargaining position is also strengthened if one government is able to threaten a unilateral move or if two governments are able to exclude a third one from the negotiations. The bargaining, however, becomes difficult if such positions are not available. In this case a government can gain some advantages if it is able to offer side-payments or concessions in less important areas, which are nevertheless desired by other governments (Moravcsik 1993a: 499-507).

It is possible to translate this complex picture of advantages and disadvantages in bargaining processes into a typology of decision-making situations based on game-theoretical language (Scharpf 1997; Zürn 1992). This typology of so-called mixed-motive games is based between non-problematic social situations (like market exchanges) on the one hand and zero-sum games on the other hand. Whereas simple market exchanges are always socially and politically undisputed since both sides benefit from the transactions, zero-sum games are basically unsolvable (in non-hierarchical, non-coercive situations), since the benefit of the one side is always identical with the cost of the other. Between these two poles it is possible to distinguish four different decision-making situations, which constitute mixed-motive games:

Table 3.2: Hypotheses of Intergovernmentalism (Zürn 1992)

Decision-making Situation	coordination games without distributional conflict	coordination games with distributional conflict	dilemma games	rambo games
Probability of Cooperation and Institutionalisation	very high	high	low	very low

(a) *Coordination games without distributional conflict:* This is the least difficult case to solve, since both sides are willing to cooperate and most of the time only missing information is barring them from doing so.

(b) *Coordination games with distributional conflict:* This is the classic case of a so-called 'chicken' game or 'battle of the sexes'. Both partners are basically willing to cooperate but they disagree about who has to shoulder the costs of this cooperation.

(c) *Dilemma games:* The famous Prisoners' Dilemma is the central example of this kind of coordination problem. Each of the partners would prefer that the other side is cooperating in order to avoid sub-optimal outcomes. However, each partner has an incentive to free-ride, that is, not to cooperate, and to avoid the costs of cooperation.

(d) *Rambo games:* This category of mixed-motive games is least likely to lead to cooperation since one of the two sides has the possibility to reach unilaterally the intended goal.

With these four categories of mixed-motive games it is possible to systematise all of Moravcsik's arguments about intergovernmental bargaining and to develop hypotheses about the probability (and speed) of reaching an agreement.

If one compares the set of hypotheses of neofunctionalism with that of intergovernmentalism it seems that the two contradict each other. Converging socio-economic structures or spill-over effects as independent variables basically exclude converging interests as explanatory factors and vice versa.[4] The first set of variables stems from a structural macro-perspective whereas the second set is basically voluntaristic and micro-oriented.

**Table 3.3: Dependent and Independent Factors of
Neofunctionalism and Intergovernmentalism**

Dimensions	Explanatory Variables	
	Dependent	Independent
Polity		Neofunctionalism
Politics		Intergovernmentalism
Policy	Neofunctionalism and Intergovernmentalism	

The Amalgamated Approach

Theoretical approaches with contradictory sets of hypotheses are usually not open to any form of merger or amalgamation. A closer look at the character of the two different sets of dependent and independent variables of intergovernmentalism and neofunctionalism, however, reveals an interesting picture.

Against the background of the well-known distinction between polity, politics and policy it becomes obvious that in both cases the dependent variable of the analysis belongs to the realm of policies. Both approaches attempt to explain the deepening and widening of European integration, which can be described as a set of formal and informal regulations, treaty provisions and institutional developments. The independent variables, however, reveal a different picture. In the case of neofunctionalism the explanatory factors are of a structural or functional nature and mostly consist of polity elements: socio-economic and political-administrative structures as well as functional necessities. By contrast, the explanation of intergovernmentalism is based on interests, preferences and the strategic ability to pursue them in a bargaining process. These are typical elements of the politics dimension.

How is it possible to combine the two sets of variables in a theoretically sound way? Against the background of the distinction between polity, politics and policy it seems to be possible to use neofunctionalism as an interest theory in which to insert an intentional decision-making theory. Even on the basis of Jon Elster's (1979, 1983) extremely demanding definition of a valid functional explanation such a combination appears to be feasible. According to Elster an empirical fact X is explained by its function Y for group Z if and only if

1. Y is an effect of X,
2. Y is advantageous for Z,
3. Y was not intended by the actors who created X,

Figure 3.1: Elster's Definition of a Valid Functional Explanation

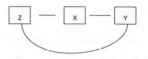

4. Y or at least the causal link between X and Y is not understood by the members of Z, and

5. Y promulgates the existence of X through a causal feedback loop, which includes Z (Elster 1979: 28).

In order to use this argument with respect to European integration it is necessary to show that the function Y of a common institution X was not—or at least not in all aspects—intended by the political actors involved in creating X. If it were possible to show that the function was entirely intended by Z the argument would constitute an intentional explanation (something like Keohane's 'functional institutionalism'); the actors Z rightly perceived the positive function of the new institution and thus created it for that purpose. However, against the background of the extensive debate on globalisation, denationalisation, the reduced ability of welfare states to regulate their social and economic affairs and the increasing importance of unintended consequences of political decisions, it does not seem unrealistic to assume that—contrary to Elster's assertion—such a functional explanation is a valid argument in social sciences. If this is the case it is certainly possible that the actors Z pursued their (different) interests when they decided about the creation of the common institution X. But the functions and effects of this institution are (although not entirely) congruent with the original intentions.

This line of reasoning enables functional explanation to allow for a voluntaristic, intentional element without jeopardising its basic functional character. It allows the formulation of a functional interest theory of European integration, which rests on the form and development of the socio-economic structures of the member states. Central hypotheses would then become:

1. The interests and preferences of important national actors are heavily influenced by the socio-economic structures of the policy area in which these actors are incorporated. The more these structures of the member states converge, and the more this convergence is based on long-term developments, the stronger the preferences are of the actors to cooperate in the EC and vice versa.

2. The stronger the functional pressure from an adjoining, already Europeanised policy area or sectors of the same policy field, the more the actors are inclined to deepen and widen the integration and to transfer more political competences from the national to the European level.

Table 3.4: Hypotheses of the Amalgamated Approach

Increasing ← → Decreasing			
Functional Spill-over and Socio-economic Convergence			
High degree of already existing socio-economic convergence		Low degree of already existing socio-economic convergence	
Coordination games without distributional conflict	Coordination games with distributional conflict	Dilemma games	Rambo games

These hypotheses can be combined with the intergovernmentalist hypotheses about the probability of co-operation.

To put it in simple terms, the higher the achieved degree of socio-economic convergence and the stronger the spill-over effects for an increasing tendency of such a convergence, the less controversial the decision-making situations are, and the easier it is to reach a cooperative solution.

Plausibility Tests:
The Werner Plan and the Necessary Decisions to Follow It Up

In order to support the validity of the amalgamated approach we will apply its hypotheses to several empirical examples. However, in the context of this chapter it is only possible to offer some very preliminary and sketchy plausibility probes. A real testing of the hypotheses has to be confined to a later, much larger analysis. We will take as prime examples for this kind of plausibility probe two cases from the history of economic and monetary integration in Europe: the successful decision for the Werner Plan in 1970 and the failure to follow up this basic decision with the necessary specific regulations in the years between 1971 and 1974.

The Werner Plan of 1970: The Decision to Create an Economic and Monetary Union in Europe

The Dependent Variable

Although the Community plunged into a major crisis during 1965-66 over the implementation of the Common Agricultural Policy—the so-called 'empty chair' crisis—it nevertheless managed to create the projected customs union by the end of 1968. The first major economic recession after the Second World War, however, convinced most of the member governments that a customs union was not enough to withstand international economic pressures, which increased during the late 1960s in the context of the Bretton Woods System. Since the treaty on the European Economic Community of 1958 already envisaged a Common Market the European governments decided in late 1969 to further pursue this perspective and to convene the so called Werner committee. It was composed of representatives of the member states (who also were member of various EC institutions) chaired by the then Prime Minister of Luxembourg, Pierre Werner. The Werner committee was to report on the possibilities of strengthening economic and monetary cooperation in Europe not least in order to reduce the hegemonic power of the US dollar in European economic affairs.[5]

The Werner committee met for the first time in March 1970 and published its report in October 1970, which included a plan for the creation of an Economic and Monetary Union in the EC by 1980. During this transitional period the Community was to increase its economic cooperation, establish a Common Market with free movement of goods, services, capital and people and, finally, create a common monetary institution to facilitate the introduction of a common currency and to decide monetary policy. The Werner plan proposed three phases for this transitional period to a common currency. During the first phase the governments were to increase their consultations in order to strengthen a common perspective on economic and monetary matters and to increase their coordination efforts. In the second phase the differences between national economic trends and developments of the member states would be reduced and economic and monetary cooperation and consultation would be intensified. The aim was to increase the number of cases in which the Council—still under unanimity—would collectively decide on important economic and monetary questions and, thus, reduce the area of purely national decision-making. This common decision-making would have been paralleled by the introduction of a common conditional, mid-term financial support system in order to help partner states with substantial financial difficulties. The third phase should have included the complete transfer of economic and monetary competences to the EC level, the introduction of majority voting in these common bodies, the irrevocable fixing of the exchange rates between the participating currencies, the pooling of the currency reserves of the member countries, and the creation a common central bank solely responsible for monetary policy decisions in the Community. The last and final—largely symbolic—step would be the replacement of the national currencies and the introduction of a common European currency.

Although the Werner Plan received considerable criticism, it was accepted by the Council in March 1971. But in their decision the ministers of the member countries did not envisage to change the treaty but ordered the institutions of the Community to care for the realisation of the goals during the following years. The Council followed up its decision with some additional measures like the introduction of the Committee of Central Bank Governors and the strengthening of short-term coordination in economic matters (Tsoukalis 1977: 110). But the decisions necessary to follow up the Werner Plan fell victim to the economic and monetary turbulences presiding and following the collapse of the Bretton Woods System (1971-73) and the effects of the first oil crisis of 1973. After these developments the integration process was effectively stalled and since 1974 the Werner Plan was considered to be a failure.

The Independent Variables

Considering the level of socio-economic convergence with respect to monetary questions[6] in the EC at the end of the 1960s one still observes considerable differences between the member states, especially regarding long-term factors. However, these differences tended to become smaller. Even in France and Italy the modernisation of the economy rapidly decreased the share of agriculture of total GDP and the number of employees. Each substantially increased its industrial production (Italy lost its status as an immigration state) and their overall productivity approached the level of the Benelux countries or Germany. Because of the Bretton Woods System, short-term factors, such as inflation and the exchange rates, were kept within narrow margins. The rates of unemployment increased during the recession of 1967-68 but were reduced and even reached the level of full employment again after the following boom became evident. Only the fiscal deficits of the member governments diverged. Italy had already accumulated a considerable level of budgetary deficit and public debt, Germany only started with small budget deficits after the recession of 1967.

Furthermore, the member states experienced the first massive spill-over effects from adjacent policy areas that were already Europeanised. For example, the Common Agricultural Policy accumulated its first large-scale surplus in several important areas of production (i.e., milk, grain) which forced the Community into establishing price guarantees for certain farm products. These guarantees, however, were based on accounting units (later ECUs), which became very sensitive to exchange rate shifts. Farmers in member countries with depreciating currencies de facto gained additional income (since the products were paid in their own currency), whereas farmers in member countries with appreciating currencies effectively lost income. These exchange rate fluctuations were substantially enhanced by the volatile US dollar since each European currency reacted differently to changes of the dollar. Thus, the Werner Plan can be seen as a reaction of the member states not only to insulate themselves from the turbulences of the world currency markets, but also to facilitate intra-Community trans-border trade by abolishing the exchange rate risk.

Against this background one can identify two different approaches to economic and monetary integration in the EC. On the one hand one can identify the so-called 'monetarists', and on the other the so-called 'economists'—or, in order to avoid misinterpretations, supporters of the 'Locomotive' and the 'Coronation' strategy for monetary integration. The first group consisted of the governments of France, Belgium and Luxembourg (Kruse 1980: 62-66).

Table 3.5: Decision-making Situation in the Case of the Werner Plan

D, NL, I F, L, B	'Locomotive' strategy	'Coronation' strategy
'Locomotive' strategy	4/3 N, P+	2/2
'Coronation' strategy	2/2	3/4 N, P+

Abbreviations: D=Germany; NL=Netherlands; I=Italy; F=France; L=Luxembourg; B=Belgium; N=Nash Equilibrium; P=Qualified Pareto Optimum.

The supporters of the 'Locomotive' strategy realised that the final goal of a monetary union included the transfer of broad economic and monetary competences to the European level. In the meantime, however, they advocated the transfer of only some of these competences for monetary policy to a new common central bank (with a common currency) but to retain most of the economic (and some monetary) competences on national level. The basic idea was to gain the advantages of a common currency very quickly without losing the political powers to influence the economy.

On the opposite side of the bargaining table were the governments of the Netherlands and Germany, partially supported by Italy. They advocated the 'Coronation' strategy in order to achieve the ultimate goal of a common currency (Kruse 1980: 66-70). For them it seemed undesirable to create a common currency in advance of the establishment of a common decision-making body in economic and monetary affairs. In their opinion it was necessary to Europeanise these political competences and, hence, to secure an ever increasing level of convergence and parallel economic development in the Community. Only after the successful achievement of this high level of convergence and continued common policy-making it seemed viable to this group to irrevocably fix the exchange rates and—as the final coronation of the economic integration process—to introduce the common currency and the common central bank responsible for its regulation.

Given the above mentioned socio-economic structures in the member states and preferences of the actors involved in the political process it is possible to model the decision-making process for the decision to accept the Werner Plan as a coordination game with distributional conflict.

The (Missing) Decisions to Follow Up the Werner Plan in the Years between 1971 and 1974

The Dependent Variable
The member governments generally had accepted the Werner Plan as the blueprint for the further economic and monetary integration process. However, with a few exceptions they did not transpose the plan into a treaty revision or at least into secondary European law. Rather, the Commission and the Council were supposed to care for the successive steps of implementation. This process of drafting legislation stalled, however, because of the economic and political turbulences after the collapse of the Bretton Woods System and the first oil crisis. Thus, no successful serious common decision in monetary affairs was made. Rather, in May 1971 the governments of Germany and the Netherlands decided to allow their currencies to float against the US dollar (and other major currencies). And even the attempt to regain regionally stable exchange rates in the EC by establishing an exchange rate mechanism ('snake' or 'snake in the tunnel') proved to be unsuccessful (Tsoukalis 1977).

The Independent Variables
While the long-term socio-economic factors of the member states showed first signs of convergence after a decade of economic integration in the Community, the collapse of the Bretton Woods System and the oil crisis forced the short-term factors into diverging directions. As early as the second half of 1971 France and Italy experienced the first signs of a renewed recession, to which the governments reacted with Keynesian, demand-oriented deficit-spending. This policy led to higher inflation and rising budgetary deficits, but did not reduce unemployment, since the world economy also slowed down and diminished the prospects of the export industries. Germany and the Netherlands, however, managed to control their rates of inflation. The two central banks

Table 3.6: Decision-making Situation for the Decisions to Follow Up the Werner Plan

F, B, I \ D, NL	exchange rate stabilisation, capital controls, interest rate politics	floating, control of money supply, fighting inflation
exchange rate stabilisation, capital controls, interest rate politics	3/2	2/4
floating, control of money supply, fighting inflation	4/1	1/3

Abbreviations: D=Germany; NL=Netherlands; F=France; B=Belgium; I=Italy.

welcomed their new freedom in monetary matters with the end of Bretton Woods, since the floating of their currencies freed them from the requirement to defend the exchange rates in the Bretton Woods System and, thus, they could move toward a monetarist strategy of controlling the money supply (Schlesinger 1983). The German Bundesbank claimed for years that the defence of the exchange rate of the deutschmark had forced it to increase the money supply beyond the reasonable economic necessity and, thus, had created an inflationary risk. Having lost this external straight-jacket both central banks reoriented their policies towards fighting inflation as the central goal of their monetary policy.

Furthermore, the spill-over pressures from adjacent policy areas lost their significance. Since the establishment of the Common Market was not in sight for the near future, the only spill-over pressure came from the Common Agricultural Policy. But these were not powerful enough to force the Community into establishing a common currency. Rather, the agricultural ministers found an internal cushion for the exchange rate problems. They invented the so-called 'Monetary Compensatory Amounts' (MCA) with which the Community tried to offset both positive as well as negative effects of the exchange rate changes (Hrubesch 1987). Additionally, the floating of the currencies freed Germany and the Netherlands from the costs of supporting the US dollar. Only when both currencies rapidly appreciated against the dollar were both governments (and central banks) again forced to intervene in order to limit the losses of their export industries on the US market.

Given these socio-economic structures of the member states in monetary matters two courses of action for the participating governmental actors were feasible: on the one hand the stabilisation of the exchange rates (capital controls, market interventions, interest rate changes), and on the other the fight against inflation (control of the money supply, floating of the exchange rates). The first option implied a cooperative strategy to strengthen the exports and to fight unemployment, while the second option focused on a unilateral mid-term perspective to lower the interest rates and to increase investments through supply-side reforms. It would certainly have been advantageous for the member state governments had they engaged in stabilising the exchange rate, which would have allowed them each to concentrate on fighting inflation at the national level. But for France, because of its weak currency, the second-best strategy still remained the cooperative option, whereas Germany and the Netherlands, in particular, with their strong currencies could resort to unilateral moves. In game theoretical terms this constitutes a rambo situation.

Conclusions

Although this chapter can only offer some very preliminary plausibility probes on the validity of the amalgamated approach to the explanation of European integration it is possible to draw some interesting conclusions. Both short empirical cases are readily explainable with the new approach. In the first decision making situation on the question of accepting the Werner Plan the long-term socio-economic factors still showed considerable divergence. However, the short-term factors clearly tended toward convergence and the Community witnessed massive spill-over pressures from adjacent policy areas like the customs union, the Common Market or the Common Agricultural Policy. This led to a specific pattern of interests of the participating governmental actors, which can be described in game theoretical perspective as a cooperation game with distributional conflict. Both groups of member governments were ready to cooperate in monetary questions but could not agree on who had to shoulder the costs of this cooperation. The result was a preliminary compromise which advocated a so-called 'parallel approach' to the question of monetary integration and effectively did nothing other than transfer the specific decisions to the appropriate European institutions. As the amalgamated approach predicts, the compromise was reached comparatively quickly and from a post-Maastricht perspective it seems to be safe to assume that the Werner Plan would have been implemented if the socio-economic conditions and the corresponding interests of the actors had not changed.

This change occurred because of the two major external economic and political shocks of the early 1970s: the collapse of the Bretton Woods System and the first oil crisis. Both ended the trend toward convergence of even the short-term socio-economic factors in the member countries and, hence, changed the interest structure of the respective governments. While France and Italy were still forced to a cooperative strategy because of their weak currencies, the central banks of Germany and the Netherlands finally saw the opportunity to gain not only their de jure but also their de facto independence and to engage in a unilateral supply-side oriented, monetarist stabilisation policy. This situation effectively ended the important cooperation in monetary matters in the Community and led to a decade of 'beggar-my-neighbour' policies. Again, the amalgamated approach predicted this result with considerable accuracy.

With this result the new amalgamated approach has shown its ability to explain the major steps of European integration in more comprehensive terms. If this very preliminary result can be supported by more thorough analyses, the amalgamated approach to European integration is prone to offer a better explanation of the process. It avoids at least three shortcomings of the classical neofunctionalist and intergovernmentalist approaches. First, it avoids the holistic and deterministic perspective of neofunctionalism, since it incorporates voluntaristic elements into its conception and offers (at least some) micro-foundations for the explanation of major political decisions in European integration. Neofunctionalism—even in its most sophisticated 'dialectical' version (Corbey 1995)—could not offer any theoretically sound explanation for integration failure. The new amalgamated approach is able to account for this. The pattern of convergence or divergence of underlying socio-economic structures influences the interest structures of the actors and, thus, creates or destroys opportunities for cooperation.

Second, it also avoids the reductionism of intergovernmentalism by offering a theory of interest development and not only a theory of interest aggregation. The major source of the interests of political actors is the socio-economic background on which they act. Here are the roots of major interests and preferences. With respect to cooperation, converging socio-economic structures remove some of the hurdles of reaching an agreement, whereas diverging socio-economic patterns necessarily lead to more difficulties for cooperative solutions. Thus, the new theoretical approach not only accounts for the aggregation of interests but also for their sources and contents.

Finally, it avoids the eclectic picture of so many 'fusion' approaches (Wessels 1997), which only advocate the combination of different theories and describe the necessary variables which have to be incorporated into the new explanation without offering clear-cut and empirically testable hypotheses. Merging theories—especially with seemingly contradictory hypotheses—is a difficult task, which cannot be solved simply by incrementally applying interesting parts of theses theories and adding their results where they fit into the picture. Rather, such a merger has to be based on (meta–)theoretical considerations in order to allow for a full-scale use of the theoretical elements and the creation of a combined, amalgamated (and not simply added) set of empirically testable hypotheses. This new approach is a first—albeit preliminary and sketchy—attempt, which has to be augmented by further research.

Notes

This chapter profited from numerous very interesting comments for which I am especially grateful to Konrad A. Cedro, Liesbet Hooghe, Erik Jones, Peter H. Loedel, Gary Marks, Ben Müller, Amy Verdun, Bernhard Zangl and Michael Zürn.

1. On the differentiation of modes of explanation see especially Elster (1979), Cohen (1982).
2. At least not until Corbey's interesting concept of 'dialectical functionalism' (1995).
3. An interesting deviation from this rejection of spill-over can be found in Sandholtz and Stone Sweet (1998).
4. This contradiction is best illustrated by the predictions of the two approaches. Whereas intergovernmentalism predicts further integration only in cases of converging interests of member governments, neofunctionalism argues that European integration might proceed even against the will of particular governments.
5. For concise introductions to the history of European monetary integration see especially Lieberman (1992), Ungerer (1997).
6. Possible parameters to observe in this case of monetary politics are, for example, the division of labour in the national economies of the member states (shares of agriculture, industry and services), the overall level of productivity, the inflation rate, the rate of unemployment, the growth rate, the interest rate or the fiscal deficit.

F33
F36

Chapter 4
WHY STATES WANT EMU:
DEVELOPING A THEORY ON NATIONAL PREFERENCES

F. A. W. J. van Esch

Neither neorealism nor neoinstitutionalism can account for the establishment of the European Economic and Monetary Union (EMU). In fact, some events that occurred in the history of EMU are the opposite of those predicted by either theory. In this chapter it will be proposed that this gap between theory and practice is due to the fact that theories on international relations assume rather than explain part of the causes of international cooperation, namely, the occurrence of a common interest. Several authors have already suggested that developing a theory on national preferences would enhance our understanding of international relations (Jervis 1988; Keohane 1993; Maoz 1995; Milner 1992; Moravcsik 1993a; Sanders 1996), but few attempts to create such a theory have actually been made. This chapter will provide a critical assessment of these attempts.

The argument will start with a brief analysis of the problems that neorealism and neoinstitutionalism face when trying to account for the establishment of the European Economic and Monetary Union. Subsequently, the proposition that these problems can be solved by the construction of a theory on national preferences will be made. An overview of the attempts to create a theory on national preferences will follow. This overview will include an analysis of the contributions of theories on international politics and theories on domestic politics. Finally, the evaluation of these approaches will lead to the conclusion that elements of both kinds of theories need to be included in a theory on national preferences.

Neorealism and Neoinstitutionalism in Trouble

Neorealism and neoinstitutionalism cannot account for several events that occurred in the history of the European Economic and Monetary Union. This section will briefly illustrate this statement (cf. Grieco 1993a; Keohane 1993).

Both neorealism and neoinstitutionalism consider a hegemonic or bipolar system to be a prerequisite for the establishment of interstate cooperation. It is said that only under the protection of the dominant power in the system or in the contesting blocs, states are safe to cooperate. Neorealism claims that when the dominance of the major power in the system declines, the existing international cooperation will not survive long. Neoinstitutionalism is more positive about the possibility of prolonged cooperation. When the main participants consider prolonged cooperation to be in their interest, institutions may survive a change in the international structure (Keohane 1993). Furthermore, neoinstitutionalists claim that increased interdependence between states can stimulate the continuation of international cooperation. They cannot, however, account for the establishment of new forms of cooperation under these circumstances.

Two major events in the history of European Economic and Monetary Union defy these theoretical claims. In the 1970s, for instance, the structure of the international system was bipolar and the West European states enjoyed the protection of the United States. Under these circumstances, both theories would expect cooperation to succeed. Nevertheless, despite a seeming common interest amongst the European states, co-operation was not established. The Maastricht Treaty also poses a problem for both theories. At the time the treaty was signed, the bipolar structure of the international system had collapsed and the hegemony of the United States was declining. In such a situation, neither neorealism nor neoinstitutionalism is able to account for the establishment of new forms of cooperation, let alone the creation of supra-national institutions. Moreover, prior to the establishment of EMU, Germany was unified. This event transformed Germany from Europe's main economic and monetary power into Europe's main political power. In theory, this event should have stimulated balancing behaviour by the other European states, which would inhibit co-operation even further (Lieshout 1995: 135-38). In spite of these constraining circumstances, the plans to create EMU succeeded.

Neorealist and neoinstitutionalist authors have attempted to solve the second empirical problem (leaving the first unattended). Grieco, for instance, has added a new thesis to the analytical core of neorealism to explain the Maastricht Treaty (Grieco 1995). This 'voice-opportunities' thesis states that:

*if states share a common interest and undertake negotiations on rules consti-
tuting a collaborative arrangement, then the weaker but still influential
partners will seek to ensure that the rules so constructed will provide for
effective voice opportunities for them and will thereby prevent or at least
ameliorate their domination by stronger partners* (Grieco 1995: 34, italics in
original).

This thesis may explain that in order to counter the German dominance on
monetary issues—which, Grieco argues, existed in the European Monetary
System (EMS)—France and Italy needed, and wanted, a supranational institution
like the European Central Bank (ECB) in which they would have some control
over policy decisions.[1] Yet, the thesis cannot explain why Germany agreed to the
establishment of EMU. Furthermore, it is unclear how the 'voice-opportunities'
thesis could enhance our understanding of the failure to establish EMU in the
1970s. Under the Bretton Woods system, the European states were dependent on
the monetary policy of the United States. The European states may have wanted
to prevent, or at least ameliorate this dependence, but since the United States
was not involved in the negotiations on EMU, the 'voice-opportunities' thesis
cannot enhance the explanatory power of neorealism in this case.

Keohane suggests that neoinstitutionalism offers a better solution to the
empirical problems than neorealism. He accepts the 'voice-opportunities' thesis
and claims it 'seems entirely consistent with institutionalist arguments' (Keohane
1993: 293). He states, however, that neoinstitutionalism can, in addition, show
how increased interdependence and the provision of economic and political
gains by the European institutions have made commitment to the European
Union 'an essential condition for Germany to be able to pursue its interests . . .
without unduly alarming its partners' (Keohane 1993: 290). Neoinstitutionalism
may therefore solve one of the remaining problems of neorealism: Germany's
motivation to establish EMU. But like neorealism, neoinstitutionalism still
cannot explain the failure of the attempt to create EMU in the 1970s.

Preferences to the Rescue

Neorealism and neoinstitutionalism traditionally focus on the constraints of
structural variables on international processes. The previous section shows,
however, that in the case of EMU the causes of failure and success cannot be
found by merely focusing on structural variables.

Apart from a favourable structure, however, neorealism and neoinstitutionalism identify another prerequisite for the establishment of cooperation: a common
interest among the participating states. Both theories tend to merely assume the
existence of a common interest instead of explaining it. In my opinion, however,
it is crucial to examine the preferences of states in order to be able to understand

the history of the EMU. For, could it not be possible that—for whatever reason—the initial common interest in the 1970s collapsed? If it did, the plan to set up economic and monetary cooperation surely could not succeed. And could it not be possible that the common interest grew so strong in the 1990s that it was able to beat the systemic odds? I think that this is exactly what happened.

Therefore, more should be learned about what actually constitutes a common interest, under which conditions it occurs, and how it develops over time. This means a theory on national preferences should be developed that could, at least, explain the content and intensity of national preferences, how they are formed, why they change, and how a common interest among states is established.

After a theory on preferences is developed, the interaction between preferences and the international negotiating process should be studied, as well as the way in which this interaction results in international outcomes, and how this is constrained by systemic factors. Although it is not the purpose of this chapter to conduct such analyses, it is necessary to state that, in my opinion, systemic factors cannot, a priori, be considered the dominant cause of international outcomes. As is stated above, a strong common interest may under certain conditions beat the systemic odds.

Theories on National Preferences

As mentioned above, some authors have suggested that a theory on national preferences may enhance the understanding of international relations. However, few efforts have been made to develop such a theory. This chapter will now offer a critical assessment of these few theories on national preferences.[2] This assessment will start with the contributions that theories on international relations may make to a theory on national preferences. Subsequently, the value of theories on domestic politics will be addressed.

International Determinants of National Preferences

This section will focus on neorealism and neoinstitutionalism. As stated before, these theories do not explicitly encompass theories on national preferences, but the current section will show that they do implicitly take a position on this subject.

There is no consensus on the position of neorealism and neoinstitutionalism on national preferences among their adherents. Some authors argue that both theories treat preferences as an assumption (Grieco 1993b; Keohane 1993; Krasner 1978; Waltz 1979), whereas others claim that preferences can be deduced from the analytical core of the theories (Jervis 1988; Keohane 1993).[3]

To assess the contribution that neorealism and neoinstitutionalism can make to a theory on preferences, both positions will be studied respectively.

National Preferences Assumed
Some adherents of neorealism and neoinstitutionalism consider preferences to be exogenous to these theories. Authors of the respective schools tend to disagree, however, about the content of this assumption. Neorealists, in general, argue that states are driven by a desire for survival (Grieco 1993b; Waltz 1979), and 'increased power may or may not serve that end' (Waltz 1979).[4] Neoinstitutionalists agree that anarchy leads states to be concerned about their survival, but they deem its effects less far-reaching than neorealists do (Keohane 1993).

More recently, the discussion between these schools of thought has focused on the difference between absolute and relative gains (Baldwin 1993). Neorealists stress that states are primarily concerned with relative gains: '*the fundamental goal of states in any relationship is to prevent others from achieving advances in their relative capabilities*' (Grieco 1993b: 127, italics in original).[5] Neoinstitutionalists, on the other hand, focus on the consequences of states' concerns with absolute gains. The question is, however, whether this difference is an analytically useful one because in practice 'bargaining for a larger share of overall benefits, and for relative gains, may be indistinguishable' (Keohane 1993: 280).

Nonetheless, whatever the substance of the assumptions, they are a far cry from a theory. Furthermore, assuming preferences results in two problems: First of all, since the content of the national preference is fixed, it cannot account for changes in international outcomes. Secondly, because neorealism and neoinstitutionalism assign the same preference to every state, differences in policies between states cannot be explained (Clinton 1994: 33). In sum, if one claims that neorealism and neoinstitutionalism treat preferences as exogenous, these theories are of no value for the development of a theory on national preferences.

National Preferences Deduced from Neorealism
Neorealism[6] states that the anarchic structure of the system shapes international politics and the strategies states use to achieve their purposes. This line of reasoning can be stretched to contain the preferences of states. So, apart from determining world politics and states' actions, anarchy may also define national preferences.

According to neorealism, the international system is one of anarchy in which the primary preference of states is to secure their survival by maximising their security. So far, this implies that the content of national preferences is fixed and universal. But the assumption is valid only under certain circumstances. For 'only if survival is assured can states safely seek such other goals as tranquillity, profit, and power' (Waltz 1979: 126). This means that the neorealist assumption about the content of national preferences is valid only if the security of states is at risk. In an anarchical system the security of states, in general, is said to be at risk. At first sight, the only way to solve this would be a change in the structure of the international system from anarchic to hierarchic. This change is not likely to occur.

However, neorealists acknowledge that there are other possibilities to change the anarchic structure of the system because: 'Anarchic systems are transformed only by changes in the organising principle and by *consequential changes in the number of their principal parties*' (Waltz 1979: 161, italics added). This statement points to two ways in which the structure may change: first, by a change in the number of the states in the system, and second, by a change in the relative power of states. Together, these two factors constitute the polarity of the system. A change in the polarity of the system would not be as drastic a change as from anarchy to hierarchy (a change in the organising principle), but it would nevertheless be consequential.

The number of states in a system affects the security of states as follows: a system that contains few states supplies those states with more information and clarity than a system that contains many states (Lieshout 1995: 179), and as Kenneth Waltz has noticed: 'Uncertainty and miscalculation cause wars' (Waltz 1979: 168). So in light of their preference for safety, states would generally prefer a system that contains fewer states.

The relative power of states is the second determinant of state safety in a system. The most powerful states are best assured of their survival: they have sufficient capabilities to protect themselves (Waltz 1979: 135) and nobody dares to defy their power. The least powerful state is also reasonably safe: it has no assets to be desired by anyone. The states with average power are least safe. They may not have enough capabilities to defend themselves, but they contain enough assets to be a desirable prey. Analysing the effects of these two factors together can lead to predictions of a state's sense of safety (Lieshout 1995:179-81), and, therefore, to a hypothesis about the general content of their preferences (security oriented or not). However, since the effects of the number of states and the capabilities of actors can be contradictory, clear assessments are difficult to make.

In sum, neorealism draws attention to several international variables that may affect the content of national preferences: it gives insight into the effects of the nature of a system on these preferences, it describes the circumstances under which security is the primary preference of a state, and it can identify structural factors that cause these preferences to contain goals other than security. However, neorealism cannot say anything about the content of national goals after their safety is ensured. Do states prefer 'tranquillity or profit' (Waltz 1979: 126)? This remains unknown. Moreover, neorealism still does not allow differences in preferences between states. Finally, although this deduction shows that preferences can change, this is said to occur only when the nature of the system changes. Since the system is said to be very rigid, national preferences are extremely constant as well. The history of EMU, however, indicates that these preferences can be quite variable.

National Preferences Deduced from Neoinstitutionalism
    Better results may be obtained by deducing a theory on preferences from the assumptions of neoinstitutionalism. The core of neoinstitutionalism[7] is very similar to that of neorealism. Neoinstitutionalists also claim that anarchy determines the nature of international politics and recognise the smoothing effects of the polarity of the structure. However, they see one more possibility to soften the effects of anarchy: international institutions. Whereas 'institutions, in first place will serve to enable states to achieve their goals' (Keohane 1993: 273), they might also alter the effects of anarchy on international relations, and—by stretching the line of reasoning—on the preferences of the state.
    Institutions have three distinct effects on relations between states. First, by supplying states with additional information and by laying down the agreements, institutions make state behaviour more predictable and the environment less elusive. Second, by facilitating linkages and bringing down the transaction costs of dealing with other states, institutions make cooperation relatively more attractive. Finally, once institutions have been set up, the investments that have been made and the benefits these institutions have created will be a barrier for terminating cooperation (sunk costs) (Keohane 1993: 274). Overall, institutions turn national preferences away from survival and independence, towards 'tranquillity and profit' (Waltz 1979: 126) and interdependence.
    This deduction leads to conclusions similar to those in the previous section: neoinstitutionalism is able to describe the circumstances under which a state prefers security, and those under which other objectives are preferred. This school of thought merely acknowledges more of those circumstances than neorealism does. This means that national preferences are said to be slightly more variable. Differences in preferences among states, however, are still not possible in neoinstitutional thought.

Similarity and Continuity of National Preferences
    In sum, it appears that both neorealism and neoinstitutionalism cannot offer a sufficient explanation of the formation of the national preference. The current section does, however, clarify how theories on international relations may contribute to a theory on preferences.
    First, theories on international relations direct attention to the international factors that influence the national preference. They explain how variables like the number of states in the international system, their relative power, or the level of institutionalisation constrain the content of the national preference by biasing preferences in a certain direction. Theories on international relations may, therefore, partly answer the question: 'Why do the European states prefer EMU?'
    Furthermore, theories on international relations are very well suited to answer questions concerning continuity and similarity of national preferences.

These questions respectively refer to situations in which the 'similarity of outcomes prevails despite changes in the agents that seem to produce them' (Waltz 1979: 39), and to situations in which states that differ significantly prefer the same things. In other words: similarity across time, and similarity across actors. This means, that in the case of the EMU, theories on international relations may be able to provide answers to questions like: 'Why does EMU appear on the international political agenda in both the 1970s and the 1990s' and 'Why did those divergent states all want to construct EMU?'

However, even a superior international theory on national preferences is, in my opinion, unequipped to explain fully the content of national preferences and the occurrence of a common interest. Theories on international relations may be able to explain similarity and continuity of national preferences, but they are unable to explain why preferences differ among states and why preferences change over time whereas the system did not. Theories on domestic politics may provide answers to these questions about difference and change, and should, therefore, be incorporated in a theory on national preferences.

Theories on Domestic Politics and National Preferences

Among theories on domestic politics, three kinds of theories on the forma- tion of national preferences can be distinguished: elitist theories, pluralist theories, and statist theories (cf. Milner 1992: 494). In this section the value of each of these kinds of theories for understanding national preferences will be addressed.

An Elitist Theory of Preference Formation
An elitist theory focuses on the background and beliefs of central decision makers, and the context in which they operate. Their preferences, or their perceptions of the national interest, will constitute the preferences on which policies are based (Milner 1992: 494-95). An example of the elitist approach to preference formation is the state identity approach of Thomas Risse. According to this approach, the content of the identity of a state and its political elite is primarily determined by historic events. Such collective identities provide a system for self-reference by which individuals define their place in society. These identities are largely formed in response to a perceived difference with another group and will change only gradually except in times of 'critical juncture'. Risse defines a 'critical juncture' as an instance in which 'the amount of perceived information which severely contradicts given identity constructions becomes unbearable' (Risse 1998: 11). In those instances, identities can change fast and drastically (Risse 2000: 8).

National identity determines the range of policies that are considered legitimate and appropriate to pursue. This does not mean that identities determine behaviour; they just guide policies in a general direction (Risse 2000: 9). According to Risse, his line of reasoning does not exclude the possibility that the initial formation of identities was a result of material preferences. Identities, however, will outlast the material preferences: they will continue to guide policy decisions after the relevant material preferences have disappeared (Risse 1998: 12).

Risse claims that a combination of the achievements of the European institutions, specific national historical memories, and 'critical junctures' have caused 'Europeanisation' of the national identities of the European elite (Risse 2000), and subsequently have 'guided policies' in a European direction. This does not mean that a single European identity has evolved which has replaced the specific national identities, for individuals hold multiple identities (Risse 2000: 1). The 'European identities' of the elite still contain distinct national elements, and some national identities are more open to 'Europeanisation' than others.

Since the 'Europeanness' of national identities varies, the 'Europeanness' of national policies will differ as well. Germany, for instance, is expected to adopt pro-European policies since it has developed an extensive 'European identity'. This identity was formed in response to its own history of authoritarianism, militarism, and anti-Semitism. The Germans turned to Europe, the representative of stability, peace, and democracy, to redefine their identity. In contrast to the German identity, the British identity lacks almost any 'Europeanness'. In fact, Risse states that the British notion of 'the other' is Europe. It identifies primarily with the United States, invoking their common Anglo-Saxon culture. This tends to make British policy anti-European. Its distinct national historical experience (which Risse identifies as including the events of 1066 and Britain's various conflicts with the continent, as well as its 'hard-fought victory over the King' (Risse 2000: 11) has made them very protective of their internal and external sovereignty. This has resulted in an aversion to supranational cooperation. Finally, the relationship between French policy towards Europe and its identity is less apparent. According to Risse, both have shifted considerably in the course of this century. He identifies four 'critical junctures' in recent French history that have caused these changes in identity and (therefore) policy: 'World War II and the German occupation'; 'the war in Algeria and the ongoing crisis of the Fourth Republic'; 'the failure of Mitterrand's economic policies in the early 1980s'; and 'the end of the Cold War'(Risse 2000: 20-21).

At first sight, Risse's expectations seem to coincide reasonably well with the attitudes of the European states towards EMU (Risse 1998). Germany has, in general, preferred the establishment of EMU, whereas Great Britain has not. Although Risse is unclear on the French identity of the mid-1970s (Risse 2000: 21), he does seem to be able to explain its pro-EMU stand in the 1990s. A closer look, however, casts some serious doubts on the value of his explanation of state's policies. The various 'specific historic events' that are said to have caused the content of the different national identities are by no means comparable in content, intensity, and impact on the nation. Moreover, the time-lags between the various events and recent attitudes towards EMU vary from 900 to two years. Yet, Risse claims, for instance, that 'a hard-fought victory over the King' that occurred 700 years ago, and 'the failure of Mitterrand's economic policies in the early 1980s' both constitute 'critical junctures', and have the same explanatory value for a state's recent attitude towards EMU. In my opinion, however, these historical events cannot constitute more than ad hoc explanations. As Mancur Olson put it: 'Only the British have Big Ben and only the Germans eat a lot of sauerkraut, but it would of course be absurd to suggest that one is responsible for the slow British growth and the other for the fast German growth' (Olson 1982: 10).

Furthermore, Risse states that identities guide state policies in general directions. But what does that really mean? That identities matter? Anarchy matters, but its existence does not explain why states sometimes fight each other, and sometimes do not. Likewise, identity can not explain why states sometimes adopt pro-European policies, and sometimes do not.

Liberal Intergovernmentalism: A Pluralist Theory of Preference Formation

A pluralist theory claims that the preferences of interest groups are central to the national preference. The sum of their preferences, weighted by their access to policy-making institutions, will shape a state's preferences (Milner 1992: 494-95). An example of a pluralist theory of preference formation is represented by Andrew Moravcsik's liberal intergovernmentalism. In this approach, he adds a liberal theory of preference formation to theories on international relations (especially neoinstitutionalism) and bargaining theories. This results in a two-stage theory, in which the first part addresses national preference formation and the second part addresses interstate interaction (Moravcsik 1997: 545). So, unlike neorealism and neoinstitutionalism, liberal intergovernmentalism explicitly tries to explain the origins of national preferences and their effects on interstate relations and the results of bargaining.

Moravcsik's theory on preference formation is based on a pluralistic view of society (Moravcsik 1997). The general idea of this approach is that domestic social groups and individuals form their preferences based on economic costs and benefits and will pressure the government to realise these goals for them (Moravcsik 1998: 35-38). In this stage of the approach, the government constitutes nothing more than a representative of the wishes of the people. Once national preferences are formed, governments will try to realise these wishes by bargaining with other governments.

Moravcsik's theory on preferences is based on three core assumptions. The first assumption states that the primary actors in international politics are rational and risk-adverse individuals and private groups, who have differentiated preferences and act under constraints like 'material scarcity, conflicting values, and variations in societal influence' (Moravcsik 1997: 516). The preferences are primarily determined by domestic factors and economic interdependence (transnational factor). When significant social groups are affected negatively, they will put pressure on their government to attend to their needs, and, if necessary, to engage in international coordination or cooperation. It is important to notice that domestic groups or individuals define their preferences independently of domestic or international politics before they try to advance those preferences. The demands of individuals and groups are, thus, analytically prior to politics (Moravcsik 1997: 519).

Moravcsik's second assumption states that: 'States (or other political institutions) represent some subset of domestic society, on the basis of whose preferences state officials define state preferences and act purposively in world politics'; this means that 'the state is not an actor but a representative institution' (Moravcsik 1997: 518). However, states are not assumed to represent every individual equally. The nature of state institutions constitutes a 'transmission belt' that selects preferences and translates the social power of individuals and groups. State institutions do not have preferences of their own. The national preference, which is a derivative of the apolitical preferences of individuals and social groups, will be 'exogenous to a specific international political environment' (Moravcsik 1998: 24-25). According to Moravcsik this means that 'the phrase "Country A changed its preferences" in response to an action by Country B misuses the term as it is defined here' (Moravcsik 1998: 24-25). International influences only enter the national preference through the transnational social contacts of individuals and social groups and their assessment of the global market.

Assumption three states that: 'The configuration of interdependent state preferences determines state behaviour' (Moravcsik 1997: 520). This means that the actions states undertake to realise their preferences are, at this point, constrained only by the preferences of other states (not by capabilities or systemic factors). National preferences are linked by patterns of 'policy interdependence' which are defined as 'the pattern of transnational externalities resulting from attempts to pursue national distinctive purposes' (Moravcsik 1997: 520). The inclination of states to cooperate varies with their vulnerability to these externalities. After the configuration of preferences is formed, states enter the second stage of the liberal intergovernmentalist approach: the stage of international strategic interaction.

In sum, Moravcsik's approach states that the national preference is determined by both the substance and the intensity of the preferences of domestic social groups and individuals, transferred by domestic political institutions. This constitutes a rather simple image of domestic politics and the formation of the national preference for two reasons (cf. Wincott 1995: 600).

First, Moravcsik claims that social groups or individuals are guided only by economic concerns. Moreover, he claims they form their preferences independently of any domestic or international political process. Whereas these assumptions give his model the advantage of parsimony, they also unrealistically exclude political considerations and the exertion of influence or leadership on the preference formation process. Secondly, in *The Choice for Europe* Moravcsik argues that the international political system is biased in favour of 'existing producer groups' and, therefore, focuses exclusively on their most important preferences. Moravcsik claims that the bias of the political system stems from the producers' 'more intense, certain, and institutionally represented and organised interests' (Moravcsik 1998: 36) and, thereby, merely touches on the most political, complex, and interesting part of the process of national preference formation: the struggle between the various social groups and individuals to 'capture' the national preference.

Furthermore, assuming that preferences are formed bottom-up might be appropriate for the analysis of some issues (such as the European agricultural policy), but seems inadequate for the analysis of an issue like monetary policy. This policy is, after all, quite complex and its distributional effects on domestic groups are so diffuse, that it is hard to imagine any social group demanding it (Wilson 1973: 332-37). In fact, unlike Moravcsik (Moravcsik 1998), neither McNamara nor Sandholtz have found evidence to support the proposition that EMU was initiated by special interest groups (McNamara 1998: 37-42; Sandholtz 1993: 23-25).

A Statist Theory of Preference Formation
Statist theories focus on domestic decision-making structures. The character of domestic political institutions constrain the preferences of the state by shaping actors' preferences and conditioning their access to decision-making forums (Milner 1992: 494-45). A typical example of a statist approach is that developed by Krasner. He explicitly distinguishes his theory from the pluralist (liberal) approach on preference formation. He believes that the state (as in 'state institutions') is an autonomous actor, standing apart from society: 'The objectives sought by the state cannot be reduced to some summation of private desires' (Krasner 1978: 5-6). This does not mean that the preferences of the state institutions merely reflect the self-interested goals of the central decision-makers, or are completely distinct from the needs of society. On the contrary: 'These goals are associated either with general material objectives or with ambitious ideological goals related to beliefs about how societies should be ordered' (Krasner 1978: 10). Krasner even suggests that the objectives of the state institutions reflect the nation's interests more genuinely than the summation of a specific group's interests since 'the summation of individual utilities and the collective well-being of the society are not the same thing' (Krasner 1978: 12). The preferences of state institutions can, therefore, appropriately be regarded as the national preference.

As opposed to a pluralist model, a statist model explicitly acknowledges that a situation can occur in which a state initiative encounters massive domestic resistance, and that states may actively try to overcome this opposition.[8] The ability of states to overcome domestic resistance depends upon the amount of control it can exercise over groups within its own society, in Krasner's definition: whether a state can be called 'weak' or 'strong' (Krasner 1978: 11). Krasner distinguishes five ideal-typical societies, which range from one in which the state apparatus is non-existent, to one in which state institutions are dominant (state institutions can remake society to fit their own preferences). The 'stronger' state institutions are, the more likely the national preference will be dominated by their preferences (Krasner 1978: 55-61).

In sum, Krasner's approach draws attention to the effects of the role and nature of the state institutions on the content of the national preferences. It remains unclear, however, how the nature of these institutions relate to the content of the national preference. Do state institutions determine the access of societal groups to the formation of national preferences, or do different types of states also prefer different things? This remains unknown. Moreover, whereas Krasner rightly points to the existence of autonomous preferences of state institutions, he does not clarify what motivates state institutions. In other words, what makes them tick? Obviously, they are not motivated by the desires of their citizens, or merely by securing their own survival. Krasner seems to suggest that they are motivated by the 'collective well-being', but he does not elaborate on what this well-being entails: the survival of the nation, or, perhaps, some other greater good like 'beauty, truth, and goodness' (Gilpin 1986: 305)? Finally, Krasner does not elaborate on why state institutions would even care about the well-being of the collective and at some occasions risk massive opposition when they do. Whatever the answers to these questions, reducing the state to a mere representative of the collective well-being would, surely, be as unrealistic as reducing it to a mere representative of special interests. So, whereas Krasner's approach does bring up some interesting matters, it will need clarification in order to explain the origins of national preferences in general and the strive for EMU in specific.

Difference and Change in National Preferences

None of the different domestic approaches to the formation of preferences that have been analysed has offered a convincing explanation of the national preferences concerning EMU. This is not to say that the respective approaches are without their merits. The approaches do identify several domestic variables that may influence the formation and content of the national preference. These factors include: the different actors that may play a role in the preference formation process (elite, interest groups and state institutions); their motivation (identity, historic events, economic or political benefits, or the collective well-being); and the relationships between these actors.

Furthermore, theories on domestic politics, in general, draw attention to the differences between the national characteristics of states. These domestic approaches are, therefore, very well suited to explain differences among states and to identify domestic sources of change (cf. Waltz 1979: chapter 3). These are precisely those questions that theories on international politics could not answer: questions concerning differences and changes in national preferences. In this case, this means that theories on domestic politics may be able to provide answers to questions like: 'Why did state's preferences change during the 1970s, whereas the system did not?' and 'Why are Great Britain's preferences significantly different from those of the other European states throughout the history of EMU?'

Conclusion

In sum, this chapter shows that some of the historic events concerning the establishment of EMU defy the expectations of neorealist and neoinstitutionalist theory. In my opinion, this is caused by the fact that neither (explicitly) theorise about the formation of these preferences. Since the existence of *both* a common interest and a favourable system (the latter *is* analysed by IR theories) are essential prerequisites for creating cooperation, these theories on international relations are not able to explain major events in the history of EMU. The combination of neorealism or neoinstitutionalism and a theory on national preferences might be able to do a better job.

In an attempt to develop a theory on national preferences, an overview of several theories on domestic politics and IR theories was given. Unfortunately, none of the approaches discussed seems to be able to explain adequately the strive for EMU. In my opinion, this is largely due to the fact that the reviewed theories are merely based on either international or domestic variables. Since only theories on domestic politics can explain change and difference, and only theories on international relations can answer questions of stability and similarity (Waltz 1979), both kinds of variables need to be included in an adequate theory on national preferences.

Notwithstanding the fact that none of the approaches discussed in this article was able to fully analyse the strive for EMU, there is no reason to be gloomy about the possibility of creating a theory on national preferences. The analysis conducted supplies many points for departure.

The different domestic approaches suggest that the *process* of preference formation is one of the determinants of the *content* of that preference. It has become clear that the outcomes of the process will vary with the actor that dominates or initiates the formation process (elites, interest groups, or state institutions) and its international and domestic goals. Which actor dominates the formation of the national preferences may partly be the result of the relative strength of different societal and statist groups, the intensity of preferences, and the institutional organisation of the national political systems. Furthermore, I have suggested that a pluralist model is not the best model to analyse a complex international policy that has unclear distributional effects on specific domestic groups. This may indicate that the characteristics of a specific issue area may partly determine the preference formation process (and therefore the content of the national preference). Studying these factors may be the starting point for development of an adequate theory on national preferences.

Theories on international relations have shown how international factors like the number of states in the international system, their relative power, or the level of institutionalisation may bias preferences in a certain direction. The international system puts constraints on some preferences, whereas it promotes others. This indicates that actors are also influenced by the international system prior to defining their interests (as opposed to what Moravcsik believes).

Notes

I would like to thank Markus Haverland, Mirjam Kars, Bob Lieshout, Bert-Jan Verbeek, Anna van der Vleuten, Anton Weenink, and the participants of the conference 'Conceptualising the New Europe' for their useful comments on previous versions of this chapter.

1. The ECB will partly be composed of the heads of national central banks, and will take decisions by majority voting.

2. Students of International Relations refer to 'national preferences' as 'state preferences'. This results from the assumption that in international relations a state acts as if it were a unitary actor (cf. Moravcsik 1998: 22). I have chosen not to make a distinction between the two terms in this article. Both will refer to the position a country will ultimately fight for in the international arena. The term 'preferences of the state's institutions' will be used to refer to the goals of members of, or organisations within the national government (cf. section on the statist theories).

3. Keohane is mentioned twice because he seems to believe that, up to now, both theories treat preferences as a assumption, but considers it possible (and necessary) that they incorporate statements about preferences in their theories.

4. As opposed to classic realists who claim states are motivated by a search for power.

5. Waltz suggests these relative gains are only important to great powers in an oligopoly, not the smaller ones (Waltz 1979: 134), a qualification Grieco fails to make.

6. In this section, the term 'neorealism' refers to the work of K. N. Waltz.

7. In this section, the term 'neoinstitutionalism' refers to the work of R. O. Keohane.

8. Events following the first Danish 'No' offer, in my opinion, an illustration of this process.

II. THEORISING MONETARY INTEGRATION: IDEAS AND IDENTITIES

F33
F36

Chapter 5
EMU:
A NEOLIBERAL CONSTRUCTION

Lloy Wylie

Economic and Monetary Union (EMU) represents a decisive step in European integration. In some respects the Treaty on European Union (TEU), which posed concrete stages toward full EMU, is the defining agreement on European integration. Many complex factors have led to this new push toward EMU. This chapter intends to answer the following questions: What are the forces stimulating the current momentum that has ended years of inertia? What is the political and economic context in which this push has occurred? How have certain key social actors been able to influence the process of integration?

European integration theorists have for decades debated the question of political power in the European Community. Yet these debates have tradition-ally been centred on the question of whether power is concentrated in the nation state or in the new supranational institutions. Seldom have these debates taken up the question of the ideological commitments of these power-wielding structures or the social purpose that they served. We must first understand the social bases of the various institutional structures in Europe, in order to understand how these structural changes represent a realignment of social forces. The process of European integration is restructuring the European political arena and creating an institutional framework along an entirely new paradigm. It embodies an ideological struggle over the character of the European

69

project and a realignment of social forces in the making of that project. Although the earlier integration theorists tend not to discuss these questions, the significance of the shifting ideological context becomes clear when one looks at the history of the integration process.

An examination of the changes in the economic and political terrain over the past two decades can help to shed light on the process of economic and monetary integration in Europe. Increased mobility has enhanced the political power of transnational capital to insist upon policy frameworks that facilitate their economic needs. The ideological dominance of neoliberalism is also a decisive factor in the policy choices of nation states. Nation states are strongly pressured to follow restrictive monetary and fiscal policies in order to maintain and attract capital investment and financing. These changes at the national level began in the early 1980s.

The approach I apply to this problem is in the theoretical tradition that sees economic changes linked to political ideas and choices. Not only is the process of European integration initiated by the political agency of key actors; the structures of the EU and of the nation states have also been created and recreated through political agency. The primacy of human agency in determining the history of European integration makes it essential to examine the role important actors play in the process. Although the institutional position of the different actors will influence their ideas, we should not assume that their ideas are thus predetermined by the structure of which they are a part.

The above discussion informs the hypothesis of this chapter, namely that the convergence around monetarist 'sound money' principles had to take place before EMU could be created; these two processes are linked. The changes at the national level created the political space for the institutionalisation of 'sound money' policies at the supranational level brought about through EMU. This so-called monetarist orientation[1] of EMU has reinforced neoliberal economic policy at the national level. The second element of the hypothesis is that social actors, namely political leaders in the nation states, the central banking community, and neoliberal ideologues, have played a defining role in determining the direction of European integration.

To examine this question I first look at the traditional integration theories and how they shed light on the integration process, and also when their relevance is questioned. Next, I look at more recent theoretical approaches to European integration, particularly constructivism, which emphasises the importance of social context of political choices. Following the theoretical section I examine European integration in the context of global transformation, both in the changes to the international political economy and ideological shifts. Part of the ideological section examines how new political ideas are spread through the socialisation of political agents and the development of influential groups in the process of political transformation. The penultimate section explores how these transformations have restructured Europe. The final section concludes.

Integration Theory

Neofunctionalism and Intergovernmentalism

During the early days of European integration the expansion of inter-regional trade through capital mobility was understood to support the increase of economic welfare for all citizens of the European Community. The initial writings in integration theory reflected this belief. David Mitrany, originally writing in 1932, suggested that integration between nations could take place in the technical aspects of government operations that were free of political controversy. He argued the elaboration of common principles that addressed human needs could inspire the formation of international institutions to bring about the universal application of these principles. In Mitrany's schema integration would take place through the functional coordination of the specific yet generalised needs of the period, i.e., free trade and peace among nations (Mitrany 1975: 100).

Neofunctionalist integration theory from the 1950s through the early 1970s emphasised the commitment to social welfare as the key legitimating aspect of European integration. Ernst Haas (1964) and Lindberg and Scheingold (1970, 1971) stressed that the expansion of economic welfare throughout Europe and the promise of even greater economic prosperity provided a 'permissive consensus' (Lindberg and Scheingold 1970) among the European populations to the goals of increased regional integration. Over time, however, these originally linked goals of further integration with a deepening in generalised social welfare were wrenched apart. Contradictory visions of the future of integration formed: one which desired an integration process leading to the creation of a 'social market' Europe, another which favoured dismantling the 'inflexibilities' of the Keynesian welfare state as part of the process of eliminating the barriers to the free movement of capital. This change in the socio-political environment is recognised by Haas in his re-evaluation of neofunctionalist analysis in which he debunks some of its theoretical assumptions (Haas 1976). In the turbulent circumstances of post-1968 Europe it was difficult for the various actors to develop stable expectations of mutual behaviour and performances, thus leading to an erosion of the patterns of consensus (Haas 1976: 179). Spill-over, which predicted an automatic progression of integration, became a decreasingly relevant concept as the integration process stalled.

The centrality of the nation state in the integration process was reasserted in 1982 by Hoffmann who focused upon the importance of the European Community in reinforcing and preserving the nation state (Hoffmann 1982: 21). According to Hoffmann, it was in the interests of the nation state to cooperate in order to create some economic stability in an attempt at self-preservation (Hoffmann 1982: 31-32). Although there was an increase in common concerns among the member states, no corresponding articulation of common goals among the member states, no corresponding articulation of common goals emerged to allow for continued innovation towards regional integration. The cooperative regime was in jeopardy when individual state action could achieve the same or preferable outcomes to the international arrangement (Hoffmann 1982: 34); throughout the 1970s many nation states chose a course that did not require the transference of decision making to the supranational level.

Andrew Moravcsik (1998) carries on the intergovernmentalist tradition. He contends that the grand bargains among nation states that developed the five treaty amending agreements (the Treaty of Rome in 1957; the customs union and the Common Agricultural policy in the 1960s; the creation of the European monetary system in 1978-79; the negotiation of the Single European Act in 1985-86; and the Maastricht Treaty in 1992) have been the moving force behind integration. Moravcsik argues that the progression of integration occurred through a series of rational choices by national leaders pursuing the economic interests of their state. The most important incentive for integration was the possibility it offered for commercial advantage through the liberalisation of trade and the stabilisation of the monetary system. When the commercial interests of production and the adjustment of macroeconomic policies converged, further integration was possible. The integration process did not overrule the political will of the national leaders, but rather reflected their will (Moravcsik 1998: chapter 1).

Intergovernmentalist and neofunctionalist theories of European integration share the common problematic assumption that political actors will behave in a predictable manner. Intergovernmentalists argue that the nation state representatives act by rational choice, looking out for the best interests of the state, while neofunctionalists argue that EU functionaries will defend integration.

Although the structures of the nation state do influence its leaders' prefer-ences, there is no 'best interest' of the nation state in the abstract. Rather there are visions of what different political actors in control of the state institutions consider the best interests based upon the kind of social intervention that they favour. Different strategies of nation state organisation have been adopted, from Keynesian to neoliberal, differing in perspective on the organisation of political, economic and social processes and priorities. Thus the 'best interest' of the nation state has shifted as the historical context has raised the necessity and possibility for different strategies, and political leaders have had different social agendas. European integration can be seen as another means by which nation states (and other sectors) aim to meet the needs of economic growth, in a more globally interdependent economy.

Not only are the analyses of the 'best interests' of the nation state posed in the abstract, the discussion of political power is also unspecified, and therefore a problematic feature in integration theory. The transfer of some of the nation state's previous functions to the supranational realm indicates a reduction of nation state power in some areas, as does the creation of free trade agreements which privilege multinational capital. But these power transfers do not represent a surrendering or withering away of the nation state. Rather they signify a change in the structure of political and economic systems, and a concomitant redefinition of institutional responsibilities. It is important to examine where the nation state continues to play a central role and where its obligations have been transferred or waived, and determine the rationale behind this transition. Such an examination would reveal that the development of the European Union is a co-operative (yet continually contested) effort between the nation state, supranational institutions, and multinational capital through the emergence and agency of a transnational elite.

Rather than discussing the transference of political power, more insight is offered through addressing how power has been transformed, and by whom. The liberalisation that is occurring on a global scale indicates that 'in every region of the world, states, economies, and political processes are being transformed *under the guidance of a class-conscious transnational bourgeoisie*' (Robinson 1992 in van der Pijl 1995: 121, italics in original). Established states continue to provide for the needs of the business community, with whom they create a 'cohesive bourgeois class' (van der Pijl 1995: 103). The current changes in economic structures could not have taken place without the political initiative of class-conscious state representatives who constitute an integral part of the transnational bourgeois elite. This separation of economic decisions from political pressure has been a guided process.

Constructivism and Critical Theory

Political science theorists often aim to address the functioning of systems of governance in order to examine the consequences of policy choices. Whether the aim is to offer prescriptions or not, the formulation of the research question to address the effectiveness of policy choices often leads to value judgements on policy, rather than on non-governmental political processes. In this sense the structural rationale of systems of governance are taken for granted and analysis is confined to choices made within this system. The assumptions of neorealist analysts, such as Kenneth Waltz (1979), that the international political order is structured but anarchic is reflected in studies of national governance systems. How the social ontologies that comprise these systems (e.g., norms, institutions, routinised practices, constitutive processes, etc.) originally came into being and are redefined is often under-theorised. This constitutive stage of the making and remaking of social ontologies is at the centre of the constructivist meta-theoretical approach.

The constructivist research agenda in European integration studies emphasises the impact of 'intersubjectivity' and 'social context', and can thus be a useful foundation for analysis that seeks to examine the question of social purpose in structural and ideational transformation (Christiansen, Jørgensen, and

Wiener 1999: 528-29; Marcussen 2000). As discussed by Bastiaan van Apeldoorn in his elaboration of Gramscian transnationalism, constructivist theory provides a good basis of social theory from which to develop an alternative perspective.

> Constructivism . . . explicitly challenges the individualistic and rationalistic understanding of social action underlying mainstream IR theory, whereas at the same time rejecting the structuralist alternative in which there is no room left for human agency. As constructivism tends to take agency seriously . . . it draws our attention to the role of consciousness and ideas in social practice (van Apeldoorn 1999a: 17).

Critical theory has a similar research agenda, and can incorporate the constructivist approach, as it also attempts to create a method for understanding how the current order came into existence, but has the further aim to identify possibilities for transcending that order (Cox 1995: 32). Critical theory aims to reintegrate political science with both economics and sociological theory, in order to construct 'a larger picture of the whole of which the initially contemplated part is just one component' (Cox 1996 [1981]: 89). Through its recognition of events and conditions as products of a historical process, critical theory emphasises the importance of contextualisation:

> [B]oth human nature and the structures of human interaction change . . . . History is the process of their changing. One cannot therefore speak of 'laws' in any generally valid sense transcending historical eras, nor of structures as outside of or prior to history. Regularities in human activities may indeed be observed within particular eras . . . though not with the universal pretensions to which [positivism] aspires (Cox 1996 [1985]: 53).

The theoretical approach that I utilise in this paper is one that aims to bring together the constructivist and critical traditions, which see ideational and material factors as intersubjective. This approach draws attention to the moment of interface between structural change and political agency (Christiansen et al. 1999: 540) to highlight the social purpose that gives rise to structural transformation. Rather than seeing structure and agency then as strictly co-determinate, this approach seeks to analyse the circumstances when structural constraints are overcome through social and political agency.

Social agents (political and social leaders) act within and are influenced by the structural terrain, but not so far that their actions are strictly determined by these structures. Individuals still have independent intentions and actions, but their ability to act upon them or to see effective consequences of their actions is constrained. Yet when the existing structures are faced with crises, social agents with competing social purposes are better able to impact upon the creation of new social ontologies than when the structures are stable, i.e., in times of crisis, the political and social structures of society can be transformed.

When new material conditions emerge, existing structures can be rendered ineffectual, or at least their ineffectuality can be exposed. This opens up opportunities for new perspectives to influence structural transformation. Effective social agents are the ones who anticipate the breakdown of the structures and develop alternative ideational perspectives prior to this collapse. While the controlling social forces are disoriented and cannot answer (or do not even know) the questions posed by the new context, developed ideational forms can offer a new paradigm for action.

European Integration and Global Transformation

An example of this phenomenon of 'policy windows' (Checkel 1999) is the transformation of economic policy paradigms in the late 1970s and early 1980s. Nationally based Keynesian economic policy became ineffectual (for the purpose of economic growth) due to increased international competition and popular expectations that outstripped growth. The political and economic pressures of the late 1960s and early 1970s led to the collapse of the Keynesian hegemonic project. Profits were squeezed as workers continued to demand wage increases that now outpaced productivity. The end of capital controls and the collapse of the fixed exchange rate regime made capital (particularly financial capital) more mobile while holders of constant capital and commodities were more vulnerable to economic volatility. This newly 'liberated' financial capital gained political power with its ability to easily relocate. Demands for liquidity forced productive enterprises to focus on short-term profit realisation. Competitive pressures from global trade compelled corporations to attempt to regain competitiveness through a redefining of the relations of production. Capital began to pressure for a relaxation of the 'inflexible' nature of the Fordist mode of production. Globally mobile capital also demanded that the nation state change its macroeconomic policies. Nation states that chose to follow Keynesian expansionary policies were attacked by capital through currency devaluation and disinvestment in the economy. Thus the hegemonic order of the post war world was thrown into crisis.

This was compounded with the collapse of the Bretton Woods system of fixed exchange rates and capital controls, combined with the oil shocks in 1973 and 1979. In the 1970s, European states followed a patchwork of economic policies. Although monetarism was embraced as the new economic paradigm, governments succumbed to the pressures of the near collapse in capital investment by adopting policies of loose credit. European nation states turned their efforts toward forming a 'neocorporatist concertation' to address the economic crisis they were facing. A managed development of technical mechanisms and policy coordination among the member states, rather than transference of decisions to the supranational level, characterised integration during this period (Taylor 1983: 107). The intergovernmentalist analysis seemed more applicable, as European nation states turned inwards and integration stalled.

The development of national strategies to address the crisis made the possibilities for a Europe-wide strategy more remote. At the same time, the subjection to economic shocks precipitated by US economic and monetary policies provided the incentive towards further integration as a protective measure; European nation states were faced with external destabilising pressures that they could not overcome alone (Hoffmann 1982: 31-32). As states became more vulnerable to the pressures of mobile capital, the basis of the neocorporatist arrangement was undermined. States that followed expansionary fiscal policies were punished by speculative attacks on their currencies and the withdrawal of investment from their economies. France's failed attempt to implement an expansionary economic program of Keynesian redistribution in 1981-82 is a clear example of the inability of states to withstand the demands of reorienting capital—'Keynesianism in one country' was not a possible alternative. This pressure effectively eroded the bargaining power of states with the unions, as they were no longer able to offer the alleviation of unemployment through fiscal stimulus (Streeck and Schmitter 1991: 145).

As the national Keynesian economic frameworks were not able to provide successful growth strategies, new policy frameworks were sought. Monetarist economic policy, as developed by Milton Friedman and Friedrich von Hayek of the Mont Pelerin Society, had become influential among political leaders in the International Monetary Fund and the World Bank, and began to win over individuals in nation states to these economic paradigms. Influential political agents like Ronald Reagan and Margaret Thatcher remade economic policy frameworks, and this transformation resulted in the restructuring of numerous sites of social relations.

The indecision that typified the economic strategies of the 1970s gave way in the 1980s to increasingly convergent efforts by European governments to encourage liberalisation and break the institutional links between money supply and government spending via deflationary monetary and fiscal policies (Sandholtz 1993: 7-9). The commitment to macroeconomic discipline 'established the necessary foundation upon which discussions of monetary union could build' (Sandholtz 1993: 5). This cooperation began with the creation of a fixed exchange rate system, the European Monetary System (EMS) in 1979. This system provided an opportunity for national states to better protect the profitability of capital investment in European industry, particularly for export manufacturers via the intervention of central banks to shore up any EMS currency under speculative attack. Coordinated currency stabilisation allowed an immediate mitigation of capital outflow crises; however, these responses alone did not deal with the underlying concerns of capitalist investment. The desire of financial markets for economies that more directly served the needs of transnationally enabled capital required a fiscal response from EU member states. This was provided for by the Deutschmark's dominant position in the

EMS. The German Bundesbank in effect set monetary policies for the region, which had a deflationary effect on fiscal policy.

The restrictive monetary policy of the Bundesbank was forced upon the other countries in the EMS to ensure the established (yet flexible) parity of exchange rates in the European Community. The pressures to stay within the framework of the EMS, as well as the increased power of capital strikes against expansionary macroeconomic policies, enforced policies of austerity throughout Europe. The crises in the EMS (1983, 1987, and 1992-93) gave credence to 'sound money' solutions, which produced an important shift in the course of EMU.

> 'Irresponsible' government use of fiscal policy, particularly reflected in the accumulation of public debt, was increasingly identified as the source of economic problems; the remedies were identified in the realm of monetary policy. The most dramatic change was the new ascendancy of 'sound money' ideas in economic theory, and a revival of interest by economists in the role of central banks in economic policy (Dyson et al. 1995: 482).

The transformation of the European Union in the 1980s and 1990s was built upon this precedent of the transformation of national economic paradigms. The liberalisation of trade and finance, already well established in Britain, was the basis for the renaissance of European integration. According to Dyson et al. (1995) there has been an internationalisation of financial markets, particularly under the auspices of the Single European Act (SEA) of 1986 that allowed for the liberalisation of capital movements. This has resulted in 'altering the systemic relationships that govern monetary policy making' (Dyson et al. 1995: 466). The creation of the SEA was a significant initial step in the process of genuine free trade in the region. EMU is the completion of that process.

Ideological Shifts

In the current period economic decisions are dictated by market pressures that require technical choices concerned with the objective needs of the economy. The disconnection of politics from economic decisions is a central part of European integration. Although it appears, and has been argued, that European integration is taking place primarily in the economic realm (Haas 1976; Lindberg and Scheingold 1971), it must be stressed that this concentration of economic decisions is a division of political control. The mandate of the European Central Bank (ECB), which determines monetary policy for all countries in the EMU, is based upon a monetarist economic paradigm. It is claimed that this is the only possible arrangement to ensure low inflation and the credibility of EMU in financial markets.

The institutional isolation of economic policies enshrined in EMU provides member states with the ability to enforce painful economic decisions while avoiding the direct political consequences. Thus EMU promises the continuance and deepening of the restrictive economic and monetary policies that nation states have been unevenly pursuing since the 1980s, through the institutionalisation of monetarist policies in the ECB.

Monetarist economic ideas developed by new right (neoliberal or neoconservative) ideologues, such as Milton Friedman and Friedrich Hayek, were a direct challenge to the basis of Keynesian macroeconomic policies (Hayek 1972). Neoliberals competed for government support throughout the Keynesian era, but it was not until after the prolonged economic downturn of the 1970s that this challenge from the new right gained political significance. The 1980s saw a stronger influence of neoliberal ideology on the policy objectives of national governments in Europe. The result was a decisive rightward shift in the ideology of the national governments of the European Union. This shift occurred through the defeat, realignment, or programmatic shift of social democratic governments in favour of more conservative forces or ideas.

Neoliberalism is able to enforce an economic adjustment dictated by the market rather than through a cumbersome state directed process that can incite political pressure from both labour and capital. Divorcing economic decisions from the public political realm and leaving market forces to restructure the economic organisation of society diffuse the responsibility for the possible negative outcomes. Reorganising society in this manner allows for a shift in the balance of political power in favour of capital, while deflecting criticism by insisting that the dictates of the market cannot be ignored.

Despite the focus on economic goals, one can define neoliberal policies as a political programme for the reallocation of society's resources. Yaghmaian's assertion that deregulation is a form of regulation which acts to facilitate accumulation for the most internationalised sectors of capitalism, challenges the discourse of the 'free market' by highlighting the deliberate and focused nature of economic decisions. Neoliberal policies extend and deepen the market logic in all social relations, which requires ending the legacy of social guarantees that are obstacles to an uninhibited market economy. In this sense one can see that the neoliberal agenda is not merely based upon a reorganisation of the economy, but also a method by which to undermine the political power of the working class by threatening social and economic security. The concerted action of nation states in restructuring the political economy is evidence that the 'self-regulated' market is a myth (Yaghmaian 1998).

Individuals within the nation state have been decisive in the shift from state interventionist Keynesian policies to the market oriented 'deregulation'. The marketisation of social services and the proliferation of social Darwinist ideology have been supported by policy shifts of nation states. This reorganisation of social relations has been legitimised through nation states' proclamations of the need for 'belt-tightening' throughout society in these tough economic times.

The neoliberal belief in the operation of capital freed from the constraints of state intervention, such as national protectionist policies, and initiatives to mitigate the distributive inequalities and unemployment generated by the market, underlay their prescriptions for free trade and restrictive monetary and fiscal policies. A key structural change in the economic decision making power of nation states led by neoliberals was the establishment of independent central banks dedicated to price stability and isolated from the political system.

The advantage of the neoliberal model is its promise to facilitate the capital accumulation process while maintaining political stability by separating economic decisions from the public political realm. This is a clear example of what Ellen Wood defines as one of the key aspects of capitalist rule: the separation of the economic from the political (Wood 1995: chapter 1). Neoliberalism combines the mission of serving the direct needs of capitalist profitability while disguising this intent with a technocratic economic mantra that insists interventionist policies are destabilising at best, but more often devastating to the economy. Neoliberal ideology has reified the market logic as an unquestionable imperative for the reorganisation of economic priorities. Economic decisions of the state are declared a matter of market pressures or technical choices concerned with the objective needs of the economy.

The specific aims of the neoliberal model for a united Europe are: the free movement of capital within Europe; monetary policy aimed at low inflation (monetarism); austerity and marketisation of the welfare state; and the restructuring of the (Fordist/corporatist) production regime. This model for Europe was aimed to enhance profitability for capital operating in the region along with rationalising the organisation of capital accumulation by eliminating all barriers (such as capital controls and wage demands) to capital's ability to pursue the best rate of return. What I will address in the following section is how European institutional structures at both the national and supranational levels were created or reformed in order to meet these goals.

The Socialisation of the Agent

Since developed ideational forms provide a more successful basis for social agency, it is necessary to analyse the process of socialisation of the agent, a key objective of social constructivism. Actors acquire new interests and preferences through the process of social learning (Checkel 1999: 548). Initially this process begins with a group that together develops ideational norms; social learning occurs when the group is faced with a crisis or failure and when there is regular interaction within the group. This group can then diffuse its ideas through society in a number of ways, including persuasion (particularly of important political actors), and by exploiting 'policy windows'—when there is a new problem for which the controlling actors have no clear answers (Checkel 1999: 549-52).

Obviously political organisations and parties play this type of role in society, as did the Mont Pelerin Society in the transformation to a monetarist economic paradigm. Groups of technical experts have been central to the 'social learning' of policy makers in the EU, acting as 'epistemic communities'. An epistemic community, as defined by Peter Haas (1992):

> may consist of professionals from a variety of disciplines and backgrounds, they have:
> 1.   A shared set of normative and principled beliefs, which provide a value-based rationale for the social action of community members;
> 2.   Shared causal beliefs, which are derived from their analysis of prac-tices leading or contributing to a central set of problems in their domain and which then serve as the basis for elucidating the multiple linkages between possible policy actions and desired outcomes;
> 3.   Shared notions of validity—that is intersubjective, internally defined criteria for weighing and validating knowledge in the domain of their exper-tise; and
> 4.   A common policy enterprise—that is, a set of common practices as-sociated with a set of problems to which their professional competence is directed, presumably out of the conviction that human welfare will be en-hanced as a consequence (Haas 1992: 3).

Since an epistemic community is asked for advice on international policy cooperation, it is situated in an influential position and thus can 'affect the outcome of the policy-making process' (Verdun 1998b: 179). Given that the advice that they offer is highly technical, it is often not scrutinised for subjectivity; thus epistemic communities are in a position to form the opinion among those who sought the policy advice. Their recommendations are advanced as professionally sensible choices; yet the community's 'advice is informed by its own broader worldview' (Haas 1992: 4).

The Delors Committee is such an example of an epistemic community, which played a key role in influencing the direction of EMU (Verdun 1999). The Delors Committee members were selected for their expertise in the area of monetary policy. Recognising their professional skills, national governments bestowed upon them the task of developing a plan for Economic and Monetary Union. Although member states would have had a vision of EMU in mind when they chose a committee of central bankers to develop the blueprint, the Delors Committee itself influenced the member states' perceptions of what would be the desirable path to EMU. Their proposal for central bank independence and a commitment to low inflation has become the mantra of monetary policy-making for the EU. As Haas has asserted, epistemic communities can establish themselves as a more permanent influence on policy-making:

To the extent to which an epistemic community consolidates bureaucratic power within national administrations and international secretariats, it stands to institutionalize its influence and insinuate its views into broader international politics (Haas 1992: 4).

The central banking and monetary community has been very successful in such a consolidation of its influence, and has thus been very effective as a collective social agent in turning its beliefs into broader, shared understandings (Checkel 1999: 552).

Central bank economic experts and the EC heads of state have played a key role in determining the direction of integration. Member states at the Hanover Council meeting in 1988 created the Delors Committee and gave it the explicit objective to 'propose concrete stages' (Dyson 1994: 132) for moving towards EMU. As a member of the Delors Committee has said, 'governments in part had this type of EMU in mind when they decided to ask a group of primarily central bank governors to draft a blueprint for EMU' (quoted in Verdun 1998b: 184-5). Thus integration is moving in the direction envisaged by member states, regardless of the different compromises each has had to make.

The central bankers of Europe have been able to fill a vacuum in the European Union. They have provided effective leadership that no other institution of the European Community has, by making concrete proposals for the realisation of deeper integration. Economic and Monetary Union represented by a single currency and thus a single monetary policy. Although the proposals of the Delors Committee are seen as a technical solution for European integration, the process that they have outlined will result in institutionalising the neoliberal goal of monetarist economic policy for the European Union.

Under the leadership of Jacques Delors, the committee situated itself at the helm of the new Europe, and laid out a clear proposal for decisive movement toward EMU that government leaders could accept. The central banking community has played an important role in creating the belief that Economic and Monetary Union is the best method to create economic stability for Europe. Not only has the proposal of the Delors Report been accepted as advancing the best route to EMU, their prescriptions (summed up in the TEU) are pronounced as the only rational means by which to have a properly functioning European Union. The high level of acceptance of the current EMU model, combined with a lack of any concrete alternative, gives the illusion of a 'spill-over' pattern of integration.

Tommaso Padoa-Schioppa (Deputy Director of the Bank of Italy and member of the Delors Committee) has stated that throughout the 1980s:

[A] latent logic . . . started to impress itself upon decision-makers in Europe. . . [F]ree trade, unconstrained mobility of capital, fixed exchange rates [aspects of the Single European Act] and independent national monetary policies cannot co-exist for long (Padoa-Schioppa 1997: 163).

Although the analogy of Odysseus 'strapping himself to the mast' has been used to describe the behaviour of the central banking community (Dyson et al. 1995: 466), this group has been much more decisive than this statement would suggest. EC central bankers have taken the helm and are setting the course of European integration. The prepared political and institutional conditions are the still waters, and the ideological victory of neoliberalism has put the wind in their sails. And, like any good navigator, they are trying to gain as much ground as possible while the conditions are favourable, by institutionalising their independent and decisive position for the European Union as a whole. Whether or not they will shift their course in the face of economic turmoil remains to be seen.

Although I would argue that the path proposed by the Delors Committee is not a fundamental shift in the strategy that member states were following, EMU offers an institutionalisation of that process. Many of the prerequisites of the central banking community's version of Economic and Monetary Union had already been, or were in process of being, carried forward by the commitment of many of the European governments. 'EMU . . . was a result of consensus among policy makers that further integration at this point was only feasible in the realm of *monetary* policy making' (Verdun 1996a: 80). The commitment to monetary integration as a defining feature of the European Union was essential as an institutional justification for central bank independence.

Restructuring Europe

After the commitment to price stability was well established in the EMS, the next phase of European integration was the extension of genuine free trade. The Single European Act (SEA) of 1986 allowed for the liberalisation of capital movements, which resulted in 'altering the systemic relationships that govern monetary policy making' (Dyson et al. 1995: 466). The increased ability of mobile capital to move even more freely in order to find the best conditions in which to invest has given them increased political power to press for the institutionalisation of rules that favour their interests.

Two inhibiting factors for *maximum* capitalist profitability are the high social wage and the barriers to free trade; both of these are legacies of the Keynesian welfare state. As van der Pijl asserts, 'this "equilibrium of compromises" in the long run undermines the discipline [capital] must impose on the labour process' (van der Pijl 1997: 36). In order for capital to realise profits in such a highly competitive environment, it must continuously re-impose market discipline upon the working class. At the same time, production itself must be rationalised to more closely meet the levels of demand. These are the bases for the imposition of flexibility on the labour process, where the burden of adjustment is levied.

As the possibilities for maintaining the national social market framework became increasingly limited, states began to dramatically restructure their national institutions. Governments implemented programmes of austerity, deflation, and liberalisation, and sought to break the institutional links between money supply and government spending (Sandholtz 1993: 7-9). Control over the restoration of economic prosperity and employment was ceded to 'the market'. This included the deregulation of the labour market, decentralisation of negotiations, the dismantling of collective bargaining, and the end of government commitment to redistributive economic policies (Streeck and Schmitter 1991: 146-48).

Despite these changes, governments were still burdened by economic obligations to welfare state expenditures. Although the adoption of neoliberal policies assumes generalised deregulation, a combination of deregulation and re-regulation through different institutions has occurred (Majone 1997: 143). State administrations have become decentralised and regionalised, and activities have been broken down into single purpose areas and delegated to various agencies. These agencies are often comprised of 'experts', thus giving more legitimacy to their regulatory strategies than the state may have had in following the same strategy (Majone 1997: 146, 154).

The shifts that took place throughout the 1980s and the 1990s clearly indicate that the social market model was being dismantled at the national level, and restructured along lines drawn by market principles. As welfare state services have become compartmentalised there has been a corresponding shift to the organisation and distribution of these services along market principles. Questions of economic efficiency are being addressed strictly through the reduction of the workforce in the institutions that provide these services. The result has been a reduction in the quality and accessibility of the services provided as well as a taming of the once powerful public sector unions.

The growing similarity of the political convictions and commitment to macroeconomic discipline of the member states has also provided an incentive for policy coordination at the supranational level. States continued to face problems meeting their economic goals, and thus sought an international (regional) arrangement under which to make that possible. The commitment to a regional solution has played an important role in legitimating the turn to monetarist policies. As Hoffmann has argued, 'the EEC has also served as an alibi for governments too weak to take unpopular measures on their own, or strengthened their hand against protectionist or inflationary pressures' (Hoffmann 1982: 35).

Despite the complete liberalisation of capital mobility in the European Union, the creators of the SEA have argued that the goal of a unified Europe could be best realised through a single monetary policy. The idea of eventual progression to monetary union was inherent in the European Community's decisive removal of any barriers to the functioning of the internal market. 'With the ratification of the SEA, EMU was enshrined once more as a policy objective' (Cameron 1995: 2). This is attributed to Jacques Delors' persistence that there was an inherent logic that connected the idea of a single currency to the facilitation of capital's freedom of movement and investment in the functioning of the internal market.

Supporters of EMU argued that a single monetary policy would provide the stability necessary for regional trade by eliminating the costs of exchange rate differentials. A single currency and monetary policy throughout the region would provide the market security for productive capitalist activity in Europe. European producers would be provided with a market in which US exchange rate manipulations would no longer be a major factor. Thus the completion of EMU is seen as having a functional linkage to the 1992 project. 'The argument is that complete capital liberalisation (undertaken in July 1990) and exchange-rate stability (in the European Monetary System [EMS]) are incompatible with divergent national monetary policies' (Sandholtz 1993: 20).

Although the SEA made definitive alterations to economic activity through-out the European Union, the Treaty on European Union (TEU) which outlined the steps to creating Economic and Monetary Union is arguably the most decisive shift in the integration process.

> The decision to assign responsibility for defining and implementing monetary policy within a group of member states to a single central bank, and to cede all responsibility in the domain of exchange-rate policy to the institutions of the EU, undoubtedly represents one of the most significant extensions of suprana-tional authority in the four decades since the Treaty of Rome (Cameron 1998: 189).

The sentiment expressed here by David Cameron in his discussion of the sources and effects of EMU reflects a commonly held opinion concerning the TEU. The fundamental change in the institutional terrain of the European Union concomitant with the TEU cannot be understated.

As discussed earlier, throughout the 1980s European governments' policy priorities shifted decisively to a monetarist doctrine that emphasised anti-inflationary policies. These same European state leaders chose the central bankers and economists for the Delors Committee that created the blueprint for EMU, knowing well that these individuals would propose the centralisation of monetary power through the creation of an independent central bank. The path that was proposed by the committee was not a fundamental shift in the strategy that member states were following, but rather an institutionalisation of that process. The progression of integration occurred through a series of rational choices by national leaders pursuing the economic interests of their state; when the interests of production and the adjustment of macroeconomic policies converged, further integration was possible (Moravcsik 1998: 3). Thus the mandate from the heads of state given to the Delors Committee clearly illustrate Moravcsik's assertion that 'the integration process did not supersede or circumvent the political will of national leaders; it *reflected* their will' (Moravcsik 1998: 4, italics in original).

The process of moving toward EMU as outlined by the TEU was mutually reinforcing for both the supranational monetary authorities and the member states. National and supranational institutions thus were not adversaries but rather partners in developing the nature of the new European economic and monetary union. The central banking community needed Europe-wide commitment to macroeconomic discipline as a basis for a single monetary policy. The institutionalisation of the commitment to price stability in the treaty and the independence of the ECB would together provide a basis of credibility for Europe's new monetary arrangement in the financial markets. It was also a guarantee for stability in the climate of uncertain economic convergence of the EMU participants (Verdun 1998b: 181-82).

Not only did this design of EMU provide credibility in the financial markets; it also provided legitimacy for governments implementing austerity policies in the domestic realm. In countries where governments face greater pressures against neoliberal economic restructuring, EMU is an important legitimising force. As Sandholtz explains, there was quite an incentive for national governments to support EMU:

> For governments that found it difficult domestically to achieve monetary discipline, EMU offered the chance to have it implemented from without. Governments could even escape the blame when tight monetary policies pinched (Sandholtz 1993: 38).

For example, Italy has found it difficult to implement a thorough restructuring of its labour market, as workers have provided significant pressure against this process. Yet the desire of the Italian population to be part of an economic project that will provide a stable currency has allowed the government to implement otherwise unpopular policies in order to meet the convergence criteria for participation in EMU (see Croci and Picci, this volume).

Amy Verdun has asserted that the monetary authorities and employers' organisations felt that restructuring the national economies to purge inefficient welfare state policies would be necessary for countries to remain competitive, and were enticed by restructuring via market principles that EMU offered (Verdun 1996a: 75). Because of the politically sensitive nature of breaking the Keynesian consensus and diminishing welfare state responsibilities these measures were carried out in the economic realm.

> Thus the strategy of relying on market forces to exert pressure on domestic political actors to restructure the national welfare state, and the subsequent harmonisation *via market forces*, was considered attractive (Verdun 1996a: 76-77, italics in original).

86 Lloy Wylie

EMU is the completion of the separation of economic policies from political pressures that was initiated with the adoption of neoliberal restructuring policies. The transfer of economic power to the supranational ECB is thus the extension of this neoliberal model of the separation of economics from formal democratic political control that was already under way at the national level among the member states of the European Union.

Conclusion

EMU is not just an economic goal. It is a political goal supported by sections of the European business community, the political elite and policy makers that want to realise the marketisation of all aspects of the economy. The direction of integration in Europe has been chosen through the conscious action of political leaders led by ideological convictions. The social agents central to the creation of EMU took advantage of the policy window opened up by the crisis of the Bretton Woods system, followed by the inability of national corporatist strategies to resolve the crisis in the face of economic instability.

This shift in policy priorities offered a new direction for European countries, and policies of 'sound money' were implemented by governments of the member states from 1979 onwards. The economic developments since the collapse of the Bretton Woods economic order, including the process of European integration, 'have led to a fundamental reorganisation of political authority in Western Europe' (Hooghe and Marks 1999: 70). The political power of mobile capital has increased dramatically and the ability of nation states to follow independent expansionary economic policies has been tightly constrained, as evidenced by the French experiment in the early 1980s. This weakened ability of the nation state has influenced the decision to the shift responsibility for economic governance to the supranational realm, through the establishment of the ECB.

EMU is a product of the convergence of neoliberal convictions within the governments of member states, transnational capital, and supranational institutions. This change in monetary and fiscal policy frameworks at the national level lessened the divergences among member states and was a prerequisite to moving toward monetary union. The economic priorities outlined in the 1992 Treaty on European Union is the institutionalisation at the European Union level of economic priorities that were already well embedded in the economic policies of the various member states. EU states have chosen to ensure the maintenance of anti-inflationary economic policies by creating a single currency and a centralised monetary authority that is less susceptible to political pressure. The decision to move toward a single currency for the European Union represents a new strategy of nation states for achieving their goal of maintaining the money system in a context of increased uncertainty, through redefining the nation state's role in economic decision-making.

Thus rather than institutionalising the social market model on the supranational level (one of the greatest fears of Margaret Thatcher), EMU provides both a legitimacy and obligation to continue dismantling the social market at the national level, while offering the ability to redirect blame for the consequences of these changes. The development of the neoliberal hegemony and the weakening of popular organisations have allowed nation-states to increase their independence from domestic popular pressures for economic policy choices. The institutionalisation of neoliberal policy goals that EMU offers is in this respect a mechanism through which states are better able to ensure policies of 'sound money'. The institutional model of EMU further entrenches the four goals of neoliberalism—free trade, monetarist economic policies, and the restructuring of both the welfare state and the production regime.

The decisive movement towards an integrated and neoliberal Europe, represented by EMU, was prompted by the impact of globally intensified economic competition and the rise of transnational neoliberal ideologues. As Stephen Gill has identified, there is 'movement towards the attempt to consolidate a new form of hegemony which has a quite different social basis to the one which preceded it' (Gill 1992: 157). This new hegemony has become increasingly consolidated since Gill's assessment in 1992; neoliberalism has become increasingly dominant in the ideological realm and better placed in both transnational and national institutions to enhance its political influence. Margaret Thatcher's claim that 'there is no alternative' seems even truer today, as this type of monetary policy-making is not challenged by a comprehensive alternative economic scheme that addresses current economic conditions.

The creation of this type of EMU is an expression of the dominant position of the neoliberal perspective over the European project. Structures have been established that institutionalise the commitment to neoliberal austerity policies. The most powerful institution of the European Union is the ECB, which ensures the commitment to price stability regardless of the social costs.

The breakdown of nationally oriented stabilisation programmes in the face of pressures from increasingly mobile capital resulted in nation states' loss of the ability to use reflationary monetary policies to increase employment and investment. Thus nation states were unable to maintain the stability of corporatist structures that facilitated national stability. The implementation of neoliberal policies on the national level represented the commitment to a new type of socio-economic governance that rejected 'social market' principles of redistribution in favour of market dictated economic governance.

The developments on the supranational level show that the facilitation of free trade and the consolidation of monetarist policies are institutionalised in the Single European Act and the Treaty on European Union. EMU has provided the member states with the legitimacy to continue the dismantling of national redistributive policies. With the European Central Bank explicitly instructed to not yield to political pressure to alter its commitment to price stability, market forces are paramount in determining economic policies throughout the region.

The reason for the continued dominance of the neoliberal agenda is that the alternative projects for European integration do not have detailed elaboration in the Community agreements. The agreements of the European Union concerning social standards outline general principles, which are only symbolic. As van Apeldoorn argues, the demands of the neomercantilist and social democratic projects for the creation of the European order are incorporated 'in such a way that these concerns are in the end subordinated to the overriding objective of neoliberal competitiveness' (van Apeldoorn 1999b: 243).

Constructivist theory provides a useful tool for conceiving of social ontologies as socially and historically produced. In this sense, constructivism highlights the importance of the contextualisation of political and social processes. When militant labour movements were able to challenge the political and economic direction of policy choices, nation states were forced to make concessions in order to maintain social cohesion. When labour movements are considerably less powerful, their concerns can be ignored or adopted in an even more partial fashion, or redefined to fit the immediate economic needs of capital. The permissive consensus of European integration has allowed for the imposition of sacrifices on labour and other social groups, who hope to see an improvement in their economic positions through EMU.

This highlights the relevance of the agency and structure debate. When structures are challenged by new economic and social conditions, social agents are better positioned to intervene and redefine the structures. Agents who are aware of the specific contexts under which structures are created are better able to effectively challenge those structures. Therefore, effective social and political actors are those that understand how the factors that lead to the creation of specific institutions have changed over time. Crises open up 'policy windows' (Checkel 1999) where organised political or social agents can effectively alter social structures. The crisis of the Keynesian model and of national corporatism opened up a policy window that was utilised by those actors politically committed to economic and trade liberalisation and 'sound money' solutions. EMU is the culmination of this neoliberal project for Europe.

Note

Thanks to Gabriel Haythornthwaite, Liesbet Hooghe, Gary Marks, Ben Müller, Bastiaan van Apeldoorn, Amy Verdun, and the participants of the conference 'Conceptualising the new Europe' for comments on earlier drafts.

1. Monetarism in this sense is different from the 'monetarist' versus 'economist' debates as discussed by Wolf in chapter 3. In this context 'monetarist' refers to the belief in 'sound money' policies.

F33 F36

Chapter 6
EMU AS EUROPEANISATION: CONVERGENCE, DIVERSITY, AND CONTINGENCY

Kenneth Dyson

Rationalist and Constructivist Accounts:
The Importance of Ideas

That Economic and Monetary Union (EMU) is radically reshaping European states has become something of a truism (Cobham and Zis 1999). The questions with which this article is concerned are: what it is doing to them, how is it affecting them, and who is being affected? The answers reveal in what ways EMU is Europeanising states. What it is doing to them is defined by the direction, scope, and depth of its effects. The direction is provided by the institutionalisation of a paradigm of 'sound' money and finance, the consequent privileging of neoliberal reform strategies, retrenchment of welfare-state provision, and difficulties of sustaining non-inflationary national wage-bargaining regimes. In consequence, social democracy is in a difficult process of redefinition. This 'top-down' Europeanisation is, however, complemented by a 'bottom-up' process in which domestic elites construct EMU by reference to distinctive domestic institutional arrangements and project these constructions at the EU level. Hence the direction of change is complex.

The scope of EMU's effects has been more evident on domestic policies, notably fiscal, wage, labour-market, and welfare, than on domestic political structures like party systems (cf. Radaelli 2000). At the same time policy change—associated with institutionalising this paradigm—has potential effects on how these structures operate, especially in empowering executive leadership and the role of technocrats in finance ministries and central banks (Dyson 1997). Even when formal structures remain unchanged, EMU may serve to trigger processes of transformation of European states affecting domestic discourse and identities as well as policies (Giuliani 1999).

The depth of EMU's effects is bound up with how it influences states. This article identifies both a strategic and a cognitive component to Europeanisation. How EMU affects states takes two forms.

Rationalist accounts highlight 'thin' causal effects on the behaviour of state elites as they respond to the new external incentives and constraints represented by EMU's norms and rules. They adapt the ways in which they pursue exogenously given, essentially egoistic interests, by pursuing strategies appropriate to their context. These strategies include accommodation, transformation, evasion, and retrenchment (Dyson 2000b; Radaelli 2000).

Constructivist accounts stress 'thick' constitutive effects on the properties of states, that is on how their elites form their identities, define their interests, and legitimate both the European integration process in general and specific policies by framing them in convincing ways (Wendt 1999: 366). Europeanisation is about the internalisation of integration values and European policy paradigms at the domestic level, shaping discourse and identities. The focus shifts to the discursive construction of EMU by domestic actors and whether, and in what ways, it facilitates or blocks domestic changes.

The former effects involve material changes in the context of state action. Thus integrated financial markets, price transparency, and loss of policy instruments like devaluation and interest-rate adjustment produce changes in corporate and labour-market behaviour. The latter effects are discernible in the cognitive dimension of policy and politics, in a policy paradigm that privileges some strategies (e.g., market liberalisation and fiscal discipline) over others (e.g., direct state provision of services and active demand management), and in selective framing of discourse to convince publics (cf. Schmidt 1999). Some actors are empowered (notably finance ministries and central banks), others disempowered (like trade unions and welfare-state institutions) (Dyson 1997).

The value of this analytical distinction is lost once it is erected into an ontological dualism between positivists and post-positivists. In consequence, we lose sight of the complex, interwoven, and interdependent relationship between strategy and the discursive construction of the constraints and opportunities associated with EMU. 'Thick' and 'thin' effects are simultaneously at work in ways that are difficult to disentangle empirically. For instance, sociological, ideational, and rationalist aspects are bound up in a highly complex way in the attempts to transform Greece and Italy to make them 'fit' for EMU (Featherstone et al. 2000).

Importing constructivism into the EMU debate offers a useful corrective to a literature overly dominated by rationalist assumptions about the nature of causality and the basic unit of analysis (states as egoists with exogenously given interests). It widens the notion of what we should seek to observe in EMU, especially how state interests, power, and identity are constructed within the process, the underlying importance of ideas as real phenomena and of their internalisation by domestic elites. It underlines the complex interweaving and mutual interdependence between the material and the ideational. It shifts the basic question from 'under what conditions do ideas matter more than interests?' to 'how do interests come to be constructed in certain ways?' It is also receptive to seeing institutions as the embodiment of ideas rather than just matrixes of incentive and constraint. Finally, it recognises the power of culture understood as shared ideas, collective knowledge, and historical memories. The cost is a greater discord and complexity in thinking about the relationship between ideas and interests, and between ideas and institutions, than more parsimoniously minded rationalists like. The gain is a more dynamic sense of the relationships at work in EMU. What follows is not an argument against rationalist approaches but a plea for not dismissing constructivism.

This article argues for taking ideas more seriously in the study of EMU than rationalist accounts typically allow. In this sense it displays a measured sympathy for constructivism (e.g., Jachtenfuchs et al. 1999), critical discourse analysis (e.g., Foucault 1980), philosophical realism (e.g., Bhaskar 1986), and sociological and historical institutionalism (e.g., DiMaggio and Powell 1991). A key question is whether EMU is a macro-cultural form, with its own systemic properties, and with independent, top-down effects on identities and interests, or whether it is discursively constructed in very different ways reflecting the institutional distinctiveness of national capitalisms. The article stresses that systemic effects are discernible. They do not, however, obliterate the individuality of states, diminish the significance of domestic stories, and imply a remorseless logic of convergence in policies, outcomes, and processes. Diversity follows from the very different ways in which state elites, embedded in their own distinctive domestic institutional contexts, construct their identities in relation to EMU and give it political meaning (Schmidt 1997). The result is differential responses (Dyson 2000a; Héritier and Knill 2000). Participation in EMU does, however, have implications for how state individuality is conceived and defined and involves new tensions and opportunities.

Two caveats need to be entered. First, the article is not trying to explain the origins of EMU as a macro-cultural form, specifically of the sound money and finance paradigm that informs it (see Dyson 1994). Its concern is with how EMU as a set of shared ideas is affecting states—in other words its cultural significance for elites and the meanings that they attach to the games they are playing within the EU. Secondly, it shares with rationalist approaches a recognition that EMU involves powerful changes to material realities, for instance to markets and to available policy instruments (no devaluation, no interest-rate adjustment), which have independent effects on state action. But it argues that the form and impact of these effects is also shaped by ideas and their discursive construction. Thus changes in the material reality of the European economy (like free capital movement and economic convergence) made EMU possible. Those changes would not, however, have had the effects that they did in the absence of a strong political commitment to European unification in the key European capitals, especially Paris and Bonn (Dyson and Featherstone 1999). Historical memory played a vital role.

In what way do ideas matter? Ideas are not just a reflection of material realities. They are themselves part of the reality that we observe and have their own real effects in privileging certain forms of argument and expression and certain courses of action over others. In this sense the institutionalisation of the paradigm of sound money and finance in EMU is both discursively and strategically selective (cf. Hay 2000). Ideas structure debate, give direction to policy development, and provide legitimating formulæ in terms of which action is made defensible. Their long-term effects are produced through their institutional embodiment which gives them a certain 'stickiness'.

Context

EMU's effects on European states did not begin on 1 January 1999. The process of putting in place the conditions for EMU can be dated to the birth of the European Monetary System in 1979. In short, the timescale is two decades. It could be argued that the crucial impacts took place before 1999, especially with the institutionalisation of sound money and finance ideas in the Exchange Rate Mechanism (ERM) (Dyson 1994). In an imperfect and variable manner, the ERM functioned as a platform for policy transfer and policy learning, based on three variables: on emulation of Germany as a monetary policy model in the 1980s; on elite socialisation through the EMS; and on an ideational leadership role for EU central bankers (Marcussen 1998). In effect, the exchange-rate discipline of the ERM was a training ground for EMU, with the Bundesbank as team trainer. The key turning points can be seen as 1979-82 in Denmark, 1983 in France, 1992 and 1996 in Italy, and post-1997 in Greece. Hence variability is apparent in the timing and tempo of EMU's effects (cf. Goetz 2000).

Secondly, it is difficult to isolate EMU's effects on European states from other effects, notably from globalisation, the single European market, and rapid technological change. Whether EMU is judged to be an important independent variable, or merely mediating other influences, is an empirical issue that may be answered differently in individual cases. But these factors are associated with a discursive shift that puts European social models on the defensive—privileging a political discourse of modernisation and restructuring (especially labour-market and welfare-state reforms), policies of deregulation and privatisation, and institution-building in market regulation and economic stability. Of significance after 1999 is the new policy-pushing role of the ECB on behalf of liberalisation of goods, services and labour markets and flexibilisation of wages policy (Dyson 2000a). The euro-zone was a stimulus to an intensified process of policy benchmarking, transfer, and lesson-drawing, epitomised by the Lisbon

European Council in 2000. This process is consistent with a wider literature that shows how the EU functions as a forum for policy transfer and learning, with dynamic effects on how domestic policies are constructed (e.g., Radaelli 1999). In this case the ECB, supported by DG Economic and Financial Affairs of the European Commission, is the key entrepreneurial player on behalf of a particular European policy paradigm of structural economic reform.

What Are the Effects of EMU on European States? EMU as a Contingent Process

The various characterisations of EMU suggest the multi-dimensional and variable nature of its effects. Three dimensions of change can be identified. First, EMU is seen variously as 'hollowing out' the state, 'rescuing' it, or—in constructivist terms—as 'redefining' the state. The state is, in one view, losing its centrality as the primary unit of action and analysis; in another view, it is being strengthened; whilst, in a third, it is actively reconstructing its role in economic policy in a new context. Secondly, EMU is pictured as a relentless logic of convergence in European policies and politics. Alternatively, it is viewed as foreshadowing a more intergovernmental Europe. In an increasingly technocratic 'monetary' Europe, states are seen as even more important in providing political legitimacy. Denied monetary and exchange-rate policies, states are seeking to develop distinctive domestic economic policy models around their specific institutional strengths (Marsh 1999). In this sense EMU is producing diversity and competition (cf. Héritier and Knill 2000). It suggests a 'bottom-up' process of Europeanisation. Thirdly, EMU highlights another surprising contrast. On the one hand, it is characterised as drawing out traditional national patterns of statehood (neoliberal, dirigiste, and corporatist states); on the other, it appears to overturn stereotypical views of statehood. States like Greece and Italy appear more effective than Germany in pushing through structural economic and budgetary reforms. These characterisations need more careful examination.

1. European states are being hollowed out in two main areas: in monetary policy with the transfer of sovereignty to the European System of Central Banks (ESCB) and the emergence of the ECB as a supranational body with key executive powers; and in fiscal policy in the form of the Stability and Growth Pact which introduces a mechanism (including sanctions) to ensure state compliance with a balanced budget over the economic cycle (Artis and Winkler 1997). In core areas traditional state sovereignty has been either abandoned (interest rates and exchange rates) or hedged (fiscal policy). But it is inadequate simply to talk of the hollowing out of the state. The continuing relevance of the state as a unit of action in economic policy is confirmed by the absence of a structure of EU fiscal federalism, the lack of independent and discretionary areas of EU taxation, the continuity of state responsibility for welfare-state, labour-

market and employment policies, and the location of collective bargaining at the state and intra-state levels. EMU embodies an asymmetry between monetary union and 'soft', 'open' coordination in economic and related policies (Dyson 2000a).

More positively, the state can be viewed as a net gainer in that EMU rescues it from its former dependence on, and vulnerability to, global financial markets (cf. Milward 1992). EMU has brought about structural change in the material conditions of state action. The euro-zone's trade dependency is very much lower than that earlier of most of its Member States. Hence they conduct their economic policies in a more secure, stable and predictable framework, in which the constraints of balance of payments and exchange-rate instability are relaxed. But the effects of this structural change—rescuing the state—are shaped by how states reconstruct their role in economic policy in this new context.

Hence a constructivist approach provides a fuller view of what EMU does to European states. Formally deprived of interest rates and the exchange rate as instruments, they have been redefining their economic policy role (Marsh 1999). Greater stress is placed on their role in micro-structural reforms (e.g., to tax and benefit systems); in opinion formation and management, especially in relation to modernisation and restructuring; and also in relation to collaboration with employers and trade unions to ensure responsible wage bargaining and welfare-state reform. This process of reconstructing their role is exemplified in the proliferation of social pacts. Tripartite, negotiated package deals seek to reward wage moderation and work flexibility (to improve productivity and reduce labour costs) with tax, training, and welfare-state measures (Ebbinghaus and Hassel 2000). The redefinition of the state's role combines measures to promote modernisation and restructuring (including deregulation, privatisation and welfare-state reforms) with efforts to sustain social consensus through negotiated change. Governments have attempted to incorporate potential losers into the process of reform.

2. EMU's effects on European states can be viewed as making convergent their policies and politics, embracing wages, labour markets, and welfare-state provision. This process of convergence is attributable to two variables—heightened material economic interdependence and the logic of the sound money and finance paradigm. First, EMU reduces transaction costs by eliminating exchange-rate risk and creating a new transparency in prices and costs. The result is fiercer competition, an intensification of internal trade, mounting pressures for restructuring of sectors and firms, and a new vulnerability to adverse policy interactions (Dyson 2000a). The risks of adverse policy interactions amongst states, and of an inappropriate policy mix at the European level, draw attention to the issue of a strong political centre of economic policy coordination—an 'economic government'. Also, it is no longer possible to insulate national capitalist systems, like Germany's Rhineland capitalism, from predatory behaviour. The result is new inroads for the model of shareholder capitalism. Secondly, EMU's sound money paradigm—consistent with global

financial markets—suggests a logic of convergence of policies based on top-down Europeanisation.

But, paradoxically, top-down Europeanisation is held in check by the sound money paradigm which rules out an explicit coordination of economic and monetary policies as threatening the independence of the ECB. Hence there is no economic government. It is also constrained by the institutional variability of national capitalisms and by how domestic actors choose to construct EMU and frame policies in its terms. Implications follow for legitimacy. An essentially technocratic union in monetary policy makes more important the role of the state in providing democratic legitimacy. In contrast to the traditional German 'coronation' theory of EMU, monetary union is not embedded in a pre-established process of political union, conferring an EU-wide democratic legitimation (Dyson 1994: 66). The problem is how to handle the politicisation of EMU as its effects become more visible and directly impact on individuals in the absence of a supranational structure of democratic legitimacy. States remain the basic fora in which the processes of politicisation associated with EMU can be handled in a manner consistent with democratic legitimacy. This division of labour remains politically sustainable because fiscal, labour-market, employment, and wage policies remain national and have more visible and direct distributive effects on individuals than monetary policy. In short, states remain vital as the key part of the solution to problems of democratic legitimacy of EMU.

Seen from this perspective, EMU exhibits two processes of Europeanisation—top-down, focused on the ECB's explicit European-level price-stability target, use of its policy instruments and the policy paradigm on which they rest; and bottom-up in structural economic reforms to labour markets, wage bargaining, and welfare states where states engage in benchmarking, policy transfer, and lesson-drawing. In this view states are competing to set best practice and gain status and power from voluntary emulation by their partners. This looser form of coordination by indirect Europeanisation is suited to the legitimacy requirements of economic policy in the context of a technocratically defined monetary union.

3. The effects of EMU appear to demonstrate an historical path dependency conditioned by the institutional distinctiveness of national capitalisms. EMU draws out this historical and cultural variability. Britain can be seen as embodying a neoliberal conception of the role of the state. Thus the Blair government is hesitant to embrace partnership in tackling structural reforms (see the Blair-Schröder paper); trade unions are not drawn into a process of negotiated change. EMU is constructed as a mechanism for forcing the pace of structural economic reforms required by the neoliberal logic of globalisation. In France, by contrast, the Jospin government talks of a regulated and controlled globalisation, in which the state—and by extension the EU—provides political direction to markets (Jospin 1999). A characteristically French *volontarisme* and *dirigisme* is discernible in French constructions of EMU. In contrast, the Danes, Dutch, Irish, Italians, and Germans favour a more consensual, non-majoritarian

construction of EMU, based on social pacts and dialogue (Ebbinghaus and Hassel 2000).

But these neat surface patterns often hide a more complex and disorganised reality. Thus German attempts to negotiate economic change by tripartism in 1995-96 and after 1998 proved exceptionally difficult and frustrating. Also, post-unification, fiscal policy behaviour showed an absence of the discipline and order that are perceived as German hallmarks. In contrast, Italy utilised national social pacts to negotiate wage, labour-market and welfare-state reforms. The Greek and Italian governments—traditionally impaired by ineffective, politicised civil services and fragile domestic support for reform—demonstrated a greater readiness to implement structural changes than their German counterparts (Cobham and Zis 1999). Hence EMU has been associated with some surprising effects. The German state demonstrated a mix of inertia and accommodation; Greece and Italy a new will for transformation.

This variation in state responses to EMU is to be explained by three variables: the goodness of fit between the sound money paradigm of EMU and domestic policy ideas and institutions; domestic beliefs about governance and the extent to which they support an integrated leadership and capacity for technocratic capture of policy; and the presence or absence of a legitimating discourse, conditioning whether elites are emboldened by belief in a permissive public consensus on European integration (Radaelli 2000). The greater the fit, in the context of a cohesive leadership and a permissive consensus, the easier it is to accommodate to EMU. Where the ideational fit is poor, but the other variables are in place, the conditions exist for a transformation of domestic policies and structures. In such circumstances EMU empowers and legitimates elite action (Dyson and Featherstone 1996a). Germany, Greece, and Italy share a permissive consensus on Europe. But in Germany there was, at least initially, little sense of a lack of goodness of fit between EMU and domestic institutions and policy ideas. Hence German state elites responded with a mixture of inertia and accommodation, assuming that no substantial modifications to domestic policies and structures were required. In Greece and Italy, by contrast, technocrats led a debate about EMU as a force for transformation of the state: in effect, for a radical change of domestic policy discourse. Consequently, the scale of change resulting from EMU has varied considerably, as has its timing and tempo (cf. Goetz 2000).

Such diversity of domestic effects qualifies the explanatory power of the concept of EMU as a macro-cultural phenomenon with its own systemic properties. This concept yields an excessively top-down approach to EMU as Europeanisation. It is pictured as a dynamic process of endogenous policy change, characterised by cognitive learning and coercive policy transfer, and its discursive mediation into domestic institutional contexts. In practice, the ideational and institutional context is much more complex, especially at the domestic level. Once again, a useful analytical distinction—between top-down and bottom-up approaches to EMU—threatens to obfuscate rather than clarify if elevated into an intellectual dualism inviting either-or choice. These twin faces of Europeanisation have a complex dynamic interrelationship. How domestic actors construct EMU is shaped not simply by their participation in its structures but also by the institutional distinctiveness of national capitalisms and by the domestic power of those few participating to reframe domestic discourse. Tensions, conflicts and unintended consequences follow. Hence the effects of EMU are contingent and political rather than the unfolding of either a logic of convergence or a logic of domestic institutional distinctiveness. Political science all too easily succumbs to over-determined views of policy and political change in Member States.

How Is EMU Affecting European States?
The Cultural Dimension

A key question is how we conceive of EMU as affecting European states. With its stress on EMU as a refashioned framework of inducements and constraints, within which state actors pursue individual self-interests, rational choice theory seems to capture well its political and contingent effects (cf. Scharpf 1999; Tsebelis 1999). Following neorealist and neoliberal views, these self-interests are defined in the framework of domestic politics and national identity. The result is a one-way image of a bottom-up politics of European integration, carefully controlled by states jealous of individual sovereignty (e.g. Moravcsik 1998). For neoliberals ideas figure as an additional variable constraining self-interested action. Under certain circumstances they may help overcome collective action problems (e.g., McNamara 1998). But what we are looking at remains fundamentally the same—powerful individual states with exogenously given self-interests, pursuing their material advantage in a condition of rivalry with other states.

   This rationalist account captures a key part of the reality of how EMU is affecting states. Its problems follow from its individualist and materialist account of European states in EMU and its underdeveloped cultural dimension. European integration is seen as embedded within a Lockeian culture of egoistic inter-state rivalry, tempered by mutual respect for each other's sovereign rights and the rule of non-intervention, notably in fiscal, employment, welfare-state, and labour-market policies (Wendt 1999). But culture has no more than behavioural effects from the way in which it constrains actors. Rationalist accounts suggest limited cooperation, with actors disposed to escape EMU's constraints at the earliest opportunity, for instance by relaxing the Stability and Growth Pact's fiscal rules or their interpretation or by activating exchange-rate policy. Absent from this one-sided bottom-up picture is how EMU as a macro-cultural formation constructs actors by shaping how they come to define their interests, form their identities and exercise power. In this sense EMU has deeper, more powerful effects as actors internalise certain standards of socially appropriate behaviour, and particular ideas and institutional forms are diffused.

These effects are on the properties of states. Their actors continue to be rationalists, pursuing their interests and engaging in game-like behaviour. But the terms on which they define those interests and play games of strategic interaction are changed with important long-term effects.

As a macro-cultural form EMU embodies a set of shared ideas about what a state is, what sovereignty means, what making the euro-zone work implies, and how power is to be exercised. Without taking this cultural dimension into account, it is not possible to comprehend fully how EMU affects states through deeper constitutive effects. Those who manage EMU are held together by collective knowledge, notably the sound money and finance paradigm, and shared memories of the damage inflicted by past crises of the ERM. Such knowledge and memories have long-term effects on how they perceive tax, welfare-state, and labour-market issues.

EMU as Transnational Policy Community: Effects on Whom?

A key question is who mediates the central ideas of EMU into domestic settings and whether EMU strengthens their power. EMU is a highly technocratic policy domain, legitimated by the shared beliefs of a sound money paradigm. These beliefs accord primacy to credibility of monetary policy and the institutional requirement of central bank independence from politics as a technical precondition (Alesina and Gatti 1995). Credibility is deeply rooted in central banking culture and illustrates the way in which EMU empowers and legitimates EU central bankers (Blinder 1999). As far as the ECB is concerned, issues of accountability and transparency—central to the debate about the EU's democratic deficit—are secondary to credibility (Issing 1999). Hence minutes of meetings of the ECB's Governing Council are not published, and differences of opinion not aired. Seen from within this economic policy paradigm, EMU is not essentially about democratic legitimacy, about accountability to representative structures. It is a matter of technocratic legitimacy, of putting in place the appropriate institutional mechanisms to guarantee economic stability in Europe. Within that framework, accountability and transparency is about giving reasons for monetary policy decisions (cf. Majone 1999). EMU accords with a model of post-parliamentary governance, characterised by the importance of non-majoritarian institutions and the 'technicisation' of public policy (Radaelli 1999).

Traditionally, and consistent with this set of beliefs, EMU is a core executive activity, limited to a very tiny group of actors, principally in EU finance ministries and central banks. In terms of domestic empowerment they are the main beneficiaries. Before 1999 they were grouped in the EC Monetary Committee (EU finance ministry officials and central bankers together) and the European Monetary Institute (till 1994 the Committee of EC Central Bank Governors). A tight policy community developed around these two fora consequent on management of the ERM after 1979. The Delors Report on EMU in 1989 and the obligation to prepare for the final stage of EMU after the Maastricht Treaty accelerated this process. From 1999 the focus is provided by the ECB, with national central bank governors now part of the ESCB and obligated to implement the ECB's decisions (in which they play a part through membership of its Governing Council). Another focus is the Economic and Financial Committee, again EU finance ministry officials and EU central bankers, with the difference that the latter are now part of the ESCB. It prepares the work of the Euro-Group, which has an informal role, and of Ecofin, which continues to be the policy-making forum. Ecofin has been upgraded, with finance ministers now joining Heads of State or Government in the European Council for EMU business.

This closed, privileged transnational policy community of core executive actors has not just retained but also reinforced its identity with the process of EMU: through managing jointly the ERM, through preparing stage 3, through the structuring of their interactions after 1999 around an ECB-centric euro-zone; and—not least—through a collective interest in keeping the European Council at bay. Their collective identity was reinforced by the challenge of the Amsterdam Treaty's employment chapter and the subsequent search of the Labour and Social Affairs Council and the new Employment Committee for a strengthened role. The ECB-centric euro-zone policy community had to absorb and accommodate the so-called Luxembourg 'process'—with its annual employment policy guidelines and national action plans—and the Cologne 'process'—the Employment Pact and the macroeconomic dialogue. These developments opened up the dialogue about EMU by transforming the definition of who was in the policy domain. But, at the ideational level, there is a crucial continuity of the ascendancy of sound money and sound finance policy ideas. Ecofin and the Economic and Financial Committee asserted their right to be the framework within which dialogue about employment policy guidelines and macroeconomic policy coordination was conducted. These exercises are seen as subordinate to consistency with the Broad Economic Policy Guidelines for which Ecofin was responsible.

What emerges is a picture of an EMU policy community bound together by a sound money paradigm and of the privileged role of EU central bankers within that community as the bearers and beneficiaries of that paradigm. Just as the construction of the single European market centralised the regulatory function at the EU level, so EMU has centralised the economic stabilisation function at the EU level. Seen in technocratic terms, the EU is no longer just a regulatory state. It is an emergent stabilisation state, dedicated to improving the economic efficiency of Europe by establishing and safeguarding economic stability (Dyson 2000a). This small, exclusive EMU policy community continues to define the meaning and boundaries of the EU as a stabilisation state.

The Long-Term Political Effects of EMU on European States

Though a narrow, closed, and privileged policy domain, EMU's effects on states are pervasive. Their scope stretches over fiscal, labour-market, welfare-state, and wage policies. They raise what appear to be in the first instance technical questions about how these policies are to be coordinated to optimise economic adjustment to asymmetric shocks in a manner consistent with economic stability. In reality these questions go deeper to include domestic beliefs about governance (especially in relation to executive leadership) and about what are 'winning' and 'lost' causes in domestic policy discourse. The belief in making EMU work has implications for the meaning of sovereignty, in particular the nature of the rules that states believe they should respect in their relations with each other. Hence, whilst technocratic in origin and ethos, EMU's effects as a macro-level cultural form stretch to the level of the polity. What are these effects?

The Semi-Sovereignty Game

Foremost, EMU has constitutive effects on what kind of sovereignty 'game' Member States think they are playing (Sorensen 1999). Already, in the wider context of the EU, Member States seem to be playing a post-Westphalian sovereignty game in which the traditional rules have been recast (Caporaso 1996; Jackson 1999; Linklater 1998). The rule of non-intervention in the domestic affairs of other states is highly qualified, whilst the rule of equity is no longer seen as simply applying to the distribution of resources between states. In a material sense, these states are bound together in a transnationally integrated economy in which adverse policy interactions threaten welfare losses. In an ideational sense, they are united by the shared historical memory of the failure of the Westphalian system to prevent mutually catastrophic war in Europe; and by the shared memory of the vulnerability of European currencies in global financial markets (especially of the collapse of the Bretton Woods system and later ERM crises), with subsequent political humiliation for state policies.

EMU reflects these material and ideational forces. It also gives a new focus and momentum to them. It is about the creation of new forms of collective identity in monetary policy and in fiscal policy that provide state elites with a rationale to persuade vested interests about the need for reforms. The processes of collective identity formation move at very different paces in monetary and fiscal policy. But the two key points are that in these areas identity is no longer exclusively tied to the state and that the ECB, abetted by the EC Commission, acts as a new catalyst for collective identity formation.

Two effects are discernible. First, Member States' conception and use of sovereignty is deeply hedged by their recognition of the policy leverage of the ECB (it can punish 'irresponsible' behaviour with higher interest rates) and by their fear of the mutual costs from damaging the ECB's credibility as an actor. In this context the ECB enjoys a greater freedom in voicing its views on the urgent need for governments to tackle structural economic reforms than governments have either in voicing their concerns about monetary policy or in threatening their own exit as a means of levering change from the ECB (cf. Hirschman 1970). The Lafontaine episode in Germany, when the German Finance Minister issued public warnings to the ECB, proved a rapid learning process for state elites about the importance of self-restraint and unity in taking up policy positions. The learning process was by no means one-way. Lafontaine's behaviour sensitised the ECB to the need for a more political definition of its role. Viewed overall, however, this period was testament to the new asymmetrical form of political power in an ECB-centric euro-zone.

Secondly, states are reinforcing and extending the scope of partnership in economic policy. In the Amsterdam Treaty, the Luxembourg process, the Cardiff process, and the Cologne process and the Employment Pact, the stress is on enhanced cooperation in economic and employment policies. The semi-sovereignty game is about cooperation and redefining what states are doing on an individual basis within an agreed framework of shared ideas. This framework is provided by the sound money paradigm and the ECB's role as a policy reform pusher on behalf of structural reforms consistent with that paradigm.

Because of differences in domestic political beliefs, some states have greater difficulties than others do in adapting to this semi-sovereignty game. Adaptation is easier for those states that are used to consensual forms of liberal democracy, like the Netherlands, Germany, and Italy (Lijphart 1984). For Britain, with its majoritarian political form and style, it poses more problems. In this sense the obstacles to British membership of the euro-zone are more political and cultural than economic, and greater than for Denmark and Sweden. British political culture is less well adapted to playing the semi-sovereignty game of the euro-zone.

States as Prime Sites and Units of Analysis

Despite this semi-sovereignty, the euro-zone is by no means incompatible with a continuingly state-centric EU. Looking at economic policy in its widest sense, European states remain the prime sites of action and units of analysis. Quite simply, it is principally through states that the effects of economic policy action are likely to be channelled into the euro-zone and beyond. But how states make economic policy in the euro-zone is embedded in a transnational EMU policy community that extends beyond policy-makers in national state governments. The progressive institutionalisation of EMU (from managing the ERM onwards) has been associated with important socialisation effects on national policy-makers, especially in central banks and in finance ministries. Their behaviour is not simply a matter of responding to new constraints. It is shaped by the internalisation of certain norms of appropriate economic policy conduct. In short, it involves the notion of obligations and responsibilities to a wider whole. States may continue to be primary. But those who act on their behalf in monetary and fiscal policies—and potentially beyond—frame their notions of self-interest and identity differently. Hence Europeanisation reaches down into domestic policy-making. The question is how does it do so?

Europeanisation and Competition for Cognitive Leadership

Europeanisation has two dynamically interrelated components, each with ideational and material elements. Top-down Europeanisation derives principally from the ECB. It seeks cognitive leadership on behalf of the euro-zone's collective interest in economic stability and makes strategic use of policy leverage for this purpose. Bottom-up Europeanisation across the wide range of economic, labour-market, wage, and welfare-state policies comprises two elements: a cognitive and dynamic process of endogenous policy learning about best practice, and the strategic search for political and electoral profile as a cognitive leader on growth and employment policies. This prevalence of bottom-up Europeanisation is consistent with the state-centric nature of the EU and with the practice of the semi-sovereignty game. With the Lisbon European Council in March 2000, EMU became associated with a new stress on an open co-ordination method. This method accepts continuing prime responsibility of states in economic and related policies. But it places emphasis on the process of benchmarking best practice, policy transfer, and lesson-drawing (Dyson 2000a). These can be seen as soft instruments of Europeanisation, providing legitimacy for domestic reformers, triggering domestic learning dynamics, and leading to a restructuring of power within and amongst domestic institutions. This process has been apparent in taxation, welfare-state, labour-market, and wage-policy reforms. It also holds out a means for states to profile themselves through the power of ideas. States seek reputation—and their governments, electoral success—from becoming models that others seek to emulate.

At the same time benchmarking, policy transfer, and lesson-drawing are fraught with complications and difficulties, consequent on ideological, institutional, and historical differences between states (Dolowitz and Marsh 1996). Reception of certain ideas is easier in some states than others: for instance, the Dutch model of growth and employment is more readily considered in Schröder's Germany than Jospin's France. The cross-currents of policy transfer and learning are very complex, underlining the picture of differential responses to EMU.

Tendencies towards several Europes within the euro-zone, or a differential euro-zone (cf. Héritier and Knill 2000), need to be set against the more generalised effects of the policy-pushing role of the ECB on behalf of structural economic reforms consistent with the sound money paradigm. Labour-market, wage-policy, and welfare-state reforms take different forms, and occur at different times and tempos, reflecting the tenacity of individual national capitalisms and contrasting opportunity structures for reform opened by domestic institutional arrangements. At the same time countervailing pressures for convergence are promoted by a powerful cross-national coalition united around neoliberal economic beliefs: the ECB, multinational companies, and the global financial markets. The difficult empirical question is at what point this coalition's effects cease to be simply causal in triggering adaptive structural reforms within domestic institutional arrangements, become constitutive of the way in which Member State governments define their interests and form their identities, and lead to elite endorsement of a logic of EMU for the wide range of economic and social policies. Such a process of political victory for EMU as a macro-cultural phenomenon defined in neoliberal terms is by no means inevitable. It depends on how national elites choose to construct EMU and the contingencies that mark EMU as a process.

Conclusions: Convergence, Diversity, and Competition

The effects of EMU on European states are complex and contingent, not least on whether domestic elites come to internalise an associated logic of neoliberalism. Hence we are looking not simply at its material effects but also at how they are constructed. This chapter seeks to clarify this complexity rather than resolve it.

First, EMU involves powerful top-down pressures for convergence. These pressures are material and involve the removal of key protective conditions for distinctive national capitalisms—devaluation and interest-rate adjustments and nationally organised financial markets. As a macro-cultural form, EMU imparts a particular direction to the substance, framing, and legitimation of domestic policies and politics, selecting certain strategies and discourses and empowering finance ministries and central bankers.

Secondly, how convergent policies and outcomes are in practice depends on the contingencies created by the interactions between these pressures and distinctive institutional arrangements and cultures of both national capitalisms and domestic politics. There are differences in ideological goodness of fit; in capacity for integrated leadership and/or technocratic capture; and in whether a permissive public consensus facilitates the framing of policy and political reforms in terms of EMU. The result is very variable effects, apparent in different timing and tempo of change. Convergence in policies and outcomes is more contingent than the manifestation of an inexorable logic of EMU or of domestic institutional conditions.

Thirdly, EMU exhibits a complex dynamic interaction between top-down and bottom-up effects. The result is that EMU is constructed in different and changing ways. Three constructions predominate: as a mechanism for forcing the logic of structural economic reforms required by globalisation; as a mechanism for retrieving political direction of globalising capitalism and rescuing the European social model; and as a mechanism for negotiating change through social dialogue. They are exemplified respectively by Blair, Jospin, and Schröder. EMU can be seen as a contest between these three constructions.

Fourthly, the variability of EMU's effects is apparent in the four different strategies that state actors pursue (Dyson 2000b). A strategy of accommodation involves skills of discourse craftsmanship in framing policies 'required' by EMU in terms that will persuade particular publics. It was evident in Germany under Chancellor Kohl before 1996. A strategy of transformation requires the skills of policy entrepreneurs, whether in the state or in the private sector (e.g., the role of the French employers' organisation Medef in unemployment benefit reform), in negotiating or imposing domestic reforms. Greece, Italy, and Spain provide examples in the 1990s. A strategy of evasion is about skills in seeking out new institutional fora as mechanisms for reshaping preferences (e.g., French efforts to give new content to employment and growth strategies at the EU level, and Lafontaine's pursuit of international exchange rate co-ordination). A strategy of retrenchment reflects the 'stickiness' of domestic institutional arrangements in the face of EMU and reflects skills in mobilising opposition. Examples include failures of pension reforms in Greece and Italy, and unwillingness to tackle labour-market reforms in Germany. The lack of effectiveness of evasion as a strategy (note Lafontaine) suggests the constraining power of the paradigm of sound money. On the other hand, retrenchment is a sign of its weakness. But what has been most impressive is the way in which elites have on the whole embraced accommodation and transformation.

Fifthly, EMU is a factor not just in cooperation but also in conflict. The statement that, to an extent, state identities and interests are endogenous to the EMU process does not amount to claiming that they do not have identities and interests that are exogenous. States bring their own individuality to EMU, and that individuality, as in the British case, may be difficult to reconcile with the systemic properties of EMU. What is interesting is the way in which the meanings or terms of that individuality are redefined within the EMU process. The result is the contest about meanings of EMU identified above. These meanings bear the imprint of different state individualities.

Contrasting definitions of state individuality are associated with different responses to EMU. In Britain, especially after 1988, the EMU process served as a key variable in redefining British (and increasingly English) identity in a way that differentiated that identity more from Europe. In Germany, by contrast, state individuality was in important ways confirmed by an EMU that emulated the German model of monetary policy. In another sense, however, EMU challenged German individuality. The design of EMU transferred the 'Frankfurt' model of German capitalism to the EU level, not the 'Rhineland' capitalism model with its stress on a strong social dimension rooted in a cooperation of employers and labour. The issue of the sustainability of that model was raised as EMU contributed to a more predatory behaviour by firms intent on pursuing shareholder value, led by Allianz, Deutsche Bank, and Daimler Benz. Hence EMU had complex and ambivalent effects on German definitions of economic identity. It generated new domestic tensions and conflicts about the future nature of German capitalism and pressures for its transformation that had not been anticipated in 1991. The ambivalence of discourse and strategies of the Schröder government in relation to the Rhineland and shareholder-value models reflects these domestic tensions and conflicts. In Greece and Italy EMU acted as a catalyst for a process of radical redefinition of state individuality, focused on strengthening its will and capability to reform and provide a framework of discipline and order. EMU was an 'external' discipline (cf. Dyson and Featherstone 1996c). But its values were also internalised by key actors. Again, sharp contrasts are apparent in the ways in which European states experienced and responded to EMU.

Processes of redefining interests and forming a collective identity generate new tensions and conflicts, especially where a gap opens between elite beliefs and attitudes and the agenda and discourses in the public sphere (Schmidt 1997, 1999). The key question is: who is being socialised into its values? EMU's effects are uneven and reveal problems of a legitimating discourse. What is striking about the EMU process is its closed technocratic nature. It takes place at a distance from public debates. In states like Italy EMU-linked reforms such as privatisation, and pension and labour-market reforms are deeply contested. Hence, post-1999, Italian elites have attempted to shift public discourse about domestic reforms away from EMU to legitimation in terms of specific domestic arguments (e.g., intergenerational fairness in pension reform). An attempt has been made to find a legitimating discourse that will protect Europe. The problem, for instance in France, is how to construct a legitimating discourse that supports the values and changes associated with EMU (Cole and Drake 2000).

Sixthly, the political effect of EMU involves a challenge to those who subscribe to a traditional 'Westphalian' outlook on sovereignty, in which states are seen in Lockeian terms as egoistic rivals for material advantage. Though the EU may be an emergent Kantian culture, it is only imperfectly so. 'Making the euro-zone work' puts greater weight on accelerating this process of cultural change. In doing so it is likely to cause, or at least reinforce, conflicts. A likely form of expression will be in national populism on the right of the political spectrum. This phenomenon has grown in the 1990s, and raises the question of whether centre-right parties in Europe can hope to form governments without bringing these political forces on board. The political problem is how to engage public debate with the process of EMU in a context of a changing balance amongst the European party 'families' in which Christian democracy is waning and the far right gaining.

Finally, EMU involves a contest amongst states for status and power as cognitive leaders, providing policy models that others will emulate. In this way they stand to gain domestic political credibility and electoral support, attract inward investment, and bolster political legitimacy. The key factor here has not been the birth of the euro-zone but the loss of persuasive power of the German Rhineland model in the 1990s over growth, employment, and job creation. EMU transferred German monetary orthodoxy to the EU but not a German-style co-operative capitalism. In this new context, subject to ideological receptivity, other states can use superior economic performance in output growth and job creation to assume a cognitive leadership role. The result is new opportunities for small states, like Denmark and the Netherlands, to influence larger states, like Germany (see Bundesfinanzministerium 2000).

Note

This chapter was previously published as Kenneth Dyson (2000) "EMU as Europeanization: Convergence, Diversity and Contingency". *Journal of Common Market Studies* 38 (4): 645-66. The editor thanks Blackwell Publishers for permission to reprint this article.

F33
(EMU)   F36 J16

Chapter 7
THE GENDERED LIMITATIONS OF EUROPEAN CITIZENSHIP AND MONETARY INTEGRATION

R. Amy Elman

The political entrepreneurs of European integration bequeathed European citizenship to the Single Market in 1992. Faced with growing economic uncertainty and a democratic deficit, Europe's current leaders rely increasingly on varied measures to grant greater legitimacy to the new EMU. 'Economic integration bore the burden of building a polity' (Laffan 1996: 92). Historically, the definitive attributes of any polity are threefold: territory, sovereignty, and citizenship. In the context of the EU, much attention has been focused on sovereignty (e.g., subsidiarity) and the expansion of territory (through extended membership); by comparison, EU citizenship is a relatively recent concern, its formal establishment in the treaty dating only from Maastricht.[1]

Within the context of growing monetary integration, this chapter explores briefly the meaning of such EU citizenship for those who have historically been excluded from state construction and transnational bargaining, principally the women of Europe. The central argument is that the status of this citizenship and the alleged benefits of EMU are dubious and thus their implementation inspires ambivalence, particularly for feminists. We shall consider the reasons for this by focusing on those women residing on the periphery of integration. Focusing on the margins enhances our sensitivities to the asymmetrical character and consequences of European monetary integration. Several scholars have conceded that the process of integration is neither inevitable nor is it uniform or unilinear (e.g., Tsoukalis 1996). However, few explicitly observe that the growing disparities of wealth within and between states are gendered and that 'many of the most severely affected are women, including women who are racialised, migrantised and/or without access to formal citizenship' (Pettman 1999: 209).

Historical Precedents

Citizenship has always entailed both privilege and exclusion, affording benefits to those who possess it and legitimising discrimination (and even destruction) against those who lack it. Its primary function has been its identification of those community members who are to be protected and rewarded. In *The Origins of Totalitarianism*, Hannah Arendt reminds us that, as stateless persons, Europe's Jews were among the first in the twentieth century to experience unrestricted police domination. For Arendt, 'only nationals could be citizens, only people of the same national origin could enjoy the full protection of legal institutions' (1979: 275). The Second World War deeply enhanced our understanding of this condition.

For many that survived the Second World War, a united Europe promised the transcendence of those national rivalries and parochial loyalties that helped make the abominable carnage of that period possible. Indeed, the Preamble to the Treaty of Paris explicitly calls upon its members 'to substitute for age-old rivalries the merging of their essential interests' and 'create, by establishing an economic community, the basis for a broader and deeper community among peoples long divided by bloody conflicts.'

Europe's wars were economically devastating and it was assumed a cohesive economic community would provoke prosperity and diminish dissension. This presumption proved false for a number of reasons, not the least of which concerns chronic unemployment, the collapse of communism in Eastern Europe, and the renewed assertion of national identities throughout the continent. More recently, the enthusiastic expectations of euro-investors have been repeatedly defied. By the fall of 2000, the euro had plummeted by over 25 percent of its original worth. While the US economy expanded at an impressive rate of 4.2 percent over the past five years, the twelve-nation eurozone grew by only 2.4 percent.

With declining influence and affluence, Europe's political actors came to appreciate that 'An emphasis only on the material benefits of integration [would] not guarantee continued commitment to the process' (Laffan 1996: 95). They thus invested in the sentiments of prestige and solidarity. European emblems (e.g., European flags, anthems, and feasts), democratic rhetoric, and European citizenship were designed to inspire such commitment. EU citizenship emerged as one of the most recent and arguably ambiguous of these devices, distinctive for the limited legal rights it confers.

Unlike conventional citizenship, defined as 'a status bestowed on those who are full members of a community,' which includes civil, political, and social rights and obligations (Marshall 1950: 14), the political status of the union citizen is presently circumscribed. 'It is a citizenship whose legal and normative bases are located in the wider community, and whose actual implementation is assigned to the member states' (Soysal 1994: 148). EU citizenship is, after all, premised in nationality, an identity determined by state, not union, policy. Union citizenship is thus extended to member state nationals, not European nationals. 'Every citizen holding the nationality of a member state shall be a citizen of the Union,' a status that entitles one to free movement within all member states (Article 8(1) EC). Though the guarantee of free movement for economic purposes dates from the Community's inception, the recent attachment of this right to the article on citizenship is significant. It suggests a desire to reaffirm the ability of member states to determine the acquisition of this transnational status.

Nation states remain the venue for the attainment of citizenship and the primary repository for the effective distribution of material benefits associated with it. Because the rights of political participation are weak and social rights are non-existent, union citizenship is, at present, neither social nor participatory. According to the European Commission, the 'purpose' of European citizenship is 'to deepen European citizens' sense of belonging to the European Union and make that sense more tangible by conferring on them the rights associated with it' (1995: 21). However, the most novel application of this 'right' is the ability of any (member state) citizen to vote and stand for office outside of one's own member state in local and European Parliamentary elections—rights several states had come close to granting already.

The EU's channels for political expression remain few and insubstantial. Considering that the European Parliament holds relatively limited influence over the politics of integration while the Council of Ministers are accountable to national governments and not the EU electorate, policy outcomes are minimally influenced by those civic acts associated with EU citizenship. This helps explain the low voter turnout in European elections as well as its steady decline, from 63 percent in 1979 to 56 percent in 1994. Voter turnout increased in 1999 to 64 percent only after a Euro 24 million (30.4 million USD) public relations campaign (begun in 1997) to promote EU citizenship. Given the expense of this 'Citizens' First' initiative, a single percentage point increase over that of two decades earlier seems unimpressive. Nonetheless, EU officials persist in attributing voter apathy to an ignorant electorate and not to a well-informed citizenry cognizant of and perhaps frustrated by its limited ability to influence matters of integration.

Unlike Europe's movements for suffrage and other rights based movements, the request for European citizenship resulted not from a call from Europe's masses but, instead, from the elite that governed them. Noting that 'ordinary' Europeans approve of it (e.g., Meehan 1993) is not the same as being able to demonstrate that they demanded it. In fact, the extension of European citizenship was hardly popular. It often sparked confusion and, at times, a powerful reaction against it. For example, in 1992, some 'felt that the citizenship proposals were not far-reaching enough' (Meehan 1993a: 184 n28) while others, like many French, who opposed the Treaty on European Union, equated the treaty with the destruction of the nation state (Laffan 1996: 89). Danes were similarly concerned over citizenship's possible usurpation of their sovereignty (Petersen 1993: 9), a concern most recently manifested in the country's rejection of the euro (see below).

In its offer of EU citizenship, the Commission has had to assure member state nationals that this status is neither in conflict with national citizenship nor is it an identity that merely functions as a preserve of the continent's elite. This task has not been easy. The relative absence of enthusiasm for unification among Europe's less privileged was clearly evidenced by the voting patterns in four national referenda on the Treaty on European Union. Moreover, at this time, a majority of Europeans asserted that they have never even felt European (Reif in Laffan 1996: 99).

Issues of European citizenship and identity are bound inextricably to the political economy of the European Union. Focusing on the EU's pursuit of EMU thus facilitates our understanding of those hesitant to identify with and embrace European citizenship and economic integration. The treaty's requirement that member states have deficits below 3 percent of GDP and outstanding public debts below 60 percent of the GDP before joining it has, in part, legitimised the chorus of post-Keynesian calls for cuts in social welfare (Ostner 2000; Rossilli 2000). Subsequent austerity measures have, in turn, led to large protests throughout the EU, most notably in France and Germany.[2] Undeterred, these two member states and nine of the fifteen others committed themselves to the single currency while failing to put the issue to a public referendum. In the fall of 2000, when the Danes held the first vote on whether to join the currency, 53 percent of the electorate opted to preserve their krone. 'The rejection appeared to contain an ominous warning to European leaders that they may have raced ahead of their electorates in adopting the euro' (Cohen 2000).

While the convergence criteria concentrate exclusively on monetary variables, the social costs of EMU cannot be underestimated. Eurocrats, scholars, and others may acknowledge the substantial social costs of closer economic integration but still insist that suffering is best alleviated by more, not less, integration (e.g., Simpson and Walker 1993). By contrast, 'workers and poorer sections of society see little benefit and many dangers in the "Europeanisation" of the contemporary state' (Laffan 1996: 89). Indeed, their dissatisfaction could increase as reforms (e.g., equality legislation) previously taken on their behalf are increasingly portrayed as 'unwarranted and unworkable infringement[s] on freedom in market transactions' (Conaghan cited in Beveridge, Nott, and Stephen 2000: 388).

Considering that women comprise both a significant majority of Europe's least privileged and service sector employees, it is not surprising that, as a group, women have been consistently less favourably disposed than men to political and economic integration. For example, a recent Eurobarometer poll revealed that 55 percent of men surveyed favour their country's membership in the EU versus 47 percent of women surveyed (2000: 34). In addition, women are less willing to vote in European elections (Eurobarometer 2000: 89), a point that should not be taken to conclude that they are apathetic. After all, women are often more prominent in campaigns to counter unification (Hoskyns 1996: 22).

Engendering Citizenship

Apart from encouraging the opportunity to vote (exercised every five years) and a Social Action Program (1991-95) designed to encourage women's entrance into politics and civil dialogue, the EU has most emphasised women's market-oriented participation. Remarking on the escalating importance of economics more generally, Dominique Schnapper notes that 'True membership in the community is no longer defined by political participation but by economic activity' (1997: 204). Patrick R. Ireland explains that 'Geographical mobility accrued to nationals of the member states not on the basis of their citizenship status but when they travelled as workers, for economic reasons' (1995: 237).[3] That is, European citizenship is grounded in free market ideology with its related rights often predicated on calculations of the bottom line and not on the intrinsic value of persons and/or sexual equality. Put differently, Europeans have long been engaged as consumers and workers, not as citizens (Laffan 1996: 94).

Efforts to enhance a sense of belonging to and improve the democratic accountability of the European Union were considered, often behind closed doors, at the 1996 Intergovernmental Conference (IGC). Having restricted access to these discussions, barely 15 percent of all Europeans even knew about the IGC. Such exclusivity has led several EU commentators, like Michel de Meulenaere, to conclude that the Commission's incessant chatter of 'giving people a voice' within a democratised Europe fails to mask its insincerity (1996: 2). Nonetheless the subterfuge persists.

Ignoring the elitist character of the Union helps maintain the illusion that equality is a goal pursued vigorously and that citizenship implies uniform access to policy influence and social rights. Until recently, women were conspicuously absent from Europe's key deliberative body, the Commission. It contained no women commissioners during the first thirty years of its operation. Member states share a similar, if not more oppressive, history of sexual exclusion. Europe was man-made; a fact often politely overlooked. Those burdened by this past are quick to list the numerous advances that women have since made. These include, but are not limited to, an increased participation in the wage labour market and greater presence within various political institutions. At present, five of the twenty European commissioners are women. Women similarly increased their percentage in the European Parliament, from 19 percent in 1989 to over 25 percent in 1994 and 31 percent since 1999, more than nearly all the national legislatures throughout the Union. While such achievements are not insignificant, assessing gender (in)equality through women's numerical presence within established political institutions and the labour market, as opposed to the substance of the policies and material conditions they promote, is as problematic as it is naive (Rossilli 2000; Vogel-Polsky 2000; Weldon forthcoming).

Emphasising women's formal rights obscures the numerous obstacles to their effective use. 'Powerful market forces are at work which can rob even the most "women friendly" policies of their full impact' (Beveridge and Nott 1996: 398). In a labour market in which women comprise 77 percent of Europe's 'low wage workers' and over half of the total unemployed in almost every member state, women are especially reluctant to initiate grievances against their co-workers and employers for fear of retribution. In addition, women often remain ignorant of the possible redress Equality Directives provide. Those that are aware may lack the time and resources needed to obtain the counsel with which to vigorously pursue their formal rights. Few states provide thorough assistance for claimants who are likely to have less power and fewer resources than their employers do.

Engendering Marginalisation

The presumption that monetary integration, affluence, and democratisation are deeply intertwined is challenged perhaps most conspicuously by a political malaise reflected in the escalation of xenophobia throughout Western Europe. Right wing politicians and press reports often portray immigrants as a key destabilising force. Indeed, this tactic proved especially effective for Austria's far right Freedom Party, which garnered nearly a third of the vote in the national election of 1999. The alleged inextricability of escalating unemployment and immigration has also been made abundantly clear in a notorious National Front poster that exclaims: 'Three million unemployed, that's three million too many immigrants.'[4] Deportation is one proposed solution; French women figure prominently in the second (see Kofman 1998). Interestingly, they are encouraged to reproduce for the 'fatherland' while foreign mothers are depicted as bearers of an onerous immigrant population. Austria's Freedom Party has adopted a position similar to that of the FN. During the 1999 election, Haider promised $400 a month to Austrian mothers as an incentive for them to stay at home to raise their children. Some years ago Tony Judt warned that both the FN and Freedom Party are a matter of concern because they do so well among the insecure elderly and unemployed youth (1996: chapter 3).

Afraid to alienate a potential voter base, politicians within Austria, France, and throughout Europe have been reticent to challenge the far right. Even Sweden's Social Democratic party challenged neither the racist rhetoric nor the agenda of a newly established (New Democracy) party which, among other things, called for additional restrictions in refugee policies in the 1991 election. Bengt Westerberg of the Liberal party was the only party leader to publicly criticise the increasing xenophobia of Swedes. He demanded that other parties also address the problem; his request was met with silence. Nearly a decade later, the fragility of the European left is expressed, in part, through its inconsistent opposition to the racism of the right (Judt 2000).

While the EU's condemnation of Austria's Freedom Party suggested that, in the aftermath of EMU, a shift towards decisive action is possible, a more considered examination implies that this is unlikely. The EU suspended normal links with Austria through limiting ambassadorial contact and withdrawing its support of Austrian candidates to international posts. Yet, because Austria did not break any specific rules and unprecedented sanctions were imposed with limited discussion, the censure lasted only seven months. The opaque and feeble foundation of the Union's response has not gone unnoticed (see Judt 2000).

Just prior to the Austrian debacle, the European Union endeavoured to take action through a range of reports, resolutions, and declarations that condemns racism and xenophobia. In addition, the European Commission proclaimed 1997 the 'European Year Against Racism' and agreed, in Amsterdam, to establish the European Monitoring Centre on Racism and Xenophobia in Vienna. Rhetorical pronouncements and monitoring aside, the EU conceded that it will not 'take specific measures to combat racism and xenophobia' nor will it 'modify the system for protecting human rights in the Community or . . . make any major change to the institutional system in the Community or any of its Member States' (COM 1996: 3). Subsidiarity poses a further constraint on effective action.[5]

While EU citizenship may augment Europe's accessibility for many member state nationals, it may also more firmly etch a boundary 'around a culturalist and physical Europe so to ensure the exclusion of non-European foreigners' as well as Europeans of colour (Feldblum 1996: 11; see also Hervey 1995).[6] Writing from Britain, John Clarke and Mary Langan remark: 'perhaps more powerfully than before, "race" came to be seen as the single most visible demonstration of "citizenship" combining the implicit racial "test" as the basis of detecting suspected non-citizens among citizen residents' (1993: 73). Writing from France, Pierre Bourdieu asks: 'What does it mean to be a citizen if at any moment proof of citizenship has to be provided?' Like Clarke and Langan, he objects to the ways in which numerous civil servants are authorised 'to cast doubt on the citizenship of a citizen at the mere sight of her face or the sound of her name' (1998: 79).

The fact that Article 13 of the Amsterdam Treaty may provide redress is encouraging, though it empowered but did not oblige the Commission to combat discrimination. The text of that article reads:

Without prejudice to the other provisions of this Treaty and within the limits of powers conferred by it upon the Community, the Council, acting unanimously on a proposal from the Commission and after consulting the European Parliament may take appropriate action to combat discrimination based on sex, racial or ethnic origin, religion or belief, disability, age or sexual orientation.

In consequence, member states did not establish a directly effective provision but, instead, left it to the Community institutions to adopt 'appropriate' measures. The Union is under no obligation to secure relief for the victims of such ('race') discrimination. Moreover, the (post-Amsterdam) Austrian debacle underscores the EU's impotence in this regard.

The price of exclusion is born increasingly among women throughout Europe, particularly third country nationals. Most recently, a majority of the survivors of Serbia's war against Bosnia-Herzegovina and Croatia are (Muslim) women seeking refuge.[7] This is, perhaps, the most significant case in point. The fact that this genocide happened in non-member states within Europe makes it no less compelling to consider (see Nenadic 1996). Years before the genocide began, the EC expressly declared its commitment to the protection and promotion of democracy and human rights not only within its community but also in non-member states (Single European Act 1986, Preamble). In its Statement on Human Rights (21 July 1986), the Community declared that, 'The Twelve seek universal observance of human rights' and insisted that such rights are 'an important element in relations between third countries and the Europe of Twelve.' Less than a decade would pass before the reality fell far short of the rhetoric. Member states responded to the genocidal war through 'concerted efforts to stop refugees from leaving' and sought 'to keep these refugees "as close to their home areas as possible,"' and within the confines of the former Yugoslavia' (Sassen 1999: 125). Although the EU has long been interested in the affairs of 'third countries,' the essentially economic character of the European Union has undoubtedly dulled its interest in fundamental human rights issues. Moreover, the absence of any specific and detailed articles concerning human rights has made it easier for the EU to evade action in this and other important areas, impressive statements notwithstanding.

Within seemingly peaceful Europe, male violence in the home also places women in a perilous position. One of the major issues confronting women's refuges throughout Europe is how best to meet the needs of newly arrived immigrant women married to batterers (e.g., Nordic Council of Ministers 1998). To escape their abusers, many women are forced from their homes and, in consequence, risk statelessness. Immigrant women, for whom it is difficult to return to their homelands, face a situation in which they are unable to stay in Member States unless they remain married for a specified number of years. In the Netherlands, for example, a woman must reside with her partner for at least five years and in Sweden she must remain with him for two years. In Britain, women are required to stay with their husbands for at least one year or return to their country of origin. Women are, thus, sometimes expected to endure abuse for the privilege of residence.

Should a third country national woman leave her EU citizen husband, she must leave 'his' country. The European Court of Justice reinforced this position in *Diatta v Berlin Land* (Case 267/83 [1985] ECR 567). The case concerned an EU national husband separated, though not formally divorced from his third country national wife. The Court ruled that the woman was entitled to the protections of Community law only until the marriage was formally annulled. Tamara K. Hervey explains, 'The effect of the ruling . . . was to give the EUN [European Union National] husband control over expulsion of his wife: on divorce she would cease to be a member of the family for purposes of Community law' (1995: 106).[8]

Several Member States have sought to mitigate the hardships of such a stateless existence by decreasing residence requirements specifically for abused women. Given the absence of any explicit legal basis in the treaty, the EU has been reticent to promote a uniform approach to this particular issue (Gradin 1999). It has, thus, only just begun to acknowledge male violence against women as political in nature and economic in consequence (Elman 1996). This shift resulted, in part, from efforts undertaken by European women's movements. Throughout Europe, feminists politicised the public nature of this seemingly private abuse by emphasising the problems battered women encountered at work (e.g., poor concentration, tardiness, and sick leaves), and politicians and corporations responded—oftentimes for reasons of health, safety, liability, legitimacy, and the bottom line. Indeed, it is unlikely that the EU would have responded to the issue of male violence against women had European women's movements not couched the issue in market and employment related terms (Ostner 2000: 31).[9]

In 1997, the European Commission released a report acknowledging that while male violence is the most endemic form of violence within all member states, the elderly, poor, and migrant women may be especially vulnerable (1997). The following year the European Parliament designated 1999 as the 'European Year Against Violence Against Women.' The Commission concomitantly proposed funding for investigations into the problem as well as an information campaign, called Daphne, to promote the notion of zero tolerance for violence against women throughout member states (OJ C 304, 6.10. 1997: 55). Daphne has since been renewed as a Community action program (2000-2004) and is funded as a public health initiative (OJ C 259, 18.8. 1998: 2). Similar efforts are being undertaken to combat (sexual) trafficking in women under a separate program called STOP (OJ C 14, 19.1.1998: 39).

As suggested earlier, this increased interest among Europe's policy makers corresponds to escalating public concern throughout the member states (Duffin 1999; Simpson 1999), a concern inspired by women's movements. Recent Eurobarometer data on violence against women reveal that over two-thirds (67 percent) of member state nationals polled believed that the EU should 'definitely' be involved in countering violence against women and only 5 percent suggested a non-interventionist approach as appropriate (1999: 103).

For those image entrepreneurs whose job it is to sell Europe, the above-mentioned efforts may facilitate support for Europe's political institutions (particularly among women) without necessarily requiring innovative policies and effective implementation. According to Bryan Wendon, the Commission has realised that its position is 'strengthened by being less responsible for policy formulation' than by 'enabling others to deal with the detail' (1998: 350). He concludes: 'In a difficult period in EU social policy DG V has found new roles in helping, funding, researching and nurturing—while staying well out of the firing line' (1998: 350).

Conclusion

The practice of citizenship has characteristically involved the assertion of claims directed toward the state that, in turn, authoritatively develops socio-economic policy for the members of its shared national community (Wiener 1997: 548). Citizenship inspires ambivalence among feminists and others seeking socio-economic justice not merely because it entails exclusion for those who do not possess it but because it legitimises the very polities able to confer it. As J.H.H. Weiler has argued: 'The importance of European citizenship is much more than a device for placating an alienated populace. It goes to the very foundations of political legitimacy' (1997: 502).

European citizenship may equip individuals with rights enforceable outside the parameters of the nation states but whether such rights strengthen the claims of privileged actors while simultaneously weakening the position of others is at issue (Sassen 1998: 99). The fact that some analysts suggest that the EU 'offers a wide range of potential venue opportunities for strategically motivated actors at various levels of governance: local, national and European' (Wendon 1998: 342; see also Pollack 1997) overlooks the power differentials between claimants. In fact, several scholars have aptly cautioned that 'the effects of the EU have been highly variable,' depending on the issues and movements under consideration (see Marks and McAdam 1996: 119).[10] Some scholarship on women's rights, particularly when confined to work-related issues, suggests that the ascendance of international venues provide an additional space where women can gain visibility (e.g., Mazey 1998; Sassen 1998: 99-100). Sonia Mazey argues: 'At the EC level, women encountered a somewhat more favourable policy-making venue to that which prevailed in most national capitals' (1998: 138). She specifically credits the Commission for the cultivation of 'close relations with the relevant policy community in an attempt to create 'constituency' support for EC intervention in a particular policy sector' (Mazey 1998: 138).

Mazey's astute recognition of the Commission's favoured ties to 'femocrats' and ostensible non-governmental actors like the European Women's Lobby (which it funds)[11] does not, however, necessarily mean that the Commission and/or other European institutions are permeable to demands originating from grassroots feminist organisations throughout Europe. Similarly, Saskia Sassen's assertion that feminists are now mobilising outside of their nation states does not mean that they will do this with any more or less success than they have had within domestic contexts. Focusing specifically on feminist organisations, Jan Judy Pettman observes that the 'fears of global power and its blatant unaccountability underlie some feminist attempts to reclaim the state, and citizenship, as still difficult, but more accessible than global power' (1999: 208). Regardless of one's preferred avenue of mobilisation, as noted throughout, the difficulty for most women is that they often lack financial and other resources with which to effectively organise at any level (e.g., within states and across their borders).

Despite the increased recognition and global institutionalisation of 'women's issues' and women's substantially increased presence in the labour market, their pay remains significantly lower than that of men while their rate of unemployment is generally much higher. 'Indirect' discrimination is persistently pervasive and gender segregation is the norm within the labour market as well as well beyond it.

Women's conspicuous exclusion from the first decades of Europe's construction, and now conditional access to its most powerful institutions, suggest that, as relative newcomers, their knowledge of and influence within the EU is likely to be limited. Despite considerable variation across member states, this factor, among many others, places the women of Europe at a particular disadvantage with regard to citizenship, the politics of integration, and the affluence it presumably affords (Elman 1996: 12). This assessment is bolstered by Charlotte Bretherton and Liz Sperling's circumspect comparative study of women's networks in the United Kingdom. They reveal that, in general, grassroots organisations have difficulty accessing the Union but that women's groups 'suffered disproportionately' (1996: 503). Furthermore, while local women's groups and national volunteer organisations for women were least favourable and knowledgeable about the EU, women connected to trade unions were more positive and had higher levels of awareness about it. The difference can, perhaps, be explained by the top-down and economic orientation of EU policy.

While union citizenship may occasionally provide an additional venue for (women's) movements to make claims, the ability of autonomous (feminist) actors to move freely between alternate avenues in an attempt to find the level most permeable to their position(s) assumes unlimited resources with which to make such determinations. Moreover, the possibility that sexual inequality and various multifaceted exclusions may best be mitigated within a Single Market, replete with intrinsic economic and social disparities, is profoundly paradoxical. Women's citizenship is inextricably bound to the socio-economic constraints that the mechanism of citizenship is not empowered to undo because EU 'equality' policy remains fastened to a 'free' market ideology that rejects the redistributive social policy needed to level the playing field. Thus, the transformative potential of EU citizenship is largely limited.

Notes

The author extends her gratitude to her colleagues in the Women and Gender Studies Program at Middlebury College and the Title VI Center for European Studies at Kalamazoo College for its partial support of this research. An earlier version of this chapter was published as R. Amy Elman (2001) "Testing the Limits of European Citizenship: Ethnic Hatred and Male Violence". *National Women's Studies Association Journal* 13(3): 49-69. The editor thanks Indiana University Press for permission to publish this revised version.

1. Although the practice of citizenship remained largely invisible before Maastricht, the roots of citizenship policy and its actual practice can be traced to the early 1970s (Durand 1979; Evans 1984; Lyons 1996; Wiener 1997).

2. French dissatisfaction erupted in a series of winter strikes (1996-97) which led President Chirac to reverse some of his deficit reducing measures. This situation also weakened his government in the parliamentary elections that followed. On June 15, 1996, 350,000 people turned out in Bonn to express their dissatisfaction. Later, in October 1999, tens of thousands of teachers, police officers, and other civil servants closed down the centre of Berlin after Chancellor Gerhard Schröder's announcement to further trim Germany's 'nanny state'. The same month, Ireland witnessed the largest work stoppage in the nation's history as 27,500 nurses went on strike for nine days over paltry wages. Women were clearly key players in these demonstrations.

3. People of independent means, students, and the families of heterosexual workers have also been geographically mobile. By contrast, 'the family unification of homosexuals is legally virtually impossible' as most member states do not recognise same sex partnerships as the equivalent of heterosexual ones (Lutz 1997: 105). For a further analysis, see Elman (2000).

4. In Germany, in 1931, the Nazi party produced a similar poster which read: 'Five hundred thousand unemployed, four hundred thousand Jews, the solution is simple.' Today, it would be foolish to underestimate the support enjoyed by the National Front. While French opinion polls indicate that most French regard the party as racist, 30 percent admit to having, at one time, voted for it. In 1995, Le Pen garnered 15 percent of the presidential ballot. In 1997, his party enjoyed the same percentage of support in the first round of parliamentary elections (Gourevitch 1997: 110-49).

5. Indeed, member states have yet to fully honour their promise (made several years ago) that they would relinquish their internal borders. Efforts taken in Amsterdam to expedite the free movement of persons while maintaining respect for border controls reflected 'a compromise between the timid and the impatient.' According to Duff, Article 73j 'allows for the progressive establishment of free movement of persons *after a five year period* in which, one hopes, a sufficient degree of trust has been built up between member states' ministries of the interior and customs authorities' (1997: 20, my emphasis).

6. In 1997, a Eurobarometer Opinion Poll revealed that of the 16,241 people questioned across the member states, 33 percent openly described themselves as 'quite racist' or 'very racist.' At the closing conference on the 1997 European Year Against

Racism, then Commission President Jacques Santer said that this revealed a 'worrying and unacceptable banalisation of the expression of racist sentiments' (in Commission of the European Communities 1998: 5).

7. 'One of the most dramatic developments in the migration field over the past decade has been the growth in the numbers of people seeking asylum. There are estimated to be 17.5 million refugees worldwide; two thirds are female and women refugees face particular difficulties at all stages of the asylum-seeking process' (Bhabha and Shutter 1994: 229). Though a majority of the world's adult refugees have been women, the majority of applicants seeking asylum in the west have been men (Bhabha and Shutter 1994: 244).

8. Hervey further explains the ways in which this position and those like it disproportionately perpetuate discrimination against migrant women. The precarious position of immigrant and migrant women more generally has been explored, in greater detail, elsewhere (European Women's Lobby 1995; Hervey 1995; Hoskyns 1996; Kofman and Sales 1992; Lutz 1997). For a discussion of guest workers and the empirical anomalies pertaining to the conventional narratives of citizenship more generally, see Soysal (1994).

9. Carl Stychin reaches a similar conclusion in his pointed exploration of European gay rights movements: 'the economic teleology of rights in the EU can "sanitise" the claim, making it more likely that a court will conclude that it can legitimately find in the claimant's favour' (2000: 290).

10. Analysts of the anti-nuclear movement, for example, observe that the refusal of member states to transfer any real policy authority to the EU has effectively circumscribed the mobilisation of this movement to the national level (Marks and McAdam 1996: 119). By contrast, focusing on Britain's gay rights movement, Carl Stychin concludes: 'in the U.K., where rights discourse is comparatively underdeveloped (for better or worse), Europe provides a new arena for social and legal struggle' (1998: 136).

11. The name European Women's Lobby (EWL) may appear misleading because the term 'lobby' suggests the organisation's independence from the very European institutions it appears to be influencing. However, the EWL represents the Commission and labours on its behalf rather than on behalf of 'women.'

III. INSTITUTIONS AND ACCOUNTABILITY

Chapter 8
MULTILEVEL GOVERNANCE AND THE INDEPENDENCE OF THE EUROPEAN CENTRAL BANK

Peter H. Loedel

> Money is more than a part of the economy. Money reflects the state,
> politics, and culture. The Euro (however) will be a denationalised and
> de-politicised currency.
>
> Hans Tietmeyer, Bundesbank President and
> former ECB Governing Board Member[1]

The European Central Bank (ECB) is perhaps the most far-reaching supranational institutional creation of the European Union (EU). The ECB's power to set interest rates and regulate the money supply for the twelve participating members specifically demands that nation states relinquish national sovereignty. Moreover, the ECB's independence from political and national control suggests that national governments will have limited influence over ECB policy-making. In this way, the ECB perhaps stands out among EU institutions and traditional forms of multilevel governance that characterise other policy arenas within the European Union—for example, agriculture, environment, industrial, and regional/structural policy. The ECB may therefore challenge traditional conceptualisations of the EU as a system of multilevel governance.

This chapter analyses the ECB's institutional independence and policy-making process. I suggest that the independence of the ECB is quite strong,

125

stronger than the Bundesbank. Despite the overriding structural and institutional framework of independence, the ECB does seek to carefully balance supranational, national, and even local levels of interest in its policy-making process. In this way, multilevel governance and the concept of an independent ECB monetary policy may be compatible, providing a model for future governance within the EU.

Multilevel Governance and the European Union

Many analysts describe the varying policy-making processes of the European Union in terms of multilevel governance (Scharpf 1994; Marks, Hooghe, and Blank 1996). For example, Andrew Jordan has analysed the transformation of environmental policy from a series of limited measures to a far-reaching multilevel governance system (Jordan 1998). Gary Marks has noted that structural policy involves a system of multilevel governance that involves continuous negotiation among several tiers, including supranational, national, regional, and local (Marks 1993). Lee Ann Patterson has also developed the concept of 'three-levels' to describe multilevel negotiation and policy formulation within the Common Agricultural Policy (Patterson 1997). This multilevel negotiation process involves supranational, national-level executives, and domestic interest associations influencing EU agricultural policy. Claus Hofhansel has recently analysed EU export controls and argues that it is a system of multilevel governance that best describes the policy-making process (Hofhansel 1999). Streeck identifies multilevel governance within the institutional configuration of EU industrial relations (Streeck 1998). In sum, the institutional design and policy-making process in a wide array of arenas of the European Union has become predominately multilevel in terms of governance.

Despite the theoretical dominance over the decades of neofunctionalist and intergovernmentalist approaches to understanding EU integration, multilevel governance perhaps offers a more systematic model of explaining how the EU policy-making process actually operates. Multilevel governance moves easily across the so-called levels-of-analysis problem of international relations and draws upon the richly detailed and textured approach of comparative analysis of institutions, processes, and policies. While some international relations scholars might object on these methodological grounds alone (the level of analysis focused simultaneously on intergovernmental, supranational, and sub-national actors, processes, and negotiations), multilevel governance develops comprehensive theoretical and analytical explanations of EU politics. As such, multilevel governance should be considered a mid-range theory; while theoretical parsimony may be lost somewhat using the multilevel governance approach, I argue that it is clearly superior as a tool for examining the European Union as it functions today. As noted above, a strong consensus exists suggesting that EU policy-making institutions entail a considerable measure of multilevel governance in a wide variety of policy arenas.

But why employ a mid-range theory when more traditional theories are available? Multilevel governance in the Euro-polity acknowledges the continued importance of individual states and intergovernmental bargains (not acceptable to the neofunctionalists or epistemic community scholars), but also recognises the shifts in decisional authority away from individual member-state control (not acceptable to the intergovernmentalists) towards institutions at the European level (Marks and Nielsen 1996). In this way, multilevel governance allows us to examine both the nature of the policy-making process and the nature of the institutional design of the actors involved in the policy-making process without being theoretically constrained by older, less flexible theories. Restated, multilevel governance characterises a system of governance through a process of shared authority in policy-making and multilevel governance can characterise the actors and institutions involved in the policy-making process. As a result, this dual function of multilevel governance theory provides a powerful lens through which one can examine European Union politics. As this chapter will show, European monetary policy and the institutional set-up designed to govern European monetary policy (the ECB) are best understood through the lens of multilevel governance.

The following defining characteristics of EU multilevel governance can be set forth (borrowing strongly from Marks, Hooghe, and Blank 1996: 346-47). While I do not suggest the list to be comprehensive, it does capture, based on a survey of the literature, the key elements of multilevel governance:

(a) Nation states have lost some of their former *authoritative* control over *policy-making* in their respective territories.

(b) *Supranational institutions* have some measure of *independent* influence, albeit with some form of democratic oversight, in *policy-making* that cannot be derived from their role as agents of states.

(c) National sovereignty is diluted within the EU *by collective decision making* among national governments and by the autonomous role of *EU institutions*.

(d) *Decision making* competencies are shared by *actors* at different levels rather than monopolised by state executives.

(e) Political arenas are interconnected rather than 'nested' at any one level of governance. Sub-national actors operate in both *the national and supranational arenas*.

(f) *The structure of political control* tends to be more variable, fluid, and not constant.

These six characteristics explicitly show the dual nature of multilevel governance theory—the emphasis on understanding the policy-making process and the institutions designed to govern that process. They also emphasise the supranational nature of EU governance, but they also offer up an understanding of EU politics that allows for national and subnational avenues for influence.

If one accepts these defining characteristics of EU multilevel governance, then one would expect that European monetary policy—as regulated by the ECB—might also conform to this dominant model of governance. But is the institutional makeup of the ECB and its policy-making process based on multilevel governance? It is to this question that the chapter now turns. First, I examine the institutional design of European monetary policy with a particular focus on the independent European Central Bank. I argue that we must have a solid understanding of the institutional structure of governance before we can fully consider the policy-making process. It is from this analysis that we can then examine whether the ECB and European monetary policy conform to the prescriptions of multilevel governance theory.

Central Bank Independence

In the negotiations leading to Maastricht, the key debate around the institutional structure and the policy-making powers of the future ECB was over the issue of the degree of central bank independence from political influence (Hasse 1990; De Haan 1997; Brentford 1998; Verdun 1998a; Loedel 1999a). More directly, would nation states have any authority and influence in the policy decisions of the future ECB? While most analysts focused on the influence of states, other possible influences—business and banking associations and labour unions, for example—would also need to be limited. The focus on central bank independence was strongly articulated by Germany and especially Bundesbank officials, given Germany's strong tradition of non-inflationary monetary policy and central bank independence (Loedel 1999b). Germany's views were also shared by a number of the leading architects of EMU, primarily within the Delors Committee (Verdun 1999).

The view from Germany and the Delors Committee was based on a series of arguments. Most empirical studies have shown that countries with independent central banks achieve substantially lower rates of inflation than countries in which the central bank is controlled directly by the government (Alesina and Summers 1992; De Haan 1997; Blinder 1998), although there is mixed evidence from some countries—primarily in the developing world (Posen 1993). Others argue that independence is important due to technical factors—policy-making from an independent central bank can be more straightforward and responsive to short-term needs of the economy in order to avoid the inevitable delays or 'decision lags' that exist in the normal political process. One can also see constitutional principles at work and envision an independent central bank as a separate branch of government that can check potentially damaging policies of other government branches. This logic could be applied to the ECB as it constantly reminds the euro-twelve governments to rein in spending under the limits set forth in the Stability and Growth Pact (SGP). Furthermore, in view of the politicians' short term motivation and propensity to spend in support of lobbies, interest groups, and other pressures, issuing money, i.e., making the central bank provide credits when needed, should be limited or capped to some ceiling.

Central bank independence and its corresponding impact on policy credibility have also been cited by many analysts as an important reason for freeing the hand of a central bank. Independence has a strong impact on policy credibility and vice versa (Blackburn and Christensen 1989; Woolley 1992; Mayes 1998). A central bank with a strong reputation for credible anti-inflationary policies may be able to resist political pressures to reform the legal structures and statutes of the bank that might threaten price stability. More importantly, perhaps, the issue of credibility centres on whether and how policy makers can make credible commitments about their future conduct. Independence and the credibility that flows from it also need to be understood in terms of actual behaviour and not just institutions. The structure of the economy and internal politics may present policy-makers with difficult trade-offs between short-run policy benefits and long-run policy costs that may impact credibility. An institution such as a central bank can be considered credible if it is willing to let the government, the public, and the economy incur the costs of their decisions.

While these arguments carry with them considerable merit, they should not go unquestioned. Perhaps the strongest argument against central bank independence is based on legal or democratic theory (Majone 1996; Verdun 1998a; Majone 1999; Berman and McNamara 1999). The theory would contend that an independent central bank could not be held democratically accountable for its politically sensitive actions. One might ask who should be held responsible for the effects on employment created by the ECB's monetary policy—the bank or the governments of the eurozone twelve? Central banks remain free from the task of legitimating their power (via elections), unlike other representative institutions. This is of central concern to the ECB and the institutions of the European Union as they grapple with questions of democratic deficits, pressures of regionalism, and issues of transparency. As Verdun notes, 'the lack of formal parliamentary control over the decision making process . . . has led to considerable concerns about democratic accountability: the aspect of secrecy, technocracy and lack of transparency' within the European Union is a significant point of contention (Verdun 1998a: 111). Such concerns point directly at the potential accountability problems of the ECB.

In principle, one can argue that the final decisions and the priorities, which are given to monetary policy, must lie with the European Parliament or some other nominally representative body—perhaps the Council of Finance Ministers. It follows that if necessary, monetary policy should be subordinated to fiscal policy or other objectives laid out by popularly elected officials. Only democratically elected officials of the government have the respective legitimacy and authority to proceed with the negotiations and reach an agreed upon solution. As powerfully stated by Berman and McNamara, allowing the ECB 'to rest unchallenged both damages democracy and begs important questions about who the winners and losers of economic policy should be' (Berman and McNamara 1999: 2). In this vein, noted economist Peter Kenen has suggested that the European Parliament be given greater authority over the European monetary policy-making process (Kenen 1995).

From an economic policy perspective, one can further argue that monetary policy be considered an integral part of the government's overall economic policy. The government's ability to successfully deal with economic difficulties would be strengthened if fiscal and monetary policy were coordinated. Working from this idea, Dyson, Featherstone, and Michalopoulos suggest that the lack of linkage between fiscal and monetary policies within the EU worsens the problem of the 'insularity' of the EMU process (Dyson, Featherstone, and Michalopoulos 1995). Although most governments now accept that low inflation is essential for sustainable growth, the trade-off between a bit more inflation and a bit more unemployment can still be made in the short term—especially with elections looming in the horizon. As a result of this short-term motivation, an independent central bank and monetary policy could very well lead to government frustration, friction and conflict. In this view, monetary policy and the central bank should be considered one important part of a government's overall arsenal in dealing with weighty economic problems.

The Independence of the European Central Bank

Given the arguments both in favour and against central bank independence, did Maastricht create an independent ECB? Specifically, there are three distinctive contexts that we can identify within which the influence of the government, societal interests and international actors must be excluded or greatly curtailed in order for a central bank to be considered independent. These three contexts are political independence, personal independence, and financial independence.[2] Within each one of these contexts, a range of possible constraints on the ECB's independence will be analysed. In order to draw some useful conclusions about the degree of ECB independence, I compare the ECB's independence to that of the Bundesbank (before the euro).

Political Independence

Perhaps the pivotal concept in the study of central bank independence is its functional or political independence. For purpose of definition, Woolley distinguishes two types of independence that prove useful here (Woolley 1984). Political independence refers to the ability of a central bank to choose a course of action independently without yielding to the pressures of others as to what that action should be. In the second sense, functional independence refers to the central bank's ability to achieve its objectives without being affected by the actions of others. Functional independence, as Woolley argues, is generally not characteristic of monetary policy (Woolley 1984: 13).[3] For my purposes, I will focus on political independence.

Political independence refers to the formal legal competence of the ECB to choose a course of action independently and without yielding to the overt or covert pressures of other political actors. By almost all accounts and universal consensus among analysts, political independence should characterise the monetary policy of the ECB. The ECB's independence is enshrined in the Maastricht Treaty—a treaty that would be extremely difficult (and unlikely) to revise. Article 107 of the treaty clearly states that 'neither the ECB, nor a national central bank, nor any member of their decision making bodies shall seek or take instructions from Community institutions or bodies, from any government of a member state or from any other body.' Furthermore, the treaty narrowly defines the ECB's primary objective as maintaining price stability (Article 105). The ECB is also required, albeit in vague terms, to support the economic policies in the European Union but 'without prejudice to the objective of price stability.' The president of Ecofin and a member of the Commission may participate on the Governing Council of the ECB, but they do not have the right to vote (Article 109b). Given the clear legal mandate, there is little chance that the ECB's political independence will be watered down in the areas it has sole responsibility.

Most significantly, the informal body made up of the euro-twelve finance ministers (Eurogroup) will likely be the most consistent political threat to the political independence of the ECB. Demanded by the new French Socialist-led government in 1997, Eurogroup concept was presented as part of an attempt to limit the austerity measures imposed by the convergence criteria, which were explicitly prolonged into Stage Three of the EMU project by the Stability and Growth pact. Within the Eurogroup, the voices and concerns of national governments regarding the ECB's monetary policies will be articulated—a necessity given the belief among the euro-twelve that non-euro members (UK, Denmark, Sweden, Greece) should not have a say over the ECB's monetary policy. Resisted by the German government under Kohl, somewhat ironically the Eurogroup has become a forum of German concerns with the ECB's monetary policy, given the persistent high levels of unemployment in Germany. From the French perspective, the euro-twelve body was their creation and fits within the traditional French view of a more politicised monetary policy serving national employment interests, not just price stability measures. The French also see the Eurogroup formulating positions on exchange rates (more below) as the French also tend to see the link between the price of a currency and competitiveness— albeit now the competitiveness of the Euro-twelve zone.

As a result, the ECB has already faced overt political pressure from national governments or within the Euro-twelve body to pursue a particular monetary policy. The governing council faced concerted pressure and attacks on its policies including heated pressure from the former German Finance Minister Lafontaine prior to a 4 March 1999 council meeting.[4] Along with some of the other left-of-centre European governments, Germany's new Socialist Government led by Gerhard Schröder has raised the issue of political independence to the forefront of debate. Schröder has stated that the ECB 'doesn't only have responsibility for monetary stability but also for economic growth in a sensible way.'[5] With a general shift to the left across many European governments, there has been a sense of an increase in the willingness of governments to use fiscal and monetary policy to stimulate growth and reduce unemployment. The euro's stability and the Stability and Growth Pact's credibility have in part been undermined by this manner of questioning—particularly from Germany. The ECB has responded to such pressure by indicating that it would be forced to act with interest-rate increases if governments were to fail in their attempts to keep government deficits under control. The credibility of this threat must have been believable, as pressure on the ECB has lessened in the last months.

Lafontaine and others have also criticised the bank's secretiveness and refusal to reveal the minutes of the governing board meetings. Christian Noe, state secretary at the German Finance Ministry accused the Bundesbank—and by extension the ECB—of engaging in 'pre-democratic' behaviour.[6] The issue of transparency and accountability is critical here. While the president of the ECB Wim Duisenberg has gone out of his way to speak openly of the ECB's policies,[7] including ongoing presentations within the Monetary Committee of the European Parliament, he has stated cogently that some measure of secrecy is needed in order to keep the market off balance. Indeed, speculation that the ECB would never lower interest rates so soon after the resignation of Lafontaine proved wrong as the bank lowered rates a full half percentage point in early April 1999. Keeping the markets and analysts guessing, and guessing wrong, are early signs of an independently minded ECB.

In summary, even with the Eurogroup body, there is no clear institutional political context within which the ECB will have to answer for its policy. As noted, the president of the ECB will be called before the European Parliament—but the Parliament lacks its own credibility among the electorate. Also as noted, the president will attend meetings of the Eurogroup where he will face questioning and possible pressure, but these meetings are also secret and will not serve as a true 'accountability' forum. Moreover, as the ECB has already firmly demonstrated, it takes its price stability mandate and its institutional protection of political independence seriously. The ECB to date has not once backed down on any serious decision it has made whether on interest rates, monetary objectives or indicators, or secrecy. The ECB has had a baptism of fire in its first year of operation, but it has largely emerged unscathed—adding to the perception of political independence and policy credibility.

Personal Independence

Personal independence is a second crucial determining factor of central bank autonomy and is intricately related to political independence. If the members of the ECB are selected for political, ideological, and/or national reasons, one would have to question the overarching independence of the ECB to pursue its price stability mandate unfettered by national or political constraints. The ECB's decision-makers will have to assume a transnational identity and act in the interests of Europe first instead of national interest. If one senses the slightest national bias in the bank's decision making, one would have to question whether it has established a transnational European identity and whether personal (read 'national') interest has trumped the interests of the institution.

Institutionally and personally, the ECB is a hybrid of transnationalism and intergovernmentalism. The two key bodies in the ECB are the executive board, made up of a president, a vice-president, and four additional members, each appointed to eight-year, non-renewable terms; and a governing council, compromising the executive board and the central bank governors of the euro-twelve members. The national central bank governors will also have, at a minimum, five-year contracts so as to ensure some continuity on the Council. Table 8.1 lists the current members. The Executive Board is appointed by

Table 8.1: European Central Bank Governing Council
Executive Board

Wim Duisenberg, President, the Netherlands
Christian Noyer, Vice-President, France
Otmar Issing, Germany
Eugenio Domingo Solans, Spain
Sirkka Hamalainen, Finland
Tommaso Padoa-Schioppa, Italy

National Central Bank Governors
Guy Quaden, Belgium
Ernst Welteke, Germany
Luis Ángel Rojo, Spain
Jean-Claude Trichet, France
Maurice O'Connell, Ireland
Antonio Fazio, Italy
Yves Mersch, Luxembourg
Nout Wellink, the Netherlands
Klaus Liebscher, Austria
Matti Vanhalla, Finland
António José Fernandes de Sousa, Portugal

agreement (consensus) of the political leaders of the European Union, after consulting the European Parliament and national central bankers. The Executive Board is clearly the transnational European part of the ECB and is seen as the leading articulators of the bank's European policies. While undoubtedly interested in supporting the ECB's European price stability mandate, the national bank governors will also be representing the concerns of their respective nations. As such, they will undoubtedly bring an intergovernmental voice to ECB deliberations.

The Executive Board has found its footing as a strong united body pursuing the interests of the euro-twelve. Unfortunately the high-profile squabble over the appointment of its first president Wim Duisenberg has given some tarnish to the personal independence of the ECB. All the member governments except for the French, who desired their own candidate, Bank of France President Jean Claude Trichet, favoured Duisenberg. At the May 1998 summit to decide euro participants and to finalise the 1999 launching date, Duisenberg was appointed for a full eight-year term, but 'volunteered' to step down after four years to allow Trichet to take over. While no one doubts the anti-inflationary credentials of Trichet, the embarrassing episode may lead some to question the future personal independence of the ECB. Nonetheless, with the lengthy eight-year terms of office and the squabble over the presidency receding in memory, one can argue that the executive board will continue to emerge as a forceful independent and transnational voice of European monetary politics.

It remains to be seen what role the national central bank governors will play in ECB deliberations. The ECB is really the European System of Central Banks (ESCB) based on a Bundesbank-modelled 'federalist' structure. Power within the Governing Council is therefore decentralised in favour, based on numbers, of the national central bank governors. Monetary policy decisions will be taken by a simple majority on the Governing Council. Small countries arguably could carry undue weight in the system. Austria, Belgium, Finland, Ireland, Luxembourg, the Netherlands, and Portugal will between them have nine of the seventeen votes on the governing council (including members of the executive board) compared with Germany's two, even through their combined GDP is only half of Germany's.[8] One would also suspect that the Bundesbank and Bank of France presidents will speak with a louder voice within the forum. One might also expect the national central bank presidents to have their own views and data. Therefore, the role of the President Wim Duisenberg will be especially important in moving the governing council in his and the executive board's direction.

One important reason for the united voice on euro-policy is due to the overriding 'economic culture' of the ECB (Kaltenthaler 1999). Economic culture can be seen as the social perceptions that structure macro-economic policy. Based on the membership of the executive board and most of the national central bank governors, one can argue that the ECB's economic culture is structured by a strong interest in fiscal rectitude and a deflationary macro-economic policy targeting price stability. The members of the governing council are what most analysts would describe as believers in the benefits of an independent central bank; almost all members retained strong anti-inflationary credentials—a bank full of Bundesbankers (residing in Frankfurt no less), but even more powerful. They believe that safeguarding the value of the euro and maintaining price stability are the preconditions to a sound European economy. Too much inflation, even at an annual rate of 2-3 percent, is seen as a cancer on the economy that will destroy the European economy over the long term. In other words, there can be no short-term tradeoffs between a little bit more inflation for a little less unemployment. Keynesian-inspired macroeconomic policy finds little if no support among the ECB's membership.

Financial Independence

The third and final important aspect determining the level and degree of central bank independence is its financial independence from either the obligatory financing of government debts (internal) or exchange rate arrangements or obligations (external) such as those that existed under Bretton Woods and more recently within the EMS.[9] The latter concern is especially relevant as the euro emerges as an international *numéraire*. The euro will likely, albeit modestly, increase its role as a unit of account, a means of payment, and a store of value (Hosli 1998). If so, the euro's influence in global monetary relations will increase pressure on the ECB to stabilise the value of the euro externally.

First, regarding government financing, a government can exercise influence over and limit the discretion of central bankers if there exists the possibility that the government can finance its expenditures either directly or indirectly via central bank credits. Access to central bank credits, especially direct access, can result in an overlapping or fiscal circular flow of money into the money supply. If such financing mechanisms exist, monetary policy is by necessity subordinated to the dictates of fiscal policy.[10]

Currently, the ECB is not directly subordinated to the fiscal demands of member states. However, the bank is necessarily concerned about the potential of national governments to increase spending during the transition phase to the full implementation of the euro by 2002. For example, the ECB fears the very real scenario in which Italy, now comfortable in its inclusion within the euro-twelve, might be tempted to fall back into past proclivities of fiscal profligacy. As a result, bolstered by the SGP, which demands continued fiscal discipline within the boundaries of the convergence criteria (with exceptions for recessions) under the threat of stiff penalties, the ECB continuously warns the euro-twelve governments to maintain fiscal discipline. While it is not impossible that member states might stray from the convergence criteria (even with Italy's additional room for fiscal spending, it remains well within the criteria), one suspects that the fear of penalties, the ongoing political commitments in each country to fiscal stability, and with the ECB ready to pounce on any divergence, states will continue to hold spending steady. It remains to be seen whether a future centralised EU fiscal policy might alter this arrangement. But for now, no such scenario looks imminent.

Most importantly the ECB may face the financial constraints associated with the intervention requirements, institutional commitments, and interest rate pressure associated with exchange rate mechanisms. Exchange rate policy for the Euro remains unclear and the debates over clarifying exchange rate policy remain extremely controversial (Henning 1997). More importantly, the ECB and the EU will face the very same choice as faced by the Bundesbank: pursue monetary autonomy (albeit within the eurozone member states) or sacrifice a measure of autonomy in return for exchange rate stability vis-à-vis the dollar, yen, or some other currency. The scenario sounds like one drawn straight from German monetary history: a powerful independent central bank with the goal of internal price stability pitted against an external monetary policy subject to the domain of the Council of Finance Ministers, Ecofin-12, or other EU actors.

Specifically, Article 109 of the Maastricht Treaty lays down the legal relationship and general parameters between the ECB and the Council of Ministers on exchange rate policy. While still not entirely clear, it is assumed that representatives of the Council hold authority to negotiate formal and informal exchange rate agreements with foreign governments under consultation with the ECB. Formal agreements that peg the euro, for example, to the dollar or yen would require a unanimous vote within the Council after it consulted with the ECB, the European Commission, and the European Parliament. Such an arduous process of agreement or ratification will likely decrease the likelihood of increased exchange rate management at the international level. Exchange rate flexibility—or European monetary autonomy at the expense of exchange rate stability vis-à-vis the dollar or yen—will likely be the result.

Nevertheless, as Henning observes, if they are cohesive, 'national governments, operating through the Council, appear to hold a strong position vis-à-vis the ECB on the matter of formal arrangements' (Henning 1997: 36). While the search for consensus on exchange rate policy is required, actually attaining consensus is not required. Moreover, it is not clear which institution, the ECB, the Council, or some other institution, would determine whether an exchange rate agreement would do damage to the price stability mandate of the ECB. In Germany, the government held the final say over such questions. A similar scenario for the EU depends on the cohesiveness of national governments—a pattern for which the EU national governments are not often known.

However, in an interesting set of exchanges in April and May of 1999, Tietmeyer and Trichet openly questioned Duisenberg's decision to take a hands off approach to the sinking euro. Tietmeyer (now replaced by Welteke as head of the Bundesbank) and Trichet were responding to domestic pressures in Germany and France, respectively, especially among the general public, which had been promised a 'strong' euro, and savings and financial interests intent on preserving euro-denominated assets. In this way, Tietmeyer and Trichet were advocating 'national' interests within the supranational Governing Council. More interestingly perhaps, within the German Länder (mainly those dominated by SPD governments) and among Germany's leading export industries, voices could be heard counter to those of Tietmeyer. Parallel interests were expressed in France. The sinking euro actually was improving the export dependent economy, creating new jobs for workers, and enhancing the general eurozone's competitiveness. As discussed below, this could have been one of the first instances of ECB multilevel governance.

Moreover, informal exchange rate arrangements such as those of Plaza and Louvre can be negotiated by the Council under the rubric of setting a 'general orientation' of exchange rate policy. The general orientation must not, however, prejudice the 'primary objective of the ECSB to maintain price stability.' This would suggest that the ECB would have a right to reject such orientations, although this again is not clear and will be subject to later determination under actual practice. If the ECB is bound to keep exchange rates stable—a political decision made by Ecofin—the ECB may be forced to automatically intervene in foreign exchange markets or may be pressured to pursue an interest rate policy so as to ensure the proper exchange rate levels. In a system of freely fluctuating exchange rates, this constraint does not hold true and the central bank can pursue a policy solely concerned with domestic affairs. However, in a system of dirty floating as exists in the international monetary system, the ECB may be placed in a situation where it might have to buy and sell foreign currency or pursue an interest rate policy in order to meet some form of external exchange rate commitments.

The ECB may also face pressure from the United States and Japan or other remaining members of the G-7 to intervene in the currency markets in order to achieve pre-arranged euro-dollar-yen rates. Already the United States has voiced concern about the euro's weakness vis-à-vis the dollar and what impact that is having on US competitiveness.[11] As noted at the beginning of this chapter, the ECB has already found that the external scope of its monetary policy range has narrowed, certainly with the increasing integration in financial markets and with greater global interdependence. Although no formal exchange rate system currently exists between the euro and the dollar, external exchange rate commitments may circumscribe the ECB's financial independence. For example, during his short tenure, Lafontaine sought to resurrect a 'target zone' scheme for the Euro. From the perspective of the ECB, the proposal fortunately disappeared along with Lafontaine.

Summarising ECB Independence

Table 8.2 compares the independence of the ECB with that of the Bundesbank.[12] The analysis in table 8.2 should be seen as preliminary and some-

Table 8.2: Comparing ECB and Bundesbank Independence

	ECB	Bundesbank	Comparison
Political	• Primary objective of price stability; • Free from "instructions" of Community institutions and member states; • Mandates enshrined in Maastricht Treaty; • Threat of Ecofin-12.	• More general mandate to "safeguard the currency"; • "Independent" of the advice of the government; • Bundesbank Law not guaranteed constitutional protection; • Government, labour, business group pressure.	• ECB has more clearly articulated mandate on price stability; • "Freedom" of ECB and "independence" of Bundesbank from government interference similar; • Hard to envision Maastricht Treaty being revised. Bundesbank Act had "constitutionality" but could be amended by simple majority.
Personal	• Executive Board selected by consensus of member states; • National Bank Governors chosen by member states (majority in the Federalist structure); • Eight-year terms (non-renewable) on Executive Board; • Influential role of President.	• Directorate has eight-year terms, strong President; • Land Bank presidents in majority on council; Federalist structure; • Strong sense of German monetary culture; • *Stabilitätsgemeinschaft* (culture of stability).	• Bundesbank subject to personal issues related to Chancellor preferences, party preferences, and Bank Presidents; • Eight-year terms; • ECB will face similar concerns but culture of central bankers will be strong, like Bundesbank; maybe no culture of stability within European public? • Duisenberg conflict embarrassing; will likely not affect independence.
Financial	• Not required to finance government debt; • Must contend with member state budgets (strengthened by Stability and Growth Pact); • No centralised European Union budget; • No formal (external) exchange rate commitments; • Possible exchange rate pressure as Ecofin controls exchange rate policy.	• Bundesbank not required to finance government debt; • Had to contend with government spending; • Required to hand over profits to government; • Finance Ministry controlled exchange rates; • Often found itself constrained by exchange rate regimes (Bretton Woods and EMS).	• Both have to deal with government spending; • Similar scenario for ECB and Bundesbank on spending since convergence criteria in place; • Bundesbank faced more exchange rate pressure within EMS; • ECB will face possible exchange rate pressure as Ecofin controls exchange rates; no strong pressure currently.

what tentative. However, the conclusions I draw do represent an accurate early examination of ECB independence.

First, in terms of political independence, we can state that the ECB has perhaps an even greater level of independence than that of the Bundesbank, at least as based on the statutes creating the ECB. The role of the Ecofin-12 remains a bit of a wild-card, but given the first examples drawn from the clash between Lafontaine and the ECB, the ECB has maintained political independence. The ECB, however, does not operate in a complete political vacuum. The bank's decision to lower rates in April 1999 by half a percentage point does show a pragmatic political side to the bank. In terms of personal independence, the ECB faces some complementary concerns that often plagued the selection of personnel on the Bundesbank. The much-cited problem with Wim Duisenberg's appointment does raise some concern about future manipulation of the selection process. But I would contend that the overriding economic culture of the Governing Council moderates any concerns about national bias.

Financial independence is a bit more complex and depends on whether one examines internal or external sources of constraint. Internal financial independence appears to be strong, given the SGP, the lack of a centralised budgetary process in the EU, and the overriding commitment not to stray far from the price stability model, especially during the transition phase to 2002. External financial constraints, in the form of exchange rate pressures, will continue to pose very difficult and serious dilemmas for the ECB. But no formal exchange rate agreement between the euro and the dollar, for example, currently exists. This should provide the ECB with greater policy latitude in the near term.

In sum, the ECB would appear in many respects—political, personal, and financial—to have at a minimum the same level of independence as the Bundesbank. In some areas, particularly political and financial independence, the ECB can be seen as perhaps maintaining even greater amounts of independence. In its brief history, the ECB has already established itself as an independent actor focused on its primary objective of price stability. However, internal pressure from Eurogroup, the euro-twelve member states, and external exchange rate pressures will make the ECB's balancing act a difficult one indeed. Here we must return to the question of credibility.

Credibility must be measured over time and must be evaluated in terms of the actual behaviour of the bank—a record that is preliminary at best. In one sense, the euro's weakness vis-à-vis the dollar (losing over 25 percent of its value since January 1, 1999) indicates to some analysts that the ECB's credibility has suffered due to the varying pressures coming from the markets, governments, and politicians. Yet, euro-bond markets have been quite strong, giving alternative evidence that the markets do indeed trust the ECB to keep inflation under control. Moreover, the actual behaviour of the ECB—especially its decision on interest rates—shows a keen presence in terms of establishing firm credibility. It appears that the ECB's reputation strengthened considerably with the resignation of Lafontaine. It is Lafontaine who paid the price for the bank's policies. Finally, the overall coherence of the macroeconomic policy of the euro-zone member states, shaped by the demands of the convergence criteria and the SGP, does indicate that the ECB has a strong grip on the overarching policies of the eurozone. Much remains unresolved and unknown at this point in time, but one can argue that the ECB is on the right track in terms of establishing credibility and maintaining a high level of independence.

Multilevel Governance and ECB Independence

Although any analysis of the ECB must be tempered with the recognition that its structures and policy-making operations are in their infancy, we can begin to set forth some basic propositions about the usefulness of the multilevel governance model as it applies to the ECB and its policy-making process. It would seem at first glance that the very notion of ECB independence precludes effective multilevel governance. While supranational in orientation, the bank's decisions are made in strict accordance to its mandate of price stability, independent of the influence of other policymakers and influences. This would suggest a neofunctionalist orientation and understanding of EMU. Central banks were not able to conduct credible monetary policies at the national level, thus, it was transferred to the European (supranational) level. There would appear at first glance to be very little room for multilevel negotiations.

There also appears to be little democratic oversight—oversight that exists within other EU policy arenas defined by multilevel governance. Political control appears to rest firmly with the ECB. Does the strongly independent position of the ECB impede meaningful state and sub-national influence and participation in the policy-making process? If so, does this suggest a moving away from multilevel governance and a state-centric model perhaps to a truly centralised, powerfully independent, supranational decision making structure? In addition, those who suggest an elite-based approach to policy-making would also draw upon the epistemic community literature to understand the ECB (Verdun 1999). Overall, policy control is more constant in the hands of the transnational, elite-based decision-makers in the ECB—rather than a more variable form of policy-making as suggested by the multilevel governance model.

These are valid concerns and indicate the potentially difficult task of employing multilevel governance to understanding the ECB. However, the argument made here is that the European Central Bank does fit a conceptualisation of multilevel governance, albeit with some modifications and reservations. First, the European central bank is an institution of governance within the European Union that pursues monetary policy within the statutes of the Treaty on European Union. Governance implies *rules and institutions*. The ECB as an institution governs the behaviour of those actors (nation states) who participate in EMU. The ECB's rules demand that

Table 8.3: The ECB as Multilevel Governance?

Characteristics of Multilevel Governance	European Central Bank
Loss of authoritative state control over policymaking *(The Rules of Governance)*	Yes—ECB has the power to set interest rates and regulate money supply. National central banks no longer set interest rates.
Supranational institutions have *independent* influence on policymaking, albeit with some measure of democratic oversight *(The Institutions of Governance)*	Yes—Key issue in the debate of ECB independence. In practice, ECB has demonstrated strong independence over policymaking, although exchange rate controversy suggests avenues for national influence. No—problems with democratic oversight
Sovereignty of state diluted by collective decision-making and shared decision making competencies at different levels *(Institutions and Rules of Governance)*	Yes—Shared governance in area of exchange rate policy-making Yes—Ecofin-12 and ECB Executive Council/Governing Council National Banks interact to formulate policy.
Political arenas are "interconnected"— subnational actors operate at both the national and supranational level *(Institutions and Rules of Governance)*	Yes—Evidence is tentative and early; but banking/savings interests and "public opinion" influencing Bundesbank and Bank of France at national level; export oriented business (and important *Mittelstand* in Germany) and industry more silent on this issue, indicative of support for Duisenberg.
Structure of political control tends to be more variable, fluid than constant *(Institutions and Rules of Governance)*	Mixed—Structure designed to be constant. Some fluidity, however, in the ongoing struggle for control between ECB, national governments (Ecofin-12), and domestic actors (national central bank governors reacting to interest associations and the general public) over monetary policy. More constant than other EU aspects governance.

it regulate and supervise European monetary policy, arbitrate disputes between member states through its decision making body, and enforce a strong measure of compliance among participating states—all with the goal of stabilising macroeconomic conditions within the member states. It is within this arena of monetary governance that the politics and policies of the ECB are played out. More importantly, it is in the politics and policies of the ECB that we find multilevel governance.

As table 8.3 demonstrates, the rules and institutions governing the ECB generally fit the characteristics of the multilevel governance model. Even with the rules and institutions of European monetary governance designed to insulate the ECB and its policy-making process from political interference, we can still argue that the ECB's monetary policy is characterised by the interaction of political actors across supranational, national, and sub-national levels. First, we have to recognise that the ECB and its monetary policy will likely be more constant than the multilevel governance model suggests—with the ECB acting as a powerful pillar of policy control. Forcefully supranational, the ECB's independence may limit national and sub-national influence and policy negotiation. This independence naturally raises longstanding concerns within the EU over transparency and democratic oversight. This concern will likely increase in importance if and when a serious dispute needs adjudication among the various EU institutions (for example, the European Parliament's Monetary Committee) and national executives whether within Ecofin-12 or other EU intergovernmental forums.

Despite the strong element of supranational independence, member state executives—whether within Ecofin-12 or the national central bank governors in the Governing Council of the ECB—do remain influential. The sovereignty of the state is clearly diluted through the ECB's policy-making process and institutional structure—but the interests of national executives (and their respective states) have *neither disappeared nor will they in the future*. The ECB's institutional structure allows for some measure of national level input into the policy-making process. Moreover, despite the apparent success of the ECB to weather the barrage of criticism from the likes of Lafontaine, we should not interpret these events to suggest that similar national-level pressures will not return in the future. As long as some of the institutional structures remain unclear in terms of design or responsibilities (Ecofin-12), the policy-making process will also remain at times unclear. The state's responsibility in terms of setting interest rates may be gone, but its interest (and those of dominant political parties) in seeing monetary policy steered in a particular direction has not gone away.

Moreover, as the exchange rate controversy over the sinking value of the euro indicated, the sub-national level may be developing as a coherent level in ECB policy-making. Business associations, savings and other financial groups, and labour organisations have been quick to identify the multiple levels of political influence inherent in the institutional structure of the ECB. These avenues will likely in the future be more sophisticatedly developed to support particular interests or causes. Through such avenues, the concerns of the public can be taken into account. It may take time, however, for a firm foundation of interconnected political arenas to become a reality. It is interesting to note that Germany's federal system may make the Germans the most comfortable with the multiple levels of influence and decision making within the ECB. Supporting this view, Hooghe (1999) has argued that officials from federal political systems are more likely to favour multilevel governance and the supra-nationalism of European institutional arrangements like the ECB.

Conclusion

The ECB retains a rather unique institutional structure within the traditionally multilevel governance structure of the EU. The ECB's strongly independent institutional structure will effect the policy-making process within the EU in ways that differ from the multilevel governance policy-making process many EU members are familiar with. For its part, the multilevel governance model may lead to a confusing process of policy-making and understanding of power for the public, policymakers, and EU officials. What 'level' of the policy-making process is truly in control or has the 'power'? This confusion adds to the EU's legitimacy problems among the EU public—witness the poor turnout in the June 1999 European Parliament elections. Shifting power and authority toward one level—in the case of the ECB toward the supranational—may clear up some of this confusion. At least the public and politicians know who is responsible for decisions—even if the ECB is not always accountable. Such a trend may suggest a new model of policy-making within the EU: maintain multilevel avenues of influence, but designate one level clearly in 'charge' of policy. I would suggest ensuring avenues of accountability as well. In this way, supranational, national, and subnational interests can be brought into the policy-making process—even if such interests are not always followed—as is the case with an independent central bank.

Notes

The author is thankful for the specific comments of Liesbet Hooghe, Gary Marks, Ben Müller, Amy Verdun, Dieter Wolf and the other participants at the conference on European Monetary Integration and Beyond. All errors in analysis and judgement remain the author's.

1. Hans Tietmeyer, 'Der Euro: ein entnationalisiertes Geld,' *Auszüge aus Pressartikeln*, December 12, 1997 (parentheses mine).

2. The use of three measures of independence is based on the author's analysis of existing literature on central bank independence. See Loedel (1999a) and Alesina and Summers (1992) for further elaboration and justification for using these three measures.

3. Typically, no actor controls all of the instruments relevant to achieving particular goals. Thus, any actor's ability to reach his or her objectives depends to some degree on the actions of others—even if the actor's own choice of action is completely free. The effects of monetary policy actions are dependent in part on fiscal policy, bank regulatory policy, and events in the private sector, among other factors.

4. The ECB's first 'independence' casualty is Lafontaine who retired after only five months on the job. While internal SPD politics and the government's tax policies contributed to his decision, Lafontaine's ongoing battle with the ECB's President Wim Duisenberg certainly contributed to Lafontaine's decision to retire.

5. See the analysis, 'Hard Money for a Softer Europe,' *The New York Times*, November 5, 1998.

6. Ibid.

7. See, for example, Duisenberg's testimony to the European Parliament's Sub-Committee on Monetary Affairs, 18 January 1999 [http://www.ecb.int/key/st990118.htm] (the ECB's website, while rather unexciting visually, is extremely valuable as a research tool).

8. See the analysis in 'EuroTowers or Faulty Towers,' *The Economist*, October 31, 1998.

9. One can argue that budgetary independence (i.e., freedom from the need to get legislative approval of the central bank's operating budget) should also be considered. Although it may be important in some countries, the issue of operating budgets has not emerged a source of contention.

10. In the last analysis the ECB, through the national central banks, must cover the financial requirements of a government that cannot be met from other sources.

11. See the comments of Treasury Assistant Secretary for International Affairs Edwin Truman, 'U.S. Official in attack on euro-zone policy,' *Financial Times*, April 8, 1999.

12. I do not include a detailed separate analysis of the Bundesbank here, but use the Bundesbank as a baseline model of a historically independent central bank. See Loedel (1999b) for further discussion of the Bundesbank's independence.

Chapter 9
MACROECONOMIC PREFERENCES AND EUROPE'S DEMOCRATIC DEFICIT

Erik Jones

The European Central Bank (ECB) is the most politically independent institution of its kind. Both its strong constitutional position outlined in the Treaty on European Union and the difficult requirements for amending the treaty make it unlikely that the ECB will be overturned.[1] Moreover, the lack of an elected counterpart equal in continental scope suggests that the ECB is unlikely to face a united and powerful political counterweight. Not all member states represented in the Council of Ministers may benefit from the day-to-day management of monetary policy, but it is difficult to imagine that they would all suffer from the ECB's actions at the same time or that they would all gain from exerting influence over the bank. Divisions within the European Parliament will be even more extreme, and so the prospect of a united political front forming in opposition to the ECB is remote. Thus, in many respects, the management of Europe's Economic and Monetary Union (EMU) operates in a realm beyond politics and so beyond political accountability.

Given the very public support of the European Union (EU) for liberal democratic values, the apolitical management of EMU suggests an important contradiction. If democracy is about process and not outcome, why should EMU be exempt from electoral oversight? If the focus is on outcome and not process, then how indispensable are democratic values? The answers to such questions are not one-sided. Put another way, the case against the political independence are not one-sided. Put another way, the case against the political independence of EMU—and in favour of a more democratic arrangement—is strong. First, following Berman and McNamara (1999), democracy *is* more about process than outcome. Therefore, any marginal improvement in economic performance may not outweigh the cost of the perceived legitimacy of the European system of governance. Second, the role of an independent central bank in producing favourable economic outcomes is dependent on other institutional conditions such as fiscal or wage-bargaining regimes. To the extent to which such conditions do not exist at the European level, a politically independent EMU may actually produce worse economic outcomes than no EMU at all (Hall and Fanzese 1998). Finally, what really matters for economic performance is a 'culture of price stability'—or a powerful vested interest in stable prices (Posen 1993)—and not an institutional formula per se. Such factors are decisively political and so should be mediated through political institutions rather than insulated from political accountability.

Nevertheless, much of the strength of the argument against the political independence of the ECB rests on a crucial assumption. Critics of the democratic legitimacy of central bank independence assume that macroeconomic outcomes, and particularly inflation and unemployment, are the subject of direct and relative political preferences within the democratic electorate. Voters want to trade-off inflation against unemployment or unemployment and inflation against other factors directly, and therefore require that monetary policy-makers be directly accountable to their wishes. Any attempt to delegate monetary policy authority beyond the oversight of national electorates will necessarily violate the most basic requirements for the democratic representation of popular preferences.[2]

Under different assumptions, the arguments against the democratic accountability of central bank independence become less compelling if not irrelevant. For example, voters may have preferences concerning macroeconomic outcomes that are direct and absolute rather than direct and relative. Under this assumption, voters do not want to trade off inflation and unemployment against anything. Rather, they prefer to have consistently low inflation and consistently low unemployment in all circumstances. The empirical possibility that voters can only have one (such as low inflation) at the expense of the other (such as low unemployment) should not be taken to negate the fact that voters would *prefer* to have both.

Under the assumption that voters have direct and absolute preferences regarding macroeconomic outcomes, the focus for political accountability would rest on establishing mechanisms to work toward the achievement of those absolute objectives. If such mechanisms involve the delegation of monetary policy authority to some extra-national agency, then so be it. Moreover, not all possibilities have to be made available. Even if there is an empirical basis for believing that the manipulation of monetary policy instruments can either facilitate or limit the achievement of direct and absolute macroeconomic objectives, that is no reason to thrust monetary policy into the public domain. Capital expropriation and forced labour also work to hold down prices and unemployment, and yet few would regard the prohibition of such practices as undemocratic. In the extreme case where monetary policy is the *only* possible means for achieving macroeconomic objectives, democracy still does not necessitate discretionary control. The requirements for popular representation or procedural accountability are limited to identifying the objectives for policy-makers. The form of this identification is open, and can fall anywhere on a continuum from direct intervention to a permanent rule. Hence, there can be no categorical objection to central bank independence on the basis of democratic principles.

Alternatively, it is conceivable that macroeconomic outcomes like unem-ployment and inflation concern members of the electorate only through their effects on the distribution of economic resources. Under this assumption, voters have direct preferences about, for example, the return to capital and labour. However, they have only indirect or instrumental preferences about the movement of macroeconomic variables. Inflation and unemployment can be good or bad depending on how they influence the income and wealth of workers and capitalists. If voters are principally interested in distributive outcomes, then there is no a priori reason for specific macroeconomic instruments—like monetary policy instruments—to be subject to political manipulation. What matters is that the electorate have some control over macroeconomic outcomes or over the influence of macroeconomic outcomes on the distribution of resources. By implication, fiscal regimes, wage bargaining institutions, or any number of other arrangements can repair the absence of a politically accountable central bank. Once again, there can be no categorical objection to central bank independence.

The argument in this paper is twofold. To begin with, critics of the democ-ratic legitimacy of central bank independence are mistaken. Independent central banks may or may not provide for superior macroeconomic performance, but that is beside the point. The assumption that macroeconomic outcomes are the subject of direct and relative preferences within the democratic electorate is simply incorrect. Voters do not seek to trade off inflation and unemployment either directly or against other macroeconomic outcomes. To the extent to which direct preferences concerning macroeconomic outcomes do exist within the electorate, they are absolute. The voters want inflation and unemployment to be as low as possible given the circumstances. An independent central bank can satisfy such preferences as easily as a dependent one. Moreover, to the extent to which an independent bank provides the appearance that such absolute objectives are not to be sacrificed on the altar of short-term political gain an independent central bank may even be more appealing.

The second argument has more fundamental importance for how we under-stand monetary integration in Europe. Essentially, what voters are concerned with is the distribution of economic resources and not the movement of macroeconomic variables per se. If movements in macroeconomic variables influence this distribution of resources, voters will adopt instrumental preferences to their own benefit. However, the structure of these preferences will be determined not just by the direction in which the macroeconomy moves, but by a variety of institutional arrangements as well. By implication, the success of Europe's economic and monetary union will not lie with the ECB alone, or even with the central bank and some other *crucial* institutional arrangement. Rather, it will lie in the complexity of distributive outcomes as mediated by a variety of institutions across the European Union and its member states. To the extent to which that welter of institutions confuses the distributive impact of monetary policy changes, coherent political cleavages may never form around the operation of the ECB. A European 'culture of price stability' could be the result.

The chapter has four sections. The first explains the emergence of assumptions about the direct and relative macroeconomic preferences of voters in the economic arguments for central bank independence. The second argues for replacing the direct and relative macroeconomic preferences with a combination of direct and absolute preferences and instrumental (or distributive) preferences. The third demonstrates that a combination of direct and absolute macroeconomic preferences and distributive preferences fits better with the empirical record than the direct and relative preferences used in the initial discussion of central bank independence. The fourth extends the argument to the European level to examine how assumptions about distributive preferences can influence our understanding of European (monetary) integration as well as the democratic legitimacy of EMU. It is this concluding section that represents the link between the chapter and the rest of the volume.

Macroeconomic Preferences

The notion that voters hold direct and relative preferences concerning macroeconomic outcomes derives from a series of facilitating assumptions used in economics. For example, economists routinely assume that politicians and voters recognise a trade-off between inflation and unemployment (the Philips curve). Alternatively, they might assume that voters and politicians regard inflation as a legitimate source of government revenue (the inflation tax). Such assumptions can be backed by empirically plausible mechanisms. A rise (fall) in unemployment can place downward (upward) pressure on wages and so lower (raise) the incentive for firms to raise prices. Alternatively, a rise in the rate of inflation can erode the value of outstanding cash balances and so decrease government liabilities. Importantly, however, there is no direct empirical support for hypotheses that voters and policy-makers attempt to trade-off inflation against unemployment or inflation against other forms of revenue. Thus while the mechanisms remain plausible, their use in the real world is unproven.

Plausibility is all that is required. Hypotheses concerning the trade-off between inflation and unemployment or between inflation and other sources of government revenue can operate as assumptions. In turn, these assumptions can allow economists to investigate other hypothetical relationships between political action and economic performance—such as political business cycles or macroeconomic credibility. Assuming that voters and politicians confront an 'exploitable' Philips curve or strive for the 'optimal' inflation tax or would want to manipulate some other plausible economic mechanism, what can we predict about the interaction between politics and economics?

The structure of the question is important. Sometime during the 1970s, economists came around to the realisation that political behaviour may have a systematic and powerful influence on the functioning of the economy.[3] The challenge for positive economic analysis, therefore, is to develop tools for formulating and testing hypotheses about this influence (Friedman 1977: 459-60). Assumptions about the exploitable Philips curve or the optimal inflation tax were originally intended to bridge the gap between theoretical analysis and empirical data. If we believe that politicians are using macroeconomic policy to further their own interests, and we can measure the movement of macro-economic variables, then it is necessary to connect the theory of manipulation and the data on outcomes.

The problem is one of motivation. Following Downs (1957), economists can start with prior assumptions that politicians want to be re-elected and voters want to be better off. However such assumptions only bridge part of the gap between theories of policy manipulation and data on macroeconomic outcomes. The rest of the distance is covered via assumptions about policies and outcomes. Politicians manipulate the macroeconomy and voters assess their well-being on the basis of government policies. Crucially, voters do not have to base their assessments on the movement of macroeconomic variables per se. All that matters is that they make the connection between government action and personal well-being.[4] In this way, assumptions about the macroeconomic policies pursued by governments do not have to make sense at face value. No politician should be expected to run on the pro-inflation platform. What matters is that assumptions about macroeconomic preferences should be reasonable given appropriate qualifications about mechanisms, etc. Politicians could run on a platform of higher wages or lower taxes with higher inflation being the result. This is a reasonable assumption with the qualification that politicians benefit from raising wages or lowering taxes and that higher wages or lower taxes would result in inflation. At the end of the story, economists can correlate inflation performance with indicators of political success in order to test hypotheses about the political-economic relationship.

Through continued use, however, assumptions about the preferences surrounding policy trade-offs such as the exploitable Philips curve and the optimal inflation tax have developed into short-hand assumptions about macro-economic preferences. The utility curves of politicians and voters are described as a function of macroeconomic outcomes. At the same time, these shorthand assumptions have also acquired such an acceptance in the economic literature as to be attributed with quasi-empirical status. Economists no longer need to describe the chain of reasoning behind their assumptions about preferences because the arguments are already well-rehearsed in the literature (much of which dates back to the 1950s). Moreover, continuous repetition of qualifications distracts from the object of the analysis—which is to test some new hypothesis concerning the relationship between political action and economic performance and not to analyse political preferences per se. This is not to suggest that economic analysis is somehow inherently wrong, sloppy, or irrelevant. Rather my point is that the qualifications surrounding such facilitating assumptions as the exploitable Philips curve or the optimal inflation tax have tended to get lost through repetition.

Consider the exploitable Philips curve. The assumption is that politicians trade-off inflation against unemployment in order to gain some political benefit. In the Downsian sense, the benefit could be to win re-election as incumbent. Here an example is Nordhaus's (1975) electoral business cycle. Incumbent politicians encourage economic growth just before the election to raise employment and so increase their chances of winning. After the election, politicians confront the rising inflation that results from the pre-electoral boom and so rein in on the economy even at the cost of rising unemployment. The assumption is that voters experience the growth and connect it with the government when they go to cast their votes: more growth, happier voters, re-election. Once the election is over, the government has to slow down growth again—and presumably alienates voters in the process—but retains the capacity to engineer another boom in time for the next election.

The manipulation of the economy does not have to follow the cycle set out by Nordhaus, although his mechanism is plausible. With a slight change of assumptions, the pattern of interaction could be altogether different. For example, the benefit to politicians could be to compete for the support of different groups in society—some who dislike unemployment more than they dislike inflation, while others dislike inflation more than they dislike unemployment. The exemplar here is Hibbs's (1977) partisan business cycle, where centre-right governments manage the economy with lower inflation but higher unemployment while centre-left governments provide for higher inflation but lower unemployment. Of course, at the basis of all this politicians still want to get elected and voters still want to be better off. All that has changed from Nordhaus to Hibbs are the assumptions about preferences that bring the two groups, politicians and voters, together.

Both hypotheses—Nordhaus's electoral business cycle and Hibbs's partisan business cycle—rely on untested facilitating assumptions about political preferences surrounding the trade-off between inflation and unemployment. For Nordhaus (1975: 181-82), the assumption is that voters prefer employment in the present even at the expense of inflation in the near future, a government retrenchment, and a return of unemployment. This assumption cannot be tested directly, and so is verified indirectly through the success of the model as a whole. Moreover, as Nordhaus admits, if this assumption of voter preferences is empirically unfounded, then his hypothesis of the electoral business cycle cannot be true.

For Hibbs (1977: 1468-70), the assumption is that wage and salary earners fear unemployment more than inflation while groups relying on profit-based income fear inflation more than unemployment. This assumption is a weak one in that it can be (and has been) tested empirically, at least in part, but does not necessarily support his claim. Hibbs discusses survey data about macroeconomic concerns by income class from Great Britain and the United States but without going into great detail about the stability of preferences over time or the link between macroeconomic preferences and partisan allegiance. Even with fully specified panel data over an extended period of time, however, it would be difficult to distinguish the direct and relative preferences of voters for specific macroeconomic outcomes from the instrumental preferences of voters for the distributive implications of these outcomes.[5] Therefore, Hibbs necessarily qualifies his analysis with an explanation of the distributional *reasons* for partisan macroeconomic preferences. Presumably, if the distributive consequences of inflation and unemployment were to change, then the partisan business cycle would change as well. If the consequences were to be the same for wage and salary earners on the one hand, and profit/income groups on the other hand, then the partisan business cycle would vanish.

Assumptions about the optimal inflation tax could be used to connect political behaviour with economic outcomes in ways that are similar to those described by Nordhaus and Hibbs. Politicians could spend their way into re-election and then inflate away the debt afterward. Alternatively, politicians could alternate between using inflation to tax creditors (or the holders of cash balances) and other instruments to tax debtors (or those who do not hold cash) depending upon which group was more important in winning the next election. The mechanisms have changed, but the qualifications remain the same. Voters have to be shortsighted for the electoral cycle to function and they would have to be divided across distributive outcomes for the partisan cycle to function.

Hypotheses such as those put forward by Nordhaus and Hibbs are particularly attractive because they can be so easily tested using macroeconomic and electoral data. Time series for inflation, unemployment, and electoral outcomes are widely available and can be made readily subject to regression analysis. The pattern of testing is the same whether the focus is on the exploitable Philips curve or the optimal inflation tax. In either case, the test of competing hypotheses is still deduced from the model as a whole—which is to say, from the extent to which macroeconomic outcomes correlate with indicators for political success. Moreover, the existence of two different sets of hypotheses— electoral cycle and partisan cycle—provides the basis for a credible research program. Given two different hypotheses, both equally plausible, which is better and under what conditions? This pattern of argument lies at the heart of economic support for central bank independence: If political behaviour creates inefficiencies in the functioning of the economy, then perhaps it is necessary to remove macro-economic policy-making from direct political influence. The difference is that while the plausible mechanisms in these arguments become ever more sophisticated, the macroeconomic preferences become ever more straightforward. Thus, Kydland and Prescott (1977) make their argument for 'the [time-] inconsistency of optimal plans' around the assumption that voters will anticipate attempts by policy-makers to exploit the trade-off between inflation and unemployment. Barro and Gordon (1983) focus on how politicians respond to the economic expectations of voters about government incentives to resort to an inflation tax as well as to changes in those expectations. Backus and Driffill (1985) work from the assumption that the public may not be aware of the government's true preferences regarding inflation and unemployment. And Rogoff (1985) argues that the government's macroeconomic preferences should be systematically different from that of the electorate. In each case—albeit for different reasons and under different conditions—one solution to the problem of politically induced macroeconomic inefficiency is the appointment of an independent central bank.[6]

The assumptions about macroeconomic preferences are not only straightforward, they are also largely untestable—at least outside of the hypothetico-deductive analysis of the models as a whole. It is one thing to look for correlations between political success or institutional design and macro-economic performance, and yet it is harder to map the macroeconomic preferences of the electorate, harder still to distinguish between different types of preference, and hardest of all to assess how strongly such preferences feature in the actions of voters and politicians. Thus the empirical debate about central bank independence focuses on large macrocorrelations and not on verifying each intermediate step in the analysis. Whether the voters are ignorant of political manipulation or government preferences, and whether governments seek to deceive the electorate or to appease it, is judged indirectly through the correlation of political institutions or successes and macroeconomic outcomes.

The use of correlations to verify whole models for political-economic interaction is so deeply ingrained in the literature that the possibility that politicians and voters would not perceive a trade-off between inflation and unemployment or between inflation and other forms of taxation—or that the distributional consequences of macroeconomic outcomes may no longer divide across partisan lines—virtually never receives consideration. In journal articles, there simply is not the space—and so, for example, Alesina (1987) starts off by assuming the existence of two parties with different macroeconomic preferences. Even in book-length analyses, however, the focus for empirical examination remains at the macro level. Alesina, Roubini, and Cohen (1997) review a wealth of data for correlations between political indicators and macro-economic outcomes, but do no more than reiterate evidence from Hibbs (updated to 1987) about the partisan-distributive consequences of unemployment and inflation in the United States. Their reason: 'most people (excluding some political scientists) would agree that different parties have different political goals' (Alesina, Roubini, and Cohen 1997: 45).

This line of analysis is not intended as a criticism of the research programme centred upon the hypothetico-deductive verification of macro-models for political-economic interaction. Both types of political business cycle—Nordhaus's electoral model and Hibbs's partisan model—have a strong intuitive appeal and it is reasonable to attempt to see which accords better with the empirical record. By the same token, more complicated game-theoretic analysis of the interaction between policy-makers and voters promises to shed important light on the problems of policy implementation—particularly when anticipation by the marketplace can produce perverse outcomes. Given the prior assumption, as in Friedman (1977), that political-economic interaction may be the principal cause for systematically poor macroeconomic performance, plausible speculation as to the form of such interaction is welcome. Any estimation of the relative plausibility of different lines of analysis is more welcome still. Finally, to the extent to which combinations of political business cycles and game-theoretic approaches help to focus attention on institutional solutions for systematically poor economic performance, that is most welcome of all.[7] Small wonder, then, that the argument for central bank independence has acquired such broad acceptance.

Exchange and Distribution

Once outside the context of macro-models for political-economic interaction, however, the case for making assumptions about the direct and relative macro-economic preferences of voters and politicians loses force. Whether weak or strong, such assumptions exist to bridge the gap between theoretical interaction and directly observable data. Therefore the standard for assessing the merits of these assumptions is a combination of plausibility and utility.[8] Do such assumptions really make sense and how much do they help to provide for a meaningful test of the hypothesis? If there is no hypothesis for explicit testing, consideration of utility ceases to have meaning. The question, then, is whether the assumption that voters and politicians have direct and relative macro-economic preferences makes sense at face value. The answer, in short, is that it does not.

It is necessary to clarify that the only important macroeconomic preferences are those held by the voters. Everything else derives from an institutional logic. This point is most easily established in the political business cycle literature, where politicians care about macroeconomic outcomes only insofar as these influence electoral fortunes—the Downsian assumption. If the voters do not care about macroeconomic performance, then the politicians do not care either. The status of elite preferences in the game-theoretic literature about policy credibility is only slightly more problematic. Politicians and monetary policy-makers may hold macroeconomic preferences that (particularly in the case of central bankers) are independent of electoral outcomes and therefore popular preferences. Nevertheless, politicians and policy-makers receive their preferences in much the same way that everyone else does. Elite preferences are no more than elevated popular preferences mediated through institutions. Therefore, most analysts assume that any systematic differences between elite preferences and popular preference are institutionally determined in some predictable manner—as a result of binding policy rules, bureaucratic incentives, epistemic communities, and the like. All non-systematic differences between elite preferences and popular preferences—which is to say, any uncertainty about elite preferences that cannot be explained away as some function of their institutional environment—are not somehow inherent to elites as such but rather derive from the location of particular elites within the distribution of popular preferences. As a result, popular preferences and institutional design are all that matter in the final analysis.

Where do popular preferences come from? The connection between policy action and macroeconomic outcome is hardly a direct cause and effect relationship. From a mechanistic standpoint, politicians cannot simply 'lower' unemployment and then wait for prices to rise, or announce a tax cut and then expect markets to hold on to depreciating cash balances or government obligations. By the same token, voters cannot stop working in the hopes of seeing prices fall, or pay premiums for goods and services in the expectation of receiving a job, or withhold some of their income tax with the promise to keep the money in cash. Even those who believe in the existence of an exploitable Philips curve or an optimal inflation tax have to admit that some intermediate process must come into play between government policy and macroeconomic outcomes.

More fundamentally, some intermediate process must come into play between perception, evaluation, accreditation, and action. Voters have to perceive the change in macroeconomic conditions, they have to translate it into some kind of personally meaningful framework, they have to accredit the change to government policy, and they have to formulate an appropriate response. This type of mechanism is at least as complicated as the economic mechanics that relate prices to employment. It is also less intuitive—as least from the standpoint of direct and relative preferences.

The problem is that macroeconomic outcomes and policy instruments are non-fungible. At a personal level, inflation and unemployment cannot be freely exchanged, and neither can inflation and other forms of taxation. Thus the trade-offs implied by the Philips curve and the inflation tax have no meaning without the introduction of an intervening value—something voters can perceive in common to both inflation and unemployment or inflation and other sources of government revenue. Downs (1957), for example, relies on the notion of utility in order to translate policy outcomes into comparable units of personal welfare. Once the existence of utility as a sort of universal currency is assumed, however, it is possible to denominate all objects and outcomes in terms of a third currency—which, for convenience, may as well be actual currency (money) rather than notional currency (utility). All that is required is a constraining assumption that the utility value of money is independent of the utility value of other objects. Everything has its price apart from money itself.

The introduction of money as an intermediate and universal value solves the first two steps in the mechanics of popular preferences. Macroeconomic change is perceived and interpreted in terms of changes in personal money—which is to say, income or wealth. As the function of money is to facilitate exchange between otherwise non-fungible goods, this impact relates to command over goods and services in the economy (real income) and not to the units of money per se (nominal income). Moreover, even if macroeconomic developments do not affect all the people all the time, we could recast the argument in probabilistic terms as expected changes without affecting the logic of the claim. Finally, the accreditation of macroeconomic change to government action can be assumed as a natural outgrowth of the political process—incumbents will always try to lay claim to what is good, while aspirants will highlight what is not. From this basis, it is easier to understand why Hibbs (1977) focuses a good part of his analysis on explaining the income effects of macroeconomic changes and Alesina et al. (1997) reiterate Hibbs's approach.

Intermediate monetary values also suggest the existence of direct and absolute macroeconomic preferences. Voters will dislike unemployment to the extent to which it reduces or threatens to reduce income. They will like growth to the extent to which it adds to the amount of goods and services available for consumption or to the extent to which it represents an increase in personal income. And they will dislike inflation to the extent to which price changes undermine the value of money or alter the relative rates of exchange between goods or services. These preferences are direct in that they attach to specific macroeconomic developments and they are absolute in that each development has a consistent effect on real income—positive for growth and employment, negative for unemployment and inflation.[9]

Beyond these direct and absolute preferences, however, two issues remain to be addressed. The first is left over from the mechanics of popular preferences—even if we can identify how voters perceive, value, and accredit macroeconomic changes, we still must consider how they will respond. For example, to what extent will the political response of different groups vary with the intensity of the personal wealth and income effects and to what extent will it vary with the expected costs and benefits of the response itself? The second is new, and derives from the existence of an intermediate and universal value. If, at

156   Erik Jones

the base of the matter, popular preferences revolve principally around (expected) changes to personal income and wealth, it makes no sense to assume that politicians are concerned with macroeconomic manipulation. Again, if voters are not inherently interested in macroeconomic outcomes, then politicians are not either. Following Downs (1957), the assumption should be that politicians will strive to manipulate whichever policy instrument is available and is most likely to secure re-election. Put another way, politicians will do whatever they can to generate a beneficial response.

These issues can only be addressed within the context of real-world constraints. To begin with, the volume of available income or wealth is limited. The economy can produce only so much—both in static terms, and in terms of real growth. Second, political action—whether directly at the polling booth, or indirectly through lobbying or campaigning—has a cost. For the electorate, this implies that the expected gain from acting should exceed the cost of doing so.[10] For politicians, the combination of these two constraints suggests the need to target their efforts. Simply, distribution matters. If politicians hope to create substantial income effects for a particular group in the electorate, they can only do so either by concentrating the effects of growth or by taking wealth from one group to give to another. In turn, this strategy of concentration raises a third constraint on political action. It is always going to be more efficient for politicians to target distribution first-hand, rather than to affect some macroeconomic change in the anticipation of second-order distributive outcomes. Targeted mechanisms not only promise to raise the income or wealth of those concerned, but they also underscore the chain of perception, valuation, and, most important, accreditation.

The notion of targeted redistribution is at least as intuitive as the notion of a political business cycle. Moreover, the two views are not mutually exclusive. They are, however, prioritised. Within the distributive context, macroeconomic manipulation is a residual. Politicians resort to macroeconomic policy only when more efficient distributive mechanisms are either unavailable or too costly to use. Following this hierarchy, the question is not whether politicians attempt to manipulate macroeconomic variables in their own interests but why. The focus is not on motivation but on constraint. In this way, what started as a question of popular preferences can thus be reduced to a set of basic assumptions about motivation and a set of more complicated institutional factors affecting the relative cost or availability of direct distributive mechanisms.

Economists have long recognised the importance of distributive outcomes to popular evaluations of policy performance. For example, Bailey (1956: 93, 110) pioneered the analysis of the 'optimal inflation tax' as a means to look beyond 'the redistributive and disruptive aspects of inflation'. Nevertheless, he concluded by emphasising the overwhelming significance of distributive effects. If governments are attempting to raise revenue via inflation, he suggests, it must 'be that the costs are at first largely hidden, whereas the costs of other forms of taxation—the costs of administration and compliance—are obvious.' Building on this position, Gordon (1975) suggested that if governments are generating inflation around elections, it is not because they want inflation per se, but rather because they have no other means to meet the distributive demands of the electorate. And, along similar lines, Stigler argued that macroeconomic performance—whether measured in terms of inflation, unemployment, or even per capita income—is unrelated either to incumbency or to party programmes.

One should not infer that economic questions are unimportant to the policies of parties or to the various groups in the population who systematically support one of the parties. . . . [Nevertheless] the economic bases for party affiliation must be sought in this area of income distribution (1973: 166-67).

The problem for economists in the 1970s was to build a research program around the political-economic dynamics of distributive outcomes. While the chain of reasoning is robust, the manifestation is more likely to be idiosyncratic. Politicians confronting diverse constituencies within the electorate are forced to make a judgement call about whose support to encourage based on the prevailing circumstances at the time. The choice may well be rational in the manner described by, for example, Dahl and Lindblom (1976), however it will be difficult to model in any detail before the fact. In commenting on Gordon's argument, Brunner stressed the overwhelming political significance of targeted distributive mechanisms only to admit that:

This analysis suggests . . . the fundamental irrelevance of most chapters in the theory of economic macro-policy and implies that systematic and deliberate macro-policies are somewhat improbable. The prevailing pattern of macro-policy results from a political process of detailed allocative struggle covered by a rhetoric occasionally borrowed from textbooks on macro-policies (1975: 853-54).

Commenting on Stigler, McCracken offers a less cynical and yet still telling synopsis:

What all this seems to suggest is that, within reasonable tolerances, changes in political sentiment are more apt to reflect the myriad of other factors that bear on voter sentiment. If the swing is outside these tolerances, or if the event is sufficiently visible or discrete, economic developments can exert a substantial effect on citizen support of the incumbent. If, therefore, the economic indicators start to waver, the economist may sleep well at night, knowing that in all probability it means little, but the politician may for very good reasons remain awake, wondering if this will be one of those cases that transforms him into a statesman (1973: 171).

Even without a forward-looking research program, however, it is possible to consolidate the argument by way of a couple of observations. To begin with, the critique of central bank independence as necessarily undemocratic lacks analytic basis. Given that voters do not have (at least inherently) direct and relative preferences for macroeconomic outcomes, there is no a priori reason to make macroeconomic policy-makers subject to democratic accountability. Ensuring the accountability of monetary policy-makers may or may not be something that the voters or politicians choose, but they do not have to do so, and neither do they have to consider the option. Second, some justification for central bank independence remains, although it is perhaps different from the traditional arguments developed by Kydland and Prescott, Barro and Gordon, Rogoff, and the like. Within this distribution-oriented political economy, having an independent central bank may help to prevent distributive conflict from undermining monetary conditions. Following Brunner: 'The role of monetary rules appears in this context in a new light. They define a constraint on the political process and are intended to move some portions of macro-policy beyond the allocative process of the "political market"' (1975: 854).

Competing Explanations

The argument that voters are more interested in distributive outcomes than in macroeconomic performance is compelling—at least on analytic grounds. Politicians want to be re-elected, and voters want to be better off. Politicians face resource constraints, and voters demand incentives to act. Therefore politicians make choices, target voters and reward them by redistributing either existing wealth or the benefits of economic growth. Such actions may have macroeconomic implications and, in moments of political desperation, may even manifest as macroeconomic policy changes. However, macroeconomic manipulation is not a usual means for politicians to seek re-election and it is not what the voters want (or are likely to respond to) in any event. This is a convincing interpretation—or at least a highly plausible one—but can it really tell us anything beyond the obvious? Recalling that the twin test for any framework of assumptions is utility as well as plausibility, what research programme can a distributive focus for political-economic interactions offer?

At this point it is important to concede that much of the existing economic analysis behind the argument for central bank independence is consistent with the distributive interpretation of political-economic interactions. For example, the political business cycle literature can be accommodated as a plausible description of the indirect effects of distributive policies (Gordon 1975; McCracken 1973), with the qualification that politicians only resort directly to macro-economic manipulation *in extremis* (Brunner 1975). Such a modification would require that analysts of political business cycles pay more attention to the distributive basis for electoral and partisan support (Okun 1973: 177). However, it would not vitiate their models per se.

The game-theoretic analysis about policy credibility is only slightly more difficult to accommodate within a distributive framework of preferences. Where the literature focuses on direct preferences for macroeconomic outcomes, a revised interpretation would focus on direct preferences for distributive outcomes with indirect macroeconomic effects. Such a change would not require rewriting any of the equations, but would imply a different notion of 'credibility'—one focusing more broadly on the consistency of government policies with the maintenance of price stability, rather than deriving from a narrow focus on commitment to a price stability rule. Within this context, politicians might lack credibility because they try to satisfy too large a constituency or too many different elements within the electorate, rather than because they (are expected to) attempt to exploit a short-run Philips curve trade-off or create a surprise inflation.

The argument for central bank independence is strengthened in both cases. From the political business cycle standpoint, the principal advantage of an independent central bank is to mitigate the influence of distributive conflict on monetary conditions and, *in extremis*, to shield politicians from the temptation to resort to destructive macroeconomic manipulation (Baily 1956). Similar advantages also operate in the realm of policy credibility. On the one hand, an independent central bank—unbeholden to any specific distributive outcome— will be consistent with a broader range of other government policies than a central bank that is assigned to satisfy a particular constituency. On the other hand, the cost of conflict between the government and the central bank will increase the likelihood that some other policy will give way rather than monetary policy in the event of a broader inconsistency in the government's distributive programmes. Such arguments already exist in the literature on central bank independence, and yet they receive renewed importance within a distributive framework.

The distributive framework also helps to integrate other arguments about central bank independence and the political determinants of macroeconomic outcomes into the mainstream of the literature. Specifically, the distributive framework helps to establish a common causal mechanism (distributive conflict) as the link between institutional arrangements and macro-economic outcomes. Thus, following Bernhard (1998), it should be possible to explain the incidence of central bank independence as a function of the (potential) importance of distributive conflict within and between political parties. Alternatively, following Calmfors and Driffill (1988), it should be possible to identify other institutional correlates of favourable macroeconomic outcomes. In turn, such institutions may complement or substitute for central bank independence (Hall and Franzese 1998; Bleaney 1996).

Focus on distributive conflict also helps to account for some of the empirical anomalies in the existing literature. Thus, for example, the revised argument for policy credibility is consistent with Beck's (1987) findings that inflation tends to accelerate during election quarters in the United States despite the political independence of the Federal Reserve. As Beck notes, such inflation does not result from the manipulation of monetary instruments but rather from the monetary accommodation of increased government outlays. The Fed's governors are not bowing to political pressure, however, neither are they pushing against the wind. The revised credibility argument is also consistent with Lohmann's (1998) claim that the behavioural independence of the German Bundesbank is an inverse function of the ease with which the sitting government could cobble together a coalition in support of reforming the bank's statutes.

However, being consistent with too many arguments is not necessarily a virtue. The claim that adoption of a distributive framework would allow us to retain the status quo is hardly a ringing endorsement—particularly as it is far from clear that adherence to a distributive framework over the past two decades would have fostered anything beyond the nihilism suggested by Brunner (1975). Even clarifying positions within the existing literature is not enough. To warrant adoption, a distributive framework has to account for something that the assumption of direct and relative macroeconomic preferences cannot. And it does.

Within the context of distributive preferences it is possible to dispense with ad hoc cultural explanations for comparative macroeconomic performance. Recall that popular preferences no longer attach to macroeconomic outcomes, but rather to distributive outcomes. As a result, the institutional intermediation of political pressures and distributive outcomes is all that necessarily differs from one country to the next. Thus, for example, the favourable record of German inflation derives not from some vague 'culture of price stability' but instead results from a complex and overlapping network of institutions for resolving distributive conflict without jeopardising monetary stability (McNamara and Jones 1996). The strength of German direct and absolute preferences for price stability may be unique—and Loedel (1999a: 26-38) makes a strong case that they are in the context of Germany's own history. However, to the extent to which all populations share direct and absolute preferences about macroeconomic outcomes, with the implication that poor performance is always an unintended consequence, the relative strength of German preferences is more relevant to understanding institutional design than performance per se (which is essentially Bernhard's [1999] claim).

A focus on distributive preferences also makes it possible to encompass changes in the pattern of macroeconomic performance across relatively consistent institutional conditions without having to invoke an ex ante change in direct and relative preferences for macroeconomic outcomes. This argument is made in general terms by Rowthorne (1992), who finds that the influence of centralised wage bargaining on macroeconomic outcomes can be moderated through the introduction of a notional variable for 'cooperative behaviour'. The more willing economic groups are to cooperate with one another, the better the macroeconomic outcomes within a constant institutional environment. The reverse is also true, and an increase in conflictive behaviour results in a worsening of macroeconomic performance. Moreover, for Rowthorne as for Gordon (1975), the motivation for conflict and cooperation is distributive.

The hypothesis that macroeconomic outcomes are affected by a change in the intensity of distributive conflict can be made subject to empirical research more easily than the alternative hypothesis concerning a change in direct and relative macroeconomic preferences or a change in cultural economic attributes. Thus, for example, it is easier to find evidence of the distributive coalition behind recent Dutch improvements in unemployment than it is to explain how the Dutch were suffused with a spirit of cooperation at the start of the 1980s (Jones 1999a). In this way, the research programme supported by the distributive framework is richer than that traditionally used to drive research into political business cycles and policy credibility. At stake is not only the appropriate institutional context or the necessary balance between rules and discretion, but also an understanding of the conditions under which distributive conflict is most likely to increase and to decrease.

European Integration, EMU, and the Democratic Deficit

Too heavy a focus on distributive preferences threatens to bias any interpretation of European integration toward state-centric explanations. So long as voters care only about distributive outcomes as mediated by national institutions, the nation-state will remain the basic framework for analysis. This is true by definition and not in empirical terms. It derives directly from the dual assumptions that all values can be made fungible and that politics is only about winners and losers. However, clearly such assumptions do not reflect the whole reality that is European integration (Dyson and Featherstone 1999). Therefore at this stage in the analysis it is appropriate to accept that analytic reliance on distributive preferences may suffer from many of the same shortcomings as the analytic reliance on macroeconomic preferences that it replaces.

Nevertheless, by working back to distributive preferences *rather than* macroeconomic preferences we can sharpen our understanding of monetary integration even if we cannot elucidate the process in its entirety. Specifically, focusing on distributive preferences reduces the discussion of EMU and Europe's democratic deficit to three questions: Was EMU underwritten by a Europe-wide distributive coalition? Does the existence of EMU somehow constrain the member states or their citizenry in their desire to undertake redistribution either at the European level or at the national level? Will the operation of Europe's monetary union likely heighten the intensity of distributive conflict within and between Europe's member states? If the answer to all of these questions is negative, then the construction of EMU has no negative impact on the democratic character of Europe's constitution. There has been no conspiracy, there are no limitations on the fulfilment of popular aspirations, and there is unlikely to be any concerted backlash against EMU, against the European Union, or against the member states themselves.

Indeed, the preponderance of evidence suggests that EMU is democratically a non-event. To begin with, it is almost impossible to find evidence of any coherent transnational coalition of interests underwriting the project to their own benefit.[11] A few authors have found a distributive basis for *national* support for EMU (e.g., Frieden 1996; Oatley 1997); however none has been able to establish coherent linkages between these distributive groups across Europe as a whole. Indeed, the pattern of European monetary integration appears best explained by the combination of ideational conformity (McNamara 1998) and distributive idiosyncrasy (Frieden and Jones 1998; Frieden 1998).

Second, EMU places no constraint on the redistribution of income at either the European or national levels. Here it may be necessary to admit a difference between the transition to EMU and the operation of Europe's monetary union. During the period of convergence, member states were encouraged to consolidate often through draconian measures. Such consolidation had clear redistributive consequences. Given the poor state of European fiscal balances, the question is whether such consolidation would have been necessary with or without EMU. If not, then the choice to pursue the conditions for membership should necessarily have been vetted through democratic channels.

Once a country is in, however, EMU imposes no necessary constraint on the redistribution of income within the national context. While the member states have agreed to limit their debts and deficits, they have neither accepted nor imposed any constraint on the size of government spending as a percentage of total output or on the size of distributive policies as a percentage of total government spending. Moreover, to the extent to which EMU does constrain national politicians from redistributing large amounts of income across time by running up deficits and debts, this constraint more closely reflects a growing awareness of the limits of social democracy in globalised financial markets than any requirements of monetary integration per se.

Third, the evidence that EMU will intensify distributive conflict is mixed. Despite a wealth of economic analysis about the possibility for asymmetries in macroeconomic performance that are exacerbated by the operation of Europe's common monetary policy, evidence of heightened distributive tensions is little apparent. Thus, while the creation of Europe's monetary union may have increased pressure for the construction of a Europe-wide tax and transfer system, the member states seem insistent that they are capable of handling any adjustment problems through domestic institutions (Jones 1998). Indeed, Europe's member states already have made considerable progress in adapting their national distributive formulas to the constraints and possibilities of monetary integration. Moreover, as with the distributive groups in support of EMU, such adaptation is more clearly idiosyncratic than trans-European in nature (Jones 1999b).

Seen through the lens of distributive preferences, the argument that EMU is somehow inherently undemocratic lacks analytic basis. Thus while it may be the case that the Maastricht Treaty fails to provide adequate means through which national and European politicians can supervise their delegation of monetary authority to the ECB—which is the central concern addressed by Verdun (1998a) and Elgie (1998)—such failings are not beyond institutional remedy. Europe's newly established monetary constitution may need reform, but that is no necessary reason for EMU to hinder the functioning of European democracy. Indeed, if anything, the adaptation of Europe's member states to EMU may yield a positive impact of monetary union on the practice of democratic accountability. Where before, national politicians may have relied on macroeconomic manipulation to absorb the externalities generated by their attempts to reward too many groups within the electorate at the same time, EMU promises to internalise the costs of excess. Moreover, thanks to the stability pact and to the independence of Europe's central bank, politicians must conduct their redistribution through fiscal means instruments that are not only more efficient but also more transparent. Echoing Bailey (1956), politicians may have resorted to excessive inflation for the simple reason that the costs were hidden from the voters. Now that is no longer the case. In this sense, at least, EMU does not threaten democracy—but rather strengthens it.

Notes

This chapter has benefited from discussions with Robert Elgie, Daniel Gros, Paul Heywood, David Howarth, Kathleen McNamara, Ben Müller, David Stevens, and Amy Verdun. The usual disclaimer applies.

1. The point is made in greater detail by Verdun (1998a) and Elgie (1998).
2. Commentators on earlier drafts of this essay have questioned the underlying notion of democracy. For purposes of this argument, however, a precise definition is unnecessary. All that is required is that democracies necessarily involve some representation of popular interests either in the exercise of sovereign authority or in the designation of agents (i.e., the delegation of such authority). The debate here is whether monetary policy inherently requires direct representation or whether it can legitimately be delegated elsewhere. My argument is that such delegation cannot be ruled out a priori.
3. For the microeconomic perspective, see Krueger (1990).
4. This point is stressed by Downs (1957: 38) who emphasises that 'only benefits which voters become conscious of by election day can influence their voting decisions; otherwise their behaviour would be irrational.'
5. This point is admitted by Hayo (1998: 249), although he goes on to argue for the existence of historically informed 'cultures of price stability'.
6. For an excellent survey of this literature, see Forder (1998).
7. See, for example, Lohmann (1992).
8. The emphasis on utility and the prior allusion to research programs are not intended to highlight detailed Lakatosian presuppositions so much as to suggest the

existence of different criteria for selecting foundational assumptions of which 'fruitfulness' ranks among the most important. See, for example, Miller (1987: 197-99).

9. For an empirical assessment of this distributive assumption, see van Leylyveld (1999).

10. Obviously, a more sophisticated version of this same point would have to account for externalities as well as the organisational problems of collective action.

11. The same claim may not apply to epistemic communities, where some evidence does exist that central bankers and monetary economists had a disproportionate influence over the design of EMU (Verdun 1999). Crucially, however, such influence reflects epistemological and not distributive considerations and so does not factor into the present analysis per se. The claim that having like-minded individuals control the process of integration beyond the influence of popular preferences is somehow inherently undemocratic may have currency, but it is outside the scope of this argument.

F33
F36

Chapter 10
THE SHAPE OF THINGS TO COME:
THE EU'S POST-EMU INSTITUTIONAL
ARCHITECTURE

Patrick M. Crowley

The launch of the euro on January 1, 1999, marked a profound change in EU institutional and economic arrangements, and probably marks the most important development in the international financial system since the Bretton Woods conference in 1944. European Economic and Monetary Union (EMU) is the final stage in the integration of European Union markets, as it effectively eliminates the last official barriers to trade in the single market.

In Brussels in 1998, Jacques Delors, in a speech to the ECSA-World conference, issued a challenge to the academic community to forecast the effects of a 'clash' of different institutional cultures in the European Union, notably the newly formed European Central Bank (ECB), a federalist type institution where representation is by country and by appointment and voting on the central bank council will be by majority vote; the European Council, an intergovernmental institution where voting is either by unanimity or by qualified majority vote; and the European Parliament, where the institution is of a representative parliamentary type along party lines and voting is by majority vote. The Amsterdam Treaty (1998) implicitly takes no absolute powers away from institutions, but grants a significant amount of new power to the European Parliament, particularly in the realm of co-decision and for recourse to inquiry. This institutional configuration, in and of itself, is interesting and in fact unique, but the 'clash' (as Delors described it) is not in terms of open conflict between institutions but rather in terms of representation and decision making. The evolution of this structure will either come about through further inter-governmental agreement or by specific events which cause more responsibilities to be passed up to a supra-national level.

Through EMU, monetary and exchange rate policies have become major macroeconomic policies decided on at a supranational level in the EU, but the EU has very limited fiscal powers, and has no fiscal sovereignty, so fiscal policy is decentralised with the Stability and Growth Pact acting as a crude fiscal co-ordination mechanism together with the surveillance procedures that were put in place as part of the Maastricht Treaty. This multi-level macroeconomic policy coordination problem could be a major source of instability and political conflict in the future and hence this is a major focus of this chapter.

In the economics literature, the Stability and Growth Pact has already been the subject of a similar debate to that which took place surrounding the fiscal criteria of the Maastricht criteria. Three schools of thought have emerged: those who agree and support the notion of supranational constraints on fiscal policy (see Artis and Winkler 1997), those that support the constraints during the transition period (Crowley 1997) and those that are against any constraints (notably Buiter, Corsetti and Roubini 1993).

Further problems arise in terms of completion of EMU and the three remaining member states who have not yet committed to joining the third phase of EMU. The third phase of EMU will not be complete until July of 2002, so there is still scope for instability and conflict in the intervening years, and some commentators claim that the recent well-documented political conflict in Germany is just a precursor for further potential conflict. Indeed caution should be the watchword over the next three years, as the success of EMU is not assured yet: although the launch of the single currency was relatively untroubled, a successful launch is no guarantee of successful completion!

Exchange rate policy could also be a source of conflict, as responsibility for this macroeconomic instrument is divided between the European Central Bank and Ecofin (the finance ministers from the member states). This model of shared responsibility is also characteristic of the arrangements for exchange rate policy in Germany, and conflict between the Bundesbank and the Ministry of Finance over exchange rate policy, among other things, is already well documented in this case (see Henning 1997).

In this chapter, economic theory is used to determine future institutional development in the EU. In essence economic theory would dictate that EMU would likely only be beneficial for certain member states, so given the actual number of member states now in EMU, scenarios are established for the stress lines that are likely to occur in the EU, and then which EU institutions will likely benefit or otherwise from a resolution to these emergent problems. The chapter makes the bold assumption that economic theory is correct, and then proceeds to derive results from this assertion. Clearly economic theory may not be correct, and this has been taken this into account by appeal to 'endogenous' solutions for EMU.

This chapter is divided into four sections. Section II looks at the allocation of policy responsibilities between EU institutions, while section III looks at state-contingent scenarios. Section IV looks at the possible institutional implications coming out of the scenarios, and then section V concludes.

Institutions

The allocation of policy responsibilities in any state structure is a matter of history, bargaining between institutions, initiatives to concentrate certain specified responsibilities under new domains, and the principles under which countries allocate responsibilities between different levels of government. The EU is rather unique in this respect, as responsibilities are not allocated between local, state and national levels of government with perhaps some constraints being imposed at an international level (IMF conditionality springs to mind here), but are allocated (with some overlap) between national and supranational levels. Wessels (1998) has explored some of the implications of EMU for political union, and specified the inter-institutional two-level relations between organisations for policy responsibility. Here the state and national responsibilities are largely ignored so that we can focus on supranational responsibilities.

The European Council is an intergovernmental decision making body, which votes by unanimity on all important issues, and by qualified majority vote on certain specified issues. The Council is responsible for the overall direction of economic policy-making, as national governments, the ECB and the Commission all report to the Council and/or participate with voting rights.

The conclusions of macroeconomic decisions at the Council are usually delegated to the Ecofin committee, which has four subcommittees—an informal, a restricted, and a plenary Ecofin, as well as the newly formed Euro-12 council (which will be dealt with separately). The Ecofin has the responsibility of co-ordinating policies among member states, and in particular has the responsibility for monitoring pan-EU fiscal policies and exchange rate policies, again either by unanimity or by qualified majority vote, depending on the issue being dealt with. Here, particular responsibility for the operation of the ERM2 also should be recognised.

Following the launch of the single currency in the third stage of EMU, a new committee, the Euro-12 committee, is responsible for the coordination of fiscal policies of member states participating in EMU. Each member state participating in EMU is represented on the committee. The ECB is also represented on this committee for obvious reasons, as it is in all Ecofin meetings. However, this ECB participation is without voting rights.

The ECB Council is the main decision making body of the ECB, and deliberates the monetary policy of the ECB, with a mandate to maintain price stability in the euro area. All member states have a vote on the Council, but several representatives are appointed from the supranational level. Voting on the

Council is by majority vote on all issues. The ECB clearly also has an interest in the exchange rate policy for the euro, and is expected to coordinate exchange rate policy with Ecofin and the Euro-12 committee.

Both the European Commission and the Parliament have little direct active role in macroeconomic policy-making, but have a large influence on the design of any new initiatives, and also have subtle ways in which they can impinge on policy-making (through preparation of requested reports, economic evaluations, and ensuring that the single market functions properly through competition policy et cetera.).

Lastly, the Stability and Growth Pact acts as a constraint on national fiscal policies for EMU participants from the supranational level. Fines can be levied by the European Council, following a detailed process, which can last for a significant period of time before such fines are imposed. A member state has to run a budget deficit of more than 3 percent of GDP for fines to be levied, but this restriction can be lifted under specific circumstances. The restriction is automatically lifted in the case where a member state experiences a fall in GDP of 2 percent or greater during the course of the year. In a case where GDP falls by between 0.5 to 2 percent for fines to be levied a unanimous vote on the Council (excluding the member state under consideration) is required. Several points should be noted here. First, the budget deficit measure in question is the non-cyclically adjusted deficit, so that in fact the pact in effect requires that the 3 percent of GDP restraint is met at the bottom of the business cycle, unless the amplitude of the business cycle is particularly large, in which case the member state will likely be granted an exception under the above 'recession' clauses. It is widely recognised that this implies that member states should aim to run a zero budget deficit over the business cycle, so that automatic stabilisers can be allowed to work. Second, if a member state has a fall in GDP of between 0 and 0.5 percent of GDP and a budget deficit of greater than 3 percent of GDP, then this is likely to cause significant tensions, as governments usually allow automatic stabilisers to act to boost government spending so as not to exacerbate the situation. This could lead to a moral hazard problem, as governments limit the response to a fall in GDP, and maybe inhibit usage of automatic stabilisers so as to ensure that the following year, if another recession is registered, then the pact restrictions on budget deficits would likely be lifted. Lastly, the pact is an intergovernmental agreement, and although binding on the current signatories, it is not clear that it carries the same weight as treaty obligations. In short, it is not clear what the legal enforceability of the pact is.

The restrictions on national fiscal policies as part of the Stability and Growth Pact are supplementary to the coordination work done in Ecofin, so it is interesting to ask what justifies the pact. Two rationales have been put forward for the pact: first that the pact is necessary as a crude mechanism for co-ordination of national fiscal policies to counter the fact that there are no other formal restrictions on fiscal policy at the supra-national level; and second that the pact is necessary and (although arbitrary) required to ensure the credibility of the ECB in carrying out monetary policy.

Theoretical Framework

In order to define state-contingent scenarios for the outcome of EMU, a theoretical framework is required. The framework used here is the optimal currency area (OCA) literature for EMU, which is voluminous, and has reached largely similar results in terms of which member states are deemed most suitable for membership of an OCA.

Two seminal articles on optimal currency areas (Mundell 1961; McKinnon 1963) outlined the conditions under which several administrative jurisdictions might be suitable to be subject to the same monetary policy. Further refinements of this approach were subsequently made by Kenen (1969) and Krugman (1990). Bayoumi (1994) also offered a formal model of optimal currency areas (OCAs) with microeconomic foundations to underscore Mundell's original thesis. The conditions for an OCA are that members of the currency union should experience mostly symmetric shocks and that economic cycles should be synchronous (see De Grauwe 1992 for a layman's summary of the optimal currency area approach and Masson and Taylor 1993 for a thorough survey of the issues). If countries experience asymmetric shocks or have asynchronous business cycles then the costs of being subject to a single monetary policy may be significant, and may outweigh the benefits. To offset asymmetric shocks or asymmetric business cycles, then certain currency area characteristics may ameliorate costs, notably i) a significant degree of labour mobility, ii) fiscal transfers through a 'federal' level of government and iii) flexible wages and prices. Part of the reason why the OCA literature has been such a focus of interest in the context of the EU has been due to the fact that 'euroland' cannot be characterised as possessing these characteristics to the same degree that say the United States does, and that participation in EMU was determined largely by satisfaction of economic criteria.

The empirical time-series literature on OCAs can be divided into three strands[1]—a strand that uses basic regional data (from a sub-national level) to evaluate whether countries use exchange rates to offset shocks, with the implication that similar exchange rate volatilities would imply similar shock magnitudes, while at the same time evaluating whether participants possess the three offsetting characteristics (see De Grauwe and Vanhaverbeke 1993); a strand that uses structural vector auto regression (SVAR) time series methodology (following Blanchard and Quah 1989) to identify demand and supply shocks (see, for example, Bayoumi and Eichengreen 1993 and 1994 for the EU and North America, and Lalonde and St-Amant 1993 and DeSerres and Lalonde 1994 for Canada) and then look at the correlation of these shocks across countries or regions. Another strand of the literature evaluates the synchronicity of business cycles across prospective currency union members (Baxter and Stockman 1989; Artis and Zhang 1997a, b) and a final approach uses cluster methods to determine membership of an OCA (see Jacquemin and Sapir 1995 and Artis and Zhang 1998).

The first strand of OCA empirical research has been criticised for being largely descriptive, while the second (SVAR) methodology has been criticised (see Buiter 1998) for being arbitrary in terms of the restrictions that are required for identification of monetary and real shocks (usually the assumption that shocks that are neutral in the long run are monetary shocks). The third strand of research also responds to another criticism of the VAR methodology: that a shock approach ignores long run business cycle synchronicity—the synchronicity approach typically uses a Hodrick-Prescott filter to discern de-trended cyclical components in GDP and then uses the correlations in business cycles to draw out implications about relative suitability as constituents of an OCA. The obvious drawback here is that this approach completely ignores the incidence of temporary shocks and does not consider the ability of exchange rates to also compensate for shocks.

A further development in the OCA literature has been the recognition that ex-ante evaluations of which countries constitute an OCA might ignore the Lucas critique, in that new members of an OCA might a) modify policy to be better suited to an OCA (see Tavlas 1993), or b) be more suited to being in an OCA ex-post (Frankel and Rose 1997). The latter approach takes into consideration factors that usually do not appear in the ex-ante OCA approach, such as trade intensity, real interest rate cycles, and fiscal policy coordination.[2]

In this chapter the theoretical framework of the OCA approach is used as a way of deriving state-contingent scenarios. Two particular lines of argument stem from this literature, and both are particularly important in the analysis presented below, so these are reviewed for purposes of clarity:

1. Most of the OCA literature finds that there is a 'hard' core of member states that satisfy the OCA criteria according to any of the approaches outlined above. This 'hard' core roughly consists of Germany, the Netherlands, Austria, Belgium, Luxembourg, France and Denmark; a 'softer' periphery is usually thought to include Spain, Italy, Sweden, Ireland, UK, Portugal, Greece and Finland. Denmark is sometimes not in the 'harder' core, and Ireland sometimes is. Nevertheless, there is virtual unanimity on Germany, the Benelux countries and Austria forming an OCA;

2. One of the criticisms of the OCA literature (made by Buiter 1998) states that it matters what types of asymmetric shocks a member state experiences. The usual distinction made in the OCA literature is between supply and demand shocks, but from the point of view of economic policy, it is more important to know whether the shocks were IS (real/goods market) or LM (financial/money market) shocks (following the usual 'Poole' analysis in macroeconomics). With a single market in capital, asymmetric LM shocks are not damaging to a member state's membership of a currency union, as long as capital can flow between member states so as to equilibrate interest rates. Asymmetric IS shocks, however, are potentially damaging, as to counter such shocks the usual arsenal of offsetting economic characteristics (wage flexibility/labour mobility) or policy programmes (fiscal transfers/equalisation) have to be in place.

The second line of argument needs extending for our purposes though. If all asymmetric shocks in the EU were IS shocks (for example very high unemployment resulting from a lack of investment and economic activity in a certain member state), then this could lead to severe problems in EMU, as the SGP would not allow government intervention unless a recession was deemed to have occurred. If all asymmetric shocks were LM shocks, then although capital can flow freely between member states to ensure that liquidity shortages were eliminated, there could be circumstances given the institutional structure of the financial services sector and the arrangements under the European System of Central Banks (ESCB) such that a member state might temporarily experience problems. One example of this might be in a country that has a fragile financial services sector and experiences a run on its banks, which might then lead to a greater need for lender of last resort facilities than are normally provided. Also, financial markets are not perfect, so even though liquidity shortages may appear in some parts of the system, capital flows may not, for whatever reason, materialise. So asymmetric LM shocks could lead to member states experiencing problems, but clearly the single market should take care of most of these. Hence LM shocks are ignored in the analysis below.

State-Contingent Scenarios

To derive state-contingent scenarios, the OCA literature is assumed to be correct. That is, the current EMU configuration is assumed to be unsustainable over the long run, unless 'euroland' turns out to be an endogenous OCA. This implies that either a) the single currency project will collapse, or b) there will be some endogenous changes to current arrangements or c) there will be new policy competencies assigned to the supranational level.

The state-contingent scenarios are as follows:

A. *'Nirvana'*—in this scenario it transpires that EMU is an endogenous OCA, in that there is symmetry of shocks and synchronicity of business cycles. Also economic convergence occurs following the 'monetarist' model of approaching a currency union;

B. *Recognition of IS asymmetric shocks*—in this scenario EMU forms an OCA for financial markets, but goods markets experience asymmetric shocks and/or there is significant asynchronicity in business cycles, neither of which is eliminated through trade linkages or other structural changes. In this instance one or several member states might call for the SGP to be relaxed or scrapped, as it puts a constraint on a national government's capacity to address shocks and asynchronicity. Here it is important to note that recognition is acknowledged by other member states so that the response is a negotiated one;

C. *Supranational initiatives*—here there is a threat of process reversal: in this scenario the SGP or ECB monetary policy causes one member state or a collection of member states (the 'soft' periphery are likely candidates) to threaten to leave unless some institutional/policy changes are made. The threat could be due to either IS asymmetric shocks, asynchronous business cycles or economic divergence. The possible changes could include, but are not limited to:

- scrapping the SGP;
- endogenous development of prescriptive fiscal policies;
- a change in exchange rate policy.

As such, appropriate changes in institutional arrangements/policies are made in order for these member states to remain in EMU. Here, it is more likely that conflict will occur as clearly there is more likely to be bargaining among participants to maintain EMU's current membership.

D. *Process reversal*—as above except that appropriate changes are not made in order for these member states to remain in EMU. This could be due to an unwillingness to be subject to either the SGP or to ECB monetary policy, with other member states insisting that the SGP and/or ECB monetary policy are essential for an effective monetary union. In addition a 'pull' factor could be at work if the current 'outs' demonstrate economic advantages to non-membership in EMU.

E. *'Collapse'*—in this scenario EMU collapses as there are emerging battles over monetary policy on the ECB Council (perhaps following a large asymmetric shock) and economic divergence in EMU. Here Feldstein's so-called 'war' scenario (Feldstein 1997) perhaps stems from a belief that fines according to the SGP could be a significant source of conflict. But in addition, if 'process reversal' began to occur, speculation in the foreign exchange market could cause significant strains on the conversion rates, breaking EMU apart.

Other variables might also be introduced, to give intermediate scenarios. The specified scenarios differ as to the severity of the problems which impinge upon EMU, but the scenarios could also be affected by the degree of flexibility exhibited by other member states. Von Hagen has explored the implications of logrolling behaviour on the ECB Council. Clearly, if such behaviour is evident at the supranational level then this may enhance flexibility to respond to the problems of any one particular member state.

One of the scenarios, the 'supranational initiatives' scenario requires further elucidation. As the SGP is a council document, it can be scrapped by a unanimous vote in Council. This would appease any member state that wishes to have a greater degree of fiscal latitude in addressing aggregate demand deficiencies.

Institutional Implications of EMU Scenarios

Implications

For each of the state-contingent scenarios defined above, we now explore what the institutional implications would be, with the caveat that these institutional implications take the current institutional configuration at the supranational level as a given.

A. *'Nirvana'*—in this scenario the EU is able to claim complete success for EMU, and integration projects can proceed in other areas (such as EDU, for example). This scenario would likely spur the integration process in other areas, but would not lead to increased economic policy competences being passed up to the supranational level.[3]

B. *Recognition of IS asymmetric shocks*—in this scenario market-determined penalties are applied to member state debt, reflective of fiscal policy stance (as in Canada and the US) through interest rates. Here, Ecofin is potentially weakened, as it would be relegated to purely an oversight role if the SGP were scrapped, and Euro-12 could, for all intent and purpose, be disbanded. Clearly responsibilities given to the Council under the SGP might also no longer be applicable.

C. *Supranational initiatives*—in this scenario scrapping the SGP would be as above in b, and a change of exchange rate policy could be enacted very easily through a qualified majority vote in Ecofin, potentially giving the Euro-12 committee a greater role. As for the endogenous development of prescriptive fiscal policies, this is a little more complex:

1. The introduction of co-insurance/equalisation payments—this would presumably be by formula (as in Canada) and would likely give the Euro-12 committee a role in designing and implementing such a program. Perhaps the Commission might have some oversight over the scheme as well (see von Hagen and Hammond 1995);

2. An expanded supranational budget—this would now have to wait until the Ecofin/EU Council review of the EU budget in 2006. If the budget were expanded then it would likely give the Commission and the European Parliament additional responsibilities and oversight;

3. Permitting supranational budget deficits—this would require an IGC to change the Treaty of Union. It might give additional responsibility to the Commission and Ecofin to ensure that the EU budget is balanced over the business cycle;

4. Supranational fiscal sovereignty—this would also require an IGC, and would probably give the European Parliament the greatest additional responsibilities, although the EU Council and the Commission may also garner further responsibilities and oversight.

174   Patrick M. Crowley

D. *Process reversal*—perhaps this may occur by referendum. Here Ecofin and the Euro-12 will clearly be directly weakened, as their failure to maintain an EMU of twelve members would clearly affect their credibility. Obviously there would be indirect ramifications for all EU institutions.

E. *'Collapse'*—here complete collapse of EMU would cause an institutional crisis in the EU, with both the Euro-12 committee and the ECB being disbanded.

Discussion

The EU is clearly not at present an OCA, but a significant part of it is (the 'hard' core). Therefore, even if we accept the OCA approach, it is likely that scenario 'e' can be ditched as improbable. But if the OCA approach is accepted as valid, then it is likely that we would also have to throw out scenario 'a' as well. This leaves scenarios 'b', 'c' and 'd' as the most likely candidates. Scenario 'b' is probably the least controversial, as it envisages a negotiated loosening of the SGP constraints. Each of the sub-scenarios under 'c' has very different implications for institutional development in the EU. An alternative way to divide these options is to distinguish between an initiative which gives more fiscal autonomy to national governments (scrapping the SGP), versus the alternative which is to pass up some fiscal competencies to a supranational level. The threat of withdrawal could be responded to by either giving more competencies to national governments or by allowing new initiatives at the supranational level to offset the constraints at the national level.

The response to a threat to leave EMU then is important to the institutional implications for the EU. It is not appropriate to speculate on the bargaining stances that might exist when a threat to leave EMU is addressed. It is likely that only the threat of a large amount of member states leaving EMU would cause a unanimous vote on the EU Council to scrap the SGP. Thus, if a small number of member states, or a single member state threatened to leave EMU, it is most likely that 'c' would be the response. But of course scrapping the SGP might still occur if a single member state threatened to block all votes (as the UK did under Thatcher).

In 'c' though, multiple equilibria are possible in terms of what the eventual institutional outcome might be. Of the possibilities considered (i-iv above), i) appears to be most likely. Here, a formula-based approach is instituted to offset a 'fiscal gap' at the member state level. Such equalisation payments were put in place in Canada to offset shocks and to promote regional convergence (Department of Finance 1997). Another less expensive possibility might be the establishment of a co-insurance scheme, which would provide funds to offset any downturn in growth so that automatic stabilisers can effectively operate (see Eichengreen 1997). In the EU context, embarking on a new program such as equalisation would require an increase in the EU budget, but the size of the budget increase would not be great (see Italianer and Vanheukelen 1997).

One large caveat must be placed on all the above analysis, however. While the OCA literature is fast expanding, there is significant disagreement as to its real applicability. It is noteworthy that both Canada and the United States are not OCAs, and yet they are completely viable political entities. Also, research by Helliwell (1999) shows that the Canadian border does matter for trade—the majority of trade that provinces do is inter-provincial, and not international. Thus the formation of the single market may be much more important for EMU than many economists anticipated, and might lead to an endogenous OCA being formed.

Conclusions

In this chapter the OCA literature was used as a theoretical basis for defining state-contingent scenarios for EMU. Once these scenarios were defined, a qualitative analysis of the institutional implications for the EU was undertaken.

The scenarios focused on how EMU would develop, with five specific scenarios being fleshed out to illustrate the events that might unfurl given specific economic trends or events. The five scenarios then gave different implications for what new competencies might be given to EU institutions, or existing ones taken away.

The most likely scenarios were for either the SGP to be scrapped due to a recognition of the difficulties of adjusting to asynchronous real business cycles or asymmetric IS shocks, or for endogenous development of prescriptive fiscal policies due to a threat for a member state or a group of member states to leave EMU. In the former case EU institutions will lose responsibilities, and in particular the Euro-12 committee, the Ecofin and the EU Council. In the latter case various combinations of different policy initiatives could yield differing new responsibilities, with different distributional implications among the EU institutions. Such initiatives might include a) equalisation payments, b) an expanded supranational budget, c) supranational budget deficits to be permitted and d) the granting of supranational fiscal sovereignty.

Notes

Previous versions of this chapter were presented at University of Missouri at Columbia at a conference organised by the EU centre on the current EU agenda, at the 1999 ECSA-US biennial conference in Pittsburgh, and at the 1999 conference 'Conceptualising the New Europe' at the University of Victoria. Thanks to Mitchell Smith (EUI and University of Oklahoma) for comments on the original version of the paper, to Merwan Engineer (University of Victoria) for useful comments when discussing the paper, and to

Amy Verdun and Lloy Wylie (University of Victoria) for comments and invaluable assistance in the final editing of the chapter. For research assistance thanks to Elizabeth Cassidy (Middlebury College) and Josh Osborne (Texas A&M). A related version of the chapter was published as Patrick M. Crowley (2001) 'The Institutional Implications of EMU'. *Journal of Common Market Studies* 39(3): 385-404. The editor thanks Blackwell Publishers for permission to publish this related version.

1. An excellent survey of recent developments in the optimal currency area literature can be found in LaFrance and St-Amant (1999).

2. Neumeyer (1998) also considers the notion that political shocks could be incorporated as another variable contributing to the factors, which might suggest an optimal currency area.

3. This appears to deny 'neofunctionalist' type rolling integration, but it is clear that there is significant resistance to further economic integration, at least until the accession of Eastern European countries is complete.

IV. COUNTRY STUDIES

(Emu, France) F33
F36

Chapter 11
EMU, INTEGRATION THEORIES, AND THE ANNOYING COMPLEXITIES OF FRENCH POLICY-MAKING

David Howarth

The purpose of this chapter is to introduce to this volume an empiricist's sceptical appreciation of the validity of the major theoretical explanations and analytical approaches presented to explain the move to EMU. These are, it is argued here, problematic due to an inadequate understanding of the development of the positions of the leading actors of the two major states involved, namely top French and German policy-makers. The theorists, often lacking a good familiarity with national political systems and policy-making traditions, invariably ignore inconvenient facts and make simplifications. This ignorance occurs even in the case of theoretical approaches, which incorporate a detailed analysis of the development of French and German policies, including two-level theoretical attempts to explain EMU (notably, Moravcsik 1998). Rooted in a study of the development of French policy on monetary cooperation and integration, this chapter[1] attempts to address this problem—at least to the extent that a study excluding Germany can manage. It seeks to explain the strengths and inadequacies of several major theoretical approaches to EMU, both the more traditional approaches which have been widely debunked, in addition to some of the newer approaches which draw on the tools of comparative politics. These include variations on neofunctionalism/spill-over; related institutionalist/path dependency approaches; those stressing the role of epistemic communities;

liberal intergovernmentalism's emphasis on powerful business interests and margin of manoeuvre in macroeconomic policy-making; revised neorealism emphasising 'voice opportunities'; approaches emphasising geo-political developments; and rational choice explanations including rational institutions building and garbage can models.

This chapter embraces the eclecticism adopted by Sandholtz (1993) and Verdun (this volume) which challenges the ability of any one theoretical approach to explain the move to EMU and emphasises the motives of the different member states, which themselves were structured by EC institutions and increasing international economic interdependence.[2] However, in his attempt to achieve a global appreciation of the motives leading to EMU, Sandholtz ignores many important features of French policy-making, which make some of his own conclusions problematic. This chapter also embraces the approach to European integration recommended by Anderson (1995) and others which emphasises the need to examine domestic politics in the formulation of national interests in addition to the grand bargains on EMU. A theoretical understanding of EMU has to grapple with the profound divisions between policy-makers regarding the project. Most theoretical approaches fail to account for these divisions and the manner in which they shape the formation of national interests—including liberal intergovernmentalism which presents national interest in terms of economic interest with little consideration of the complexity of national policy-making. Moreover, without limiting itself to an agency-centred approach, this study emphasises the important role that leading actors played in the development of French policy: crucially the role played by President François Mitterrand in ensuring that the negotiations would result in a project that made the move to EMU irreversible.[3]

The claim that French motives are crucial to understand EMU depends upon three points: first, EMU would not have been proposed by the West German Foreign Minister Hans-Dietrich Genscher and backed by Chancellor Helmut Kohl, if the French had not been insistent in their demands for EMS reform; second, the decision to move ahead with discussions on EMU relied upon an agreement between President Mitterrand and Chancellor Kohl who met at the Franco-German summit at Evian on 2 June 1988 just prior to the Hanover European Council which agreed to establish the Delors Committee; and third, EMU would not have proceeded if the French had not agreed to accept the institutional design for the project imposed by the Germans, whereas opt-outs by the other countries, although undesirable, would not have jeopardised the project. Only the first point is somewhat controversial. The second and third are incontrovertible.

The first relies on an appreciation of France's position within the international and European economy, but ultimately depends upon an understanding of the motives of the German Foreign Minister and Chancellor, which is beyond the scope of this chapter. Of all the European countries, only France was in a sufficiently powerful position to encourage the Germans to start discussions and accept EMU. Increasingly virulent French demands on EMS reform—even after the September 1987 Basle-Nyborg accords designed to diminish the impact of EMS asymmetry—and the risk of an eventual crisis in Franco-German relations encouraged greater German flexibility. The French minister of finance, Edouard Balladur, presented an 8 January Memorandum to his Ecofin colleagues calling for greater symmetry. While most of the other EMS member states suffered from asymmetry, most were relatively small German monetary satellites not in a position to challenge EMS asymmetry. The British pound was not in the ERM and Italy's demands for a more symmetric system lacked virulence and credibility given high inflation. Thus French demands were crucial to encourage German action.[4] Less than two months after Balladur's memorandum, on 26 February 1988, Genscher produced a memorandum with the ambitious title 'A European Currency Area and a European Central Bank'—apparently to the surprise of most French officials. It is possible that the pro-integrationist Genscher might have presented his memorandum without French pressure for reform. However, the pressure almost certainly encouraged his action.

This misunderstanding of French motives and precise policy positions is due to three factors: 1) the divergence of attitudes of leading policy-makers on EMU and its institutional design; 2) the positive rhetoric of the French government regarding a vaguely defined EMU throughout the discussions and negotiations of the late 1980s and early 1990s; and 3) the enforced rally of Socialist Government ministers in favour of the EMU project agreed upon at Maastricht and the repression of all dissent in the administration. The first factor of confusion has been difficult to resolve because of the second and third factors. Theorists have largely ignored the battles that took place within the French state and government on the formulation of policy on European monetary integration. Moreover, many, including Sandholtz (1993), emphasise the views of presidents and foreign ministers, and completely ignore the views of other leading policy-makers, notably ministers of finance and treasury officials. Crucially in France, there was widespread and well entrenched opposition to EMU in the government and the French Treasury (the powerful section of the Ministry of Finance which controlled monetary policy). President Mitterrand imposed the project very late in day, only weeks prior to the Maastricht Summit.

Neofunctionalism

The official French and European argument in favour of EMU has been rooted in a neofunctionalist approach, which has been widely challenged by both economists and political scientists (including Moravcsik 1998 and Sandholtz 1993).[5] According to this, EMU represents a logical economic spill-over from the trade liberalisation of the 1992 process. Such claims have been challenged by those who demonstrate that the 1992 process strengthened the logic behind monetary integration, but did not make EMU necessary. The inclusion of the goal of EMU in the SEA has led to claims that policy-makers saw a necessary link between the two. While this might have been the case for some officials, from the French perspective there is no evidence of premeditation involved. No Treasury study, public or private, on the economic implications and feasibility of EMU exists prior to 1991—or at least none that French Treasury officials are willing to admit to (interviews).

Several theorists, including Sandholtz (1993), Grieco (1995), Moravcsik (1998) and Østrup (1995), also challenge neofunctionalist claims of spill-over from capital liberalisation to EMU. These authors argue that decisions about EMU took place prior to the removal of capital controls in 1990. In fact, the decision on capital liberalisation was made at the same 2 June 1988 Franco-German summit when Mitterrand and Kohl agreed to proceed with discussions on EMU.[6] Mitterrand imposed liberalisation upon a reluctant Treasury and minister of finance. The agreement was necessary to start discussions on EMU, given German demands. Following the Maastricht Summit, the neofunctionalist 'triangle of incompatibility' was presented as the official technocratic justification in favour of EMU. According to the 'triangle', a state cannot have monetary autonomy, free capital flows and fixed exchange rates at the same time. One must be surrendered. As a justification for EMU, the 'triangle' also assumed that, even though the operation of the asymmetric EMS left French policy-makers little room to manoeuvre and that French interest rate decisions followed those of the Bundesbank, the liberalisation of capital meant that even tighter convergence in the EMS was not enough to ensure stable parities.

There was no necessary spill-over. However, it might be possible to argue that there was a *perception* of necessary spill-over from the SEA to EMU via capital liberalisation. Revisionist neofunctionalists place increased emphasis upon the role of ideas and actors: spill-over is not only about what is necessary but what people believe is necessary. In this way, neofunctionalism can be partially salvaged if 1) the decision on capital liberalisation was *seen* as absolutely necessary following the SEA and 2) French policy-makers *anticipated* spill-over when they agreed to accept capital liberalisation. Mitterrand and his advisers most likely thought that capital liberalisation created an economic dynamic encouraging EMU, in addition to it being the German pre-condition for starting the EMU negotiations. (Several officials close to Mitterrand, including Elisabeth Guigou [interview 16.5.94] have confirmed this.) However, it is unlikely that they agreed to start the negotiating process on EMU *because* they accepted the need for capital liberalisation and saw a necessary link between the two. Still, neofunctionalism at the level of perception remains a possibility.[7] Moreover, the recognition of EMU as a long term objective in the SEA encouraged this perception.[8]

Historical Institutionalism and 'Epistemic Communities'

From the French perspective, neofunctionalism works somewhat better in the context of an historical institutionalist path dependency approach which emphasises both domestic and international institutional and economic constraints as well as the institutionally embedded political and economic ideas that shaped policy-making: notably the *realpolitik* and opposition to floating currencies that drove French policy on European monetary cooperation following the collapse of the Bretton Woods System in the late 1960s and early 1970s (Dyson 1999b; Howarth 2000). Nonetheless, this approach is weakened by the same counter-factuals presented above and does not consider the prevalence of other political attitudes which discouraged support for EMU which are outlined below. The French wanted the EMS in order to contain German monetary power, stabilise the franc and reinforce the 'sound money' policies pursued by the financial administrative elite (Treasury and Bank of France officials). Strong state leadership (*volontarisme*) in the post war period created a reluctance to accept liberal economic principles, notably that currencies should be treated like any other economic good in the market. Currencies were not to be left to the control of financial operators but rather should be one of the panoply of state tools to manipulate the economy (Howarth 2000). This tradition of *volontarisme* helps to explain the French search for monetary stability within European exchange rate mechanisms. However, it also encouraged many French politicians and officials to oppose EMU (see below).

The prevalence of 'sound money' ideas made EMU possible (McNamara 1998; Dyson 1994; Sandholtz 1993), notably because it enabled the French to accept the institutional design and rules that entrenched 'sound money', whereas during the early 1970s the French were not willing to do so. However, this did not make EMU necessary. Top Bank of France officials have argued that the maintenance of low inflation was always at risk in France given political pressures and insufficiently committed governments (interviews, including de Larosière, 26.8.94). The definitive reinforcement of 'sound money' ideas in France thus relied upon EMU, the convergence criteria and independent central banks. neoliberal institutionalist theory (for example, Axelrod 1984 and Keohane 1984) would explain the design of EMU in these terms. French Treasury officials have also argued this publicly since the Maastricht Summit. However, during the discussions and negotiations on EMU, they generally did not see the constitutionalisation of 'sound money' as a sufficiently convincing reason to move to monetary union. As shown below, other attitudes were just as strong and discouraged French support for the project.

Another application of historical institutionalism emphasises 'transgovernmental relations'—the cooperation of political and technocratic elites of different countries, notably central bankers and Treasury officials—in the move to EMU (Dyson 1994 discusses this). The argument here is that those officials with the most influence over monetary policy had become used to working with each other, and shared more in common than with their respective national colleagues. The forums for this cooperation were the meetings of EMS central bank governors following those of the Bank for International Settlements in Basle, Ecofin (finance ministers), the EC Monetary Committee (treasury and central bank officials) and the Franco-German economic council (treasury and central bank officials from the two countries). This cooperation made the move to EMU more feasible but did not make it necessary. There remained considerable divergence in the opinions of national treasury officials as to problems of the EMS and the desirable design of the EMU project (which is discussed below). Cooperation between European central bankers was probably of greatest importance given their role on the Delors Committee. However, their agreement on the design for EMU was due more to their similar views with regard to central bank independence and 'sound money' economic policies. Put otherwise, the central bank governors were more likely to agree to the imposition of the German model which was the sine qua non to advance the EMU discussions. From the French perspective, these contacts were important in terms of strengthening the position of the governor of the Bank of France, Jacques de Larosière, and other central bank officials in relation to the French Treasury, during the internal government debates as to the desirability of EMU and its institutional design.

Verdun (1999) accurately examines the role of the central bank governors in the Delors Committee as an 'epistemic community'.[9] Given the central importance of the governors to the success of the EMU negotiations, this would suggest the importance of this epistemic community to understanding the process leading to the Maastricht Summit. However, this only helps to explain French support for EMU—and acceptance of the German designed EMU project—if it can be proved that de Larosière and other leading Bank of France officials led French policy on the matter. This does not appear to be the case. Mitterrand embraced EMU and then agreed to the participation of central bankers in order to avoid derailing the process given the opposition of the French Treasury to the German design.

Dyson (1994) examines the importance of an epistemic community to the spread of 'sound money' ideas across several countries, concluding that this approach to policy-making fails to explain the decision by key member state governments to support the EMU project. Rather 'the national basis for economic policy ideas remained solidly entrenched' (Dyson 1994: 251). However, it is also possible to discuss the importance of a domestically based epistemic community which helped to enforce 'sound money' attitudes in France from 1976, which in turn made it possible for French governments to accept the imposition of the German standard and the EMU project (Howarth 2000). This community included, principally, the financial administrative elite, consisting of current and former Treasury officials—notably, members of the elite Financial Inspectorate—financial policy advisers to the president, the prime minister and the minister of finance, and leading Bank of France officials working on external monetary policy. However, its influence is of limited use in explaining French support for EMU. The financial administrative elite was split on EMU because of the institutional implications of the project. Moreover, there is no evidence of any pro-EMU activity by financial policy advisers close to President Mitterrand or leading Treasury officials prior to June 1988 and the latter continued to oppose the project over the next three years.

Powerful Economic Interests/Domestic Distributional Issues

The emphasis of some theoretical approaches upon the importance of big business interests to explain the move to EMU—including liberal intergovern-mentalism (Moravcsik 1998; see also Giovannini 1993)—can be challenged by an examination of the role of these interests in shaping French policy. Moravcsik (1998: 380) correctly challenges claims that business support did not exist. However, this should not lead to the conclusion that business interests created the momentum behind the project. In late 1986, Giscard d'Estaing and Schmidt established the Committee for the Monetary Union of Europe which included government officials, industrialists and bankers. The directors of several large EC corporations, including Rhône-Poulenc, also created the Association for Monetary Union in Europe in 1987. Both were created with the aim to lobby governments to support EMU. However, neither actually did very much prior to the Maastricht Summit. Moreover, pro-EMU ideas had been circulating in banking and business circles since 1969. Sandholtz (1993: 24-25) appears to be correct when he argues that the interest group approach fails to explain why these groups were heard in 1988-91 and not previously (see also Eichengreen and Frieden 1993). In France, François Perigot, the president of the leading employers' association, the CNPF (Conseil National du Patronat Français), came out in support of EMU only in April 1989, and the CNPF did not produce any study on the impact of EMU until after the Maastricht Summit. UNICE, the EC-wide employers' association, endorsed EMU only in December 1990 (*Agence Europe* 1.12.90, 5382). For large importers and exporters, EMU was seen as less important a development than the Single Market Programme.[10] In France, business opinion—as well as public opinion more generally—was generally positive, but not actively so, which gave the government room to manoeuvre on the matter. Policy was led by the French political and technocratic elite, not societal actors. Nonetheless, consistently high levels of business support help to explain why the project was kept on track despite numerous negotiating obstacles. This support provided a useful justificatory weapon for those in favour of EMU which could be wielded against those who opposed the project. According to a January 1989 poll, 97 percent of French employers and 86 percent of all European employers supported the EMU goal, although the precise design of the project had yet to be determined (*Quotidien de Paris*, 20.1.89).

Voice Opportunities

From the French perspective, Grieco's (1995) emphasis upon the search for 'voice opportunities' as the core motive driving French policy on EMU appears more accurate (see also Sandholtz 1993 and Dyson 1999b). Grieco uses this approach to salvage neorealism, albeit problematically.[11] He writes:

> if states share a common interest and undertake negotiations on rules constituting a collaborative arrangement, then the weaker but still influential partners will seek to ensure that the rules so constructed will provide sufficient opportunities for them to voice their concerns and interests and thereby prevent or at least ameliorate their domination by stronger partners (Grieco 1995: 34).

Germany's EMS partners wanted EMU in order to increase their voice in the determination of monetary policy, given that the asymmetric operation of the EMS forced them to follow German policy. Sandholtz (1993) incorrectly claims that the Basle-Nyborg reforms demonstrated that the EMS could have been reformed to satisfy French demands for a more symmetric system. In fact, the French saw the Basle-Nyborg reforms—which increased Bundesbank loans for intra-marginal interventions and improved interest rate coordination and thus helped to stabilise the system without undermining the fundamental asymmetry of the EMS—as a sorely inadequate expansion of 'voice opportunities'. The Germans refused further negotiations on EMS reform to create a more symmetric system, which explains the virulence of Balladur's statements regarding the unfair operation of the EMS only a few months later.

Grieco assumes that dissatisfaction with the operation of the EMS meant the necessary embrace of EMU. Top Bank of France officials argued along these lines (interviews, including de Larosière, 26.8.94). However, it is important to note that while the Bank of France governor at the time, de Larosière, represented France on the Delors Committee, he did not make French policy. Moreover, following the Maastricht Summit, many French policy-makers also argued along these lines as a justification for EMU, including Pierre Bérégovoy, then-prime minister.[12] However, even given the German refusal to reform the EMS, Grieco's assumption is highly problematic.

Several arguments can be presented to demonstrate that, although the search for 'voice opportunities' provides a reason why EMU was a logical move for the French, this does not explain why the French embraced the project. The search for 'voice opportunities' competed with other French attitudes and goals during the discussions and negotiations on EMU and did not convince many policy-makers of the need for the project. First, several politicians and officials—including the minister of finance at the time, Pierre Bérégovoy—believed that EMU and an independent ECB would not lead to a true sharing of policy-making power at the European level (interviews with former Bérégovoy staff members and Treasury officials; Balleix-Banerjee 1999; Bauchard 1994). Rather it was their belief that EMU would further reinforce the dominance of the Bundesbank in the determination of European monetary policy—principally because most of the likely participating member states were in effect German monetary satellites, or were insufficiently large to challenge German monetary influence. In this respect, their opinions aligned more closely with those publicly expressed by the Thatcher Government (Baun 1995-96). More importantly, many French politicians and Treasury officials did not believe that EMU along with the irrevocable surrender of de jure monetary sovereignty was a desirable goal in itself, regardless of the extent to which French de facto sovereignty was restricted in the EMS. Moreover, they refused to accept the independence of central banks upon which the Germans insisted and which was thus a sine qua non of progress in the EMU negotiations.

The most directly concerned policy actors which should have been most preoccupied with the search for 'voice' (viz., the French Treasury and the minister of finance) sought a very different EMU project which would have provided less 'voice' but would have nonetheless hopefully ensured less German monetary dominance as well. The French had supported the expanded use of the ECU since the early 1980s to provide an alternative source of borrowing to the Deutschmark and thus weaken the German currency's dominant position and the asymmetry of the EMS (Howarth 2000). The Germans, however, consistently blocked the expanded use of the ECU on the grounds that it was inflationary. They had claimed that their willingness to emit bond issues in ECU and to modify national legislation to permit its expanded private use, depended upon the removal of capital controls in the other member states. For the French this was an important reason to agree to the removal of remaining capital controls. However, the Germans continued to refuse to adopt measures to increase the use of the ECU in Germany, short of the creation of a single currency in Stage Three of the EMU project.

Opposed to German EMU proposals and de Larosière's preference for the single currency approach, Bérégovoy and Treasury officials continued to argue in favour of a 'common' currency approach to expand the use of the ECU which would circulate in addition to national currencies and eventually replace them. They sought the immediate creation of an ECB to emit and manage the European currency.[13] Their efforts to promote this approach were undermined by de Larosière and the other central bank governors who agreed in the Delors Report that this strategy for the expanded use of the ECU was economically problematic. Given the demands of the German government and the Bundesbank, the failure of the French to conform would have blocked all progress in the negotiations. During the course of the IGC negotiations on EMU in January 1991, Mitterrand suppressed internal opposition to the approach advocated by bank governors.

Nonetheless, Bérégovoy and the Treasury did not reject the 'common' currency approach, but rather incorporated it into their January 1991 draft treaty.

They argued—albeit vaguely—in favour of the promotion of a *"strong and stable"* currency which would be a factor of acceleration towards the adoption of a single currency' (article 5-6 of the draft treaty). Bérégovoy and the Treasury presented several arguments in favour of this approach. First, they claimed that it was preferable to expand gradually the use of the ECU than to introduce it rapidly in Stage Three of the project, although they failed to present developed economic arguments to defend this claim. Second, they argued that German concerns about inflation were less valid in the context of the EMU project, given the necessity of national governments to adopt economic policies in order to ensure respect of the convergence criteria. The ECU would be an increasingly stable currency because *all* the European currencies, which contributed to the ECU's value, would become more stable. Third, the French argued that the adoption of a de facto parallel currency approach during the first two stages of the EMU project would encourage the British government—which supported this approach rather than monetary union—to participate (interviews with former Bérégovoy staff members and Treasury officials; Bauchard 1994). The draft treaty advocates an EMI with substantial powers to be established at the start of Stage Two, on 1 January 1994 (article 5-4.1). This was to promote the use of the ECU and manage a pool of exchange reserves with which it could intervene vis-à-vis third currencies (article 5-5.1).

Bérégovoy and the Treasury sought the automatic move to Stage Two at the start of January 1994 with all the member states, in order to ensure that the Germans would not block the expanded use of the ECU. The Germans had sought to place conditions on the participation of member states in this transitory stage—notably respect for the convergence criteria. They agreed to automaticity only when the French accepted that the ECB would have minimal powers.[14] The draft treaty also demonstrates that the French Treasury was in no hurry to move to the single currency of Stage Three. Article 5-9 requires the Heads of Government and State to meet prior to the end of 1996 to determine by *unanimity* the length of a subsequent transition period prior to the final decision on the move to Stage Three.[15] The Treasury likely sought an indefinite Stage Two, in which a European monetary institute would emit ECU as a 'common' currency and all national legal obstacles to its use would be removed.

Macroeconomic Margin of Manoeuvre

The position of the French Treasury in favour of the parallel currency approach suggests that the principal concern was not 'voice opportunities' per se but rather what Moravcsik (1998) presents as 'margin of manoeuvre in macro-economic policy-making'. Moravcsik's claim appears sound because it conforms to the monetary and economic power motives that have driven French policy-making on European monetary cooperation since the late 1960s (Howarth 2000).

Moravcsik effectively recognises the importance of economic and monetary power when he writes:

> The central French economic goal—greater macro-economic *flexibility* through restraints on the Bundesbank and multilateral financing of central bank intervention—remained the same regardless of whether the forum was regional, bilateral or multilateral (1998: 412, italics added).

However, Moravcsik confuses goals with power. To be precise, the French sought the economic (monetary) *goal* of lowering domestic interest rates (et cetera) by increasing their economic and monetary *power* (flexibility) in relation to the Germans. The French sought to maximise national control over monetary and macroeconomic policy-making by minimising the impact of American and German monetary policies upon the franc and the French economy, and by maximising French influence over the establishment of American and German monetary policy. Their objective was to preserve national control in an increasingly integrated world economy, in which developments in larger national economies had increasing effect on the French economy. The failure to improve monetary cooperation at the international level increased French efforts to compensate for this within Europe.

During the EMU negotiations in the early 1970s—despite vague, forward-thinking rhetoric—the French sought the creation of a 'common' currency (the so-called 'monetarist' approach which is frequently misrepresented as French support for a single currency) but more immediately wanted improved European support mechanisms to defend the franc against speculation (Tsoukalis 1977). Such goals also correspond to French interest in the creation of the EMS (the creation of the ECU and the strengthening of European support mechanisms) (Ludlow 1982) as well as French demands on EMS reform. Throughout the 1980s, the French sought to expand the use of the ECU in order to challenge the dominance of the mark in the EMS. Crucially, in the context of the asymmetrical operation of the EMS, French policy-makers found unacceptable the need to follow the Bundesbank's lead in monetary policy and the uneven burden of maintaining the franc-mark parity in the system.

However, the goal of increasing French 'margin of manoeuvre in macro-economic policy-making' did not—contrary to the argument presented by Moravcsik—encourage the French to embrace EMU, to pool monetary power at the European level, in the hope that the monetary policy adopted would better suit French economic preferences. Rather, Treasury interest in the EMU negotiations corresponded to traditional French interest in European monetary cooperation: not to move towards integration and the pooling of sovereignty, but rather to regain power over monetary and economic policies, lost in the context of international monetary instability and relative American and German monetary power. Furthermore, this suggests that Treasury motives (as demonstrated in the French draft treaty) correspond much more closely to a neorealist perspective and a Milwardian analysis: European cooperation and 'integration' was sought in order to preserve the nation-state (Milward 1992). EMU was opposed because of competing values: crucially the defence of republican principles and opposition to the loss of state control over the levers of economic policy-making.

Geo-Politics

Most theorists examining EMU (Sandholtz, Moravcsik, Grieco) discount the geo-political changes in Central and Eastern Europe in 1989-90 as a reason for French and German support for EMU. Geo-political changes are entirely irrelevant if the 2 June 1988 agreement of Kohl and Mitterrand to push ahead with EMU was truly definitive.[16] However, it is important not to discount the significance of these changes. Baun (1995-96) demonstrates their importance in keeping the EMU negotiations on track. From the French perspective, geo-political changes helped to convince many leading politicians of the necessity of EMU to tie Germany to the EU in order to prevent it from turning to *Mitteleuropa* as its zone of influence. It is impossible to determine whether or not Mitterrand's resolve on EMU would have been enough to force French acceptance without German reunification. However, it is clear that geo-strategic changes helped him to convince a French political class motivated by *realpolitik* and greatly preoccupied by German power (Garcin 1993).

Another geo-political motive—challenging American monetary dominance—motivated French support for an expanded European currency from the creation of the ECU in 1979 (Howarth 2000). In the 1970s, French interest in European monetary cooperation was initially sparked by the collapse of the Bretton Woods System and the inability of the French to convince the Americans to re-establish an International Monetary System which maintained stability between the dollar and European currencies. The French sought intra-European monetary stability in order to diminish the impact of dollar fluctuations (and American interest rate policy) upon the French economy. These international monetary power motives should be seen in the context of the larger French geo-political goal of diminishing American economic and political hegemony in the international system. The French also wanted to avoid the creation of a tri-polar monetary world between the dollar, the yen and the Deutschmark. They argued that the mark could never compete with the dollar as an international reserve currency whereas the ECU had more potential. This logic of monetary power and the use of the term 'écu' in France—always spelled inaccurately with an accented small 'e': the name of a mediaeval French currency—made the expanded use of the European currency acceptable even to some of the most nationalist opponents of European integration. EMU and the single currency can also been seen from this perspective. Permanently fixed European parities ended the speculation created by dollar fluctuations. It is impossible to speculate against the euro given its size. Verdun (1996a, 2000a) notes that a large majority of French Treasury, central bank officials, and trade union and business representatives interviewed emphasised this motive of challenging American monetary hegemony. Indeed, this was consistently repeated as one of the major reasons for proceeding with EMU. However, support for the expanded use of the ECU as a 'common' currency to rival the dollar did not necessarily translate into support for a *single* European currency. Moreover, it is impossible to determine how important this motive was in convincing leading policy-makers (especially Mitterrand) of the need for EMU. It was clearly not sufficiently important for many French Treasury officials.

Rational Choice

Different versions of rational choice have also been applied to explain the move to EMU. This includes rational institutions building. Sandholtz (1993) argues in favour of the importance of the search for monetary credibility through tying the hands of national policy-makers. The key premise in this approach was that the adoption of 'sound money' policies was

> the foundation for growth and employment in the long term. One of the critical challenges for governments pursuing price stability is establishing credibility [Sandholtz cites extensive literature]. . . . Part of the debate about central bank independence is that central banks subject to instructions or demands from political authorities will not be credible in pursuing low inflation because politicians will inflate for electoral advantage (1993: 34).

In this sense, the EMS represents a partial tying of the French government's hands. However, the EMS did not prevent several franc devaluations up to 1987. Given German insistence upon convergence criteria and independent central banks, EMU went further, completely shielding European monetary policy from political influence. This perspective echoes the logic for EMU presented by Bank of France officials (interviews). Another version of rational choice theory has been adopted by Østrup (1995) who applies March and Olsen's (1986) garbage can model to explain the decision to move to EMU: national governments sought to transfer responsibility in a policy area that had become too politically difficult to manage.[17]

The application of both versions of rational choice theory to French policy on EMS makes sense. Giscard sought an external constraint to resist domestic political pressures to reflate the economy. Also, given that the franc tended to suffer from speculation, and devaluations were normally perceived to be a sign of managerial inadequacy, French governments had a clear political interest in monetary stability. However, the application of the rational institutions building and 'garbage can' models to French policy-making on EMU and the decision to transfer powers to the ECB is problematic. French policy-makers did find monetary policy politically difficult to manage. However, they blamed this difficulty upon the asymmetric functioning of the ERM—which contributed to speculation against the franc—not upon their control per se. The opposition of most leading French politicians to central bank independence and the attempt to establish some form of political control over the framework of monetary policy-making at the European level, indicates their preference to maintain *as much* control over monetary policy-making as possible.

The application of rational choice to explain French policy-making ignores the very strong republican tradition of political control over all elements of policy-making, as well as the opposition of the actors most affected by devaluation—the minister of finance and the prime minister—to central bank independence at both the national and European levels. Moreover, during the three year period prior to the Maastricht Treaty, there were no major speculative attacks against the franc, no franc realignments—after January 1987—and the French economy was performing well, in spite of high interest rates, at least until the end of 1990. The Socialists blamed the speculative attacks of the 1986-88 period on the economic policies of the previous government.

French Treasury officials did not accept the argument that independent central banks were necessary to maintain 'sound money' policies (Aglietta 1988).[18] French monetary history was presented in order to challenge the numerous Anglo-American econometric and statistical studies which have shown a strong correlation between central bank independence and lower inflation rates. According to these studies, politicians are likely to adopt monetary policies which do not lead to optimal results on inflation because they are motivated by more than just monetary goals (Goodhart 1988, 1993). Some in France did support these claims, notably leading Bank of France officials who, from the period of increased inflation in the late 1960s, repeatedly attempted to convince party leaders of the logic behind increased autonomy (Prate 1987). Correspond-ingly, the bank presented the argument that independence would increase confidence in the franc, diminish speculation and allow the lowering of interest rates. Such economic arguments had greater political appeal apparently and convinced Chirac and other RPR leaders of the logic behind independence prior to the 1986 elections when they supported the Pasqua private member's bill (1985) which granted a large degree of autonomy to the Bank of France. Once in power, however, Chirac's position changed. In the face of the determined opposition of the Treasury and the minister of finance, Edouard Balladur, Chirac's own position on the matter was insufficiently strong to lead to a change in policy (Balleix-Banerjee 1999; Prate 1987).

Posen (1993) argues that political support for low inflation is responsible for both low inflation and central bank independence. He attributes this political support to the influence of a narrow financial or banking interest group. In the French case, this group can be defined as the financial administrative elite mentioned above in the discussion on epistemic communities. In the Treasury, it was also generally believed that the argument linking central bank independence and inflation did not take into consideration the rationalised French model of monetary and economic policy-making in which the financial administrative elite had considerable influence over the formation of policy (interviews). Relative French success in controlling inflation during the post-war period—from 1958 to 1968 and from 1976 to the present (with the brief exception of 1981-83)—was achieved with minimal central bank influence over government policy-making. The inflationary tendencies in the French economy were linked to the excessive dependence of French public and private sector companies upon state-allocated credit, not inadequate Bank of France autonomy (Loriaux 1991; Aglietta 1988).[19] Given these achievements, French governments and the Treasury were reluctant to surrender control on the grounds that they were prone to excess. The admiration of the German economic model—and its low inflationary economic growth—*did not* extend to the institutional structure of German monetary policy-making.

From the start of the discussion on EMU in 1988, Bérégovoy and the Treasury argued in favour of the establishment of a political counter-weight (*'gouvernement économique'*) to ECB control over monetary policy. In the French draft treaty of January 1991 they insisted:

> Everywhere in the world, central banks in charge of monetary policy are in dialogue with the governments in charge of the rest of economic policy. Ignore the parallelism between economic and monetary matters . . . and this could lead to failure.[20]

Moreover, they proposed that the European Council, on the basis of Ecofin Council reports, define the broad orientations for EMU and the economic policy of the Community. Within these orientations, Ecofin would coordinate the policies of member states and make recommendations to individual governments and the ECB would manage European monetary policy. Bérégovoy claimed that the French draft treaty did not seek to challenge the independence of the ECB and the pursuit of the goal of price stability—which the Germans would have refused to accept. However, the draft treaty sought to limit the European bank's margin of manoeuvre as much as possible.

The French draft treaty had to respect the basic conclusions of the Rome I European Council which granted independence to the ESCB. Its Article 2-3.2 therefore states that the ESCB will neither solicit nor receive the instructions of the Council, the Commission, the European Parliament or the member states. However, this list omits mention of the European Council which elsewhere in the draft treaty (Article 4-1) is given the power to define the major orientations of EMU. In addition to appearing self-contradictory, the French project thus seemed to be in direct contradiction with the conclusion of the Rome I Summit, which stated that the ESCB would be independent of *all* instruction. The draft treaty very much reflects Treasury attitudes regarding the goal of price stability and French monetary policy tradition. It maintains a double language in favour of both the primacy of monetary stability (article 2-3.1) while giving the European Council and Ecofin the means to challenge this primacy.

The Mitterrand Factor: The Importance of Political Leadership

From the French perspective, a potentially valid theoretical approach must account for Mitterrand's personal role in forcing a pro-EMU position upon a very reluctant political and financial administrative elite. It is useful to present the specific ways in which Mitterrand demonstrated political leadership in shaping French policy on the EMU project (drawn from Dyson 1997: 64-68; Balleix-Banerjee 1997: 320-54; Howarth 2000). EMU fell clearly into the 'reserved domain' of the president, both as a subject of Community affairs and as a key agenda issue for Franco-German summits. He was assisted by two close advisers, Roland Dumas, the minister of foreign affairs, and Elisabeth Guigou, the head of the SGCI, member of the president's staff, and then junior minister for European affairs. The prime minister, Michel Rocard, initially hostile to the project and mistrusted by the president, was largely excluded from policy-making on the matter and his public opposition suppressed.

In order to advance the discussions and negotiations on EMU, Mitterrand took several key decisions and initiatives, often in the face of strong domestic and foreign political and technocratic opposition. First, in June 1988, at the Evian Franco-German summit, he accepted freedom of EC capital movements—despite Bérégovoy's reluctance on the issue—in order to avoid any obstacle to the relaunch of EMU negotiations at the Hanover Council. Second, prior to the start of the Delors Committee, he accepted de Larosière's arguments that ECB independence would eventually have to be adopted into the French position as a necessary development to ensure progress in the negotiations. Third, during the French Council Presidency, Mitterrand appointed Guigou to chair the High Level Group created to forward the discussions on EMU and accustom national Treasury officials to the Delors Report. Fourth, the president pushed Kohl to establish clarifying dates for the IGC—set at the Strasbourg Summit in December 1989. Fifth, Mitterrand convinced Kohl to accept the automatic move of all the member states to Stage Two at the start of 1994. Sixth, Mitterrand actively supported Andreotti's efforts to push for a more flexible interpretation of the convergence criteria in order to ensure that the Southern European member states would not block the project. Seventh, at the 28 November 1991 interministerial committee—the only one held specifically to discuss EMU—Mitterrand imposed support upon reluctant ministers for an irreversible move to Stage Three for those member states that fulfilled the convergence criteria. He joined with Andreotti at Maastricht to insist upon this irreversibility. Eighth, he ensured that the final decision on the start of Stage Three would be taken in the

European Council, not in Ecofin, in order to ensure continuing political direction.

Finally, Mitterrand imposed French support for independent central banks and a rejection of the parallel currency approach. The president first publicly stated his position when agreeing to the Conclusions of the Rome II European Council. He insisted upon Bérégovoy's acquiescence at a 26 January 1991 meeting at the Elysée and imposed French support for the minimalist German vision of the elements of Stage Two prior to the 23 September 1991 Apeldoorn meeting of the Ecofin Council (Aeschimann and Riché 1996: 227).

Given the president's sibylline nature, it is impossible to understand his precise motives and the precise development of his thinking on EMU. The diversity of his pronouncements over the years on European integration encourage scepticism in treating claims as to his true views. (Several studies demonstrate this ambiguity: Nay 1988; Paolini 1993; Attali 1993, 1994, 1995.) It is likely that his top advisers on EMU (notably Guigou) were in favour of the project—at least they claim to have been *after* the Maastricht Summit. However, their influence over the president—who was largely ignorant on economic matters—is far from certain. To what extent did he see EMU as a stepping stone to further political integration? To what extent did he accept limited progress towards political union only because of German insistence? To what extent was the president—as suggested by Dyson (1999b)—motivated by larger historical considerations which he felt able to bring to fruition in the context of a second presidential term (which perhaps explains the timing of his historic meeting with Chancellor Kohl on 2 June 1988)? These larger historical considerations suggest the importance of geo-strategic considerations and Mitterrand's desire (rooted in his direct experience of war) to bind France and Germany together within the EU through the classic economic route towards European integration. Even prior to German reunification, growing German economic and political power in Europe during the 1970s and 1980s may have encouraged Mitterrand to push for EMU in order to ensure continued strong French influence. From this perspective, it could be argued that the president's historically inspired version of *realpolitik* won out over the monetary power/'sovereignty' considerations of the French Treasury.

It is important to stress that the development of French policy in favour of a fixed date for the move to EMU and irreversibility did not originate in the Treasury. Rather, in October 1991, Guigou, and a negotiator from the Ministry of Foreign Affairs, Pierre de Boissieu, proposed a two step voting procedure to move to Stage Three. The first step was similar to the proposal in the Treasury's draft treaty: with the heads of governments and states voting by *qualified majority* prior to the end of 1996 to determine if a majority of the member states met the convergence criteria and to decide upon a future date on which the final decision—also by *qualified majority* voting—on the move to Stage Three would take place (TEU 109J.3). By replacing unanimity with qualified majority voting, this proposal decreased the likelihood of blocking votes. However, Guigou and de Boissieu anticipated that this deadline would not be respected. They, therefore proposed a second step, prior to the end of 1998, at which the heads of governments and states would be required to determine by *qualified majority vote* the member states which met the convergence criteria and could proceed automatically to Stage Three of the EMU project (TEU 109J.4).[21] In addition to ensuring irreversibility, this two stage voting procedure had the merits of meeting German demands but also helping member states to prepare themselves to respect the criteria.

An important question remains to be answered: if Mitterrand wanted EMU from 1988, why did he allow the Treasury to formulate policies which presented major stumbling blocks in the road to a deal with the Germans on the project details? This should be seen in the context of negotiating tactics. Regarding *'gouvernement économique'*, it is likely that the president allowed the Treasury to make its demands because he would have preferred to qualify for the central bank independence demanded by the Germans, although he recognised that the Germans would most certainly not budge on this principle. This is also likely the case regarding Treasury attempts to expand the use of the ECU in Stage Two. However, Mitterrand and his advisers had no say over the French Treasury's draft treaty. Therefore, the potentially indefinite Stage Two included in it should not be interpreted as hesitation on the part of the president with regard to the single currency.

Conclusion

Despite the impossibility of determining Mitterrand's precise motives, the historical conditions in which the decision to move to EMU was made can still be analysed. The initiatives took place in 1988 rather than earlier or later and this must be explained. However, confusion arises—which Sandholtz and others ignore—because it is not certain what the different actors had in mind as the end goal of the EMU negotiations. The aims of central bankers, treasury officials, ministers of finance, foreign affairs and heads of government and state both within each member state and between the member states differed. Sandholtz recommends an approach that focuses on the various national preferences, and challenges the validity of any one theory. This chapter upholds this modest eclecticism. It demonstrates the limited applicability of both the more traditional theories and several of the more recent theoretical and analytical approaches. It is necessary to explore the complexity of national preference formation in order to appreciate the extent to which the different theoretical approaches apply. Moreover, by targeting President Mitterrand's motives, this chapter upholds a personalities-centred approach which emphasises the role of top political leaders in the integration process—in the context of what Peterson (1995) describes as history-making decisions. Nonetheless, it remains valid to speculate about these leaders' motives in a theoretical manner.

Notes

1. The interviews mentioned in this chapter were conducted in the context of a much larger study of French policy on European monetary cooperation and integration. A full list is provided in Howarth (2000).

2. The constraints created by increasing economic interdependence and the position of France within the global economy are not considered in detail in this chapter. However, these structural factors clearly shaped the motives and attitudes of leading French policy-makers, and the various theoretical explanations incorporate them in different ways.

3. Anderson refers specifically to the need to examine the ratification process (1995: 451). This chapter does not do so because this process is less relevant in the French case. Attitudes towards EMU in France were very favourable prior to the Maastricht Summit and no politicians anticipated political difficulties in ratifying the treaty. Strong political opposition to EMU only developed in the post-Maastricht Period.

4. The interviews with leading German officials and politicians conducted by Ivo Maes (1999) confirm the importance of French complaints to explain Genscher's initiative and Kohl's decision to push ahead with discussions on EMU.

5. For the leading statement of neofunctionalist spill-over see Commission of the EC (1990). For examples of economic arguments that challenge claims that a fully liberalised EC market requires a single currency, see Begg and Wyplosz (1992) and the debates in De Cecco and Giovanni (1989).

6. On 13 June, following the Hanover Summit, when the Delors Committee was established, the Ecofin ministers adopted the directive calling for the removal of all remaining obstacles to capital movements by 30 June 1990 for eight countries and the end of 1992 for the poorer four member states. France succeeded in abolishing capital controls from 1 January 1990, six months in advance of the 30 June deadline.

7. It has also been suggested that French officials were more willing to remove capital controls in 1988 because French success at lowering inflation meant that the franc would be more stable within the ERM. The limited speculation against the franc during the year prior to June 1988 would have strengthened this perception.

8. The Commission under Delors sought to tighten the explicit link between the Single European Market and EMU in the SEA.

9. Haas (1990: 55) defines epistemic community as:

> a professional group that believes in the same cause-and-effect relationship, truth tests to assess theory and shares common values. As well as sharing an acceptance of a common body of facts, its members share a common interpretative framework, or 'consensual knowledge', from which they convert such facts, or observations, to policy-relevant conclusions. . . . An epistemic community's power resource, domestically and internationally, is its authoritative claim to knowledge. To the extent that its members can penetrate the walls of government and maintain their authority, new orders of behaviour are possible.

10. Verdun (1996a and 2000a) outlines how the CNPF membership was split on the question of EMU.

11. The problems with Grieco's (1995) attempt to salvage neorealism are not explored here.

12. Bérégovoy argued that 'the Maastricht path represents a path in which France, far from losing independence, can regain a degree of control over monetary affairs at present largely ceded to the Bundesbank' (*Financial Times*, 13 May 1992, p. 16).

13. Interviews with Treasury officials and members of Bérégovoy's support staff; H. Bourguinat, *Le Figaro*, 17/18 December 1988; P. Fabra, *Le Monde*, 5 July 1988. The French vision differed from British proposals on a 'parallel' currency, which relied more on the operation of the free market without the creation of a European monetary institute to emit ECUs.

14. This was agreed with the Germans at the Ecofin Apeldoorn meeting on 23 September 1991. The EMI would only be allowed to submit opinions and recommendations to the Council on certain matters—including the use and development of the ECU—while the pooling of reserves would remain voluntary. The role of the EMI, it was finally agreed, was to reinforce the coordination of monetary policies, oversee the operation of the EMS, promote the development of the ECU, and prepare for a single monetary policy. On the European currency, Article 109f.2 of the treaty states that the EMI should 'facilitate the use of the ECU and oversee its development, including the smooth functioning of the ECU clearing system'. Meeting in Basle on 29 October, the Central Bank Governors left open certain aspects of the statutes of the EMI, including the structure of the direction; the voting procedures within the Institute; the constitution of its capital and its location. Given the considerable disagreement between member states, decision on these matters was left until later.

15. The French draft treaty (Article 5-10) proposes that at the subsequent vote to determine which countries would participate in the final stage, the member states would decide by qualified majority to determine if at least eight of the member states were able to proceed.

16. According to Elisabeth Guigou, who attended the summit, the agreement was definitive, although both leaders understood that there were many obstacles en route (interview, 16 May 1994; in *Nouvel Observateur*, 1782, 31 December-6 January 1999, pp. 31-32).

17. This claim has a certain intuitive appeal: on the Delors Committee and at the Madrid European Council, those countries most in favour of EMU were the Latin ones—France, Italy and Spain—none of which had distinguished themselves over the previous decades by their exchange rate policy successes.

18. Interviews with French Treasury officials and Michel Aglietta, a leading French monetary economist and consultant to the Bank of France (13 and 18 June 1994).

19. Reforms throughout the late 1970s, the financial deregulation of 1984 and European competition rules substantially diminished this dependence. Aglietta (1988) claims that the relationship between the state and the central bank is not the real problem:

> Monetary systems each have their own particular history. It is only in federal countries that central banks need to be independent of government. To create such a relationship in a highly centralised nation would be totally artificial and would not at any rate provide a real guarantee of anti-inflationary monetary policies, which is economic not juridical. What is essential is that the central bank is not the prisoner of a financial structure that requires it, under pain of destabilising this structure, to monetise public or private debts. It is

the financial structure, which must be transformed so that the central bank is not required to finance financial institutions. The policy must define the general conditions of the liquidity for all of the national economy. To achieve this judicial change is insufficient: what is needed is financial deregulation. This has been achieved in France. . . . The dependence that existed was not vis-à-vis government but rather a structural dependence which limited the Bank of France's margin of manoeuvre. . . . The aim was to organise an open financial market in which the banks could lend without perturbing excessively the interest rates. . . . Internal deregulation and the raising of the external controls on capital movements go together (19, author's translation).

20. *Agence Europe*, 28/29.1.91, 5419. Much of the following information was also outlined by Treasury and Bérégovoy's support staff officials in interviews. This also demonstrated the control exercised by Bérégovoy as leader of the French negotiating team during the IGC and the control of Treasury officials over the preparation of the draft treaty. Previously, Bérégovoy had struggled with Roland Dumas, the minister of foreign affairs, in shaping the project (Dyson 1997: 57-77; Aeschimann and Riché 1996; and Balleix-Banerjee 1997: 332-54, 372-77).

21. According to French negotiators, even without a qualified majority, several countries wishing to move to Stage Three could not be prevented from doing so (interview cited in Balleix-Banerjee 1997: 512).

F33 F36

(EMU, Germany)

Chapter 12
GERMAN INFLUENCE IN SHAPING EMU:
STILL A TAMED POWER?

William M. Chandler

Progress toward European integration has been marked by two recurrent and divergent impulses—a commitment to supranational goals and the defence of national interests. In lock-step with such political tension among states/actors, one also may note a corresponding intellectual 'great debate' between intergovernmentalists and neofunctionalists. For more than four decades, analysis and interpretation on both sides in this controversy have produced significant refinements, yet the underlying contestation of validity remains largely unresolved. Neo-functionalists contend that transnational, functional spill-overs will, over the long haul, increase interdependence and supranationality. Intergovernmentalists, for their part, anticipate that integration will always be constrained by the primacy of national interests. (For more detail, see the chapters by Verdun and Wolf in this volume.)

It is certainly true that unilateral interventions by national governments for the protection of national sovereignty have often produced confrontational stalemates. Famous examples include de Gaulle's empty chair crisis, Thatcher's demand for a budgetary rebate, Danish popular rejection of Maastricht, Greek blockage of normalising relations with Macedonia and Turkey, Spanish obduracy in defence of regional subsidies, and British obstructionism to institutional deepening.

The question of the impact of national interests in shaping the direction and progress of European integration has remained central to the entire range of interpretations of European integration. This chapter, while not intending to revisit this great debate, takes on the challenge of examining the character and effect of German power projection within the ambitious challenge of fulfilling economic union through the creation of a single currency.

European Contexts

The question of German power in Europe has preoccupied diplomatic and military strategies, as well as scholarly inquiry, for over a century. Defeat and occupation in 1945 marked the end of unilateral actions and classic bilateral diplomacy for Germany. From its establishment in 1949, the Federal Republic's external role was profoundly limited by its semi-sovereignty (Paterson 1996). Under conditions of subordination and dependence, multilateral contacts began to emerge, encouraging a general post-war German openness to transnational arenas.

Both international and domestic developments have shaped the anchoring of Germany within Europe. In the immediate post-war era, the embedding of Germany was driven primarily by the security interests of European neighbours, especially France, which had strong incentives to bind Germany into Europe— starting with the Schuman Plan for the European Coal and Steel Community (ECSC) and culminating with the signing of the Treaty of Rome in 1957.

From within German politics, embeddedness was grounded in Adenauer's *Westbindung* strategy for regaining legitimacy via reconciliation and integration. His disciple, Helmut Kohl, has many times invoked the doctrine that Germany must be deeply embedded in irrevocable networks of multilevel governance, international alliances and economic interdependence.

The institutionalisation of German interests within Europe occurred primarily within the Atlantic alliance and within an emergent European community. Over four decades the multilateralisation of Germany's external relations fostered reconciliation and cooperation with its western neighbours. In short, as Katzenstein and his collaborators argue, the Federal Republic had been tamed— due to the reinforcing effects of both external pressures and its own wishes.

Then suddenly the Soviet world collapsed, and almost instantly German reunification took place. The largest EU state and economy now stood in the middle of Europe, with an unknown potential for some greater autonomy, perhaps even for a new hegemonic role, in European affairs. These shocks forced a rethinking of the 'German Question'. First reactions among Germany's European allies to the prospects of re-unification, as expressed by Margaret Thatcher and François Mitterrand, belied dormant anxieties about a new German *Sonderweg* (Merkl 1993: 318-24; Pond 1993: 156-61). The fear, in short, was that now Germany would lose its tameness. Thus the incentives for binding in Germany recurred in the wake of the revolutionary events of 1989-90. The

Maastricht Treaty on European Union (and especially its provisions for EMU) constituted a 'concerted attempt on the part of France, Germany and other European states to create a stronger institutional network to further embed a united Germany in an integrating Europe' (Katzenstein 1997: 252). The question of German influence must certainly be judged within this broader context. Peter Katzenstein's image of 'Tamed Power' expresses a widely accepted interpretation of German external relations over the past fifty years (Katzenstein 1997: 1-6). What may seem most remarkable from this perspective is the relative absence of high-profile initiatives emanating from the largest and most important European state. Indeed, German leaders have typically preferred to believe that German national interests coincide with European integration goals (Pond 1999: 7, 11). Because of the decisive turning points in the development of the European Union during Chancellor Kohl's sixteen years in power, this preference became particularly crucial. Even in situations where the German government might have found itself out of line with prevailing wishes of other member states or of the Commission in Brussels, it has eschewed unilateral interventions to achieve its own goals.

However, given recent developments within Germany and across Europe, there is a need to re-evaluate the utility and completeness of this view. To what extent does 'Tamed Power' still constitute a convincing assessment of Germany's European role? Tameness has been engrained on the basis of embedded multilateralism and is typically expressed through a muted, highly constrained pattern of power projection. However, because tameness remains an elusive and complex concept, its meaning and relevance can be better understood by distinguishing its two underlying dimensions (see figure 12.1).

By combining the dimensions of multilateralism and power projection, we may distinguish among degrees of tameness in power projection. The concept of multilateralism derives from Ruggie (1993). Applied in the German/European context, Bulmer's premise is that 'a faltering but ongoing integration process has multilateralised German diplomacy'. German elites have perceived multiple benefits derived from integration, which has led to the deepening of elite commitment resulting in 'an institutional embeddedness' This is both a constraint and a source of indirect influence (Bulmer 1997: 49). This idea is taken a step further by Anderson, who explains that the German elite commitment to multilateralism has been linked to domestic interest politics and to the politics of national identity: 'European multilateralism diffused throughout Germany and became embedded in the very definition of German state interests and strategies' (Anderson 1997: 85).

There is a broad consensus among experts on the primacy and endurance of multilateralism in German external affairs (for example, Anderson 1997; Bulmer and Paterson 1996; Katzenstein 1997). However, multilateral relations may vary between an active cooperation and a passive dependence, involving an aversion to being isolated on any important policy. Certainly the EU constitutes the most pervasive and fundamental of these power-sharing institutions. In encapsulating the essential points of Bulmer and Anderson, Katzenstein notes the 'surprising

Figure 12.1: Variation in Power Projection

Mode of Interaction
Multilateral

<pre>
                              -
                              -
    "Tamed" Power   -   Mixed
                              -
                              -
                              -
    Compliance --- Assertiveness
                              -
                              -
                              -
        Mixed   -   Raw or "Untamed"
                              -              Power
                              -
</pre>

Unilateral

tact and lack of pressure that mark German power in Europe.' This flows 'from the multilateral institutionalisation of power relationships' (Katzenstein 1997: 294).

Projection of power refers to actions of governments in which we may distinguish degrees of directness and assertiveness. Tamed power connotes a subtle form of power projection characterised by indirect/non-assertive patterns of action (Katzenstein 1997: 4-5). At least until 1989-90, 'Germany's modal approach . . . was not to maximise its return of material benefits' due to a 'profound concern with two other 'hard' interests: (1) strengthening the broader framework of European multilateralism . . . and (2) creating a supportive external environment within which the German domestic model of political economy could flourish' (Anderson 1997: 81-82). German influence, as Anderson notes, 'takes an odd form . . . Germany has projected its power softly' (1997: 80), reflecting a 'reflexive multilateralism', and an ingrained interdependence (Anderson 1997: 85; Katzenstein 1997: 4-5; see also Goetz 1996).

Figure 12.1 proposes a two-dimensional formulation designed to identify the conditions of tameness by combining multilateralism on the vertical axis, which identifies differences in mode/arena and activism, with a horizontal axis that distinguishes between governing styles.

Dynamics of Change

Externally, the end of the Cold War generated uncertainty and crisis within much of central Europe. These changing realities have obviously exposed new potential dangers and security concerns for EU states like Germany. Internally, as well, we find at least two inter-related sources for greater activism and assertiveness in German influence.

First, a unified and thus larger Germany, with its new domestic pressures, has its own identifiable agenda on key integration issues. The internal east-west divide involves new challenges including the enormous costs of unification that have reduced the German capacity and inclination to engage in soft power, e.g., cheque-book diplomacy (Sperling 1994). If German governments are decreasingly willing and able to defer to the priorities of others, we should expect that assertiveness would displace compliance within multilateral bargaining. This might imply, as well, greater tension in the Franco-German entente. Indeed, the health of the Franco-German relationship may itself be indicative of the changing character of German power projection.

Second, post-war German leadership has been consistently averse to obvious expressions of unilateralism, especially compared to other large states like France, Britain or Spain, whose leaders have often defended national interests openly and in confrontational ways. However, a growing German sense of 'normalcy' due in part to the regaining of full sovereignty in European affairs predicts a converging of German exercise of power projection towards that of other member states (Pulzer 1996: 311-16). Normalisation connotes a shift from soft 'exaggerated multilateralism' to a modified, re-balanced multilateralism. The commonplace view is that the end of the Kohl era and the arrival of the Schröder government mark a shift to a more assertive Germany. The generational shift associated with the new majority suggests further that elites, less constrained by the past, are now more willing to assert German national interests.

A Note on Measurement Problems

The obstacles to assessing power projection are considerable. First, beyond definitional controversies, we also face the practical difficulty of measuring expressions of national influence, i.e., power projection, within the often slow-moving decision-making processes of the EU that are inherently closed and opaque. Limited transparency, associated with the democratic deficit, makes observation of power projection particularly difficult.

The basic problem for analysis is one of assessing national influence within a multilateral and supranational world. Constitutive policy, including major choices on integration, corresponds to 'high politics' within the EU. Such decisions evolve through several levels but crystallise at the highest ministerial levels, with heads of government operating in private, often bilateral, discussions followed by summit-like decision meetings in the European Council. We can identify without much doubt the key players and key decision points. But we rarely, if ever, have direct evidence on the inner negotiations leading up to a compromise or consensus. We must acknowledge that assessments of national influence at this level inevitably remain imprecise (Moravcsik 1998: 388).

EMU as a Policy Test of Power Projection

The justification for selecting policy problems and challenges to assess German influence is two-fold: primacy and recency. Primacy refers to the centrality and importance to both the EU and member states. Recency gives the best opportunity to identify changes in influence relationships. In both cases—EMU and Agenda 2000—questions of the extent and mode of German influence arise. There are, of course, important differences among them, but both constitute crucial turning points for the development of Europe. Our task is not to describe them in detail but rather to extract from them an estimate of Germany's changing role.

Battlegrounds

The early 1970s saw steps towards a currency union, notably the ambitious Werner Plan, followed by the common float (Snake). Both foundered in the wake of the OPEC induced economic crises. More enduring was the EMS instigated by Giscard and Schmidt in 1979. By creating a de facto Deutschmark zone, it assured the dominance of the Bundesbank over European interest rates and implied the exercise of German power on issues of monetary policy, visible in the unilateral adjustments of other national banks. As Katzenstein has noted, given this advantage, it is puzzling, 'why Germany's government has been so strongly committed to achieve full monetary integration in the EMU' (Katzenstein 1997: 283).

The failure of the 1981 French Socialist agenda for radical reforms provoked François Mitterrand to accent an activist European strategy as of 1983. Following Jacques Delors' appointment as president of the Commission and under favourable economic circumstances, a new phase in the development of the EC took off. With momentum gained from the SEA and the success of the EMS, impetus for the single currency option gained weight in the 1980s. Critical to understanding why national leaders opted for monetary union was their conversion to monetary discipline through which acceptance of the German Bundesbank's anti-inflationary priority became, in effect, a consensus view (Dinan 1999: 455-56; Sandholtz 1993: 5-10). The push for EMU further accelerated when French anxiety about the implications of German unification intensified the perceived need to bind Germany more tightly into Europe. Although Chancellor Kohl still wavered on the idea, in the critical year 1989 he, too, committed himself at the Strasbourg summit and seized the initiative

(Dyson 1998: 38). From that point on, EMU developed into the dominant issue for the EU in the 1990s.

Prior to Kohl's conversion, the prevailing governmental and Bundesbank position on EMU had been defined by the 'coronation' theory. This view, closely associated with Hans Tietmeyer, the then state secretary in the Ministry of Finance, held that EMU would be the crowning achievement only following completion of economic and political union. But Kohl, by advancing to a virtual fast track, challenged this orthodoxy (Dyson 1998: 39). EMU then became central to the vital linking of German unification to the European integration process. Following his mentor's maxim that German unification and European integration were two sides of the same coin, EMU became a personalised commitment that the chancellor came to see as, after re-unification, his primary legacy.

The road to EMU proved to be full of potholes in part because the politics of EMU repeatedly put French and German interests at odds. France saw EMU as a way of harnessing the economic power of a united Germany, while Helmut Kohl saw it as a way of normalising German influence within a supra-national Europe. Kohl's largely political rather than economic preoccupation with EMU guaranteed that it would emerge as the centre-piece of the 1991 Maastricht Treaty, which staked out monetary union as a binding commitment, setting 1997, or at the latest 1999, as the deadline for achieving this goal.

Leading scholars, have previously evaluated in depth the multiple factors shaping the Maastricht negotiations (Baun 1996; Dyson 1998, 1999c; Katzenstein 1997; Milner 1997; Moravcsik 1998; Sandholtz 1993; Verdun 1996a, 1998a, 1999). This discussion confines itself to exploring further the question of German influence through a set of conflict situations that have marked the uneasy progress towards the single currency.

'Not All Germans Believe in God. But They All Believe in the Bundesbank' *(Jacques Delors)*

The way to EMU was prepared by the emergence of an economic approach long propounded by the Bundesbank. Thatcher's Britain had already rejected Keynesian principles, but when France after 1983, and later Italy, also shifted towards anti-inflationary values, a new policy consensus that advocated a monetarist, anti-inflation strategy emerged (Sandholtz 1993). Franco-German bilateral relations set much of the agenda for EMU, initially between Kohl and Mitterrand, where they were able to privately work out the path to EMU just prior to the 1988 Hanover European Council (Dyson 1999c: 30-31). This summit assigned the Delors Committee, composed mostly of central bankers, the task of drawing up a plan for the single currency. In formulating core principles, contentious matters were confined to a closed process of experts, preventing a possible contagion of conflict. The Delors Report already corresponded with much of the Bundesbank's thinking and pre-settled many basic issues of principle prior to Maastricht (Verdun 1999).

The Bundesbank's credibility meant that its ambivalence and scepticism about EMU was bound to be influential in shaping German negotiating priorities. It demanded a guarantee of stability that the 'alternative must be as good as the Deutschmark' (Baun 1996: 66-70). The core treaty provisions on EMU included: a) Irrevocability, with Kohl himself placing great importance on an initial commitment to the irreversibility of EMU (Dyson 1998: 45); b) Stringent conditions for qualifying in the form of the convergence criteria, which were central to the German agenda; c) An independent central bank, with a statutory priority to ensure price stability free of political pressures, a key issue from the German perspective; and d) An automatic deadline of 1999, at which point EMU would go into force for the qualifying states. On this, the Bundesbank's preference for not setting a firm timetable did not prevail. With this important exception, the overall design of EMU conformed to essential German priorities (Moravcsik 1998: 379; Verdun 1998a: 107-10). France's strategic goal of containing the power of the Bundesbank by creating a European central bank succeeded but only by accepting German terms.

The Exchange Rate Mechanism under Stress

Plans for EMU foresaw currency coordination through the ERM of the EMS as a necessary preparation for full currency union. But immediately on the heels of Maastricht ratification, Europe quickly lurched into the 1992-1993 currency crises. In the context of the enormous costs of German unification, high German interest rates made weaker currencies ripe for devaluation (Sandholtz 1993). In the week just prior to the 1992 French referendum, panic struck European money markets creating turmoil and uncertainty. Anticipation of eventual devaluations sparked speculation in which millions of dollars were made in a rush to buy the strong Deutschmark. Several of the weaker currencies, notably the Italian lira and British pound, were pushed to the lower bounds of the ERM. The British first tried higher interest rates, but Black Wednesday, 16 September 1992, signalled the ejection of sterling from the ERM, a traumatic shock that left deep divisive scars on the then governing Conservative party. The Spanish peseta and Swedish krona were also devalued. The Italians devalued and also left the ERM. The survival of the European Monetary System appeared in doubt. The French and British were most explicit in blaming the Bundesbank for high interest rates and for triggering devaluations. German and other experts replied that more basic causes were to be found in weak economies elsewhere— especially in Britain and Italy.

With the second crisis in July 1993, the French franc also came under pressure. This further accentuated distrust and inflamed a Franco-German dispute over high interest rates. This was defused by a compromise solution to allow currencies to float within a 15 percent range relative to the Deutschmark (except the Dutch guilder), but the Bundesbank was accused of a 'Germany-first policy'. This crisis pitted France directly against Germany and tested the strength of the Franco-German partnership (Wood 1996: 225-28). The crisis was seen as a vote of no confidence in the EMS and in the projected plan for monetary union as laid out in Maastricht. Until then, the European monetary system had created a zone of economic stability, but now the fear was that instability in floating rates would lead to the end of common economic discipline. This crisis increased opposition to Maastricht and exposed previously latent anti-German sentiments in France and Britain and more generally across Europe. In the end, however, this crisis did not alter the German conditions for moving towards EMU.

Ins or Outs?

The official German view on who should join was consistent with a broad consensus found among central bankers and economists on the necessity of reducing social and economic disparities among member states. Success in meeting the Maastricht convergence criteria would determine prospects for joining EMU with the possibility that some states might not qualify. This challenge meant unpopular austerity, in other words, short-term pain (some mix of spending cutbacks and higher taxes) for long-term gain. Especially painful in times of increasing unemployment, the political danger was that convergence anxieties would create a public backlash. In the short run, meeting the criteria slowed growth, with drastic negative political consequences, particularly in France, where massive strikes and protests paralysed the Juppé government.

The unstated German preference was for a small 'hard-core' Europe. Talk of a two-speed Europe reflected a shift in mood from 1992-94 when it looked like the single currency would apply only for a small group of up to six states. German assertiveness manifested itself in the unofficial Lamers/Schäuble paper, which reflected government thinking on the future of the EU, crucially with Italy left out of EMU (Dinan 1999: 174-75). However, France was unwilling to exclude Italy and Spain, despite German claims that inclusion of 'Club Med' countries would force up interest rates of the core Euro countries. It remained uncertain how well member states would meet the crucial budgetary discipline criteria. Several of the various criteria for joining EMU proved difficult to achieve, especially the total accumulated debt and budgetary deficits (both measured as a percent of GDP). As of 1996, only Luxembourg, Denmark, Ireland, and the Netherlands had met all criteria. Because failure to converge would have delayed EMU and provided a severe shock to European integration, between 1995-97 Kohl exerted pressure on both Chirac and Prodi, in bilateral meetings, urging them to push forward with structural and budgetary reforms to meet the criteria.

The fear of being left out was intensely felt in Italy, Spain, Finland and Belgium as the deadline for first cut members neared. The major battlefield for convergence was Italy where Prodi's Olive Tree coalition made heroic efforts to meet the deficit criterion. France remained committed to Italy and Spain joining, while Germany continued to prefer a smaller core Europe. On this important matter, the French view was confirmed.

Negative economic conditions, especially rising joblessness, made the criteria difficult even for Germany. According to the commissioner for monetary affairs, Y-T. de Silguy, grave consequences would ensue if the 1999 timetable were missed. Country efforts at austerity would be relaxed, interest rates would go up, and the Deutschmark could soar. As in both France and Italy, finance minister Waigel was tempted to try 'creative accounting' with an ill-advised attempt to revalue the Bundesbank gold holdings (Duckenfield 1999).

As the deadline drew near, optimism rose that most would qualify. Coupled with strong effort by member states to meet the criteria, prospects for EMU were boosted by the 1997 economic recovery in the EU. Increased tax revenues made it easier to meet the budget criterion. The situation was also aided by a record long spell of low interest rates in Germany, with the Deutschmark relatively weak against the US dollar. The crucial decision (at Mondorf-les-Bains) to announce in May 1998 the rates at which individual currencies would be fixed avoided the perverse effects of currency traders.

The 1998 Report of the European Commission on economic performance indicated that eleven would join in the first round, based on the reduction in deficits. With only Greece failing the deficit test, the European commissioner for the internal market and taxation, Mario Monti, had no doubts that all could start as planned. The European Monetary Institute (EMI) report was slightly more cautious, but also approved the inclusion of the eleven states. The Bonn government, too, approved the joining of all eleven. However, central bankers still held reservations, as reflected in the critical remarks of Hans Tietmeyer, Bundesbank president, testifying before the Bundestag Finance and European committees (4 April 1998). He questioned whether the culture of stability was established in all eleven states and voiced concern about the massive debt ratios of Italy and Belgium. Although Belgium and Italy remained far above the total accumulated debt criterion maximum of 60 percent of GDP, a provision in the treaty allowed for flexibility in the interpretation of debt so that a downward movement could allow a state to qualify, effectively diminishing the impact of this criterion. The New World of EMU was clearly emerging, but its exact shape and impacts were still unclear.

The Stability Pact—A German Preoccupation

The German plan for draconian sanctions for those with excessive fiscal deficits resulted in a confrontation between France and Germany at the Dublin

Summit, November 1996. Only the Netherlands supported the German insistence on firm rules. Finance Minster Waigel played the role of hard-liner by insisting on near automatic penalties for countries running excess deficits. But France, with the Juppé Government at an all time low in popularity, found itself under pressure to resist this, with the UK, Italy and Spain also wanting a less rigid approach.

French finance minister Arthuis insisted on national sovereignty, meaning that ministers not central bankers would have the last word on imposing sanctions. In short, France wanted maximum discretion in applying sanctions for excess deficits. A second point of contention was the definition of 'exceptional circumstances' in a recession when deficits could temporarily exceed 3%. On this, Germany wanted a high threshold and restrictions on the discretion of the Commission and the Council. But fully automatic sanctions could not be achieved without re-writing the Maastricht Treaty. The marathon session (12 December 1996) at Dublin achieved a breakthrough agreement that closed the fundamental divide between Germany and France (supported by most other states). The crucial mediating role played by Luxembourg prime minister, Jean-Claude Juncker, led to a compromise that balanced the German demands for semi-automatic sanctions and French/majority demands that ministers would have the last word on whether an excessive deficit existed. Renamed the Stability and Growth Pact, the result still tilted toward basic German positions. It represented a tough settlement in which the definition of 'exceptional circumstances' under which penalties can be escaped would be narrow.

A new phenomenon in these negotiations was that, although still an elitist process, they now were increasingly driven by domestic public opinion. Although the deal fell short of Waigel's demand for automatic sanctions, which was criticised as a 'fiscal straitjacket and job-killer', for public consumption he was able to claim the deal assured that the euro would be as hard as the Deutschmark.

Subsequent to these compromises, the 1997 election victory for the French Left created the prospect of a widening gap between French and German EMU priorities. Jospin's campaign had hinted at a new stance on EMU, with possible challenges to the Stability and Growth Pact for fiscal discipline, and to the independent role of the new ECB. A crisis was averted at the Amsterdam Summit where Jospin accepted the Stability and Growth Pact.

The Independence of the ECB

The French desire for political input in monetary policy led to a compromise agreement to establish a Euro Council of Finance Ministers (Euro-12) of those states joining EMU, in order to give political direction and advice prior to regular meetings of Ecofin. However, at the insistence of the Kohl government, it gained only informal, i.e., no statutory, powers. It may consider tax and spending issues, structural reforms, policies on wages, and labour market issues, and still could become an influential political force. This marks a partial fusion of the economics and politics of the European currency (Dyson 1999c: 39-42).

One of the last battles prior to the start of the single currency on 1 January 1999 was over the selection of the president of the European Central Bank—the most important non-elected post in Europe. This selection is a closed elite process by heads of government and is subject to unanimity and thus a veto threat (in this case from the French president, Jacques Chirac, or the Dutch prime minister, Wim Kok). Chirac's proposal for a French nominee to head the European Central Bank created a sore point from November 97 through May 1998. This Gaullist impulse carried the implicit message that the accelerating process towards monetary union should not be left to German hegemony. The dispute over the Dutch candidate, Wim Duisenberg, for the ECB presidency led to a nasty showdown between Chirac and Kohl, two weakened leaders with little room for manoeuvre. Kohl found himself under pressure from Tietmeyer and Waigel not to give in. This led to a war of nerves at the May 1998 European Council meeting, which Kohl called 'a dog fight'. In the end, unrelenting French pressure forced Duisenberg to publicly agree to step down after four years, sometime during 2002, for 'personal reasons' (Barber 1998).

Perspectives on German Influence:
The Fading of Tamed Power?

Germany, as Europe's economic locomotive and largest state, is bound to have considerable influence. However, over the post-war era of European integration the extent of such national influence has been clouded by the considerable coincidence of German interests within the European project and its broad agreement with the pro-integration inclinations that German leaders have shared with their counterparts in a majority of the EU states. Identifying German interests has been doubly difficult because of an ingrained commitment to multilateral cooperation, reinforced by a predilection for a non-confrontational style, as encapsulated in the concept of tamed power.

To a considerable extent, German influence has been institutionally pre-scribed. This appears to be especially true for major landmark and constitutive decisions, like EMU (Bulmer 1997: 66). With crucial decisions being made by heads of government/state, summitry tends to be user-friendly for the larger members, especially if they are working together. Germany has tended to be well placed principally because bilateral Franco-German pre-decisions have reinforced its economic weight and political voice. By contrast, Britain has usually been isolated, fighting defensive battles (at least until Blair's coming to power). Italy, which has typically shared many pro-integration values with Germany and the Benelux states, has often remained passive due to its fragile coalition governments. Of course, the primacy of multilateralism has always been conditioned by the presence of bilateralism, especially in the form of the Franco-German entente, which German elites consistently and explicitly prioritise in their approach to European politics. The single currency project demonstrated the primacy of such bilateral contacts. In general, the prevailing German preference remains in place for building consensus and for averting isolation (Anderson 1997: 83) through both multilateral and (primarily Franco-) bilateral initiatives.

The prevailing interpretation of German power holds that, consistent with 'reflexive multilateralism', and on the basis of an engrained commitment to the ideal of a united Europe, which was initiated under external pressure, Germany allowed itself to be tamed. Thus Germany's strong commitment is 'best explained by the European identity of the German state' (Katzenstein 1997: 284). Consistent with this commitment, in designing EMU Germany sought to avoid isolation on confrontational issues. Crucial to German influence was the fact that Kohl 'doggedly advocated EMU' (Dinan 1999: 159). Because of his overarching belief that European peace could be guaranteed through integration, his government found a long-term interest in 'relinquishing the unilateral power ... in the determination of interest rates' (Katzenstein 1997: 293).

However, analysis of EMU also suggests an activist strategy, which became visible during the crucial Maastricht bargaining as well as subsequently in the rigorous interpretation of the convergence criteria, the insistence on enforcing fiscal discipline through the Stability and Growth Pact and in safeguarding the autonomy of the ECB. When necessary, both Chancellor Kohl and Finance Minister Waigel were willing to pressure others, especially the French and Italians (Dyson 1998: 51-60). It should also be remembered that the German government enjoyed certain institutional advantages in the EMU bargaining. Opponents of EMU were not well positioned, and no positive alternatives to the German model were presented in the Maastricht negotiations. Thus, the alternative view of Germany's influence on EMU suggests an instance of assertiveness in which the German negotiators were 'united by a norm of constructive engagement in building European unity' (Dyson 1998: 59).

Sources of change in German influence are, in part, related to internal political change. The watershed 1998 elections created a new majority on the centre-left. It also brought about an important generational change. By the end of the decade all the key leaders who had pushed for EMU had left the stage. The new chancellor, Gerhard Schröder, has articulated a new assertiveness in defending German interests, implying a new, more direct expression of national interests in foreign/European issues (Cohen 1998, 1999; Dinan 1999: 160). This new style, first surfacing during the 1999 German presidency, suggests a conditional limit on tamed power.

The old unobtrusive style was dependent on cheque-book diplomacy (Sperling 1994). Germany is now less able to foot the bill and less willing to defer to the agendas of others. The 'tamed' power characterisation is evolving as a now sovereign (but Europeanised) Germany normalises. Indications of more overt manifestations of German interests and more direct pressure on EU partners are evident in the bargaining over EMU and Agenda 2000. In other words, we may be witnessing a shift from 'gentle giant' to 'less gentle giant' (Bulmer and Paterson 1996). German multilateralism persists but in a more assertive form.

Although the broad consensus on tamed power remains unbroken, with Euro-Atlantic multilateralism still defining Germany's external relations. Anderson has observed that many of the ingredients of power projection remain in place, still based on an 'exaggerated multilateralism and a culture of restraint'. Yet he also notes that the post-unification 'deterioration of the domestic consensus' has enhanced the potential for change in 'a new set of hard interests, overlaid' on the old ones (Anderson 1997: 105). This is consistent with subtle shifts indicative of a greater initiative and some rebalancing of German influence as noted in this analysis.

We are beginning to see shifts in power projection, which seem at odds with a pure 'tamed power' view of influence. Recent evidence suggests that German elites are prepared to play a more activist role and correspondingly have reduced their willingness to defer to partners. As the purely reflexive character of multilateralism has diminished, the German exercise of influence has begun to move from tamed power.

It remains uncertain whether the evidence reported here lends convincing credence to either side in the historic debate between intergovernmentalists and neofunctionalists. The framing of the question of national interests and influence necessarily tilts observations towards the enduring role of nation-states and inevitably directs attention towards intergovernmental processes, especially summit decision-making. Even so, one cannot help but be struck by the paradoxical reality that while the process of arriving at EMU has tended to be primarily intergovernmental, the outcomes have been distinctly supranational.

Chapter 13
EUROPEAN MONETARY INTEGRATION AND INTEGRATION THEORY: INSIGHTS FROM THE ITALIAN CASE

Osvaldo Croci and Lucio Picci

The steps taken in the 1990s towards the formation of an Economic and Monetary Union (EMU) represent a qualitatively new stage in the process of European integration. The transfer of responsibility for monetary policy to the European Central Bank (ECB) means that integration has reached a policy area long considered at the heart of national sovereignty. Besides generating a heated controversy about its consequences, EMU has also given a new impulse to the debate concerning the dynamics of the process of European integration, a debate that had already been rekindled in the late 1980s by the Single European Act (SEA).

To contribute to this debate, this chapter examines the politics of Italian participation in the process of European monetary integration. Section one offers a brief summary and evaluation of the evolution of integration theory. It argues that the two classical, and rival, integration paradigms (neofunctionalism and intergovernmentalism) have reached a theoretical impasse. It suggests that to overcome this impasse integration theorists should cease to be concerned with asserting the primacy of one's preferred variables and concentrate instead on examining *how* different variables interact in concrete cases. Section two retraces the politics of Italian participation in the different attempts at European monetary integration by means of an 'interactive' approach, that is, one paying attention to the interaction between domestic and supranational variables. The concluding section discusses the theoretical implications of this case study.

The Evolution of Political Integration Theory

The term 'political integration' refers both to a process of becoming and to its final outcome. Integration theory is therefore concerned with that rather elusive phenomenon that is political change. The difficulties associated with the analysis of change as well as the uncertainties of the speed and, at times, even direction of the process have often led to the intrusion of subjectivity and political preferences in the analysis of political integration. Indeed, two of the original approaches to the study of political integration—federalism and functionalism—were primarily normative. The two classic scientific approaches to the study of political integration are neofunctionalism and intergovernmentalism. Neofunctionalism was developed in the 1950s as part of the behavioural revolution in the social sciences. Intergovernmentalism was developed in the 1960s as a reaction to neofunctionalism. Both approaches are rooted within the two main traditions of writings in international relations: idealism and realism, respectively.

The Neofunctionalist School

Neofunctionalism can be said to have transformed the largely prescriptive moral philosophy that was functionalism into a scientific methodology concerned with explaining and predicting actual political behaviour. It was the result of an attempt to develop a scientific explanation of the successes and failures of the early steps of European integration and to predict its future developments (Haas 1958).

In the process of European integration neofunctionalists saw a dynamic at work that would eventually qualitatively transform, or even completely supersede, European nation states and replace them with a new political community whose precise institutional character was left, however, largely unspecified (Lindberg 1963). Nation states would fade away not because they were pernicious (as argued by functionalists and federalists alike) but because they were no longer functional as a form of political organisation. Neofunctionalists regarded the growth of economic interdependence, changing welfare expectations, and the technocratic imperatives that went with them as the source of the integration process. They identified the main agents of such a process not so much in the national political and administrative elite (although these were certainly seen as capable of accelerating or delaying the process) but in the social and economic elite. As they had once transcended local identities and allegiances to build nation states, now they would transcend national identities and allegiances and cooperate across borders to build a new political community. The reason for action and the objective to be attained would be the same: to improve the management of the economy in order to increase collective welfare.

Neofunctionalists recognised that at the beginning of the integrative process the decision to join in or abstain from any project would be made and justified on the basis of national interests. Once central common institutions were set up, however, neofunctionalists maintained that a complex pattern of interaction between national and supranational beliefs and between the nationally oriented political elite, on the one hand, and office-holders in the central institutions, on the other, would come about. Such an interaction was expected to lead to an increasingly general political reorientation away from the nation state and towards the new supranational institutions and over time change, if not erode, any exclusive sense of national identity. This development would be all the more likely since to benefit fully from integration in one economic sector would require the integration of additional sectors, economic at first, but also political as the process continued. Such a process, defined as functional and cultural spill-over, was central to neofunctionalist theorising. It was expected that, once set in motion, spill-over would inevitably propel the process of integration forward.

The neofunctionalist approach lost some of its appeal when the process of European integration began to stall in the mid-1960s and thus ceased to lend support to its central proposition. The policies of General De Gaulle culminating in the Luxembourg compromise of 1966 led neofunctionalist scholars to revise and loosen some of their claims, particularly those connected with the concept of spill-over (Lindberg and Scheingold, 1970, 1971). Finally, the period known as 'Euro-sclerosis' led Ernst Haas (1975), the scholar that had first developed the neofunctionalist paradigm, to declare its 'obsolescence.'

The Intergovernmentalist School

As neofunctionalism entered its revisionist phase, some realist scholars who had always been sceptical of neofunctionalist claims began to formulate their own alternative explanation of European integration (Hoffmann 1966). They came later to be known as intergovernmentalists. For them, the process of regional political and economic integration did not betray a progressive and substantial refashioning of international politics and, least of all, the eventual transcendence of the nation state. Integration was a phenomenon that could be easily accommodated within the realist vision of international politics, as a process of cooperative interaction among national interests. As conceived by intergovernmentalists, integration was a way for states to advance their national interests in a situation of increasing economic interdependence in which conflicts could be costly. For Alan Milward (1992), an historian who looked at the process of European integration as a stage in the long evolution of European states, the integration process was simply the adaptive response of small and medium sized states to global challenges they could not face individually. Far from replacing the nation state, integration was a strategy to consolidate it in this new economic environment. Milward thus maintained that the state elite, much like one of the characters in the Tomasi di Lampedusa's novel *Il Gattopardo*, realised that they had to make some changes in their behaviour so that, overall, things could remain the same.

Intergovernmentalists did not discount the presence and role of Community institutions. They simply did not think that they represented a threat to the continuation of the nation state since in the last analysis the latter was in control of the integrative process. On balance, one could affirm that the function of the Community was to help the nation state survive and prosper. As Hoffmann (1982: 21) put it: 'Indeed, the relations between the Community and its members are not a zero sum game; the Community helps preserve the nation state far more than it forces them to wither away'.

Realist scholars who were less inclined to regard Community institutions as being functionally subservient to member states defined the Community as an advanced type of 'international regime' (Haggard and Simmons 1987), as a 'confederation' (Forsyth 1981), or 'consociation' (Taylor 1983). Although these characterisations suggested a more sophisticated analysis of member states/Community relations, they all referred to particular ways of setting up co-operative arrangements among sovereign states and thus also these scholars could be said to remain firmly within the intergovernmentalist paradigm. From the mid-1970s to the late 1980s, however, theoretical writings on European integration progressively lost their specific identity, and, given also the retreat of neofunctionalism, they became part of the larger field of 'interdependence' studies (Keohane and Nye 1975).

The Emergence and Challenge of a Syncretic Approach

The debate on European integration underwent a resurgence in the late 1980s as a result of the new dynamism experienced by the Community. Predictably, attempts to explain the signing of the SEA were, on the surface at least, couched in the language of neofunctionalism and intergovernmentalism. Thus, Sandholtz and Zysman (1989) regarded the SEA primarily as the result of the work of the Commission, and the pressure of European interest groups, the industrialists in particular. Moravcsik (1991), on the other hand, highlighted the role of national governments contending that the SEA was the result of an interstate bargain between France, Britain and Germany. Although these authors emphasised their commitment to their respective paradigms, a more attentive reading clearly reveals that the terms of the debate were undergoing a subtle but important change. Sandholtz and Zysman, for instance, acknowledged that the receptiveness of national governments to the initiative of the Commission (the

1985 White Paper) depended on their assessment of the domestic situation and on the perceived effects of the SEA on domestic politics.[1] By doing so, they were clearly moving away from the neofunctionalist claim that the integrative process, once under way, acquired a kind of internal inevitability and would always move forward. Moravcsik, for his part, accorded 'an important role to supranational institutions in cementing existing interstate bargains as the foundation for renewed integration' although he remained sceptical about their relevance 'in the process of opening new issues' (Moravcsik 1991: 56). He also moved away from some of the traditional realist assumptions of intergovernmentalism. He did not, for instance, derive national interests from the relative power position held by states in the international system but looked for them in the domestic politics of member states. Here, he thought, one could find some important 'roots' of European integration.[2]

This revisionist trend in the literature has continued in the 1990s. Indeed, it would not be an exaggeration to speak of a progressive, albeit reluctant, emergence of a syncretic approach. We say reluctant because as the two classic schools have continued to revise their approaches, and in the process to converge, there has been a concurrent proliferation of new labels to describe the resultant modified approaches as well as the political nature of the Community. They include 'co-operative federalism' (Scharpf 1988), 'confederal consociation' (Chryssochoou 1995), 'multilevel governance' (Marks, Hooghe and Blank 1996), and 'historical institutionalism' (Pierson 1996). A consensus, however, seems to have emerged on at least three basic points: 1) The political agents of integration are diverse, they are situated both at the national and supranational level, and they act for different motives; 2) Their interaction is complex and context-specific, that is, it varies according to the issue(s) on the agenda, as well as the contingent configuration of political forces at work within and between member states and the Community's institutional centre; and 3) The process of integration is non-linear and its speed is not constant. What distinguishes these new approaches is the different emphasis they put on some variables and disagreement on the causal direction of some interactions. As stated in a recent contribution of two partisans of revised neofunctionalism: 'Our theory accounts for causal relationships between variables that are systematically downplayed or de-emphasised by intergovernmentalism and, we argue, these relationships will regularly produce outcomes that significantly impact the trajectory of integration' (Stone Sweet and Sandholtz 1998: 26).

One of the consequences of this attempt to assert the primacy of one's preferred variables is that integration theory has fragmented in many different directions and lost sight of its main research question, namely: 'Why and how does integration occur?' This situation, however, also provides an opportunity for the re-launching of theorising because of the minimal and reluctant consensus that has been attained. Rather than continuing to debate the relative power of different, but all relevant, variables one should concentrate on examining *how* they interact in different contexts, both in terms of issue areas and configuration of political forces.

A point of departure could be the application of the 'two-level game' conceptual framework developed by Robert Putnam (1988) to a series of case studies using the method of structured-focused comparison (George 1979). According to Putnam's framework, domestic and international politics are closely entangled. Agreements at the international level are therefore the result of a two-level game. The first game is played at the domestic level where governments cannot simply act according to their preferences but have to take into consideration also those of a variety of groups. The second game is played at the international level. Under conditions of economic interdependence—and hence in the case of Community member states almost constantly—government officials have to act at the international (Community) level. Often, in fact, the solution to domestic problems can most easily be found through the co-ordination of national policies or the development of common ones. While negotiating at the international (Community) level, government officials are constrained by their domestic-level politics because the agreement they reach must eventually be ratified by national parliaments or through popular referenda. At the same time, however, government officials have the opportunity to use the politics of negotiations at the international (Community) level to help them achieve domestic policy objectives that would be more difficult to achieve otherwise.

Although it has been argued that Putnam's framework is consistent with the intergovernmentalist approach (Verdun 1996a: 62) this needs not necessarily be the case. It is true that empirical applications of the two-level game framework have focused primarily on the possibilities for action by national statesmen (Evans, Jacobson and Putnam 1993). Yet, as stated by a convinced intergovernmentalist such as Moravcsik, Putnam's framework 'also implies that domestic groups have opportunities to develop similar strategies and counterstrategies' (Moravcsik 1993b: 32). Hence, the application of such an approach allows for the study of both national and supranational variables and their interactions in shaping outcomes.[3]

We now turn to an examination of the politics of Italian participation in the process of European monetary integration guided by Putnam's two-level game conceptual framework. We focus on three aspects: 1) The preferences held by Italian governments when engaging in European exchange rate cooperation; 2) the domestic political climate; and 3) the Community negotiating environment. The purpose of this exercise is the inductive production of generalisations that one could then test and refine in other case studies.

The Politics of European Monetary Cooperation and Integration: The Italian Case

The 'Snake': Entry and Rapid Exit

The European Community first envisaged the idea of beginning to work towards a monetary union at The Hague meeting of the European Council in 1969.[4] Two years later the Council adopted the Werner Report, an ambitious plan for economic and monetary union to be achieved in stages by 1980. In the end, however, the Community was unable to move beyond the first stage of the plan, i.e., a modest scheme known as the 'snake' that aimed at limiting the range of exchange rate fluctuations of the participating currencies. Launched in April 1972, the 'snake' ran immediately into trouble due to a wave of currency speculations that pushed outside the established exchange rate margins first the British pound, and then the Danish krone,[5] the Italian lira, and the French franc. By the beginning of 1974, the 'snake' was reduced to nothing more than a limited deutchmark zone and the Community's goal of achieving economic and monetary union by 1980 was also abandoned.[6]

The Italian government had a positive attitude towards the objective of monetary integration and aspired to be part of what represented the most ambitious integration project since the Treaty of Rome.[7] It was, however, sceptical about its ability to adopt the type of restrictive monetary policies that an early locking of exchange rates (or even a narrowing of their margins of fluctuations) would require. Thus, in the so-called 'monetarist' versus 'economist' debate that emerged during the negotiations, Italy sided with the 'economists', i.e., those who maintained that the process of monetary integration should begin with a gradual convergence of national economic policies. Italy also pressed for the creation of a system of unlimited mutual assistance to deal with external imbalances, and the establishment of a regional fund to reduce structural differences among members' economies. The final agreement, however, was a compromise between the 'monetarist' (French) and 'economist' (German) views and represented the worst of both worlds for Italy. It provided for the limiting of exchange rate flexibility in the first stage but with a system of only limited and discretionary mutual assistance (Dyson 1994: 83-84).[8]

Even if the outcome had been more consonant with the preferences of the Italian government, however, it would have been unlikely that Italy could have remained in the 'snake' for much longer than it did. The domestic relationship of forces between labour and capital were decisively in favour of the former. Beginning in the autumn of 1969 (the so-called 'Hot Autumn'), Italy experienced a wave of social unrest and labour militancy that marked the beginning of what came to be known as 'the era of union centrality' (Lange 1986). A succession of weak and bickering coalition governments (there were six between August 1969 and July 1973), lacking the institutional and political capacity (Walsh 1994) to adopt the type of fiscally restrictive adjustment policies that the 'snake' required, responded with a strategy of accommodation (Craveri 1995: 361-480). This resulted not only in real wage increases but also in a profound transformation of labour relations. In particular, it led to the passing of the 'Workers' Statute' that consolidated workplace representation and workers' rights and to an enhancement of the *scala mobile* benefits that came to provide for the full indexation of wage increases to the inflation rate (Locke 1995: 186). Eventually the government sought to buy some wage moderation in exchange for economic expansion but wage increases continued to be in excess of productivity improvement (Flanagan, Soskice and Ulman 1983: 540). Economic policy, meanwhile, came increasingly to be characterised by 'fiscal dominance and budget deficit monetisation' (Fratianni and Spinelli 1997: 215). This set into place a wage-price spiral that yielded current account deficits, downward pressures on the lira, and periodical de-valuations aimed at restoring international competitiveness. In 1974, and again in 1976, the Italian government was obliged to resort to IMF loans, and to implement the stabilisation plans that came with them (Spaventa 1983). Only then did the Italian government begin to utter with increasing insistence the word 'austerity'.

The EMS: Entry through a Larger Door

Monetary cooperation in Europe was re-launched at the April 1978 European Council meeting in Copenhagen at the initiative of the German Social Democratic Chancellor Helmut Schmidt and French President Giscard D'Estaing.[9] It resulted in the formation of the European Monetary System (EMS) that began to operate in March 1979. Its central component was the Exchange Rate Mechanism (ERM) that limited exchange rate fluctuations of member currencies to plus or minus 2.25 percent of predetermined parities.

The Italian government (a Christian Democratic *monocolore* led by Giulio Andreotti and relying on the external support of the Republicans, Social Democrats, Socialists, and Communists) again aspired to be part of the project from its very beginning. There was some minor disagreement among members of the governmental coalition, and within the Christian Democrats themselves, concerning the conditions under which participation would be desirable or even possible. Andreotti, however, handpicked a negotiating team composed of people who were very sympathetic to the EMS project and favoured restrictive monetary and fiscal policies at home.[10]

What had changed since the early 1970s were not the Italian economic conditions that had indeed considerably deteriorated. The new element was political, namely a tentative, but nevertheless broad-based, multiparty consensus about the need for economic stabilisation. The 'politics of national solidarity', as such a consensus was known, had at its base the Communist effort to form a 'historic compromise', that is, to become part of a governmental coalition with the Christian Democrats. To increase their legitimacy and gain governmental credibility the Communists began to preach economic 'austerity.' In exchange for formal participation in government the Communists were ready to support a more restrictive monetary policy and use their connection with the CGIL (the most radical of the union confederations) to obtain wage moderation. And indeed in 1978 the Italian federation of trade unions adopted the so-called EUR-programme that called for a policy of sacrifices and austerity in exchange for employment support policies. In the wake of this agreement, the government moved to develop a stabilisation plan (the Pandolfi Plan) whose central points were the curbing of public sector borrowing and the containment of labour costs. The plan, however, met the criticism of some sectors of the governmental majority and the trade unions because of the inequitable distribution of costs that it would entail (Craveri 1995: 625-62). It was within this domestic political context that the Italian government began to examine the question of participation in the EMS.

On the one hand the government hoped that the external constraint provided by the ERM would facilitate the implementation of the Pandolfi stabilisation plan by making it more palatable to recalcitrant social and political forces. The 'sacrifices' called upon by the Pandolfi plan could be sold as necessary in order for Italy to retain its rightful place in Europe since neither the Communists nor the trade unions would be willing to take an anti-European stance. On the other hand, the government and the Bank of Italy (BoI) were aware that if deflationary policies were too severe they could backfire, both politically and economically. As the BoI's governor put it rather philosophically:

> In the conditions prevailing today, monetary policy cannot replace the exercise of discipline in the decisions and behaviour of the whole of society. When [monetary policy] has been successful it has guided and confirmed the decisions that have been reached on the basis of reason and experience (quoted in Oatley 1997: 68).

In simpler words this meant that deflationary policies would be successful only if a reasonable degree of consensus could be built around them. Linking the Pandolfi plan to Europe would certainly help but might not be enough. The sacrifices that the plan would demand of Italian society needed also be reasonable. EMS features had to be realistic and take into account how much some key Italian economic indicators diverged from those of its northern partners, and Germany in particular.[11]

At the European table, therefore, the Italian government made two sets of requests. The first set concerned the technicalities of the ERM. The system should grant the lira wider margins of oscillation, provide adequate credit facilities, and place explicit obligations for the maintenance of parity on the strong as well as the weak currencies. The second set contained a number of requests (the so-called 'parallel measures') concerning the overall functioning of the Community. Their overall aim was to increase intra-Community transfer of resources to economically weaker countries. The Italian government, however, did not seem to attach equal importance to these two sets of demands. The first set (and especially obtaining a wider band for the lira) was considered essential for Italy to have a chance to remain in the ERM (Baffi 1989). The second set, on the other hand, seems to have been included primarily for domestic consumption, the vision of the Community it advanced being largely that of the Communists. This explains why Italian negotiators were firm about their demand for a wider band, but 'evasive and vague' about their requests for transfers, none of which 'advanced much beyond the stage of rhetoric', something that Ludlow (1982: 257-58) found puzzling.

To support their requests at the European table, Italian officials magnified the level and extent of domestic reservations and opposition to the project, often to the annoyance of their European counterparts (Talani 2000: 24). To consolidate domestic support for entry, it strove to present participation in the EMS as the key to future Italian prosperity. The Community, the argument went, was beginning to work towards stricter monetary discipline and Italians had either to take the bitter pill of 'austerity' or reconcile themselves to being pushed toward the margins of Europe.[12] The government would try its best to convince its European partners that Italy needed some sugar coating but in the end the pill would have to be swallowed.

The sceptical public comments expressed by some prominent Italian political and economic leaders closely linked to the governmental majority— something that annoyed European partners and baffled some observers— become much more understandable when seen with the lenses of the two-level game. The comments were not so much evidence of divisions and hesitations within the governmental majority that made negotiations more difficult for the government, as argued for instance by Ludlow (1982: 208). Rather they were subtle and less subtle remarks uttered in support of the government on both the Community and domestic fronts. Thus, former BoI's governor Guido Carli (at the time head of the *Confindustria*) stated with an eye to the Community table that he was against entry into the EMS because the system was skewed in favour of surplus countries. At the same time, however, he could affirm with an eye to the domestic front that 'if Italy [was] too weak to participate in the EMS, it [was] also true that she [was] too weak not to participate' (Ludlow 1982: 208-11).

Indeed, apart from the Communists, there was hardly anyone within the governmental majority that had serious doubts about joining the EMS. The peculiar dynamics of a multiparty system and coalition government, however, obliged each party, and even factions within them, to distinguish their positions through subtle differences and nuances.[13] The critical stance of the Communists, moreover, was not directed at the monetary integration project per se, but concerned the distributive features of the system that was being negotiated. They maintained that in the absence of counterbalancing mechanisms those features would increase unemployment and lower the living standards of the weaker sectors of society. Among socio-economic groups, all the industrial, commercial, and financial sectors, both private and public, supported entry. The trade unions were more divided. The CISL was for immediate entry, while the CGIL, and to a lesser extent the UIL, shared the same reservations as the Communist party (Talani 2000: 27-38).

The outcome of the EMS negotiations was determined by the bargaining power of the participants. In the end, the credibility of the Bundesbank's commitment to price stability, and its independence, enabled it to reject any proposal that would even indirectly result in its diminished ability to control monetary policy in Germany.[14] Hence, the system finally agreed upon (a parity grid as opposed to a divergence indicator) placed the costs of adjustment on the policy makers of the depreciating currencies rather than on those of the currencies whose exchange rates diverged from the EMS average regardless of whether they were appreciating or depreciating. Italian negotiators, however, were able to obtain the concession they considered crucial, i.e., a wider fluctuation band for the lira of plus or minus six per cent. Concerning the so-called 'parallel measures' all they obtained was the promise of loans for development projects.

Andreotti did not take the decision to join at the Brussels Council meeting on 4-5 December. He chose instead to hold everybody in suspense for a week and then announced his decision on 12 December. This 'pause for reflection' was intended for domestic purposes, as demonstrated by the fact that there were no further negotiations between the Italians and their European counterparts during the 'pause' (Ludlow 1982: 271), and aimed at forcing a political clarification within the governmental majority. More precisely, given the traditional pro-European stance of the Italian electorate, Andreotti presented the Communists with the difficult choice of having either to revise their position and accept the EMS as it was or to withdraw from the governmental majority on an issue that was more likely to cost than to gain them domestic consensus (Spaventa 1980; Ferrera and Gualmini, 1999: 134).

Notwithstanding the wider margins of fluctuation, the lira was able to remain within the ERM only thanks to frequent realignments and the use of such a vast array of capillary capital controls as 'only bureaucrats of planned economies could conceive' (Fratianni and Spinelli 1997: 224). This is not surprising since Italian governments continued to find it difficult to implement restrictive fiscal policies and had to rely almost exclusively on monetary policy for exchange rate stabilisation. Adhesion to the EMS, however, triggered a slow but steady change in the domestic relationship of political and social forces. At the political level, the Communists returned to opposition from where they would re-emerge only in the 1990s as a liberal party. The Socialists progressively distanced themselves from the Communists and in April 1980 returned to take their place in traditional centre-left coalitions. Disagreements and infighting within the Christian Democrats and between the members of rapidly succeeding coalition governments (there were eight governments between March 1979 and August 1983) prevented the implementation of radical stabilisation packages, and the curbing of public spending in particular. Yet, thanks also to Italy's participation in the EMS, the momentum continued to be on the side of those political and social forces that pushed for macroeconomic discipline. At the political-economic level the ERM placed an external constraint on monetary policy. The BoI ceased to be 'subservient to the financing needs of the fiscal authorities', as starkly put by Fratianni and Spinelli (1997: 212) and began to pursue an anti-inflationary monetary policy that would have been more politically difficult to implement had Italy stayed out of the EMS (Giavazzi and Pagano 1988).[15]

After the elections of 1983 the main centre-left parties committed them-selves to a three-year coalition government, headed by Socialist leader Bettino Craxi that made reductions of the public sector deficit its first priority. The government began to resist pressures from the industrial sector for devaluation and urged it to restructure instead. At the same time, the progressive decline in union membership and the consequent ebbing of union power (Accornero 1994), coupled with the increased credibility of the government's commitment to price stabilisation, prepared the ground for a reform of the *scala mobile*. The process was far from easy. It led to the breaking-up of the CGIL-CISL-UIL federation, as well as a split between the Communist and Socialist components within the CGIL. A reform was passed in January 1983 followed by a second one, imposed through governmental decree, in 1984. The CGIL and the Communists reacted by promoting a popular referendum but the results favoured the government (Lange 1986; Locke 1995). At the same time the government also began to liberalise capital movements, a process that was completed in 1990. Having progressively restricted its ability to use those tools such as currency devaluation and capital controls that allowed it to maintain inflation rates higher than those of its European partners, the government proceeded to tie its hands even further. In 1990, in fact, it abandoned the wider band to join the other currencies in the 2.25 percent band, in the hope that this would also contribute to bringing about political pressure for a reduction of the fiscal deficit (Walsh 2000: 132).

The effects of the EMS on Italy are well summarised by the comments of a prominent Community and Italian economic official. In his opinion, the EMS 'reinforced policy co-operation both among member countries and *within* member countries, between such policy-making bodies as central banks, fiscal authorities, trade unions and employers organizations' (Padoa-Schioppa 1988: 372). The significance of the EMS effects in the case of Italy is provided by the judgment of two economists who compared the process of adjustment in France and Italy at the beginning of the 1990s. While France, 'in taking EMS discipline seriously, was able to converge to German performance without the EMS exerting a crucial role', Italy 'was inconsistent in her attitude to EMS discipline and reached partial convergence *mainly because of the effects exerted by EMS*' (Onofri and Tomasini 1992: 96).

The 1992 Crisis: Reluctant Exit

Before we turn to examine Italy's role in EMU it is worthwhile to devote some attention to the controversial timing of Italy's exit from the ERM since it represents yet another example of the use by Italian governments of European monetary integration for domestic policy purposes. The permanence of Italy in the ERM ended after a wave of speculation on the lira that, on 13 September 1992, led to a 7 percent devaluation of the Italian currency vis-à-vis the deutchmark and three days later to its official exit from the ERM.[16]

The 1987-1992 period is usually defined as the 'hard' phase of the EMS given that, unlike what had happened in the 1979-87 phase, no exchange rate realignments took place.[17] However, within this same time period, important differentials in some economic variables between Italy and its main European partners significantly eroded the foundations of the lira's exchange rate stability within the ERM. A higher rate of inflation than the European average, for instance, led to a loss of competitiveness for Italian exports, a decline in profitability of Italian firms, and a trade deficit (OECD 1994: 27). It also led to high interest rates that were instrumental for the capital inflows needed for exchange rate stability, and for the servicing of the huge and still increasing public debt in the presence of a perceived default premium.[18]

The biggest domestic economic problem faced by the Italian government, led at the time by the Socialist Giuliano Amato, was the reduction of the public deficit. This was perceived necessary in order to give a clear signal to the markets of its commitment to reduce a runaway public debt that by 1991 amounted to 111 percent of GDP. Such a signal was eventually provided by an emergency budget introduced in July, just one month after the government took office. In the same month, the government also agreed with the trade unions and the *Confindustria* to an important income policy agreement that eliminated almost completely wage indexation and blocked wage bargaining at the plant level for the whole of 1993 (Locke 1995: 190-93). Finally in October, Parliament approved a bill that delegated to the government authority to reform four areas that were considered structural sources of deficit, namely health, pensions, public sector employment, and local government finance (Della Sala 1997: 25).

The BoI was first obliged to use its reserves to prop up the lira in February 1992. This defensive action had to be stepped up in July because of an ill-conceived public statement by the Italian authorities on the liabilities of EFIM, a bankrupt state holding company, and a wealth tax on deposits (Buiter, Corsetti and Pesenti 1998: 54-55). At the end of August, the lira came under intense speculative attacks and reached the lower edge of the currency band. The BoI continued its tenacious defence of the lira for two more weeks before deciding for devaluation and exit from the ERM.

It is hard to explain why Italian authorities, despite the economic fundamentals, decided to hold on for such a long time to a monetary policy that, besides being obviously doomed, was very expensive in terms of foreign reserves. It is quite possible, as Buiter, Corsetti and Pesenti (1998: 55) point out that 'the stability of the ERM had become an article of faith.' A general shift towards monetarist and rational expectation theories took place across European policy circles during the 1980s, and the importance of credibility within a context where policies could be time inconsistent was firmly believed within the BoI, the government, and the economic profession. Yet, as Amato himself would later recall:

> As early as June 1992 the whole of Europe knew that Italian real exchange rates were overvalued and that the stability was maintained only through excessively high interest rates. It was a situation similar to when the blow of *Scirocco* announces the storm: everyone was expecting a devaluation of the lira (Talani 2000: 179).

Why then, did Italian policymakers hold on to the exchange rate parity until mid-September, when earlier action would have meant a much lighter bill in terms of lost official reserves? Amato again provides the answer: 'We [Amato and BoI governor Ciampi] were not interested in a devaluation of the lira in July 1992 since we wanted the agreement on labour costs and a devaluation would have been an obstacle to it' (Talani 2000: 184). The *Confindustria,* while acknowledging the close link between decline in profitability and an overvalued exchange rate, maintained an official position that was closely aligned to that of the government. As clearly stated by Mario Monti (at the time rector of the Bocconi University in Milan), devaluation should not take place before 'a deep change in the relations between the state and the labour market was put forward, approved and implemented.' A devaluation, in fact, would diminish 'the pressure necessary to overcome the opposition to the definition and realization of the measures' needed to bring about such a change (Monti 1992). The financial sector, while worried by a general deterioration in the financial position of ailing firms, benefited from high interest rates that they translated into high spreads and profits and supported the government position. The trade unions were deeply divided on the issue of the income policy agreement. In the end, however, also the CGIL gave its adhesion since it too, as explained by secretary general Bruno Trentin, worried about 'the extremely difficult economic and financial situation of the country' (Talani 2000: 189).

In conclusion, the government decision to remain in the ERM for as long as it did was motivated by domestic political considerations. Economic fundamentals suggested an early exit. The government, however, stayed in to keep a sense of urgency to facilitate the passing of the emergency budget, to pressure divided trade unions into accepting a hard deal on wages, and to reinforce its ability to tackle the deficit by convincing Parliament to delegate legislative powers. Soon after exiting, moreover, both Amato and Ciampi declared that re-entering the ERM and stabilising the exchange rate at its new level remained government priorities since Italy needed to restore international confidence in its economy and did not want to risk being left out of EMU. This, they hoped, would convince Parliament of the need to continue cutting the deficit and implementing labour market reforms (Walsh 1994: 256).

EMU: Entry through Sacrifices

The European Council held at Maastricht in December 1991 approved a plan for a three-stage approach to EMU to be completed by the end of the decade. In stage one all prospective participants were to join the ERM. In stage two, set to begin on 1 January 1994, the European Monetary Institute (EMI), forerunner of a full-fledged ECB that would eventually acquire full control over monetary policy, would be set up in Frankfurt. Its major responsibility would be to oversee the process of economic convergence of member states. In order to be eligible for stage three, in fact, the Maastricht treaty specified a set of five convergence criteria concerning inflation and interest rate differentials, public deficits and debt, and exchange rate stability within the EMS. Stage three would see the irrevocable fixing of exchange rates and the adoption of a common currency known as the Euro. Notwithstanding the 1992 summer crisis, the eventual de facto temporary demise of the EMS in the following year[19] and a process of convergence that proved difficult, stage three began as planned on 1 January 1999.

In its initial phase (1988-91) the EMU project was largely shaped by technocrats, and by central bank officials in particular.[20] Italian preferences were for a transition to a common currency to be managed by an independent, central monetary institution having supranational powers. Such a transition, moreover, should take place according to a clear timetable, and be irreversible (Dyson and Featherstone 1999: 486-507). The discipline of the EMS had not enabled Italy to reach economic convergence with its northern partners but had certainly contributed to the adoption of a more restrictive monetary policy. Italian officials therefore, regarded the EMU project as an occasion and an instrument—as a *vincolo esterno* (external constraint) to use the terminology adopted by Dyson and Featherstone (1996c)—that could help Italy maintain momentum towards the achievement of economic virtuosity by supplying clear objectives for fiscal policy and a supranational surveillance upon progress to attain them. As Treasury minister Carli, the chief negotiator at the intergovernmental conference (IGC), would recall in his memoirs: 'Our agenda at the table of the IGC represented an alternative solution to problems which we were not able to tackle via the normal channels of government and parliament' (Carli 1993: 435). This meant that Italy's bargaining power at the IGC was even weaker than it had been at the time of the 'snake' or the EMS. In their study of EMU negotiations Dyson and Featherstone (1999: 509), for instance, concluded: 'Overall the distinctively Italian impact on the IGC was modest. The deal was largely determined by others.' The Italians were undoubtedly side players to the dominant French-German axis, yet they were able to obtain what they considered absolutely necessary even if this did not come in the form they preferred.

Aware of their relative bargaining weakness, Italian officials concentrated on what they considered the most important objective: to make sure that Italy would not be excluded from EMU and thus appear to be drifting away from Europe's core.[21] To increase Italy's chances of qualifying for stage three, they opposed strict and numeric criteria for fiscal convergence (Ferrera 1991). They argued for indicative criteria that would take into account different national circumstances and protect the EMU project from unforeseen developments such as external economic shocks or an adverse business cycle. German adamant insistence on clear quantitative criteria, however, eventually prevailed and Italy had to content itself with the introduction of a dynamic and flexible interpretation of a member state's deficit and debt as contained in Article 104c.2 of the treaty (Dyson and Featherstone 1999: 508-33).

On the domestic front, all the Italian governments that were in power during the period leading to the time of decision concerning which countries would be eligible for stage three used the Maastricht criteria to make more palatable the type of restrictive fiscal policies whose implementation could not in any case be delayed.[22] The convergence parameter that seemed more critical was the ratio of public deficit over GNP, which was not supposed to exceed 3 percent. Between the special budget of the Amato government of July 1992 and the eve of the decision on which countries would qualify for stage three, Italian governments reduced the public deficit from 8.8 to 2.7 percent of GDP (Vassallo 2000; Verzichelli 1999). Amato implemented deep cuts in public expenditure, introduced a controversial 'minimal tax' to combat tax evasion, and began the reform of the pension system. The process of deficit reduction continued through the Ciampi and Dini governments. In July 1993, Ciampi renewed the Amato income policy agreement by inscribing it into a wider 'concertation' agreement whereby in exchange for consultation the unions agreed to restrain wage demands to productivity increases (Hellman 1998: 7-8). The Berlusconi government attempted, but failed, to complete the reform of the pension system because of its disregard for 'concertation'. It was thus left to the Dini government to accomplish this task successfully (Castellino 1996; Ferrera and Gualmini 1999: 148-49).

However, it was under the centre-left Prodi government that dramatic improvements took place, to the point that, at least judging from official rhetoric, this government at times seemed to be a single issue one. Upon taking office the Prodi government aimed for a reduction of the deficit to 4.5 percent in 1997, hoping that this would suffice to convince other member states to let Italy in EMU. He publicly opposed any hint of a compromise solution whereby Italy would enter EMU with a delay and repeatedly announced that he would resign should Italy fail entering EMU from the beginning (Walsh 1998: 117-25; Walsh 2000: 136). While it is not easy to evaluate Prodi's intentions in taking such a stance, such behaviour is consistent with the desire to raise the price for Europe not to accept Italy as a member of EMU from its inception. Italy's failure to become an original member of EMU, given its strong link with the political fortune of both Prodi and his coalition, would have given political ammunition to the separatist Northern League that would have placed responsibility for exclusion on Rome and the backward South (Levitt and Lord 2000: 70). Exclusion would have also implied a degree of uncertainty about Italy's political ability to continue with its policies of deficit reduction and would, therefore, have risked pushing a traditionally strong supporter of European integration to the margins of Europe. When it became clear that Spain would also meet the deficit parameter, Prodi abandoned the option of relying on a benevolent interpretation of the parameters by France and Germany and decided to embark on the ambitious project of reducing the deficit to less than 3 percent already in 1997.

Prodi was of course only the last in a long string of Italian political leaders who used, or even abused, the European integration process as a kind of 'salvation myth.'[23] 'Remaining in Europe' was this time around the common slogan linked to meeting the Maastricht criteria. For a while it seemed as if all of Italy had gone back to school and was applying diligently to solve the Maastricht test in order not to be 'flunked' or, as a frequently used football metaphor went, 'relegated to the second division.' The Maastricht parameters entered the public debate to the point that in February 1997 a television program was named 'Maastricht-Italia' and the imposition of an income tax surcharge created no major problem for the government thanks to its 'Euro-tax' label. Prodi's task was facilitated by the fact that throughout the 1990s and including the period when Italy was forced to exit the EMS, the domestic consensus for participation in EMU was impressively strong. The percentage of respondents favouring EMU in Italy in the 1990s oscillated between 66 and 77 percent. This was consistently and considerably higher than the average in the Community as a whole, which hovered around the 50 percent mark (Dalton and Eichenberg 1998: 277). Indeed, such a support appeared to increase as the legitimacy of the Italian political class diminished following the *mani pulite* inquiry. The less Italians came to trust their own politicians, in other words, the more they approved the transfer of important responsibilities upward toward Brussels.

Outside perception of Italian progress towards convergence also influenced the public debate. The doubts publicly expressed by German Finance Minister Theo Wagel and the German press in September 1995 concerning the ability of Italy to meet the Maastricht criteria on time (Dastoli 1996: 169-70) had the effect of rallying public support for austerity policies.[24] It is difficult to retrace the motivations of German officials in making these statements and the role, if any, of Italian officials in them. It can nevertheless be affirmed that German officials could not have chosen a better way to encourage Italians to tighten their belts with gusto. Indeed, had the Germans not made those statements, one could argue that Italian officials should have solicited them in order to consolidate consensus at home around its restrictive fiscal policies.

Besides the favourable attitude of the public in general, the task of meeting the Maastricht criteria was also facilitated by the cooperative attitude of organised groups. The devaluation of 1992 had allowed firms to improve both their profitability margins and financial positions. Thanks to the income accord of July 1992 and to sagging aggregate consumption, the devaluation did not rekindle inflation, and translated into an important competitiveness gain for Italian exports and beginning in 1993, the Italian trade balance recorded important surpluses. While Italian industrialists obviously benefited from the 1992 devaluation of the lira, they nonetheless staunchly supported the process of monetary integration. They regarded EMU as providing a unique occasion to obtain a coherent institutional framework able to force the Italian authorities to that kind of political economic virtuosity that they so often had lacked in the past.[25] The financial sector also exhibited a positive attitude towards EMU, which it perceived as a tool capable of eliminating the problem of 'disintermediation' or 'crowding out of the private credit sector' by putting a permanent cap on the public deficit (Bowles, Croci and MacLean 1998: 74; Talani 2000: 255-58).

Trade unions, for their part, rather than trying to stop the building of a more liberal economic Europe, chose to devote their efforts to making sure that such a Europe would have a social and democratic dimension as well. Since workers would shoulder a disproportionate share of the sacrifices needed to meet the Maastricht criteria, over the 1990s trade unions tried with some success to bargain their support for EMU with an advancement of social issues both at home and within the Community. At home, they received the promise that the savings made on debt servicing would be channelled towards employment creation (Ciampi 1998). At the Community level, they were able to have a new title inserted in the treaty of Amsterdam. It was conceived as a counterweight to EMU and made the attainment of 'a high level of employment' a new Community objective (Walsh 1998: 126-27). They also pressed for the creation of a European space for trade union action, in part through a strengthening of the European Trade Union Confederation (ETUC). In brief, one can affirm that following the shift to Brussels and Frankfurt of responsibility for most economic policies, the unions realised that major struggles would now have to be conducted at a European-wide level. Trade unions' support for the Prodi government was such that when in 1997, the small extreme left party of *Rifondazione Comunista* threatened to bring his coalition government down over the budget, it was primarily criticism from the unions that forced *Rifondazione* to back down (Hellman 1998: 4, 13).

In conclusion, it would seem that both government and major social-economic groups seemed convinced that Italy needed austerity and that entry into EMU was the only way to wed the country to permanent fiscal discipline. Government and trade unions also seemed confident that if 'disciplinary neo-liberalism' (Gill 1998) would prove too constraining, they, in alliance with like-minded forces in Europe, would be able to loosen its strictures.

Conclusion

This chapter has argued that integration theory has reached a theoretical impasse since the modified approaches that traditional schools have spun concentrate on arguing the primacy of their privileged variables. Intergovernmentalists are certainly right when they claim that integration progress depends on the willingness and ability of states to reach interstate bargains. Although prepared by the Delors Committee, for instance, the final blueprint for EMU was after all negotiated at an intergovernmental conference. Yet seeing nation states as the key actors in negotiations, however, does not tell us much about the process of negotiation itself, how state preferences were constructed, nor how they were linked to domestic politics. Intergovernmentalists are also right when they argue that European integration strengthens the state if strengthening is understood as 'hardening' of the decision-making capacities of the state in the sense that the latter becomes less permeable to societal interests. The process of 'hardening' however is complementary to that of 'hollowing out', that is the transfer of traditional areas of competence upward to the Community (as well as laterally to autonomous technical agencies and the complete retreat from other areas of social and economic life) (Della Sala 1997). Hence, the state might be strengthened by integration, but it is also being profoundly transformed.

Neofunctionalists, for their part, are correct in pointing out that variables other than member state executives play an important role in the integration process. To show that a certain variable plays a significant role in a process, however, is not the same thing as explaining why that process has taken place, succeeded, or failed. There is no doubt, for instance, that the road chosen to attain EMU reflected a new ideational consensus on limited government intervention in the economy, fiscal responsibility, and multilateral surveillance. That, however, does not tell us much about integration processes since attempts at monetary integration had taken place also in the absence of such a consensus. Thus, ideational consensus might be a variable capable of explaining the relative success of a specific project but not why that project is launched.

We have argued that a way to overcome this impasse and re-launch integration theorising is to adopt an approach that concentrates on *how* different variables interact in different contexts and have suggested the adoption of Putnam's 'two-level game' framework as a point of departure. We have then used such a framework to examine the role of Italy in the process of European monetary integration. Insights derived exclusively from one case study and concerning one issue area are not sufficient to contribute to a general theory of political integration. Our purpose, however, was more limited and aimed only at deriving some preliminary generalisations. These need to be tested in other case studies before one can decide whether the 'two-level game' approach can contribute to the re-launching and refinement of integration theory.

At the most general level, our inquiry confirms the current consensus concerning the multiplicity of variables that must be used to explain integration processes. Italian participation and relative successes and failures in European monetary integration do not follow from any precise set of factors. The engine of integration does not seem to reside in any of the single variables at play but in the rich interplay among them. Putnam's conceptual framework of the 'two-level game' captures well the Italian experience. Domestic considerations are important in defining the governmental position in bargaining at the Community level and Community agreements are evaluated in terms of the contribution they make to the achievement of preferred domestic policy objectives.

The Italian government has certainly used domestic constraints to try to promote its preferences at the Community table but not too forcefully and with limited success given Italy's relative bargaining weakness. This feature makes Italy more similar to the smaller countries of the Community than to Germany, France or Britain, with which it is often compared. Monetary or other significant economic integration projects could not, in fact, have been possible without Germany and France reaching a mutually satisfying agreement. Britain, for its part, is likely to have this type of influence, amounting to an effective veto power, on integration in areas such as foreign affairs and defence.

Italian officials have also often and effectively used the need to embrace Community agreements to build support for domestic policies that would otherwise have been more difficult to implement as well as restructure domestic interest coalitions. This has been done to the point that European integration projects have often been turned into a 'salvation myth.' One should note, however, that the general public has probably been quite happy to be lulled into this myth, given that its most direct consequence is to constrain a domestic political elite in which Italians often show to have little trust. If this interpretation is correct, the European myth is to some extent a lie that both sides, the rulers and the ruled, have been quite happy to accept. Domestic groups, after all, certainly regard being in the Community as an 'acquis'. As we have seen, for instance, Italian trade unions have not urged the Italian government to remain outside EMU, even temporarily, but have chosen to counterbalance some of its negative consequences by acting at the European level in co-operation with like-minded groups in other member states.

As noted by Dyson (1994: 316) who uses a conceptual framework modelled on that of Putnam to retrace the history of European monetary integration, 'the *willingness* and *capability* of the key actors involved . . . in other words their strategic view and their implementation capacity' was 'central' to the dynamic process of monetary integration. In the Italian case, one can affirm that there is always a generalised favourable predisposition to any integration project. This generalised favourable predisposition becomes *willingness* especially when Italian officials perceive the Community project as capable of helping them attain desired domestic objectives that would be difficult or more costly to attain otherwise. Thus, Italy had a limited interest in the 'snake' primarily because at the time neither the government nor the BoI considered that domestic stabilisation policies were immediately necessary, and in any case thought them politically unworkable. Ten years later, a few key officials (both in government and at the BoI) had changed their views.[26] Hence they strongly and eagerly pushed for entry into the EMS, which they perceived as an external lever capable of helping them redirect the course of Italian monetary and fiscal policies.

Unlike Dyson, however, we would argue that there is no direct relationship between *willingness* and *capability*. Indeed, in the EMS case at least, the Italian willingness to join depended in no small measure on the awareness that its political capability to adopt restrictive fiscal policies was limited. External constraints were needed precisely to strengthen such a capability. The degree of greater independence granted to the BoI in 1981, for instance, in the short run simply reinforced the capability to implement monetary austerity. In the long run, however, it contributed to the fall of those political parties that derived their support primarily from 'payments' to their clienteles through the credibility of the anti-inflation policy that an autonomous BoI created.[27] The fact that *willingness* and *capability* are not necessarily related is also shown by the fact that the Italian governments most willing to tie their monetary hands were politically rather weak.[28] The Andreotti government that adhered to the EMS depended on the support of a quarrelsome majority that included even the Communists. The Spadolini government that took the first step towards granting autonomy to the BoI was a 'transitional government' (Bowles, Croci and MacLean 1998). The Amato, Ciampi and Dini governments that took bold initiatives to meet the Maastricht criteria were formed primarily by 'technicians' and their legitimacy, at least in the case of the last two, rested more on a mandate from the president of the Republic than from Parliament (Morel 1997). The fact that *willingness* might be related to domestic objectives rather than to *capability* also explains the apparent paradox that countries that had the economic capability to participate in EMU, such as Germany and Britain, were either reluctant or adverse, whereas countries that had little capability, such as Italy, were eager to join.

Successful integration projects seem therefore to be the result of international and domestic political factors and circumstances and of the relative power and ability of political actors to manipulate them and build 'winning packages' both at the Community and the national levels. For national governments, this means the ability to be in tune with the concerns of their partners at the European level, and to build what Gramsci called 'historic blocs' around specific integration projects at the domestic level. In the case of monetary integration, for instance, the Italian government did not stress its preferences too forcefully at the European table, given its relatively weak bargaining power, contenting itself only with small side-payments, which it used to build consensus at home around the project that had emerged at the European table. Consensus building at home was made easier by the declining power of labour and by the fact that even labour was opposed only to some features of the project as opposed to the project per se. Although we have not looked at other cases in any depth, we can hypothesise that the German government developed the willingness to move decisively forward on the monetary integration project to respond to its partners' anxieties about reunification. In order to do so, however, it had to overcome the Bundesbank's reluctance at home. Given the relatively strong power of the latter at home and the strength of the German government at the European table, the project that emerged was one that almost fully satisfied the preferences of the Bundesbank. The British government, on the other hand, had the economic capability to participate but lacked willingness because of its limited political capability, both major political parties being divided on the issue of EMU.

Our case study leads us to conclude that the 'two-level game' approach integrates the variables privileged by both neofunctionalists and intergovernmentalists and examines them in a dynamic fashion, that is it can account not only for why an integration project is launched but also for why, once launched, it fails ('snake'), simply staggers along (EMS), or succeeds (EMU?).[29] The approach also suggests that the dynamics and outcomes of integration projects might not be the same for all issue areas, for all countries, or for the same country in different issue areas and time periods. With respect to the future of European integration, the approach also suggests that a 'Europe at different speeds' will be one of the inevitable by-products of enlargement. As the number of 'two-level games' to be played increases, in fact, integration projects including all member states at the same time will become progressively more difficult to launch and bring to successful completion.

Notes

1. As they put it:

> Any explanation of the choice of Europe and its evolution must focus on the actors—the leadership in the institutions of the European Community, in segments of the executive branch of the national governments, and in the business community. . . . Each of these actors was indispensable, and each was involved with the actions of others. The Community remains a bargain among governments. . . . The initiatives came from the EC, but they caught hold because the nature of the domestic political context had shifted' (Sandholtz and Zysman 1989: 108).

2. He wrote: 'Domestic analysis is a precondition for systemic analysis, not a supplement to it. The existence of significant cross-national variance in state policy preferences and diplomatic strategies invites further research into the domestic roots of European integration' (Moravcsik 1991: 55). Because of the importance given to the dynamics of domestic political configurations in determining state interest Moravcsik (1993a) has called this approach 'liberal intergovernmentalism'.

3. In this respect, Putnam's framework can be said to differ from traditional intergovernmentalism the same way as the model developed by Bulmer (1983) differed from neofunctionalism (see Verdun 1996b: 6-7). Wolf and Zangl (1996) have developed Putnam's framework into a formal model and have applied it to the case of European monetary integration to try to predict EMU's institutional design. Oatley (1997) has

advanced a model of exchange rate co-operation that links policy makers' domestic monetary policy objectives to the type of international (supranational) exchange rate institutions they create. Although Oatley does not refer to Putnam, his model can be regarded as an adaptation of Putnam's conceptual framework to the study of exchange rate negotiations.

4. The Community did not devote much attention to monetary questions in its early years because the common market operated with at least one main component of a monetary union, i.e., fixed exchange rates, by virtue of its being part of the Bretton Woods system. When this system began to collapse in the late 1960s, it became evident that exchange rate fluctuations posed a problem for what was becoming a progressively more integrated market, and were particularly disruptive for the administration of the Common Agricultural Policy (CAP).

5. The four countries that were to join the Community in 1973 also participated in the 'snake'.

6. This first attempt at monetary integration derailed primarily for two reasons. First, there was the objective difficulty of trying to establish a regional zone of stability in the midst of global monetary turbulence. Second, there was the fact that in the 1970s European governments held very different opinions and preferences about the choice of appropriate economic policies to deal with inflation and economic recession. While Germany pursued a restrictive monetary policy, for instance, the British, French, and Italian governments implemented expansionary policies to try to encourage growth and employment. In 1975, asked to review the prospects for achieving economic and monetary union by 1980, former commissioner Marjolin concluded:

> Europe is no nearer to EMU than in 1969. In fact, if there has been any movement it has been backward. The Europe of the 1960s represented a relatively harmonious economic and monetary entity which was undone in the course of recent years; national economic and monetary policies have never in 25 years been more discordant, more divergent, than they are today (quoted in Dyson 1994: 77).

For the history of this first attempt at monetary integration, see also Tsoukalis (1977) and Kruse (1980).

7. It should be noted, however, that at first Italy tended to regard European monetary integration as an addition, as opposed to an alternative, to monetary cooperation at the Atlantic level. The Italian government wanted to avoid the danger that monetary integration be an obstacle to British entry and thus become an instrument of Franco-German domination of the Community. This attitude changed when in 1970 the Italian current account showed a deficit after years of surpluses. The Italian government then began to look favourably upon the idea of creating a Community reserve currency that would counterbalance the role of the US dollar as well as the establishment of Community monetary support mechanisms (Tsoukalis 1977: 81, 89).

8. The compromise reflected the strength of Germany, and the Bundesbank in particular, in the negotiations. As a surplus country, Germany feared that it might not be able to force deficit countries to take any corrective measures and be stuck with the 'awkward dilemma of either financing the deficit of other countries or accepting a higher rate of inflation at home' (Tsoukalis 1977: 93).

9. According to Oatley (1997: 48-56), the initiative of Schmidt and Giscard was based primarily on their domestic policy preferences. Schmidt was inclined to implement an expansionary policy in view of the 1980 elections and to accommodate labour demands to stimulate employment. He was constrained by his coalition government and by the Bundesbank's traditional commitment to price stability. He therefore regarded a European exchange rate cooperation system as an instrument that could help him attain his domestic objective. As he saw it, a European exchange rate system would slow the appreciation of the deutchmark, and thus help German industry retain competitiveness without any need to act on wages. If properly designed, moreover, such a system might also constrain the Bundesbank and push it to adopt a looser monetary policy. It was for this reason that Schmidt's proposal contained a number of provisions for the common support of exchange rates, most notably a partial pooling of official reserves and the creation of a new European reserve asset (Ludlow 1982: 92). In the case of France, Giscard and his prime minister Barre had embarked on a radical policy of price stability based on monetary targeting in an effort to tackle the wage-price spiral that had characterised the French economy after 1968. For Giscard, to commit the franc to a European exchange rate system was a way to enlist French industry in the struggle against inflation by convincing it that it could no longer rely on devaluations. Since trying to pass on wage increases through higher prices would have reduced its competitiveness on the world market, French industry could be expected to resist any wage increase not reflecting improvements in productivity.

10. According to Ludlow (1982: 148), 'Italian negotiators, from Mr. Andreotti downwards, began with the presumption that participation in any new Community initiative was the proper objective, which could only be abandoned if the material obstacles were such that even special transitional arrangements could not overcome them'. The main members of the negotiating team were Treasury Minister E. M. Pandolfi, the governor and deputy governor of the central bank, C. Baffi and C. A. Ciampi, and former EC commissioner R. Ruggiero.

11. In the period 1974-78, for instance, the annual rate of inflation in Italy had averaged 17.2 percent against 4.9 in Germany. The annual growth rate of productivity had averaged 0.8 percent against the 3.5 percent of Germany. See Oatley (1997: 50, Table 3).

12. Given the traditional pro-European stance of Italian political forces and public in general, joining the EMS was presented as 'the necessity of not missing the European train', 'the appointment with Europe', 'proof of Italian maturity and/or responsibility', et cetera.

13. Sceptical statements similar to those made by Carli were made also by foreign trade minister R. Ossola and agriculture minister G. Marcora, both of whom represented social sectors that would be directly affected by the outcome of negotiations. Besides supporting the government at the European table they undoubtedly also had in mind their own constituencies.

14. See Oatley (1997: 62-63) for a recollection on the part of a member of the Monetary Committee of the Bundesbank officials' utter commitment to their position.

15. Basically the EMS allowed the BoI to tackle inflation by letting the real value of the lira appreciate relative to the currencies of other EMS members. Between 1978 and 1990, for instance, cumulative inflation was 98 percent higher in Italy than in Germany while the nominal depreciation of the lira in relation to the deutchmark was 56 percent.

Hence the lira appreciated with respect to the deutchmark by 42 percent (Fratianni and Spinelli (1997: 236). It should also be pointed out that in July 1981, the BoI was relieved of the obligation to act as a residual buyer at Treasury bills auctions and began its slow process of acquiring complete independence from the government (Bowles, Croci and MacLean 1998).

16. The crisis of September of 1992, in various degrees, affected all the currencies within the EMS as well as those that, while formally outside the monetary system arrangement, were linked to it (such as the currencies of the Nordic countries). The lira joined again the ERM on 25 November 1996, in order to fulfil one of the requirements of the Maastricht treaty for eligibility in the EMU, namely a two-year period of exchange rate stability within the EMS bands.

17. Some analysts (McNamara 1998: 160-61; Dyson 1994: 121-23) attribute this increased stability of the EMS in this period to the 1987 so-called Basle-Nyborg agreement that eased a bit the burden of adjustment on the weak currency states.

18. Moody ratings on Italian public debt were lowered, for the second time in little more than one year, in August 1992 (OECD 1992). This situation was worsened by the consequences of German reunification that led to, among other things, an increase in the German interest rate (Buiter, Corsetti and Pesenti 1998).

19. In August 1993, most of the countries still in the ERM agreed to a widening of its bands to 15 percent. Only the deutchmark and the Dutch guilder remained in the 2.25 percent band.

20. BoI governor Ciampi was the chief Italian official involved in the working of the Delors Committee. Once the EMU project entered the sphere of Ecofin and the European Council its dossier became the responsibility of a steering group comprising BoI deputy director general T. Padoa-Schioppa, Treasury director general M. Sarcinelli (later replaced by M. Draghi), director general for economic affairs in the foreign ministry V. D'Archirafi (later replaced by U. Jannuzzi) and diplomatic councillor to the prime minister U. Vattani (Dyson and Featherstone 1999: 490).

21. Unlike what had happened in the case of the 'snake' and the EMS, this time Italy did not make any request for parallel measures that would provide economic aid from EC funds to help weaker member states with the convergence process. The reason for this, however, might have been that given the level of its GDP per capita Italy could hardly expect to qualify for any such monies.

22. As an Italian observer has noted:

> In Italy, the prospect of joining the EMU and hence the obligation of meeting the Maastrich criteria has concentrated attention on the need for fundamental structural reforms that otherwise did not have and would not have found consensus. . . . The prospect of EMU has legitimised unpopular measures that otherwise would have met with even bigger resistance by the pressure groups touched by them (Nuti 1997: 16).

23. Former BoI's governor, *Confindustria*'s president and treasury minister G. Carli (1993) would point out in his memoirs that it was this 'myth' that compelled, and enabled, Italian governments to modernise and liberalise the Italian economy.

24. Former Italian ambassador Paolo Janni (1999) has called this 'the Guadalupe syndrome.' The reference is to the meeting French president Giscard D'Estaing convened in Guadalupe in the 1970s and to which Italy was not invited. That exclusion was seen as

an insult by Italian public opinion and gave new impetus to Italy's quest for recognition at the same level as the UK and France. The Italian reaction is also an example of what Putnam (1988) calls 'reverberation', i.e., a reaction by domestic groups to an action by a foreign country (in this case a public statement by German officials).

25. Giovanni Agnelli co-founded the international Association for the Monetary Union of Europe in the late 1980s. Sergio Pininfarina, then *Confindustria*'s President, was its managing director in Italy (Talani 2000: 249-50).

26. There is hardly any doubt that these officials developed their views primarily as a result of their participation in many Community and other international forums dealing with monetary issues. Also in the Italian case, in other words, monetarist epistemic communities played an important role, as some neofunctionalists would argue, in convincing the political elite to embrace neoliberal policies.

27. Both Bufacchi (1996) and Guzzini (1995) provide an explanation of the political turmoil of the early 1990s based on similar arguments.

28. This finding is consistent with the theory advanced by Goodman (1991) that the governments most willing to grant independence to central banks are (monetary and fiscally conservative) governments that do not expect to be re-elected or stay in power for long. Hence derives their preference for tying not only their hands but also, and most importantly, those of their successors.

29. On the outcomes of integration projects, a topic neglected by neofunctionalists and intergovernmentalists alike, see Mattli (1999). Although couched in rational choice terminology, Mattli's approach represents a combination of neofunctionalism and intergovernmentalism.

$F33$
$F36$

Chapter 14
CONCLUSION:
LESSONS FROM EMU FOR THEORISING
EUROPEAN INTEGRATION

Amy Verdun and Lloy Wylie

The process of European integration is a complex one. It takes place at different levels, with different actors at different points in time. The range of the theories of European integration that have been developed over the past four decades display the diversity of this process. This volume has shown that creating an Economic and Monetary Union in the European Union is an equally complex matter.

This volume started off with a question concerning the usefulness of the traditional integration theories. The analyses in various chapters show that neofunctionalism and intergovernmentalism are each capable of describing parts, though not all, of the process. The chapters identify the need to be eclectic, to be willing to draw on different theoretical traditions to explain different parts of the many-sided process. The more recent integration theories, such as the multilevel governance approach and historical institutionalism, offer a useful addition to the neofunctionalism/intergovernmentalism dichotomy. The more recent approaches provide additional theoretical lenses when putting parts of the process under our proverbial scientific microscope. Each of these approaches, traditional and newer ones, aim at understanding the integration process. Sometimes they focus on the meta-level, other times they merely aspire to understand the process by looking at it from a certain angle (e.g., the role of particular actors, or of a particular part of the process, et cetera). Thus from

242 Amy Verdun and Lloy Wylie

these analyses we draw the conclusion that European integration scholars need to be open-minded and conscious of the risks of rigorously applying one theory or another to the integration process. One needs to remain sensitive to theoretical differences and to the need to broaden our horizon, in light of the material presented, and, where necessary, dare to adopt an eclectic approach.

The case of EMU also shows that there are a wide variety of issues at stake, many of which are intertwined with wider global trends. EMU also impacts differently at the various levels. One needs merely to reflect on the difference between what happens within member states and at the EU level to appreciate the impact of EMU. At the domestic level, EMU fits into the broader change of policy-making regimes regarding the role of monetary policy-making. Some refer to this as neoliberalism, others as a focus on price stability and sound finance. EMU also has come at a time when various structural changes were deemed necessary at the domestic level, regardless of the need to deepen European integration. Such changes were with regard to restructuring the labour market, but also the role of the government. The privatisation and deregulation process of the 1980s preceded and followed the EMU initiative. EMU, of course, also changes the formal and actual policy-making relationship between the domestic monetary authorities (i.e., the minister of finance and the central bank). With monetary policy-making autonomy transferred to the European Central Bank (ECB) in Frankfurt, and with the terms of the Stability and Growth Pact, individual domestic governments have fewer tools at their disposal to address imbalances in the domestic economy. At the European level the coming of the euro leads to questions about who is responsible for the overall outcome of macroeconomic policy-making in the EU. What happens if things go wrong? Who will then be accountable? What kinds of relationships should there be between the ECB, the other EU institutions, and the Ecofin Council? As the chapters in this volume have shown, EMU impacts the institutions and policies of the EU in a broad sense. Let us now turn to the main arguments made in those chapters.

The first section of the book looks at integration theory and its ability to explain the process of European integration. The chapters in this section all agree that no single theoretical approach is adequate to explain all parts of the integration process. Instead, the three authors in this section argue the need for a mix, which considers the important factors and mechanisms identified by different theoretical traditions.

In chapter 2, Verdun argues that rather than determining an overall theoretical framework that identifies a set of important actors and mechanisms, it is more useful to take a flexible approach that uses empirical case studies to determine the driving forces behind integration. Verdun asserts that these will be different for different areas and periods in the process of European integration. In this sense, it is necessary to consider all the significant actors and processes identified in the two schools of integration theory, namely intergovernmentalism and neofunctionalism, to ensure a more complete understanding of the complex and multifaceted nature of European integration. At the same time, in adopting this eclectic theoretical approach, one must go further than either of these schools of thought by including additional factors such as changes in the global political economy.

Wolf continues with the theme set by Verdun that the two theoretical approaches can be brought together, as they address different parts of the integration process. Wolf argues that interests and preferences are heavily influenced by socio-economic structures, which tend to be overlooked by traditional intergovernmentalist and neofunctionalist analysis. These structural factors determine the willingness of nation states to co-operate. The more divergent socio-economic factors are, the less likely nation states will see co-operative solutions as a viable alternative. When there is greater convergence, spill-over effects seem logical and national interests are brought closer together, thus leading to an increased likelihood of further integration. Wolf argues that by looking at the voluntary elements of actor preferences, and by theorising interest development, an amalgamated approach avoids the determinism of neofunctionalist theory and can address integration failures. The incorporation of international economic factors into the understanding of preferences of nation state leaders, which tends to be overlooked by intergovernmentalists, also allows for a more complete analysis.

The chapter by van Esch further addresses this issue of the weakness of theories of national preferences. She argues that preferences are assumed rather than systematically theorised. International relations theories assume that international cooperation occurs when a common interest arises, but theories these fail to explain the cause of this convergence of interests. The reason for this theoretical weakness is that international relations theorists only examine international factors, whilst domestic approaches only look at national characteristics. Once again the argument here is that an amalgamated approach that considers more variables will lead to a more thorough analysis, in this case of how national preferences develop.

This theoretical section sets an agenda for the rest of the chapters to adopt a more open and inclusive theoretical approach, in which multiple factors are considered. Verdun reminds us that some actors and mechanisms are more important than others, and that these should be determined through case study analyses, rather than by a predetermined set of significant factors, which influence the direction of the research. Wolf argues that we need to analyse the socio-economic background for patterns of convergence and divergence, which can provide us with an appreciation for the actors' sentiment for or against co-operative solutions. Van Esch reiterates that neither national nor international factors alone can explain national preferences, and therefore that we must consider both realms in order to develop a comprehensive understanding of the choices made by nation states to further the integration process.

These authors remind us that EMU, a complicated arrangement within the broader process of European integration, has not been adequately analysed by a single theory. Theoretical flexibility—evidenced in the approach of mid-range theories such as multilevel governance—combined with the willingness to

Amy Verdun and Lloy Wylie

examine multiple factors can lead to a more comprehensive understanding, if only of part of the integration process.

Section II of the book examines the role of ideas and identities in the development of the integration process. Wylie argues that neoliberal economic preferences combined with a common interest in creating economic stability under the pressures of the global economy brought about a convergence among nation states in Europe. Cooperative action would allow nation states to fare better in the socio-economic conditions that they all were facing. Therefore, Wylie argues that the development of EMU can be seen partly as a result of a process of not only socio-economic convergence, but also of ideational convergence along a neoliberal economic paradigm.

Dyson's chapter recognises this same trend of neoliberal convergence in the development of EMU, but stresses that it represents a two-way process. Nation states are being Europeanised through the development of EMU and the criteria leading up to it, while at the same time, nation states are constructing EMU at a national level that is distinctive to domestic institutional arrangements. EMU has systemic effects on member states and creates an internalisation of certain practices, but is not obliterating national characteristics.

The chapter by Elman addresses how certain identities, namely those of women, have been excluded from the process of defining Europe. Elman's examination of citizenship in the European Union shows that it is built upon the exclusion of those who do not possess it and provides the legitimation of the polities that have the authority to bestow this identity. The ability of the EU equality policy to overcome sexual inequalities is constrained by the commitment to free market ideology, which rejects the need to address distributive issues through the adoption of a meaningful social policy. In this sense, the equality supposedly entrenched in EU citizenship is merely a form with no real substance.

The book then moves away from the examination of the processes of integration and its effects into the analyses of how institutions are able to provide accountability and legitimacy for EMU. The central institution for analysis in section III is the European Central Bank and its relationship with its various 'partners'—national central banks and economic and finance ministers.

Loedel asserts that the ECB is the most far-reaching and powerful institution of the EU, whose very formation has required member states to give up autonomy in the area of monetary policy. Yet despite the independence of the ECB, Loedel argues that it does contain a degree of multilevel governance in its operations. Other interests are brought into the decision making process through such channels as the Euro-group of national finance and economics ministers and the central bankers from the nation states. A good example of the importance of national interests permeating ECB structures is the row that took place over the appointment of its president. Loedel argues, though, that the multilevel governance of the ECB is more circumscribed than in other EU institutions, but that this mode of governance can be beneficial in that it is clear who is making the decisions. Other interests can be brought closer into the process by the extension of accountability requirements for the ECB, such as consultation processes.

The chapter by Jones, following Loedel, also states that the ECB has ultimate decision making power over monetary policy in Europe. Yet Jones questions the argument that having this power centralised in the ECB creates a democratic deficit. Jones argues that macroeconomic preferences should not be based upon a trade-off between inflation and unemployment, but rather should follow guidelines of rational economic policy making based upon price stability. The ECB is set to follow strict guidelines on monetary policy determined by the member states, a situation which Jones argues is more democratic than leaving these decisions in the hands of governments, where they can be used for short-term political gains, i.e., re-election. The distributional problems that could arise in the EU should not be addressed through monetary policy, but rather need to be taken on by a separate institution of the EU.

Some of the points brought up by Loedel and Jones are examined further in Crowley's discussion of the institutional implications of EMU. A significant problem of the design of EMU, as identified by Crowley, is that there is multileveled control over macroeconomic policy, which makes coordination difficult, and becomes a potential cause of instability within the eurozone. Monetary policies are decided on at a supranational level, but fiscal policy is still nationally determined, with only minimal fiscal coordination surveillance in the Stability and Growth Pact (SGP). Crowley argues that institutional adjustments, such as the abandonment of the SGP, may become necessary in the face of asynchronous business cycles or asymmetric shocks. Other reforms could include the development of various combinations of policy initiatives such as equalisation payments, an expanded supranational budget, supranational budget deficits to be permitted and the granting of supranational fiscal sovereignty. Crowley asserts that just because the launch of the euro was relatively smooth, this fact does not guarantee its success. In fact he argues that the potential for future instability is great if institutional reform is ruled out.

The final section of the book consists of three country studies, which empirically address the 'two way' process of EMU identified earlier in the chapter by Dyson. Clearly, national governments, in particular Germany and France, have an influence on the type of EMU adopted. At the same time the EMU process has similar, yet nationally distinct effects on member states. The chapters on France and Germany look closely at how these countries influenced EMU and reconciled themselves with the project, while the study on Italy looks at how EMU allowed the acceleration of domestic institutional reform.

Howarth adopts an eclectic approach in analysing the motives of the French government in moving toward EMU. He emphasises that the institutional culture of the EU and increased economic interdependence structure the motives of the member states. Yet because the end goal of monetary integration was not clear, confusion arises in the theories of actor preferences. France's close relationship with and ability to influence Germany led to institutional change in the EU based on its demand for reform of the EMS. At the same time, the French government was in the strongest position to jeopardise monetary integration if it had rejected Germany's institutional design of EMU. Howarth argues that in the case of EMU a personalities-centred approach that emphasises the role of top political leaders is better able to comprehend the rationale behind countries' willingness to move toward EMU.

Chandler analyses Germany's power projection and its effect on the process of EMU, considering the opposing forces of supranational commitments and national interests that have characterised the integration process. Identifying German interests is difficult because, despite its ability to influence the process due to its position as the largest economic power, German interests have been mediated by its commitment to the ideal of a united Europe. At the same time the commitment to fiscal discipline enforced in the Stability and Growth Pact represents German assertiveness and institutional advantage. Chandler concludes that the case of EMU shows that intergovernmental processes paradoxically arrive at supranational outcomes. Therefore he questions the sensibility of the divide between intergovernmentalism and neofunctionalism in explaining the integration process.

The analysis of the Italian case differs from those of Germany and France, because EMU has impacted domestic politics in Italy much more than Italian preferences have influenced the shape of EMU. Croci and Picci argue that the Italian government has had limited success using domestic constraints to try to promote its preferences given Italy's relative bargaining weakness. Yet Italian officials have used the need to embrace Community agreements to build effective support for otherwise unpalatable domestic restructuring policies. Croci and Picci therefore conclude that successful integration projects are the result of the ability of political actors to manipulate international and domestic political factors. They suggest that the 'two-level games' approach is a useful analytical tool that examines the many variables highlighted by neofunctionalism and intergovernmentalism.

This volume has provided ample evidence that one should be careful to adopt one theory over another. Often a mixture of theories offers better insights. Also, by focusing one's attention on one set of actors over another is likely to cause one to neglect the activities of other actors. Likewise, emphasising the importance of one mechanism over another implies the risk of missing out on the effects of other mechanisms. Thus, theoretical lenses and subjects of study need to be adopted with care, and in full consideration and appreciation of their limits.

The chapters also highlight how EMU is tightly connected with numerous other aspects of integration. The 'spill-over' of the effects of EMU on other areas of policy-making and on modes of governance is clear, and was discussed in various chapters of this volume. The broader conclusion we draw from these analyses is that EMU shows that integration theory is here to help us understand the wider process as well as the minute details of integration, but not necessarily to predict outcomes. In other words, theory cannot be an end in itself. Future research will show how we can best balance rigorous theorising with understanding the specific particularities of European economic and monetary integration.

References

Accornero, Aris. (1994) *La parabola del sindacato*. Bologna: Il Mulino.

Aeschimann, Eric, and Pascal Riché. (1996) *La guerre de sept ans: histoire secrète du franc fort, 1989-1996*. Paris: Calmann-Lévy.

Alesina, Alberto, and R. Gatti. (1995) 'Independent Central Banks: Low Inflation at No Costs'. *American Economic Review* 85(2): 196-200.

Alesina, Alberto. (1987) 'Macroeconomic Policy in a Two-Party System as a Repeated Game'. *Quarterly Journal of Economics* 102(3): 651-78.

Alesina, Alberto, and Lawrence Summers. (1992) 'Central Bank Independence and Macroeconomic Performance: Some Comparative Evidence'. *Journal of Money and Credit* 25(2): 151-62.

Alesina, Alberto, Nouriel Roubini, and Gerald D. Cohen. (1997) *Political Cycles and the Macroeconomy*. Cambridge: MIT Press.

Alter, Karen J. (1998) 'Who Are the "Masters of the Treaty"? European Governments and the European Court of Justice'. *International Organization* 52(1): 121-47.

Anderson, Jeffery J. (1997) 'Hard Interests, Soft Power, and Germany's Changing Role in Europe'. In Peter Katzenstein (ed.), *Tamed Power: Germany in Europe*. Ithaca, N.Y.: Cornell University Press, pp. 80-107.

———. (1995) 'The State of the European Union: From the Single Market to Maastricht, from Singular Events to General Theories'. *World Politics* 47: 441-65.

Andrews, David. (1993) 'The Global Origins of the Maastricht Treaty on EMU: Closing the Window of Opportunity'. In Alan W. Cafruny and Glenda G. Rosenthal (eds.), *State of the European Community: the Maastricht Debates and Beyond*. Harlow, Essex and Boulder, Colo.: Longman and Lynne Rienner, pp. 107-24.

———. (1994) 'Capital Mobility and State Autonomy: Toward a Structural Theory of International Monetary Relations'. *International Studies Quarterly* 38: 193-218.

Arendt, Hannah. (1979) *The Origins of Totalitarianism*. New York: Harvest/HBJ Book.

Aron, Raymond. (1964) 'Old Nations, New Europe'. In Stephen R. Graubard (ed.), *A New Europe?* Boston: Houghton Mifflin, pp. 38-61.

Artis, Michael, and Bernhard Winkler. (1997) 'The Stability Pact: Safeguarding the Credibility of the European Central Bank'. *CEPR Discussion Paper* 1688.

Artis, Michael, and Wenda Zhang. (1997a) 'International Business Cycles and the ERM: Is There a European Business Cycle?' *International Journal of Finance and Economics* 2: 1-16.

————. (1997b) 'On Identifying the Core of EMU: An Exploration of Some Empirical Criteria'. *CEPR Discussion Paper* 1689.

————. (1998) 'Core and Periphery in EMU: A Cluster Analysis'. *EUI Working Paper RSC No.* 98/37. Florence: EUI.

Attali, Jacques. (1993, 1994, 1995) Verbatim I, II, III. Paris: Fayard.

Axelrod, R. (1984) *The Evolution of Cooperation*. New York: Basic Books.

Backus, David, and John Driffill. (1985) 'Inflation and Reputation'. *American Economic Review* 75(3): 530-38.

Baffi, Paolo. (1989) 'Il negoziato sullo SME'. *Bancaria* 45: 67-70.

Bailey, Martin J. (1956) 'The Welfare Cost of Inflationary Finance'. *The Journal of Political Economy* 64(2): 93-110.

Baldwin, David A. (1993) *Neorealism and Neoliberalism. The Contemporary Debate.* New York: Columbia University Press.

Balleix-Banerjee, Corinne. (1997) *La France et la Banque Centrale Européenne: débats politiques et élaboration de la décision, janvier 1988-septembre 1992.* Ph.D. dissertation. Paris: University Panthéon-Assas, Paris II, 10 January.

————. (1999) *La France et la Banque Centrale Européenne.* Paris: PUF.

Barber, Lionel. (1998) 'The Euro: Single Currency, Multiple Injuries'. *Financial Times*, 5 May.

Barro, Robert J., and David B. Gordon. (1983) 'Rules, Discretion, and Reputation in a Model of Monetary Policy'. *Journal of Monetary Economics* 12: 101-21.

Bauchard, P. (1994) *Deux ministres trop tranquilles.* Paris: Belfond.

Baun, Michael J. (1996) 'The Maastricht Treaty as High Politics: Germany, France, and European Integration'. *Political Science Quarterly* 110(4): 605-24.

————. (1996) *An Imperfect Union.* Boulder, Colo.: Westview.

Baxter, M., and A. Stockman. (1989) 'Business Cycles and the Exchange-Rate Regime'. *Journal of Monetary Economics* 27: 377-400.

Bayoumi, Tamim. (1994) 'A Formal Model of Optimum Currency Areas'. *IMF Staff Papers* 41(4): 537-54.

Bayoumi, Tamim, and Barry Eichengreen. (1993) 'Shocking Aspects of European Monetary Unification'. In Francesco Giavazzi and Francisco Torres (eds.), *Adjustment and Growth in the European Monetary Union.* Cambridge: Cambridge University Press, pp. 193-229.

————. (1994) 'One Money or Many?: Analyzing the Prospects for Monetary Unification in Various Parts of the World'. *Princeton Studies in International Finance* 76, Princeton University.

BDI. (1990) *Economic and Monetary Union. A Challenge for Europe.* Cologne: BDI, January.

BDI and CNPF. (1990) 'Gemeinsames Arbeitspapier zur Wirtschafts- und Währungsunion der Europäischen Gemeinschaft'/'Document Conjoint du BDI et du CNPF'. Cologne and Paris, 2 October.

BDI and DGB. (1990) 'Gemeinsame Erklärung BDI/DGB zur Europäischen Wirtschafts- und Währungsunion'. Düsseldorf and Cologne, 22 August.

Beck, Nathaniel. (1987) 'Elections and the Fed: Is There a Political Monetary Cycle?' *American Journal of Political Science* 31(1): 194-216.

Begg, David, and Charles Wyplosz. (1992) 'The European Monetary System: Recent intellectual history'. Unpublished paper, presented at the Conference on '*The Monetary Future of Europe*', La Coruna, 11-12 December.

Berman, Sheri, and Kathleen R. McNamara. (1999) 'Bank on Democracy: Why Central Banks Need Public Oversight'. *Foreign Affairs* 78(2): 2-8.

Bernhard, William T. (1998) 'A Political Explanation of Variations in Central Bank Independence'. *American Political Science Review* 92(2): 311-27.

Beukel, Erik. (1994) 'Reconstructing Integration Theory: The Case of Educational Policy in the EC'. *Cooperation and Conflict* 29(1): 33-54.

Beveridge, Fiona, Sue Nott, and Kylie Stephen. (2000) 'Mainstreaming and the Engendering of Policy: A Means to an End?' *Journal of European Public Policy* 7(3): 385-405.

Beveridge, Fiona, and Sue Nott. (1996) 'Gender Auditing–Making the Community Work for Women'. In Tamara Hervey and David O'Keeffe (eds.), *Sex Equality Law in the European Union*. New York: John Wiley & Sons, pp. 383-98.

Bhabha, Jacqueline, and Sue Shutter. (1994) *Women's Movement: Women Under Immigration, Nationality and Refugee Law*. Staffordshire, UK: Trentham Books.

Bhaskar, Roy. (1986) *Scientific Realism and Human Emancipation*. London: Verso.

Blackburn, Keith, and Michael Christensen. (1989) 'Monetary Policy and Credibility'. *Journal of Economic Literature* 27: 1-45.

Blanchard, Olivier, and Danny Quah. (1989) 'The Dynamic Effects of Aggregate Demand and Supply Disturbances'. *American Economic Review* 79: 655-73.

Bleaney, Michael. (1996) 'Central Bank Independence, Wage-Bargaining Structure, and Macroeconomic Performance in OECD Countries'. *Oxford Economic Papers* 48(1): 20-38.

Blinder, Alan. (1999) 'Central Bank Credibility: Why Do We Care?' Paper presented at ASSA meetings. Boston, Massachusetts, January 3-5.

———. (1998) *Central Banking in Theory and Practice*. Cambridge, MA: MIT Press.

Börzel, Tanja. (1997) 'What's So Special about Policy Networks? An Exploration of the Concept and of Its Usefulness in Studying European Governance'. *European Integration Online Papers* 1(16). [http://eiop.or.at/eiop/texte/1997-016ahtm]

Bourdieu, Pierre. (1998) *Acts of Resistance: Against the Tyranny of the Market*. New York: The New Press.

Bowles, Paul, Osvaldo Croci, and Brian K. MacLean. (1998) 'The "Banca d'Italia" and the Question of Autonomy in Monetary Policy. Towards a Comparative Understanding of Central Bank Independence'. *Italian Politics and Society* 50: 66-83.

Brentford, Philip. (1998) 'Constitutional Aspects of the Independence of the European Central Bank'. *International and Comparative Law Quarterly* 47(1): 75-116.

Bretherton, Charlotte, and Liz Sperling. (1996) 'Women's Networks and the European Union: Towards an Inclusive Approach?' *Journal of Common Market Studies* 34(4): 487-508.

Brunner, Karl. (1975) 'Comment [on Gordon (1975)]'. *Journal of Law and Economics* 18(3): 837-57.

Bufacchi, Vittorio. (1996) 'The Success of "Mani Pulite": Luck or Skill?' In Robert Leonardi and Raphaella Y. Nanetti (eds.), *Italy: Politics and Policy*, Volume 1. Aldershot: Dartmouth, pp. 189-210.

Buiter, Willem. (1997) 'The Economic Case for Monetary Union in the European Union'. *Review of International Economics* 5(4): 10-35.

Buiter, Willem, Giancarlo Corsetti, and Paolo Pesenti. (1998) *Financial Markets and European Monetary Cooperation*. Cambridge: Cambridge University Press.

Buiter, Willem, Giancarlo Corsetti, and Nouriel Roubini, (1993) 'Excessive Deficits: Sense and Nonsense in the Treaty of Maastricht'. *Economic Policy* 16: 58-60.

Bulmer, Simon. (1983) 'Domestic Politics and European Community Policy-making'. *Journal of Common Market Studies* 14: 349-63.

———. (1994) 'The Governance of the European Union: A New Institutionalist Approach'. *Journal of Public Policy* 13(4): 351-80.

————. (1997) 'Shaping the Rules? The Constitutive Politics of the European Union and German Power'. In Peter Katzenstein (ed.), *Tamed Power: Germany in Europe.* Ithaca,N.Y.: Cornell University Press, pp. 49-79.

Bulmer, Simon, and William Paterson. (1996) 'Germany in the European Union: Gentle Giant or Emergent Leader?' *International Affairs* 72: 9-32.

Burley, Anne-Marie, and Walter Mattli. (1993) 'Europe before the Court: A Political Theory of Legal Integration'. *International Organization* 47(1): 41-76.

Calmfors, Lars, and John Driffill. (1988) 'Centralization of Wage Bargaining: Bargaining Structure, Corporatism, and Macroeconomic Performance'. *Economic Policy* 6: 13-61.

Cameron, David. (1998) 'Creating Supranational Authority in Monetary and Exchange-Rate Policy: The Sources and Effects of EMU'. In Wayne Sandholtz and Alec Stone Sweet (eds.), *European Integration and Supranational Governance.* Oxford: Oxford University Press, pp. 188-216.

————. (1995) 'Transnational Relations and the Development of European Economic and Monetary Union'. In Thomas Risse-Kappen (ed.), *Bringing Transnational Relations Back In: Non-State Actors, Domestic Structures, and International Institutions.* New York: Cambridge University Press, pp. 37-78.

Caporaso, James A. (1996) 'The European Union and Forms of State: Westphalian, Regulatory or Post-Modern?' *Journal of Common Market Studies* 34(1): 29-52.

————. (1998) 'Regional Integration Theory: Understanding Our Past and Anticipating Our Future'. In Wayne Sandholtz and Alec Stone Sweet (eds.), *European Integration and Supranational Governance.* Oxford: Oxford University Press, pp. 334-51.

Carli, Guido. (1993) *Cinquant'anni di vita italiana.* Bari: Laterza.

Castellino, Onorato. (1996) 'Pension Reform: Perhaps Not the Last Round'. In Mario Caciagli and David I. Ketzer (eds.), *Italian Politics: The Stalled Transition.* Boulder, Colo.: Westview, pp. 153-67.

Checkel, Jeffrey. (1999) 'Social Construction and Integration'. *Journal of European Public Policy* 6(4): 545-60.

Christiansen, Thomas, Knud-Erik Jørgensen, and Antje Wiener. (1999) 'The Social Construction of Europe'. *Journal of European Public Policy* 6(4): 528-44.

Chryssochoou, Dimitris N. (1995) 'European Union and the Dynamics of Confederal Consociation: Problems and Prospects for a Democratic Future'. *Journal of European Integration* 18: 279-305.

Ciampi, Carlo Azelio. (1998) 'Risanamento e sviluppo, due momenti inscindi-bili della stessa politica'. In special issue on *L'Euro e le politiche per lo sviluppo e l'occupazione, Info/Quaderni:* 198-203.

Clarke, John, and Mary Langan. (1993) 'Restructuring Welfare: The British Welfare Regime in the 1980s'. In Allan Cochrane and John Clarke (eds.), *Comparing Welfare States: Britain in International Context.* London: Sage, pp. 49-76.

Clinton, W. David. (1994) *The Two Faces of National Interest.* Baton Rouge: Louisiana State University Press.

Cobham, David, and George Zis (eds.). (1999) *From EMS to EMU: 1979 to 1999 and Beyond.* London: Macmillan.

Cohen, Gerald A. (1982) 'Functional Explanation, Consequence Explanation, and Marxism'. *Inquiry* 25(1): 27-56.

Cohen, Roger. (2000) 'Danish Voters Say No to Euro: A Blow to Unity'. *New York Times* 29 September: 1.

————. (1999) 'A New German Assertiveness'. *New York Times,* 12 September.

————. (1998) 'Germany is Bolder, Irritating Its Allies'. *New York Times* 12 December.

Cole, Alistair, and Helen Drake. (2000) 'The Europeanization of the French Polity: Continuity, Change and Adaptation'. *Journal of European Public Policy* 7(1): 26-43.

Corbey, Dorette. (1993) *Stilstand is Vooruitgang: De Dialectiek van het Europese Integratieproces.* Assen and Maastricht: Van Gorcum.

———. (1995) 'Dialectical Functionalism: Stagnation as a Booster of European Integration'. *International Organization* 49(2): 253-84.

Cox, Robert. (1995) 'Critical Political Economy'. In Björn Hettne (ed.), *International Political Economy: Understanding Global Disorder.* Halifax: Fernwood Books, pp. 31-45.

———. (1996) *Approaches to World Order.* Cambridge: Cambridge University Press.

Cram, Laura. (1996) 'Integration Theory and the Study of the European Policy Process'. In Jeremy J. Richardson (ed.), *European Union: Power and Policy-making.* London: Routledge, pp. 40-58.

Craveri, Piero. (1995) *La Repubblica dal 1958 al 1992.* Milan: TEA.

Crowley, Patrick. (1996) 'EMU, Maastricht and the 1996 IGC'. *Contemporary Economic Policy* XIV(2): 41-55.

Dahl, Robert A., and Charles E. Lindblom. (1976) *Politics, Economics, and Welfare: Planning and Politico-economic Systems Resolved into Basic Social Processes.* Chicago: University of Chicago Press.

Dalton, Russel J., and Richard C. Eichenberg. (1998) 'Citizen Support for Policy Integration'. In Wayne Sandholtz and Alec Stone Sweet (eds.), *European Integration and Supranational Governance.* Oxford: Oxford University Press, pp. 250-83.

Dastoli, Pier Virgilio. (1996) 'The Stone Guest: Italy on the Threshold of European Monetary Union'. In Mario Caciagli and David I. Kertzer (eds.), *Italian Politics: The Stalled Transition.* Boulder, Colo.: Westview, pp. 169-85.

De Grauwe, Paul. (1992) *The Economics of Monetary Integration.* Oxford: Oxford University Press.

De Grauwe, Paul, and P. Vanhaverbeke. (1993) 'Is Europe an Optimal Currency Area: Evidence from Regional Data'. In Paul Masson and Mark Taylor (eds.), *Policy Issues in the Operation of Currency Unions.* Cambridge: Cambridge University Press, pp. 111-29.

De Haan, Jakob. (1997) 'The European Central Bank: Independence, Accountability and Strategy: A Review'. *Public Choice* 93: 395-426.

DeSerres, Alain, and René Lalonde. (1994) 'Symétrie des chocs touchant les régions canadiennes et choix d'un régime de change'. *Document de travail* 94-9, Banque du Canada.

Della Sala, Vincent. (1997) 'Hollowing Out and Hardening the State: European Integration and the Italian Economy'. *West European Politics* 20: 14-33.

Delors Report. (1989) *Report on Economic and Monetary Union in the European Community.* Committee for the Study of Economic and Monetary Union, Luxembourg: Office for Official Publications of the E.C., April.

Department of Finance. (1997) 'The Equalization Program'. Federal-Provincial Relations Division, Government of Canada, July.

DGB. (1990a) 'Diskussionspapier zur Wirtschafts- und Währungsunion aus der Sicht des Deutschen Gewerkschaftsbundes' in DGB *Abteilung Strukturpolitik,* Düsseldorf, 16 January.

———. (1990b) 'Europäische Währungsunion: Start in eine ungewisse Phase'. *Jahres-Gutachten 1990/91,* pp. 424-37.

Diatta v. *Land Berlin.* (1985) Case 267/83, ECR 567.

Diez, Thomas. (1999) 'Speaking "Europe": The Politics of Integration Discourse'. *Journal of European Public Policy* 6(4): 598-613.

DiMaggio, Paul and Walter Powell (eds.). (1991a) *The New Institutionalism in Organizational Analysis.* Chicago: Chicago University Press.

Dinan, Desmond. (1999) *Ever Closer Union*, 2nd ed. Boulder, Colo.: Lynne Rienner.

Dolowitz, David, and David Marsh. (1996) 'Who Learns What from Whom: A Review of the Policy Transfer Literature'. *Political Studies* 44(2): 343-57.

Downs, Anthony. (1957) *An Economic Theory of Democracy.* New York: Harper and Row.

Duckenfield, Mark. (1999) 'The *Goldkrieg:* Revaluing the Bundesbank's Reserves and the Politics of EMU'. *German Politics* 8(1): 106-30.

Duff, Andrew. (1997) *The Treaty of Amsterdam: Text and Commentary.* London: Federal Trust.

Duffin, Simon. (1999) Private interview conducted by David Howarth. Brussels, 28 July.

Durand, A. (1979) 'European Citizenship'. *European Law Review* 4: 3-14.

Durkheim, Emile. (1893) *De la Division du travail sociale: Etude sur l'organisation des sociétés supérieures.* Paris: F. Alcan.

Dyson, Kenneth. (2000a) *The Politics of the Euro-Zone.* Oxford: Oxford University Press.

———. (2000b) 'Creativity and Constraint in Politics: The Case of EMU'. Paper presented at the Conference on Ideational Institutionalism, University of Birmingham, June.

———. (1999a) 'France, Germany and the Euro-Zone: From "Motor" of EMU to Living in an ECB-Centric Euro-Zone'. Paper presented at conference 'France, Germany and Britain—Partners in a Changing World', University of Bradford, UK, 21 May.

———. (1999b) 'EMU, Political Discourse and the Fifth French Republic: Historical Institutionalism, Path Dependency and "Craftsmen" of Discourse'. *Modern and Contemporary France* 7(2): 179-96.

———. (1999c) 'The Franco-German Relationship and Economic and Monetary Union: Using Europe to "Bind Leviathan"'. *West European Politics* 22(1): 25-44.

———. (1998) 'Chancellor Kohl as Strategic Leader: The Case for Economic and Monetary Union'. *German Politics* 7(1): 37-63.

———. (1997) 'La France, l'union économique et monétaire et la construction européenne: Renforcer l'executif, transformer l'Etat'. *Politiques et Management Public* 15(3): 57-77.

———. (1994) *Elusive Union: The Process of Economic and Monetary Union in Europe.* London: Longman.

Dyson, Kenneth, and Kevin Featherstone. (1999) *The Road to Maastricht: Negotiating Economic and Monetary Union.* Oxford: Oxford University Press.

———. (1996a) 'France, EMU and Construction Européenne: Empowering the Executive, Transforming the State'. Paper presented at the Eight International Conference of the Journal Politiques et Management Public, Paris, 20-21 June.

———. (1996b) 'Interlocking Core Executives: Explaining the Negotiation of Economic and Monetary Union'. Paper presented at the 24th European Consortium of Political Research, Joint Sessions of Workshops, Oslo, 29 March-3 April.

———. (1996c) 'Italy and EMU as Vincolo Esterno: Empowering the Technocrats, Transforming the State'. *South European Society and Politics* 1(2): 272-99.

Dyson, Kenneth, et al. (1994) *Reinventing the French State.* Report Number 2, European Briefing Unit, Department of European Studies, University of Bradford, UK, August.

Dyson, Kenneth, Kevin Featherstone, and George Michalopoulos. (1995) 'Strapped to the Mast: EC Central Bankers between Global and Regional Integration'. *Journal of European Public Policy* 2(3): 465-87.

Ebbinghaus, Bernhard, and Anke Hassel. (2000) 'Striking Deals: Concertation in the Reform of Continental European Welfare States'. *Journal of European Public Policy* 7(3): 44-62.

Eichengreen, Barry. (1997) 'Saving Europe's Automatic Stabilizers'. *National Institute Economic Review* 159: 92-98.

Eichengreen, Barry, and Jeffry Frieden. (1993) 'The Political Economy of European Monetary Unification: An Analytical Introduction'. *Economics and Politics* 5(2): 85-105.

Eising, Rainer, and Beate Kohler-Koch (eds.). (1999) *The Transformation of Governance in the European Union.* London: Routledge.

Elgie, Robert. (1998) 'Democratic Accountability and Central Bank Independence: Historical and Contemporary, National and European Perspectives'. *West European Politics* 21(3): 53-76.

Elman, R. Amy. (2000) 'The Limits of Citizenship: Migration, Sex Discrimination and Same-Sex Partners in EU Law'. *Journal of Common Market Studies* 38(5): 729-49.

———. (1996) *Sexual Politics and the European Union.* Oxford: Berghahn Books.

Elster, Jon. (1979) *Ulysses and the Sirens: Studies in Rationality and Irrationality.* Cambridge: Cambridge University Press.

———. (1983) *Explaining Technical Change. A Case Study in the Philosophy of Science.* Cambridge: Cambridge University Press.

Engelmann, Daniela, Hans-Joachim Knopf, Klaus Roscher, and Thomas Risse-Kappen. (1997) 'Identity Politics in the European Union: The Case of Economic and Monetary Union'. In Petri Minkkinen and Heikki Patomäki (eds.), *The Politics of Economic and Monetary Union.* Helsinki: Ulkopoliittinen Instituutti, The Finnish Institute of International Affairs, pp. 104-30.

ETUC. (1990) *Economic and Monetary Union in the European Community.* Info 31, Brussels: ETUI.

———. (1991) 'Economic and Monetary Union: ETUC Submission to Intergovernmental Conference', 2nd draft. Brussels: ETUC.

———. (1992) 'The Delors II Package: a Cooperative Growth and Employment Strategy must be added'. ETUC Statement adopted on 11-12 June, Brussels: ETUC.

Eurobarometer. (2000) *Eurobarometer.* Report Number 52, Brussels.

———. (1999) *Europeans and Their Views on Domestic Violence against Women.* Brussels: DG X.

European Women's Lobby. (1995) *Confronting the Fortress—Black and Migrant Women in the European Community.* Luxembourg: European Parliament.

Evans, A. C. (1984) 'European Citizenship: a novel concept in EEC Law'. *American Journal of Comparative Law* 32: 679-715.

Evans, Peter, Harold K. Jacobson, and Robert D. Putnam (eds.). (1993) *Double-Edged Diplomacy: International Bargaining and Domestic Politics.* Berkeley: University of California Press.

Featherstone, Kevin, George Kazamias, and Dimitris Papadimitriou. (2000) 'The Limits of Empowerment: EMU, Technocracy and the Reform of the Greek Pension System'. Paper presented at the Workshop on Europeanization, University of Bradford, May.

256 References

256 References

Feldblum, Miriam. (1996) 'Reconstructing Citizenship in Europe: Changing Trends and Strategies'. Paper presented at the American Political Science Association Annual Meeting, San Francisco, 28 August –1 September.

Feldstein, Martin. (1997) 'The Political Economy of the European Economic and Monetary Union: Political Sources of an Economic Liability'. *Journal of Economic Perspectives* 11(4): 23-42.

Ferrera, Maurizio. (1991) 'Italia: aspirazioni e vincoli del "quarto grande"'. In Maurizio Ferrera (ed.), *Le dodici Europe: I paesi della Comunità di fronte ai cambiamenti del 1989-1990.* Bologna: Il Mulino, pp. 73-92.

Ferrera, Maurizio, and Elisabetta Gualmini. (1999) *Salvati dall'Europa?* Bologna: Il Mulino.

Fielder, Nicola. (1997) *Western European Integration in the 1980s: The Origins of the Single Market.* Bern: Peter Lang.

Flanagan, Robert J., David W. Soskice, and Lloyd Ulman. (1983) *Unionism, Economic Stabilization, and Incomes Policies: European Experience.* Washington, D.C.: The Brookings Institution.

Forder, James. (1998) 'Central Bank Independence—Conceptual Clarifications and Interim Assessment'. *Oxford Economic Papers* 50: 307-34.

Forsyth, Murray. (1981) *Union of States: The Theory and Practice of Confederation.* New York: Homes & Meier.

Foucault, Michel. (1980) *Power/Knowledge.* New York: Pantheon.

Frankel, Jeffrey A., and Andrew K. Rose. (1997) 'Is EMU more justifiable ex post than ex ante?' *European Economic Review* 41: 753-60.

Fratianni, Michele, and Franco Spinelli. (1997) *A Monetary History of Italy.* Cambridge: Cambridge University Press.

Frieden, Jeffry. (1998) 'The Political Economy of European Exchange Rates: An Empirical Assessment'. Manuscript. Cambridge: Harvard University, Department of Government, August.

———. (1996) 'The Impact of Goods and Capital Market Integration on European Monetary Politics'. *Comparative Political Studies* 29(2): 193-222.

Frieden, Jeffry, and Erik Jones. (1998) 'The Political Economy of European Monetary Union: Toward a Framework for Analysis'. In Jeffry Frieden, Daniel Gros, and Erik Jones (eds.), *The New Political Economy of EMU.* Lanham, Md.: Rowman & Littlefield, pp. 163-86.

Friedman, Milton. (1977) 'Nobel Lecture: Inflation and Unemployment'. *Journal of Political Economy* 85(3): 451-72.

Gabriel, Jürg Martin. (1995) 'The Integration of European Security: A Functional Analysis'. *Aussenwirtschaft* 50(1): 135-60.

Garcin, T. (1993) 'L'unification allemande et la classe politique française'. *Hérodote* 68: 112-24.

Garrett, Geoffrey. (1995) 'The Politics of Legal Integration in the European Union'. *International Organization* 49(1): 171-81.

———. (1993) 'The Politics of Maastricht'. *Economics and Politics* 5(2): 105-25.

———. (1992) 'International Cooperation and Institutional Choice: The European Community's Internal Market'. *International Organization* 46(2): 533-60.

George, Alexander. (1979) 'Case Studies and Theory Development: The Method of Structured-Focused Comparison'. In Paul G. Lauren (ed.), *Diplomacy: New Approaches in Theory, History, and Policy.* New York: Free Press, pp. 43-68.

Giavazzi, Francesco, and Marco Pagano. (1988) 'The Advantage of Tying One's Hands: EMS Discipline and Central Bank Credibility'. *European Economic Review* 32: 1055-82.

Gill, Stephen. (1998) 'European Governance and New Constitutionalism: Economic and Monetary Union and Alternatives to Disciplinary Neo-liberalism in Europe'. *New Political Economy* 3: 5-26.

———. (1992) 'The Emerging World Order and European Change: The Political Economy of European Union'. In Ralph Miliband and Leo Panitch (eds.), *New World Order? Socialist Register 1992*. London: Merlin Press, 157-96.

Gilpin, Robert G. (1986) 'The Richness of the Tradition of Political Realism'. In Robert O. Keohane (ed.), *Neorealism and Its Critics*. New York: Columbia University Press, pp. 301-21.

Giuliani, Marco. (1999) 'Europeanization and Italy'. Paper presented at the 6th Conference of the European Community Studies Association, Pittsburgh, 2-5 June.

Goetz, Klaus. (2000) 'Europeanizing the National Executive?' Paper presented at the UACES 30th Annual Conference, Budapest, 6-8 April.

Goetz, Klaus H. (1996) 'Integration Policy in an Europeanized State: Germany and the Intergovernmental Conference'. *Journal of European Public Policy* 3(1): 23-44.

Goodhart, Charles A. E. (1993) *Central Bank Independence*. London: LSE Financial Markets Group.

———. (1988) *The Evolution of Central Banks*. Cambridge: MIT Press.

Goodman, John B. (1991) 'The Politics of Central Bank Independence'. *Comparative Politics* 23(3): 329-49.

Gordon, Robert J. (1975) 'The Demand for and Supply of Inflation'. *The Journal of Law and Economics* 18(3): 807-36.

Gourevitch, Paul. (1997) 'The Unthinkable: How Dangerous Is Le Pen's National Front?' *The New Yorker* 28 April-5 May: 110-49.

Gradin, Anita. (1999) Telephone interview conducted by David Howarth. London-Brussels, 19 July.

Grieco, Joseph M. (1996) 'State Interests and Institutional Rule Trajectories: A Neorealist Interpretation of the Maastricht Treaty and European Economic and Monetary Union'. In Benjamin Frankel (ed.), *Realism: Restatements and Renewal*. London: Frank Cass, pp. 261-306.

———. (1995) 'The Maastricht Treaty, Economic and Monetary Union and the Neorealist Research Programme'. *Review of International Studies* 21(1): 21-40.

———. (1993a) 'Anarchy and the Limits of Cooperation: A Realist Critique of the Newest Liberal Institutionalism'. In David A. Baldwin (ed.), *Neorealism and Neoliberalism: The Contemporary Debate*. New York: Columbia University Press, pp. 116-40.

———. (1993b) 'Understanding the Problem of International Cooperation: The Limits of Neoliberal Institutionalism and the Future of Realist Theory'. In David A. Baldwin (ed.), *Neorealism and Neoliberalism: The Contemporary Debate*. New York: Columbia University Press, pp. 301-38.

Gros, Daniel, and Niels Thygesen. (1998) *European Monetary Integration: From the European Monetary System to Economic and Monetary Union*, 2nd ed. Harlow Essex/New York: Longman.

Guzzini, Stefano. (1995) 'The "Long Night of the First Republic": Years of Clientelistic Implosion in Italy'. *Review of International Political Economy* 2: 27-61.

Haas, Ernst B. (1976) 'Turbulent Fields and the Theory of Regional Integration'. *International Organization* 30(2): 173-212.

————. (1975) *The Obsolescence of Regional Integration Theory*. Research Studies 25. Berkeley: Institute of International Studies.

————. (1968) 'Technology, Pluralism, and the New Europe'. In Joseph S. Nye (ed.), *International Regionalism*. Boston: Little Brown, pp. 149-76.

————. (1964) *Beyond the Nation State*. Stanford: Stanford University Press.

————. (1958) *The Uniting of Europe: Political, Social, and Economic Forces 1950-1957*. Stanford: Stanford University Press.

————. (1955) 'Regionalism, Functionalism, and Universal International Organizations'. *World Politics* 8(2): 238-63.

Haas, Peter M. (1992) 'Introduction: Epistemic Communities and International Policy Co-ordination'. *International Organization* 46(1): 1-35.

————. (1990) *Saving the Mediterranean*. New York: Columbia University Press.

Haggard, Stephan, and Beth A. Simmons. (1987) 'Theories of International Regime'. *International Organization* 41: 491-517.

Hall, Peter A., and Robert J. Franzese Jr. (1998) 'Mixed Signals: Central Bank Independence, Coordinated Wage Bargaining, and European Monetary Union'. *International Organization* 52(3): 505-35.

Hall, Peter, and Rosemary Taylor. (1994) 'Political Science and the Three New Institutionalisms'. *Political Studies* 44: 936-57.

Hasse, Rolf. (1990) *The European Central Bank*. Gütersloh: Bertelsmann Foundation.

Hay, Colin. (2000) 'Globalization, Regionalization and the Persistence of National Variation'. *Review of International Studies* 26(4).

Hayek, Friedrich A. (1972) *A Tiger by the Tail*. Tonbridge: Institute of Economic Affairs.

Hayo, Bernd. (1998) 'Inflation Culture, Central Bank Independence and Price Stability'. *European Journal of Political Economy* 14: 241-63.

Hellman, Stephan. (1998) 'The Italian Left in the Era of the Euro'. *Italian Politics and Society* 49: 4-20.

Henning, Randall. (1997) *Cooperating with Europe's Monetary Union*. Washington, D.C.: Institute for International Economics.

Héritier, Adrienne, and Christoph Knill. (2000) 'Differential Responses to European Policies: A Comparison'. *Max Planck Projektgruppe Recht der Gemeinschaftsgüter*, Bonn, March.

Hervey, Tamara. (1995) 'Migrant Workers and their Families in the European Union: the Pervasive Market Ideology of Community Law'. In Jo Shaw and Gillian More (eds.), *New Legal Dynamics of European Union*. Oxford: Oxford University Press, pp. 91-110.

Hibbs, Douglas A. (1977) 'Political Parties and Macroeconomic Policy'. *American Political Science Review* 71(4): 1467-87.

Hirschman, Albert. (1970) *Exit, Voice, and Loyalty*. Cambridge: Harvard University Press.

Hix, Simon. (1999) *The Political System of the European Union*. New York: St. Martin's Press.

————. (1996) 'CP, IR and the EU! A Rejoinder to Hurrell and Menon'. *West European Politics* 19(4): 802-4.

————. (1994) 'The Study of the European Community: The Challenge to Comparative Politics'. *West European Politics* 17(1): 1-30.

Hoffmann, Stanley. (1993) 'French Dilemmas and Strategies in the New Europe.' In Robert O. Keohane, Joseph S. Nye, and Stanley Hoffmann (eds.), *After the Cold War: International Institutions and State Strategies in Europe, 1989-1991*. Cambridge: Harvard University Press, 127-47.

————. (1982) 'Reflections on the Nation-state in Western Europe Today'. *Journal of Common Market Studies* 21: 21-37.

————. (1966) 'Obstinate or Obsolete? The Fate of the Nation-State and the Case of Western Europe'. *Daedalus* 95(3): 862-915.

————. (1964) 'Europe's Identity Crisis: Between the Past and America'. *Daedalus* 93(4): 1244-97.

Hofhansel, Claus. (1999) 'The Harmonization of EU Export Control'. *Comparative Political Studies* 32(2): 229-57.

Hollis, Martin, and Steve Smith. (1991) *Explaining and Understanding International Relations.* Oxford: Clarendon.

Hooghe, Liesbet. (1999) 'Supranational Activists or Intergovernmental Agents?' *Comparative Political Studies* 32(4): 435-64.

Hooghe, Liesbet, and Gary Marks. (1999) 'The Making of a Polity: The Struggle over European Integration'. In Herbert Kitchelt et al. (eds.), *Continuity and Change in Contemporary Capitalism.* Cambridge: Cambridge University Press, pp. 70-97.

Hoskyns, Catherine. (1996) 'The European Union and the Women Within: An Overview of Women's Rights Policy'. In R. Amy Elman (ed.), *Sexual Politics and the European Union: The New Feminist Challenge.* Oxford: Berghahn Books, pp. 13-22.

Hosli, Madeleine O. (1998) 'The EMU and International Monetary Relations: What to Expect for International Actors?' In Carolyn Rhodes (ed.), *The European Union in the World Community.* Boulder, Colo.: Lynne Rienner, pp. 165-91.

Howarth, David. (2000) *The French Road to European Monetary Union.* Basingstoke: Macmillan.

Hrubesch, Peter. (1987) '30 Jahre EG-Agrarmarktsystem. Entstehungs-geschichte—Funktionsweise—Ergebnisse'. *Aus Politik und Zeitgeschichte* B 18/87: 34-47.

Huelshoff, Michael G. (1994) 'Domestic Politics and Dynamic Issue Linkage'. *International Studies Quarterly* 38(2): 255-79.

Ireland, Patrick. (1995) 'Migration, Free Movement, and Immigration in the EU: A Bifurcated Policy Response'. In Stephan Leibfried and Paul Pierson (eds.), *European Social Policy: Between Fragmentation and Integration,* Washington, D.C.: The Brookings Institution, pp. 231-66.

Issing, Otmar. (1999) *The Eurosystem: Transparent and Accountable or "Willem in Euroland".* CEPR Policy Paper 2.

Jabko, Nicolas. (1999) 'In the Name of the Market: How the European Commission Paved the Way for Monetary Union'. *Journal of European Public Policy* 6(3): 475-95.

Jachtenfuchs, Markus, Thomas Diez, and Sabine Jung. (1999) 'Which Europe? Conflicting Models of a Legitimate European Political Order'. *European Journal of International Relations* 4(4): 409-45.

Jachtenfuchs, Markus, and Beate Kohler-Koch. (1996) 'Regieren im dynamischen Mehrebenensystem'. In Markus Jachtenfuchs and Beate Kohler-Koch (eds.), *Europäische Integration.* Opladen: Leske + Budrich, pp. 15-44.

Jackson, Robert. (1999) 'Sovereignty in World Politics: A Glance at the Conceptual and Historical Landscape'. *Political Studies* 47(3): 431-56.

Jacquemin, Alexis, and André Sapir. (1995) 'Is a European Hard Core Credible? A Statistical Analysis'. CEPR Discussion Paper 1242.

Janni, Paolo. (1999) 'The European Monetary Union and the Single Currency: A Gateway for the Political Modernization of Italy'. In Paolo Janni (ed.), *Italy in the European Monetary Union.* Washington, D.C.: The Catholic University of America and The Council for Research in Values and Philosophy, pp. 49-73.

Jervis, Robert. (1988) 'Realism, Game-theory, and Cooperation'. *World Politics* 40(3): 317-49.
Jones, Erik. (1999a) 'Is "Competitive" Corporatism an Adequate Response to Globalization? Evidence from the Low Countries'. *West European Politics* 22(3): 159-81.
———. (1999b) 'European Monetary Union and the New Political Economy of Adjustment'. Manuscript. Nottingham: School of Politics, University of Nottingham.
———. (1998) 'Economic and Monetary Union: Playing with Money'. In Andrew Moravcsik (ed.), *Centralization or Fragmentation? Europe Facing the Challenges of Deepening, Diversity, and Democracy.* Washington, D.C.: Brookings, pp. 59-93.
Jones, Erik, Jeffry Frieden, and Francisco Torres. (eds.) (1998) *Joining Europe's Monetary Club: The Challenges for Smaller Member States.* New York: St. Martin's Press.
Jordan, Andrew. (1998) 'EU Environmental Policy at 25'. *Environment* 40(1): 14-27.
Jospin, Lionel. (1999) *Modern Socialism.* London: Fabian Society.
Judt, Tony. (2000) 'Tale from the Vienna Woods'. *The New York Review of Books* 23 March: 8-9.
———. (1996) *A Grand Illusion: An Essay on Europe.* New York: Penguin Books.
Kaltenthaler, Karl. (1997) 'The Sources of Policy Dynamics: Variations in German and French Policy Towards European Monetary Co-operation'. *West European Politics* 20(3): 91-110.
Katzenstein, Peter (ed.). (1997) *Tamed Power: Germany in Europe.* Ithaca, N.Y.: Cornell University Press.
Kaufmann, Hugo M. (1995) 'The Importance of Being Independent: Central Bank Independence and the European System of Central Banks'. In Carolyn Rhodes and Sonia Mazey (eds.), *The State of the European Union: Building a European Polity?* Boulder, Colo.: Lynne Rienner, pp. 267-92.
Kenen, Peter B. (1969) 'The Theory of Optimal Currency Areas: An Eclectic View'. In Robert Mundell and Alexander Swoboda (eds.), *Monetary Problems of the International Economy.* Chicago: University of Chicago Press.
———. (1995) *Economic and Monetary Union in Europe.* Cambridge: Cambridge University Press.
Keohane, Robert O. (1993) 'Institutional Theory and the Realist Challenge after the Cold War'. In David A. Baldwin (ed.), *Neorealism and Neoliberalism: The Contemporary Debate.* New York: Columbia University Press, pp. 269-300.
———. (1984) *After Hegemony: Cooperation and Discord in the World Political Economy.* Princeton: Princeton University Press.
Keohane, Robert O., and Joseph S. Nye. (1975) 'International Interdependence and Integration'. In Fred Greenstein and Nelson Polsby (eds.), *Handbook of Political Science.* Vol. 8. Reading, Mass.: Addison-Wesley, pp. 363-414.
Kofman, Eleanore, and Rosemary Sales. (1992) 'Toward Fortress Europe?' *Women's Studies International Forum* 15(1): 29-39.
Kofman, Eleanore. (1998) 'When Society was Simple: Gender and Ethnic Divisions of the Far and New Right in France'. In Nickie Charles and Helen Hintjens (eds.), *Gender, ethnicity and political ideologies.* London: Routledge, pp. 91-106.
Kohler-Koch, Beate. (1996) 'Catching up with Change: the Transformation of Governance in the European Union'. *Journal of European Public Policy* 3(3): 359-80.
Krasner, Stephen D. (1978) *Defending the National Interest: Raw Materials Investment and U.S. Foreign Policy.* Princeton: Princeton University Press.
Krugman, Paul. (1990) 'Policy Problems of Monetary Union'. In Paul de Grauwe and Lucas Papademos (eds.), *The European Monetary System in the 1990s.* London: Longman, Harlow, pp. 48-64.

Kruse, D. C. (1980) *Monetary Integration in Western Europe: EMU, EMS and Beyond.* London: Butterworths.

Kydland, Finn E., and Edward C. Prescott. (1977) 'Rules Rather than Discretion: The Time-Inconsistency of Optimal Plans'. *The Journal of Political Economy* 85(3): 473-92.

Laffan, Brigid. (1996) 'The Politics of Identity and Political Order in Europe'. *Journal of Common Market Studies* 34(1): 81-102.

LaFrance, Robert, and Pierre St-Amant. (1999) 'Optimum Currency Areas: A Review of the Recent Literature'. *Working Paper, Bank of Canada* 99-16. Paper presented at the Canadian Economics Association meetings, Toronto, Ontario, 28-30 May.

Lagayette, Philippe. (1991) 'La Dynamique de l'Union Economique et Monétaire'. Text of a conference held on November 23, 1990. *Revue d'économie politique* 101(1).

———. (1990) 'Vers l'Union Economique et Monétaire'. Text of a conference of the German federation of industrie (BDI), Bonn, 15 October.

Lange, Peter. (1986) 'The End of an Era: The Wage Indexation Referendum of 1985'. In Robert Leonardi and Raphaella Y. Nanetti (eds.), *Italian Politics: A Review*, Vol. 1. London: Pinter, pp. 29-46.

Leigh-Pemberton, Robin. (1990a) 'Beyond Stage 1 of EMU'. Speech given to the European Parliamentarians and Industrialists Council, Strasbourg, 11 July. *Bank of England Quarterly Bulletin* August: 378-79.

———. (1990b) 'The United Kingdom's Proposals for Economic and Monetary Union'. Speech given to the European Currency Inter-Group of the EP and the European Parliamentarians and Industrialists Council Strasbourg, 11 July. *Bank of England Quarterly Bulletin* August: 374-77.

Levitt, Malcolm, and Christopher Lord. (2000) *The Political Economy of Monetary Union.* London: Macmillan.

Lieberman, Sima. (1992) *The Long Road to a European Monetary Union.* London: University of America Press.

Lieshout, Robert H. (1995) *Between Anarchy and Hierarchy: A Theory of International Politics and Foreign Policy.* Aldershot: Edward Elgar.

Lijphart, Arend. (1984) *Democracies: Patterns of Majoritarian and Consensus Government in Twenty-One Countries.* New Haven: Yale University Press.

Lindberg, Leon N. (1963) *The Political Dynamics of European Economic Integration.* Stanford: Stanford University Press.

Lindberg, Leon N., and Stuart A. Scheingold (eds.). (1971) *Regional Integration: Theory and Research.* Cambridge: Harvard University Press.

———. (1970) Europe's Would-be Polity: Patterns of Change in the European Community. Englewood Cliffs, N.J.: Prentice Hall.

Linklater, Andrew. (1998) *The Transformation of Political Community.* Oxford: Polity Press.

Locke, Richard. (1995) '*Eppur si tocca*: The Abolition of the *Scala Mobile*'. In Carol Mershon and Gianfranco Pasquino (eds.), *Italian Politics: Ending the First Republic*. Boulder, Colo.: Westview, pp. 185-95.

Loedel, Peter. (1999a) *Deutsche Mark Politics: Germany in the European Monetary System.* Boulder, Colo.: Lynne Rienner.

———. (1999b) 'The Lasting Legacy of Fifty Years of Deutsche Mark Politics'. *Debatte* 7(1): 24-36.

Lohmann, Susanne. (1998) 'Federalism and Central Bank Independence: The Politics of German Monetary Policy, 1957-1992'. *World Politics* 50: 401-46.

————. (1992) 'Optimal Commitment in Monetary Policy: Credibility versus Flexibility'. *American Economic Review* 82(1): 273-86.

Loi no. 98-170 (1998) Articles 19-1; 21-7; 21-11, 16 March 1998. On line, Internet, http://www.legifrance. Accessed 16 July 1998, 1-2.

Loi no. 93-933. (1993) *Journal Officiel* 23 July: 10342-48.

Ludlow, Peter. (1982) *The Making of the European Monetary System: A Case Study of the Politics of the European Community*. London: Butterworth.

Lutz, Helma. (1997) 'The Limits of European-ness: Immigrant Women in Fortress Europe'. *Feminist Review* 57: 93-111.

Lyons, Carole, (1996) 'Citizenship in the Constitution of the European Union: Rhetoric or Reality'. In Richard Bellamy (ed.), *Constitutionalism, Democracy and Sovereignty: American and European Perspectives*. Aldershot: Avebury, pp. 96-110.

Maes, Ivo. et al. (1999) 'EMU from a Historical Perspective'. Unpublished paper.

Majone, Giandomenico. (1999) 'The Regulatory State and Its Legitimacy Problems'. *West European Politics* 22(1): 1-24.

————. (1997) 'From the Positive to the Regulatory State: Causes and Consequences of Changes in the Mode of Governance'. *Journal of Public Policy* 17 (2): 139-67.

————. (1996) *Regulating Europe*. London: Routledge.

Maoz, Zeev. (1995) 'National Preferences, International Structures and Balance-of-Power Politics'. *Journal of Theoretical Politics* 7(3): 369-93.

March, James G., and Johan P. Olsen (eds.). (1982) *Ambiguity and Choice in Organizations*, 2nd ed., Oslo: Oslo Universitetsforlaget.

Marcussen, Martin. (2000) *Ideas and Elites: The Social Construction of Economic and Monetary Union*. Aalborg: Aalborg University Press.

————. (1998a) *Ideas and Elites: Danish Macro-Economic Policy-Discourse in the EMU Process*. Ph.D. dissertation. Aalborg: Aalborg University, Institute for Development and Planning, ISP-Series, No 226, April.

————. (1998b) 'Central Bankers, the Ideational Life-Cycle and the Social Construction of EMU'. *EUI Working Papers, RSC* N° 98/33. Florence: European University Institute.

————. (1997) 'The Role of "Ideas" in Dutch, Danish and Swedish Economic Policy in the 1980s and the Beginning of the 1990s'. In Petri Minkkinen and Heikki Patomäki (eds.), *The Politics of Economic and Monetary Union*. Helsinki: Ulkopoliittinen Instituutti (The Finnish Institute of International Affairs), pp. 75-103.

Marks, Gary. (1993) 'Structural Policy and Multilevel Governance in the EC'. In Alan Cafruny and Glenda Rosenthal (eds.), *The State of the European Union, Vol. 2: The Maastricht Debates and Beyond*. Boulder, Colo.: Lynne Rienner, pp. 391-410.

Marks, Gary, Liesbet Hooghe, and Kermit Blank. (1996) 'European Integration Since the 1980s: State-centric versus Multi-level Governance'. *Journal of Common Market Studies* 34(3): 343-78.

Marks, Gary, and Doug McAdam. (1996) 'Social Movements and the Changing Structure of Political Opportunity in the European Union'. In Gary Marks, Fritz W. Scharpf, Phillippe Schmitter, and Wolfgang Streeck (eds.), *Governance in the European Union*. London: Sage, pp. 95-120.

Marks, Gary, Francois Nielsen, Leonard Ray, and Jane Salk (eds.). (1996) 'Competencies, Cracks, and Conflicts'. *Comparative Political Studies* 29(2): 164-93.

Marsh, Ian. (1999) 'The State and the Economy: Opinion Formation and Collaboration as Facets of Economic Management'. *Political Studies* 47(5): 837-56.

Marshall, Thomas H. (1950) *Citizenship and Social Class*. Cambridge: Cambridge University Press.

Masson, Paul, and Mark Taylor. (1993) 'Currency Unions: A Survey of the Issues'. In Paul Masson and Mark Taylor (eds.), *Policy Issues in the Operation of Currency Unions*. Cambridge: Cambridge University Press, pp. 3-51.

Mattli, Walter. (1999), 'Explaining Regional Integration Outcomes'. *Journal of European Public Policy* 6: 1-27.

Mattli, Walter, and Anne-Marie Slaughter. (1998) 'Revisiting the European Court of Justice'. *International Organization* 52(1): 177-209.

Mayes, David. (1998) 'Evolving Voluntary Rules for the Operation of the European Central Bank'. *Bank of Finland Discussion Papers*, no. 2.

Mazey, Sonia P. (1998) 'The European Union and Women's Rights: From the Europeanization of National Agendas to the Nationalization of a European Agenda?' *Journal of European Public Policy* 5(1): 131-52.

McCracken, Paul W. (1973) 'The Practice of Political Economy'. *The American Economic Review* 63(2): 168-71.

McNamara, Kathleen. (1998) *The Currency of Ideas: Monetary Politics in the European Union*. Ithaca, N.Y.: Cornell University Press.

McNamara, Kathleen, and Erik Jones. (1996) 'The Clash of Institutions: Germany in European Monetary Affairs'. *German Politics and Society* 14(3): 5-30.

Meehan, Elizabeth. (1993) 'Citizenship and the European Community'. *The Political Quarterly* 64(2): 172-86.

Merkl, Peter. (1993) *German Unification in the European Context*. University Park: Pennsylvania State University Press.

Meulenaere, Michel. (1996) 'Citizenship: Will a Conference Suffice?' *Women of Europe Newsletter* 60: 2.

Miller, Richard. (1987) *Fact and Method: Explanation, Confirmation and Reality in the Natural and Social Sciences*. Princeton: Princeton University Press.

Milner, Helen. (1997) *Interests, Institutions and Information*. Princeton: Princeton University Press.

————. (1992) 'International Theories of Cooperation among Nations: Strengths and Weaknesses'. *World Politics* 44(3): 466-96.

Milward, Alan. (1992) *The European Rescue of the Nation State*. London: Routledge.

Ministère de l'Economie, des Finances et du Budget. (1991) 'La contribution française aux progrès de l'union économique et monétaire' (French draft treaty), 16 January. In English see *Agence Europe*, 28/29 January, 5419.

Mitrany, David. (1975) *The Functional Theory of Politics*. London: London School of Economics and Political Science and Martin Robertson.

————. (1966) *A Working Peace System*. Chicago: Quadrangle.

————. (1948) 'The Functional Approach to World Organization'. *International Affairs* 24(3): 350-63.

Monti, Mario. (1992) 'Perché oggi non si puó svalutare'. *Corriere della Sera* 20 June.

Moravcsik, Andrew. (2000) 'The Origins of Human Rights Regimes: Democratic Delegation in Postwar Europe'. *International Organization* 54(2): 217-52.

————. (1999) 'The New Statecraft? Supranational Entrepreneurs and International Cooperation'. *International Organization* 53(2): 267-306.

————. (1998) *The Choice for Europe: Social Purpose and State Power from Messina to Maastricht*. Ithaca, N.Y.: Cornell University Press.

————. (1997) 'Taking Preferences Seriously: A Liberal Theory of International Politics'. *International Organization* 51(4): 513-53.

————. (1994) 'Why the European Community Strengthens the State: Domestic Politics and International Cooperation'. Center for European Studies, Working Paper Series 52. Cambridge: Harvard University Press.

————. (1993a) 'Preference and Power in the European Community: A Liberal Inter-governmentalist Approach'. *Journal of Common Market Studies* 31: 473-524.

————. (1993b) 'Introduction: Integrating international and domestic theories of international bargaining'. In Peter B. Evans, Harold K. Jacobson, and Robert D. Putnam (eds.), *Double-Edged Diplomacy: International Bargaining and Domestic Politics.* Berkeley: University of California Press, pp. 3-42.

————. (1991) 'Negotiating the Single European Act: National Interests and Conventional Statecraft in the European Community'. *International Organization* 45(1): 651-88.

Moravcsik, Andrew, and Kalypso Nicolaidis. (1999) 'Explaining the Treaty of Amsterdam: Interest, Influence, Institutions'. *Journal of Common Market Studies* 37(1): 59-85.

Morel, Laurence. (ed.) (1997) *L'Italie en Transition: Recul des partis et activation de la fonction présidentielle.* Paris: L'Harmattan.

Mundell, Robert. (1961) 'A Theory of Optimum Currency Areas'. *American Economic Review* 51: 657-75.

Mutimer, David. (1989) '1992 and the Political Integration of Europe: Neofunctionalism Reconsidered'. *Journal of European Integration* 13(1): 75-101.

Nay, C. (1988) *Les Sept Mitterrand, ou les métamorphoses d'un septennat.* Paris: Grasset.

Nenadic, Natalie. (1996) 'Femicide: A Framework for Understanding Genocide'. In Diane Bell and Renate Klein (eds.), *Radically Speaking: Feminism Reclaimed.* North Melbourne: Spinifex Press, pp. 456-64.

New York Times 1998-2000.

Niemann, Arne. (1998) 'The PHARE Programme and the Concept of Spillover: Neo-functionalism in the Making'. *Journal of European Public Policy* 5(3): 428-46.

Nordhaus, William D. (1975) 'The Political Business Cycle'. *The Review of Economic Studies* 42(2): 169-90.

Nordic Council of Ministers. (1998) *Shelters for Battered Women and the Needs of Immigrant Women.* Copenhagen: Nordic Council of Ministers.

Nuti, Domenico M. (1997) 'Euro 1999? Costi e benefici dell'unificazione monetaria'. *Europa Europe* 6(0): 9-25.

Oatley, Thomas. (1997) *Monetary Politics: Exchange Rate Cooperation in the European Union.* Ann Arbor: Michigan University Press.

OECD. (1992) *Economic Outlook,* December.

————. (1994) *Economic Survey, Italy.*

Okun, Arthur M. (1973) 'Comments on Stigler's Paper'. *The American Economic Review* 63(2): 172-77.

Olson, Mancur. (1982) *The Rise and Decline of Nations.* New Haven: Yale University Press.

Onofri, Paolo, and Stefano Tomasini. (1992) 'France and Italy: A Tale of Two Adjustments'. In Ray Barrell (ed.), *Economic Convergence and Monetary Union in Europe.* London: Sage, pp. 70-97.

Ostner, Ilona. (2000) 'From Equal Pay to Equal Employability: Four Decades of European Gender Policies'. In Mariagrazia Rossilli (ed.), *Gender Policies in the European Union.* New York: Peter Lang, pp. 25-42.

Østrup, Finn. (1995) 'Economic and Monetary Union'. *CORE working paper.* Copenhagen: CORE, June.

Padoa-Schioppa, Tommaso. (1997) 'Engineering the Single Currency'. In Perry Anderson and Peter Gowan (eds.), *The Question of Europe.* London: Verso, pp. 162-72.

——. (1988) 'The EMS: A Long Term View'. In Francesco Giavazzi, Stefano Micossi and Marcus Millar (eds.), *The European Monetary System.* Cambridge: Cambridge University Press.

Paolini, J. (1993) 'Les deux politiques européennes de François Mitterrand'. *Rélations Internationales et Stratégiques* 9(printemps): 124-34.

Patat, Jean-Pierre, and Michel Lutfalla. (1986) *Histoire monétaire de la France au XXe siècle.* Paris: Economica.

Paterson, William. (1996) 'Beyond Semi-Sovereignty: The New Germany in the New Europe'. *German Politics* 5(2): 167-84.

Patterson, Lee Ann. (1997) 'Agricultural Policy Reform in the European Community: A Three-Level Analysis'. *International Organization* 51(1): 135-66.

Pauly, Louis W. (1992) 'The Politics of European Monetary Union: National Strategies, International Implications'. *International Journal* 47: 93-111.

Petersen, Nikolaj. (1993) *Game, Set, Match: Denmark and the European Union after Edinburgh.* Aarhus: University of Aarhus.

Peterson, John. (1995) 'Decision-Making in the European Union: Towards a Framework for Analysis'. *Journal of European Public Policy* 2(1): 69-93.

Pettman, Jan Jindy. (1999) 'Globalisation and the Gendered Politics of Citizenship'. In Nira Yuval Davis and Pnina Webner (eds.), *Women, Citizenship and Difference.* London: Zed Books, pp. 207-20.

Pierson, Paul. (1996) 'The Path to European Integration: A Historical Institutional Analysis'. *Comparative Political Studies* 29(2): 123-63.

Pollack, Mark A. (1997) 'Representing Diffuse Interests in EU Policy-making'. *Journal of European Public Policy* 4(4): 572-90.

Pond, Elizabeth. (1999) *The Rebirth of Europe.* Washington, D.C.: Brookings.

——. (1993) *Beyond the Wall: Germany's Road to Unification.* Washington, D.C.: Brookings.

Posen, Adam. (1993) 'Why Central Bank Independence Does Not Cause Low Inflation: There Is No Institutional Fix for Politics'. In Richard O'Brien (ed.), *Finance and the International Economy: 7.* Oxford: Oxford University Press, pp. 40-65.

Prate, Alain. (1987) *La France et sa monnaie: Essai sur les relations entre la Banque de France et les gouvernements.* Paris: Julliard.

Pulzer, Peter. (1996) 'Model or Exception—Germany as a Normal State?' In Gordon Smith, Stephan Padgett, and William Paterson (eds.), *Developments in German Politics.* Durham: Duke University Press, pp. 303-16.

Putnam, Robert D. (1988) 'Diplomacy and Domestic Politics: The Logic of Two-level Games'. *International Organization* 42(3): 427-61.

Radaelli, Claudio M. (2000) 'Whither Europeanization? Concept Stretching and Substantive Change'. Paper presented at the Annual Conference of the Political Studies Association, London, 10-13 April.

——. (1999) *Technocracy in the European Union.* London: Longman.

——. (1995) 'The Role of Knowledge in the Policy Process'. *Journal of European Public Policy* 2 (2): 159-83.

Risse, Thomas. (2001) 'A Europeanization of Nation-State Identities'. In Maria Green Cowles, James Caporaso, and Thomas Risse (eds.), *Europeanization and Domestic Change.* Ithaca, N.Y.: Cornell University Press, pp. 198-216.

————. (2000) 'A Europeanization of Nation-State Identities'. In Maria Green Cowles, James Caporaso, and Thomas Risse (eds.), Europeanization and Domestic Change. Manuscript [http://www.iue.it/personal/risse].

Risse, Thomas, Daniela Engelmann-Martin, et al. (1998) 'To Euro or Not to Euro? The EMU and Identity Politics in the European Union'. Florence: European University Institute, Robert Schuman Centre [http://www.iue.it/ personal/risse].

Risse-Kappen, Thomas. (1996) 'Exploring the Nature of the Beast: International Relations Theory and Comparative Policy Analysis Meet the European Union'. *Journal of Common Market Studies* 34(1): 53-80.

Rogoff, Kenneth. (1985) 'The Optimal Degree of Commitment to an Intermediate Monetary Target'. *Quarterly Journal of Economics* 100(4): 1169-89.

Rosamond, Ben. (2000) *Theories of European Integration*. Basingstoke: Macmillan.

————. (1995) 'Mapping the European Condition: The Theory of Integration and the Integration of Theory'. *European Journal of International Relations* 1(3): 391-408.

Ross, George. (1995) *Jacques Delors and European Integration*. New York: Oxford University Press.

Rossilli, Mariagrazia. (2000) 'Introduction: The European Union's Gender Policies'. In Mariagrazia Rossilli (ed.), *Gender Policies in the European Union*. New York: Peter Lang, pp. 1-23.

Rowthorne, R. E. (1992) 'Centralization, Employment, and Wage Dispersion'. *The Economic Journal* 102(412): 506-23.

Ruggie, John. (1993) 'Multilateralism: The Anatomy of an Institution'. In Ruggie (ed.), *Multilateralism Matters*. New York: Columbia University Press.

Sabatier, Paul. (1998) 'The Advocacy Coalition Framework: Revisions and Relevance for Europe'. *Journal of European Public Policy* 5(1): 98-130.

Sabatier, Paul, and Hank C. Jenkins-Smith. (eds.) (1993) *Policy Change and Learning: An Advocacy Coalition Approach*. Boulder, Colo.: Westview Press.

Sanders, David. (1996) 'International Relations: Neo-Realism and Neo-Liberalism'. In Robert E. Goodin and Hans Dieter Klingemann (eds.), *A New Handbook of Political Science*. Oxford: Oxford University Press, pp. 428-46.

Sandholtz, Wayne. (1996) 'Membership Matters: Limits of the Functional Approach to European Institutions'. *Journal of Common Market Studies* 34(3): 403-29.

————. (1993) 'Choosing Union: Monetary Politics and Maastricht'. *International Organization* 47 (1): 1-39.

————. (1992) 'Institutions and Collective Action: The New Telecommunications in Western Europe'. *World Politics* 45(2): 242-70.

Sandholtz, Wayne, and Alec Stone Sweet. (1999) 'European Integration and Supranational Governance Revisited: Rejoinder to Branch and Ohrgaard'. *Journal of European Public Policy* 6(1): 144-54.

Sandholtz, Wayne, and John Zysman. (1989) '1992: Recasting the European Bargain'. *World Politics* 41: 95-128.

Sassen, Saskia. (1999) *Guests and Aliens*. New York: New Press.

————. (1998) *Globalization and Its Discontents: Essays on the New Mobility of People and Money*. New York: New Press.

Scharpf, Fritz W. (1999) *Governing in Europe: Effective and Democratic?* Oxford: Oxford University Press.

————. (1997) *Games Real Actors Play: Actor-Centered Institutionalism in Policy Research*. Boulder, Colo.: Westview.

————. (1994) 'Community and Autonomy: Multilevel Policy-Making in the EU'. *Journal of European Public Policy* 1(2): 219-42.

————. (1988) 'The Joint-Decision Trap: Lessons from German Federalism and European Integration'. *Public Administration* 66: 239-78.

Schlesinger, Helmut. (1983) 'Die Geldpolitik der Deutschen Bundesbank 1967-1977'. In Ehrlicher Werner and Dieter Duwendag (eds.), *Geld- und Währungspolitik im Umbruch*. Baden-Baden: Nomos, pp. 59-83.

Schmidt, Vivian. (1999) 'Discourse and the Legitimation of Economic and Social Policy Change in Europe'. Paper presented at Association Française de Science Politique, 6è Congrès, Rennes, 28-31 September.

————. (1997) 'Discourse and (Dis)integration in Europe: The Cases of France, Germany, and Great Britain'. *Daedalus* 126(3): 167-97.

Schmitter, Philippe C. (1969) 'Three Neo-Functionalist Hypotheses about International Integration'. *International Organization* 23(1): 161-66.

Schnapper, Dominique. (1997) 'The European Debate on Citizenship'. *Daedalus* 126(3): 199-222.

Simpson, Allen. (1999) Private interview conducted by David Howarth. Brussels, 28 July.

Simpson, Robin, and Robert Walker. (eds.) (1993) *Europe: For Richer or Poorer*. London: CPAG.

Sorensen, Georg. (1999) 'Sovereignty: Change and Continuity in a Fundamental Institution'. *Political Studies* 47(3): 590-604.

Soysal, Yasemin N. (1994) *Limits of Citizenship: Migrants and Postnational Membership in Europe*. Chicago: University of Chicago.

Spaventa, Luigi. (1983) 'Two Letters of Intent: External Crises and Stabilization Policy, Italy 1973-77'. In John Williamson (ed.), *IMF Conditionality*. Washington, D.C.: Institute for International Economics.

————. (1980) *Italy Joins the EMS: A Political History*. Occasional Paper no. 32. Bologna: Bologna Center of the Johns Hopkins University.

Sperling, James. (1994) 'German Foreign Policy after Unification: The End of Cheque Book Diplomacy'. *West European Politics* 17(1): 73-97.

Stigler, George J. (1973) 'General Economic Conditions and National Elections'. *The American Economic Review* 63(2): 160-67.

Stone Sweet, Alec, and Thomas L. Brunell. (1998) 'Constructing a Supranational Constitution: Dispute Resolution and Governance in the European Community'. *American Political Science Review* 92(1): 63-81.

Stone Sweet, Alec, and Wayne Sandholtz. (eds.) (1998) *European Integration and Supranational Governance*. Oxford: Oxford University Press.

————. (1997) 'European Integration and Supranational Governance'. *Journal of European Public Policy* 4(3): 297-317.

Strange, Susan. (1994 [1988]) *States and Markets: An Introduction to International Political Economy*. London: Francis Pinter.

Streeck, Wolfgang. (1998) 'The Internationalization of Industrial Relations in Europe'. *Politics and Society* 26(4): 429-60.

Streeck, Wolfgang, and Philippe Schmitter. (1991) 'From National Corporatism to Transnational Pluralism: Organized Interests in the Single European Market'. *Politics and Society* 19(2): 133-64.

Stychin, Carl F. (2000) '*Grant*-ing Rights: the Politics of Rights, Sexuality and European Union'. *Northern Ireland Legal Quarterly* 51(2): 281-302.

————. (1998) *A Nation by Rights: National Cultures, Sexual Identity Politics, and the Discourse of Rights*. Philadelphia: Temple University Press.

268 References

Talani, Leila. (2000) *Betting for and Against EMU: Who Wins and Loses in Italy and in the UK from the Process of European Monetary Integration.* Aldershot: Ashgate.
Tallberg, Jonas. (2000) 'Supranational Influence in EU Enforcement: The ECJ and the Principle of State Liability'. *Journal of European Public Policy* 7(1): 104-21.
Tavlas, George. (1993) 'The "New" Theory of Optimum Currency Areas'. *The World Economy* 16: 663-85.
Taylor, Christopher. (1995) *EMU 2000? Prospects for European Monetary Union.* London: Royal Institute of International Affairs.
Taylor, Paul. (1983) *The Limits of European Integration.* London and Canberra: Croom Helm.
Tranholm-Mikkelsen, Jeppe. (1991) 'Neo-Functionalism: Obstinate or Obsolete? A Reappraisal in the Light of New Dynamism of the EC'. *Millennium* 20(1): 1-22.
Treaty on European Union. (1992) CONF-UP-UEM 2002/92. Brussels: Office of the European Communities.
Tsebelis, George. (1999) 'Contribution to ECSA Review Forum on Approaches to the Study of European Politics'. *ECSA Review* Spring: 4-6.
Tsoukalis, Loukas. (1977) *The Politics and Economics of European Monetary Integration.* London: George Allen and Unwin.
———. (1996) 'Economic and Monetary Union: The Primacy of High Politics'. In Helen Wallace and William Wallace (eds.), *Policy Making in the European Union.* Oxford: Oxford University Press, pp. 279-99.
Ungerer, Horst. (1997) *A Concise History of European Monetary Integration: From EPU to EMU.* Westport, Colo.: Quorum Books.
UNICE. (1990a) 'Economic and Monetary Union in the European Community: A Business Perspective'. Brussels, 27 March.
———. (1990b) 'Statement in View of the Intergovernmental Conference on Economic and Monetary Union in the European Community'. Brussels, 15 November.
Vassallo, Salvatore. (2000) 'La politica di bilancio: le condizioni e gli effetti istituzionali della convergenza'. In Giuseppe Di Palma, Sergio Fabbrini and Giorgio Freddi (eds.), *Condannata al successo? L'Italia nell'Europa integrata.* Bologna: Il Mulino, pp. 287-323.
van Apeldoorn, Bastiaan. (1999a) *Transnational Capital and the Struggle over European Order.* Ph.D. dissertation. Florence: European University Institute.
———. (1999b) 'The Political Economy of European Integration: Transnational Social Forces in the Making of Europe's Socio-Economic Order'. In Richard Stubbs and Geoffrey Underhill (eds.), *Political Economy and the Changing Global Order.* London: Macmillan, pp. 236-45.
van der Pijl, Kees. (1997) 'The History of Class Struggle'. *Monthly Review* 49(1): 28-44.
———. (1995) 'The Second Glorious Revolution: Globalizing Elites and Historical Change'. In Björn Hettne (ed.), *International Political Economy: Understanding Global Disorder.* Halifax: Fernwood Books, pp. 100-28.
Verdun, Amy. (2000a) *European Responses to Globalization and Financial Market Integration: Perceptions of Economic and Monetary Union in Britain, France and Germany.* International Political Economy Series. Basingstoke: Macmillan/New York: St. Martin's Press.
———. (2000b) 'Governing by Committee: The Case of the Monetary Committee'. In Thomas Christiansen and Emil Kirchner (eds.), *Committee Governance in the European Union.* Manchester: Manchester University Press, pp. 132-45.
———. (1999) 'The Role of the Delors Committee in the Creation of EMU: An Epistemic Community?' Journal of European Public Policy 6(2): 308-28.

———. (1998a) 'The Institutional Design of EMU: A Democratic Deficit?' Journal of Public Policy 18(2): 107-32.

———. (1998b) 'The Increased Influence of the EU Monetary Institutional Framework in Determining Monetary Policies: A Transnational Monetary Elite at Work'. In R. Reinalda and B. Verbeek (eds.), Autonomous Policymaking by International Organizations. London: Routledge, pp. 178-94.

———. (1996a) 'An "Asymmetrical" Economic and Monetary Union in the EU: Perceptions of Monetary Authorities and Social Partners'. Revue d'intégration européenne/Journal of European Integration 20: 59-81.

———. (1996b) 'EMU and Domestic Politics: How "Core" Countries Cope with the Convergence Criteria'. Paper presented at the 68th Annual Conference of the Canadian Political Science Association, Brock University, St. Catharines, Ontario, 2-4 June.

Verdun, Amy, and Thomas Christiansen. (2000) 'Policy-making, Institution-building and European Monetary Union: Dilemmas of Legitimacy'. In Colin Crouch (ed.), After the Euro: Shaping Institutions for Governance in the Wake of European Monetary Union. Oxford: Oxford University Press, pp. 162-78.

Verzichelli, Luca. (1999) La Politica di Bilancio. Bologna: Il Mulino.

Vogel-Polsky, Eliane. (2000) 'Parity Democracy—Law and Europe'. In Mariagrazia Rossilli (ed.), Gender Policies in the European Union. New York: Peter Lang, pp. 61-85.

von Hagen, Jurgen, and G. Hammond. (1995) 'Regional Insurance Against Asymmetric Shocks: An Empirical Study for the European Community'. CEPR Discussion Paper 1170.

Wallace, William. (1983) 'Less than a Federation, More than a Regime: The Community as a Political System'. In Helen Wallace, William Wallace, and Carole Webb (eds.), Policy Making in the European Community, 2nd ed. Chichester: Wiley, pp. 403-36.

Walsh, James I. (2000) European Monetary Integration and Domestic Politics: Britain, France and Italy. Boulder, Colo.: Lynne Rienner.

———. (1998) 'L'incerto cammino verso l'Unione monetaria'. In Luciano Bardi and Martin Rhodes (eds.), Politica in Italia: I fatti dell'anno e le interpretazioni. Edizione 98. Bologna: Il Mulino, pp. 109-30.

———. (1994) 'International Constraints and Domestic Choices: Economic Convergence and Exchange Rate Policy in France and Italy'. Political Studies 42: 243-58.

Waltz, Kenneth. (1979) Theory of International Politics. New York: Random House.

Webb, Carole. (1983) 'Theoretical Perspectives and Problems'. In Helen Wallace, William Wallace, and Carole Webb (eds.), Policy-Making in the European Community, 2nd ed. Chichester: Wiley, pp. 1-41.

Weiler, Joseph H. (1997) 'To be a European Citizen—Eros and civilization'. Journal of European Public Policy 4(4): 495-519.

Weldon, Laurel. (2001) Social Movements, Political Institutions and Government Response to Violence Against Women. Pittsburgh: Pittsburgh University Press.

Wendon, Bryan. (1998) 'The Commission as Image Venue Entrepreneur in EU Social Policy'. Journal of European Public Policy 5(2): 339-53.

Wendt, Alexander. (1999) Social Theory of International Politics. Cambridge: Cambridge University Press.

Werner Report. (1970) 'Report to the Council and the Commission on the Realization by Stages of Economic and Monetary Union in the Community'. Council and Commission of the EC, Bulletin of the EC, Supplement 11, Doc 16.956/11/70, 8 October.

Wessels, Wolfgang. (1997) 'An Ever Closer Fusion? A Dynamic Macropolitical View on Integration Processes'. *Journal of Common Market Studies* 35(2): 267-99.
Wiener, Antje. (1997) 'Making Sense of the New Geography of Citizenship: Fragmented Citizenship in the European Union'. *Theory and Society* 26: 529-60.
Wilson, James Q. (1973) *Political Organizations*. New York: Basic Books.
Wincott, Daniel. (1995) 'Institutional Interaction and European Integration: Towards an Everyday Critique of Liberal Intergovernmentalism'. *Journal of Common Market Studies* 33(4): 597-609.
Wolf, Dieter, and Bernhard Zangl. (1996) 'The European Economic and Monetary Union: "Two-level Games" and the Formation of International Institutions'. *European Journal of International Relations* 2(3): 355-93.
Wood, Ellen Meiksins. (1995) *Democracy against Capitalism*. Cambridge: Cambridge University Press.
Wood, Pia Christina. (1996) 'The Franco-German Relationship in the Post-Maastricht Era'. In Carolyn Rhodes and Sonia Mazey (eds.), *The State of the European Union*, Vol. 3. Boulder, Colo.: Lynne Rienner, pp. 221-43.
Woolley, John. (1984) *Monetary Politics*. Cambridge: Cambridge University Press.
Wright, Georg Henrik von. (1971) *Explanation and Understanding*. London: Routledge and Kegan Paul.
Yaghmaian, Behzad. (1998) 'Globalization and the State: The Political Economy of Global Accumulation and Its Emerging Mode of Regulation'. *Science and Society* 62(2): 241-65.
Zangl, Bernhard. (1999) *Interessen auf zwei Ebenen. Internationale Regime in der Agrarhandels-, Währungs- und Walfangpolitik*. Baden-Baden: Nomos.
Zürn, Michael. (1995) 'The Study of European Integration in Political Science'. Paper prepared for the GAAC Summer School, University of California at Berkeley, August.
———. (1992) *Interessen und Institutionen in der internationalen Politik. Grundlegung und Anwendungen des situationsstrukturellen Ansatzes*. Opladen: Leske and Budrich.

Index

1992 programme/project/process, 4, 84, 181. *See also* Single European Act (SEA)

accountability, 100, 111, 113, 129, 132, 143, 145-47, 158, 163, 242, 244-45
advocacy coalition, 12
agency and structure, 58, 70, 73-76, 79, 81, 86, 88, 180, 216, 218
Agenda 2000, 206, 214
amalgamated approach, 30-31, 40-42, 47-49
Andreotti, Giulio, 195, 222, 225, 235
Arendt, Hannah, 110
Arthuis, 211
Association for the Monetary Union of Europe (AMUE), 28n2, 240n25
austerity, 77, 79, 85, 87, 112, 131, 210, 223, 231, 232
Austria, 114-16, 134, 170
automaticity, 13-15, 24, 71, 188, 194, 196

Balladur, Edouard, 181, 186, 192
Balladur memorandum, 181
Banca d'Italia. *See* Bank of Italy (BoI)
Bank for International Settlements, 184
Bank of England, 20-21, 23, 24
Bank of France, 23, 24, 134, 142, 183-84, 186, 191, 192
Bank of Italy (BoI), 223, 224, 226, 227, 228, 234, 235
Banque de France. *See* Bank of France
Basle-Nyborg Accords, 181, 186, 239n17
Bayoumi, Tamim, 169

Belgium, 44, 45, 46, 133, 134, 170, 210
benchmarking, 94, 97, 104
Bérégovoy, Pierre, 186-88, 193, 194, 195
Berman, Sheri, 129, 146
Boissieu, Pierre de, 195
Bretton Woods System, 43-44, 46-48, 53, 75, 86, 102, 135, 138, 165, 183, 190, 237n4
Buiter, Willem, 170, 228
Bulmer, Simon, 203, 236n3
Bundesbank: economic policy and performance, 47, 77, 94, 166, 182, 186, 208; hegemony/power of, 18, 33, 134-35, 187, 189, 206, 209, 225; transparency and independence of, 132, 138, 139, 160; views on EMU, 23, 24, 128, 187, 207-8, 210, 236
Bundesverband der Deutschen Industrie (BDI), 22, 23
Burley, Anne-Marie. *See* Slaughter (Burley), Anne-Marie

Cameron, David, 84
capital mobility, 70, 71, 81, 83
Carli, Guido, 224, 229
central bank independence, 128-43; democratic deficit,146-48; design of EMU, 5, 80, 84, 100, 184, 186-87, 192, 208; market legitimacy, 6n1, 79, 82, 100, 152-53, 159, 183, 192-93, 195-96; newly independent, 20, 46
central banks: common, 43-46, 84; Delors Committee, 80, 184, 207;

271

About the Contributors

WILLIAM M. CHANDLER is professor of political science at the University of California, San Diego. His publications include *Public Policy and Provincial Politics* (1979), *Federalism and the Role of the State* (1987), *Challenges to Federalism: Policy-Making in Canada and West Germany* (1986), and numerous journal articles and book chapters on party government, Christian democracy, party system change, and immigration policy. His current research interests focus on the politics of German unification, European integration, and immigration/citizenship issues. He has also served as a visiting professor in Germany at Tuebingen and Oldenburg Universities. He is a member of the editorial advisory board of *German Politics* and is regional director (west) for the *Conference Group on German Politics*.

OSVALDO CROCI is an associate professor of political science at Memorial University in St. John's, Newfoundland, where he teaches international and European politics, and international political economy. He has published articles on the 1953 Trieste crisis, Italian interventions in Somalia and Kosovo, Canadian–US and Canadian–EU relations, central bank independence, and monetary unions. He is currently editing two volumes with Amy Verdun that deal with the process of European enlargement and institutional reform, and the lessons of Kosovo for the development of a European security and defence policy. His current research interests are in the field of sport governance and the political economy of international sport organisations.

PATRICK M. CROWLEY is an associate professor of economics at Texas A&M University in Corpus Christi, Texas. He has published in *Contemporary Economic Policy*, *Journal of Common Market Studies*, and *Journal of European Integration* and is editor of *Before and Beyond EMU: Historical Lessons and Future Prospects* (forthcoming). He specialises in international macroeconomics with an emphasis on economic and monetary policy in the European Union and in the NAFTA region.

KENNETH DYSON is professor of European studies at the University of Bradford, United Kingdom. He is a Fellow of the British Academy and an Academician of the Learned Society of the Social Sciences. His main research interests are post-war German politics and policies, the political economy of Europe, and comparative public policy. Recent books include *European States and the Euro* (2001), *The Politics of the Euro-Zone* (2000), and (with Kevin Featherstone) *The Road to Maastricht* (1999). He is currently working (with Klaus Goetz) on *Germany and Europe: A Europeanized Germany?* (Proceedings of the British Academy 2002). Earlier books include *The State Tradition in Western Europe* (1980), *Party, State and Bureaucracy in West Germany* (1977), *The Politics of German Regulation* (1992), and *Elusive Union* (1994). He was adviser for the BBC2 documentary series on the birth of the euro.

R. AMY ELMAN is an associate professor of political science at Kalamazoo College where she is an associate codirector of the Title VI Center for Western European Studies. She is author of *Sexual Subordination and State Intervention: Comparing Sweden and the United States* and editor of *Sexual Politics and the European Union: The New Feminist Challenge* (both published in 1996). She has published widely on state policies pertaining to violence against women. Her recent publications consider the gendered meanings of EU citizenship in *Journal of Common Market Studies* and *NWSA Journal*.

DAVID HOWARTH is a lecturer (assistant professor) in European politics at Queen Mary College, University of London. His principal research interests include French and EU economic and social policy-making, political economy, French European policy, and the operation of French and European political institutions. He has written *The French Road to European Monetary Union* (2000) and coedited a special edition of *Current Politics and Economics of Europe*, 'The State of Art: Theoretical Approaches to the EU in the Post-Amsterdam Era', 2000. He is currently writing (with Peter Loedel) *The European Central Bank: The New European Leviathan?* (2002).

ERIK JONES is Jean Monnet Senior Lecturer in European Politics at the University of Nottingham. He is author of *The Politics of EMU: Integration and Idiosyncrasy* (2002) and coeditor of *The New Political Economy of EMU* (1998) and of *Joining Europe's Monetary Club* (1998).

PETER H. LOEDEL is an associate professor in and chair of the Department of Political Science at West Chester University. His research interests are European and German monetary policy, the European Monetary Union, and the politics of the European Central Bank. He has published several articles and book chapters on German and European monetary policy and is the author of *Deutsche Mark Politics: Germany in the European Monetary System* (1999). He is currently working on a coauthored book with David Howarth on the European Central Bank to be published by Palgrave Press.

LUCIO PICCI holds a Ph.D. in economics from the University of California at San Diego and teaches at the University of Bologna. His recent publications include: 'Explaining long- and short-run interactions in time series data', *Journal of Business Economics & Statistics* (January 2001); 'Saving, Growth and Investment: A Macroeconomic Analysis Using a Panel of Countries' (with O. Attanansio and A. Scorcu), *Review of Economics and Statistics* (May 2000), and *La Sfera Telematica* (Baskerville, Bologna, 1999), a book on the economic and organisational consequences of the Internet. His home page is http://www.spbo.unibo.it/picci.

FEMKE (F. A. W. J.) VAN ESCH is a Ph.D. student at the Department of Political Science, Nijmegen School of Management, at the University of Nijmegen, the Netherlands. She is writing a thesis on the formation of national preferences concerning the establishment of the European Economic and Monetary Union. She has published 'Defining National Preferences. The Influence of International Non-State Actors' in *Non-State Actors in International Relations* (2001).

AMY VERDUN is an associate professor of political science and director of the European Studies Programme at the University of Victoria, B.C., Canada. She also holds a Jean Monnet Chair in European Integration Studies. She is the author of many articles and book chapters on issues related to European economic and monetary integration. She has published in journals such as *Journal of Public Policy, Journal of European Public Policy, Current Politics and Economics of Europe,* and *Journal of European Integration.* Two of her recent books are *European Responses to Globalization and Financial Market Integration: Perceptions of Economic and Monetary Union in Britain, France and Germany* (2000) and the coedited anthology *Strange Power: Shaping the Parameters of International Relations and International Political Economy* (2000) (with Thomas Lawton and James N. Rosenau).

DIETER WOLF is a research fellow and lecturer at the Technical University Munich, Germany. His research focus is European integration and comparative political economy. His recent publications include *Integrationstheorien im Vergleich* (1999) and (with Bernhard Zangl) 'The European Economic and Monetary Union: "Two-level Games" and the Formation of International Institutions', *European Journal of International Relations* (1996).'

LLOY WYLIE is a graduate student in political science at the University of Victoria. Her research focuses on European integration and international political economy. She has published in the *Journal of European Integration* and *Revue Économie et Solidarité*, and has presented at international conferences on issues of European monetary integration and the North American Free Trade Agreement.